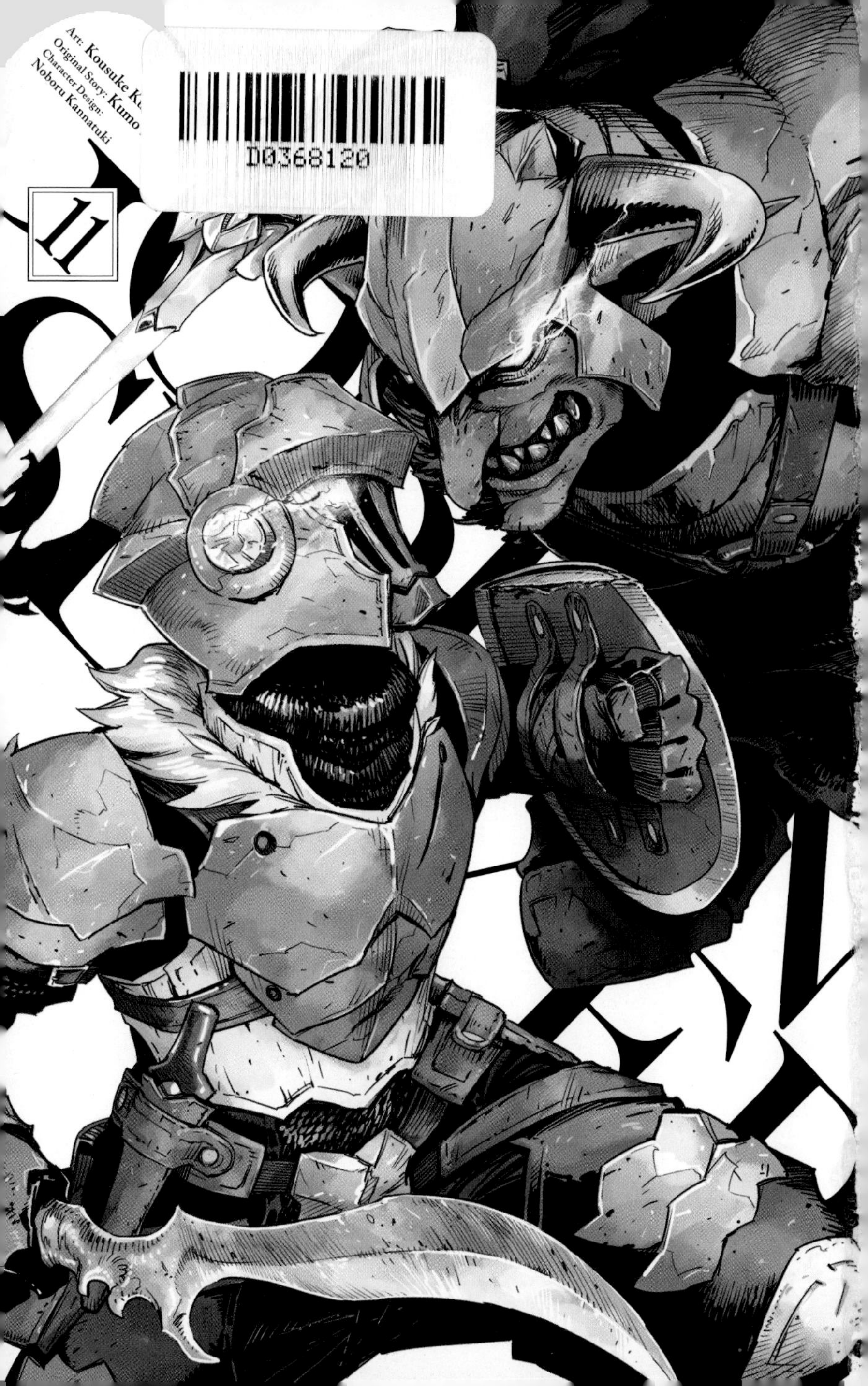
Art: Kousuke Ku
Original Story: Kumo
Character Design:
Noboru Kannatuki
11

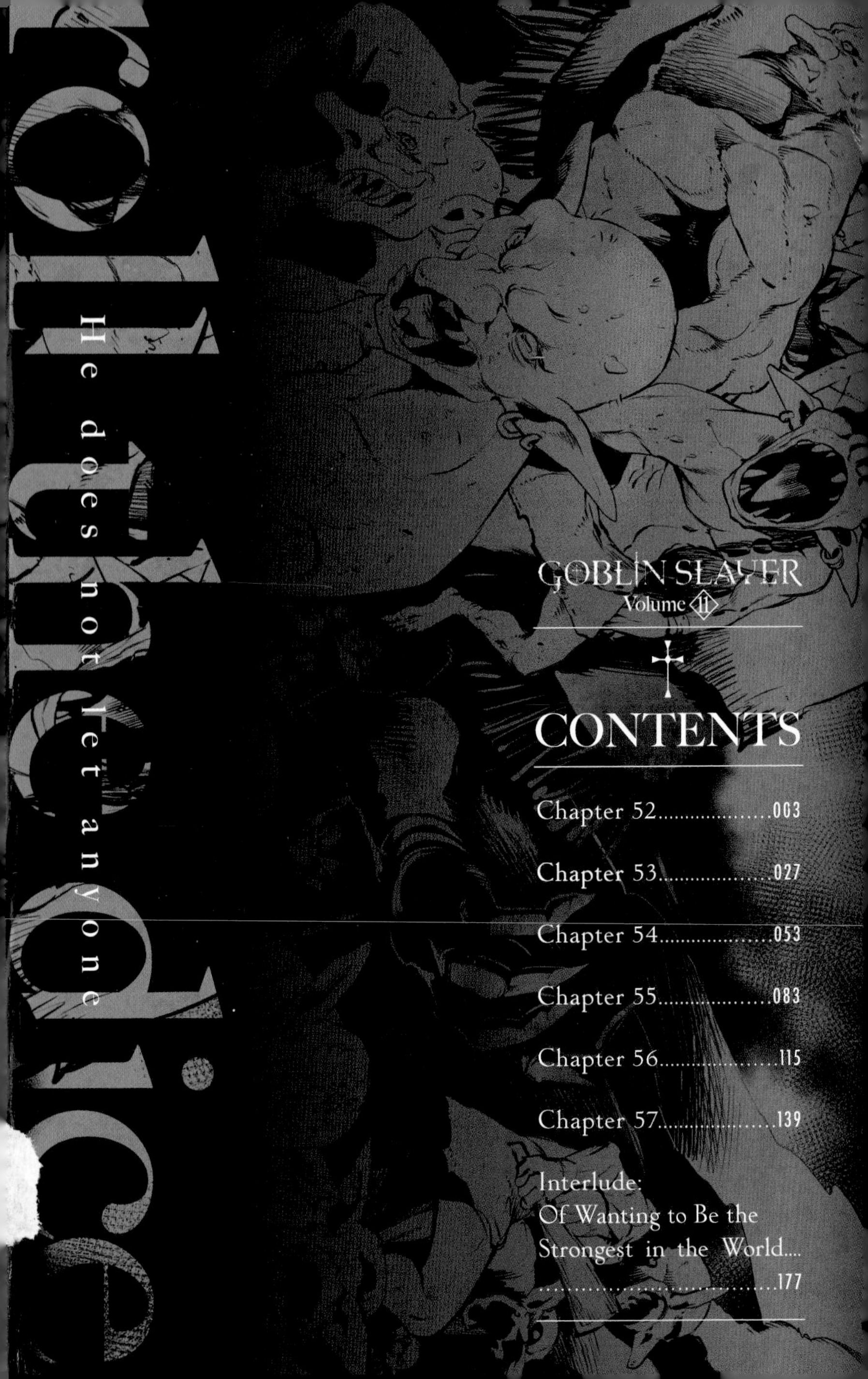
He does not let anyone

GOBLIN SLAYER
Volume 11

CONTENTS

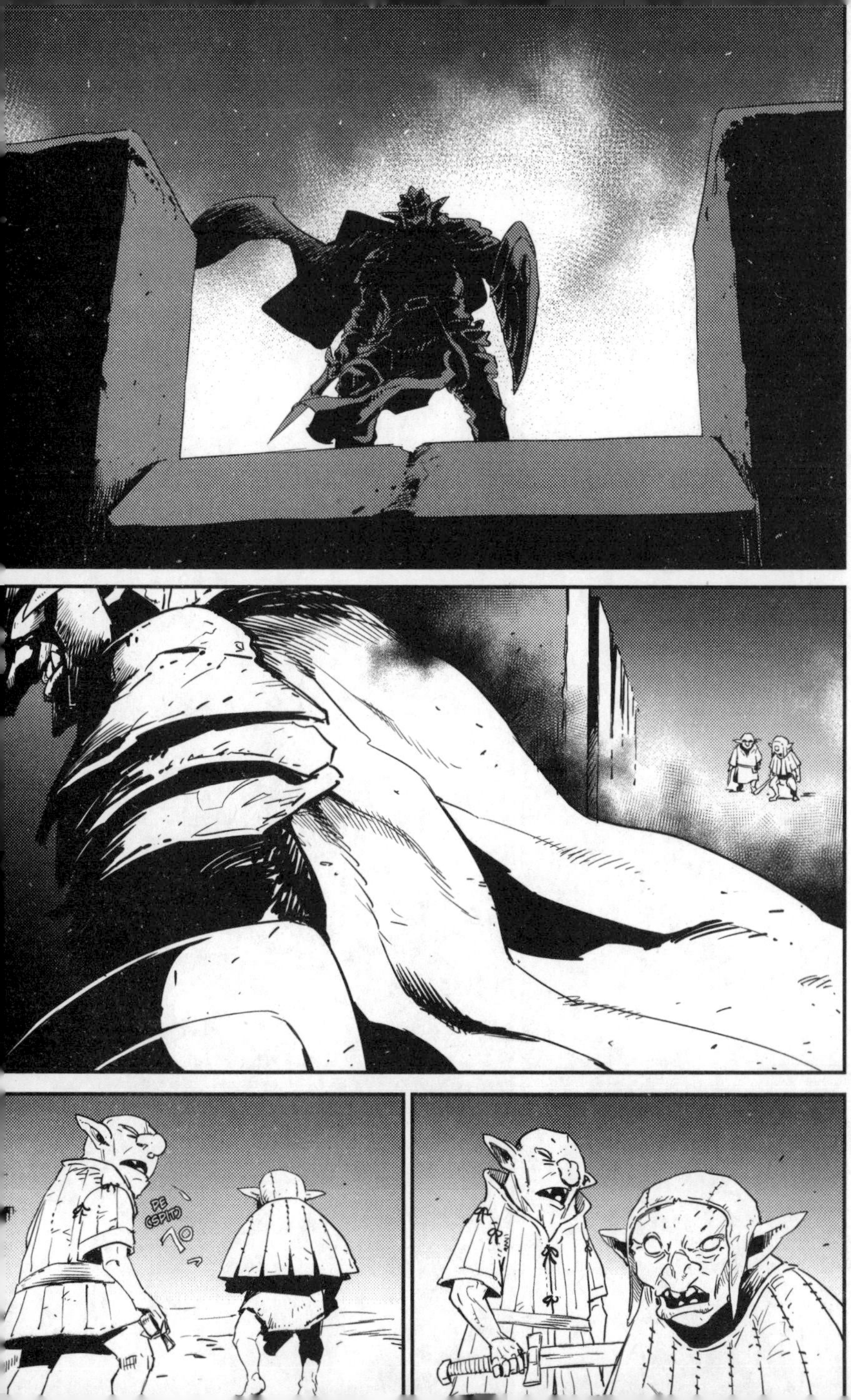
PE
(SPIT)

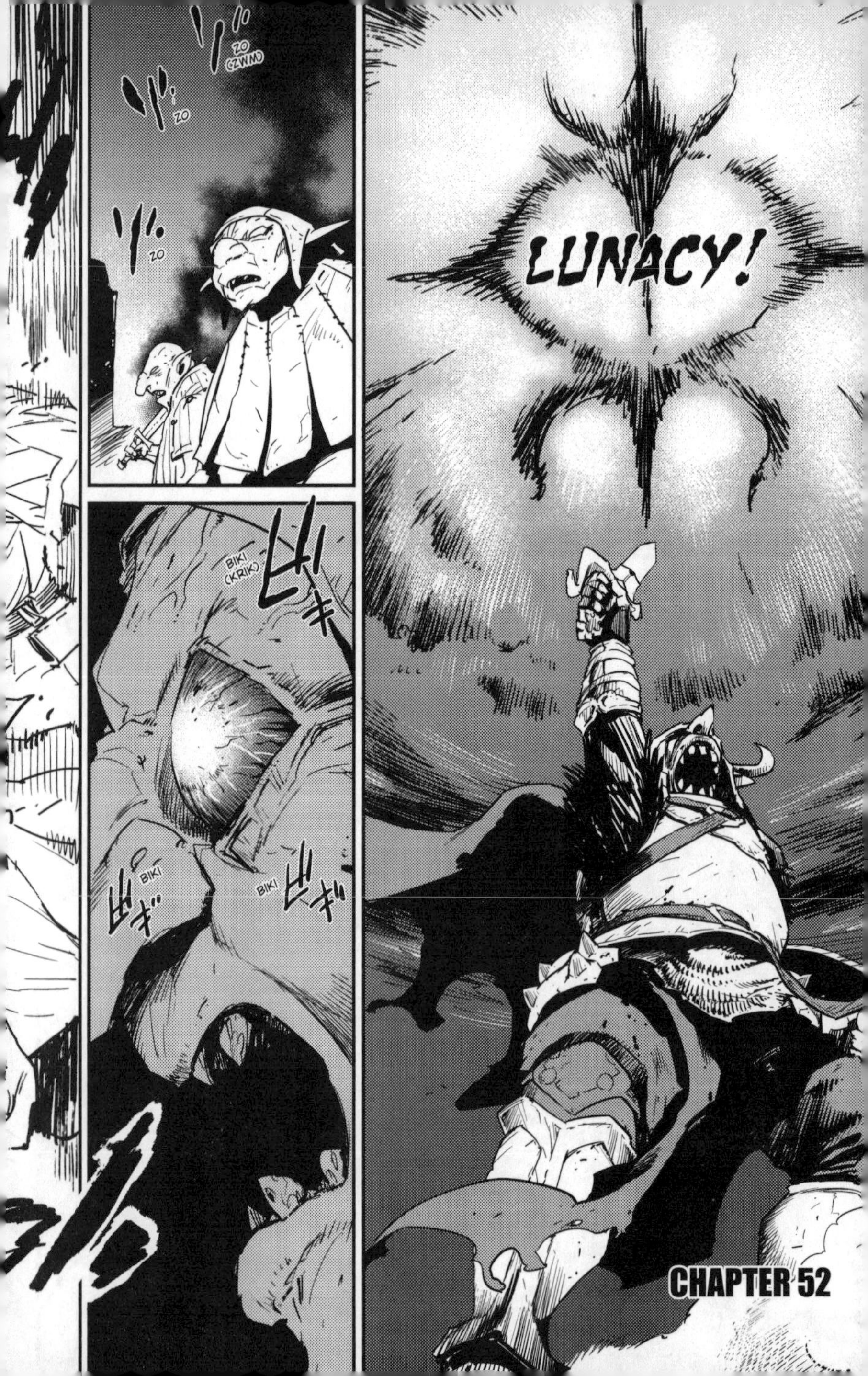

LUNACY!
CHAPTER 52
ZO (ZWM)
ZO
ZO
BIKI (KRIK)
BIKI
BIKI

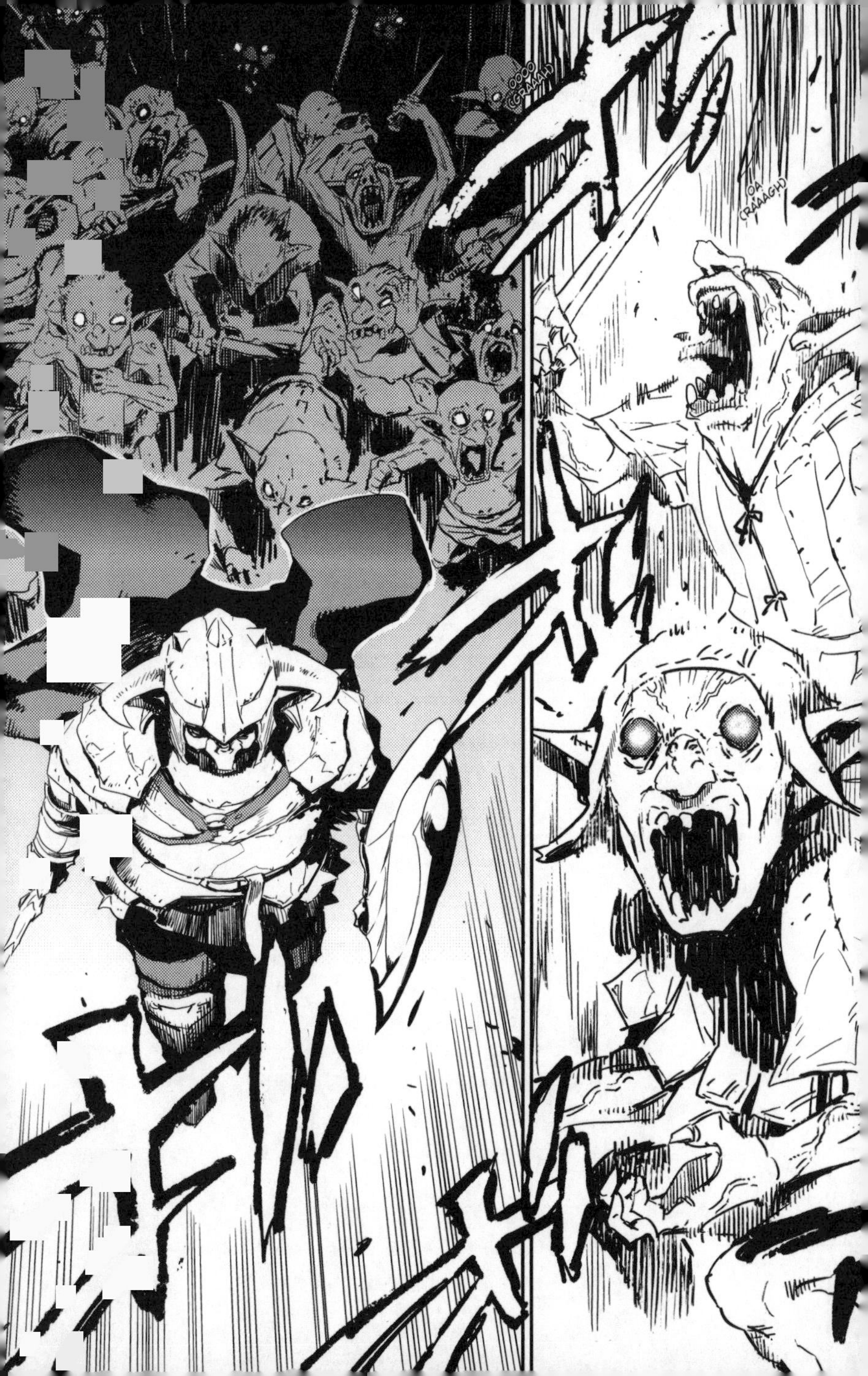
OA (RAAAGH)
OOOO (GRAAAH)

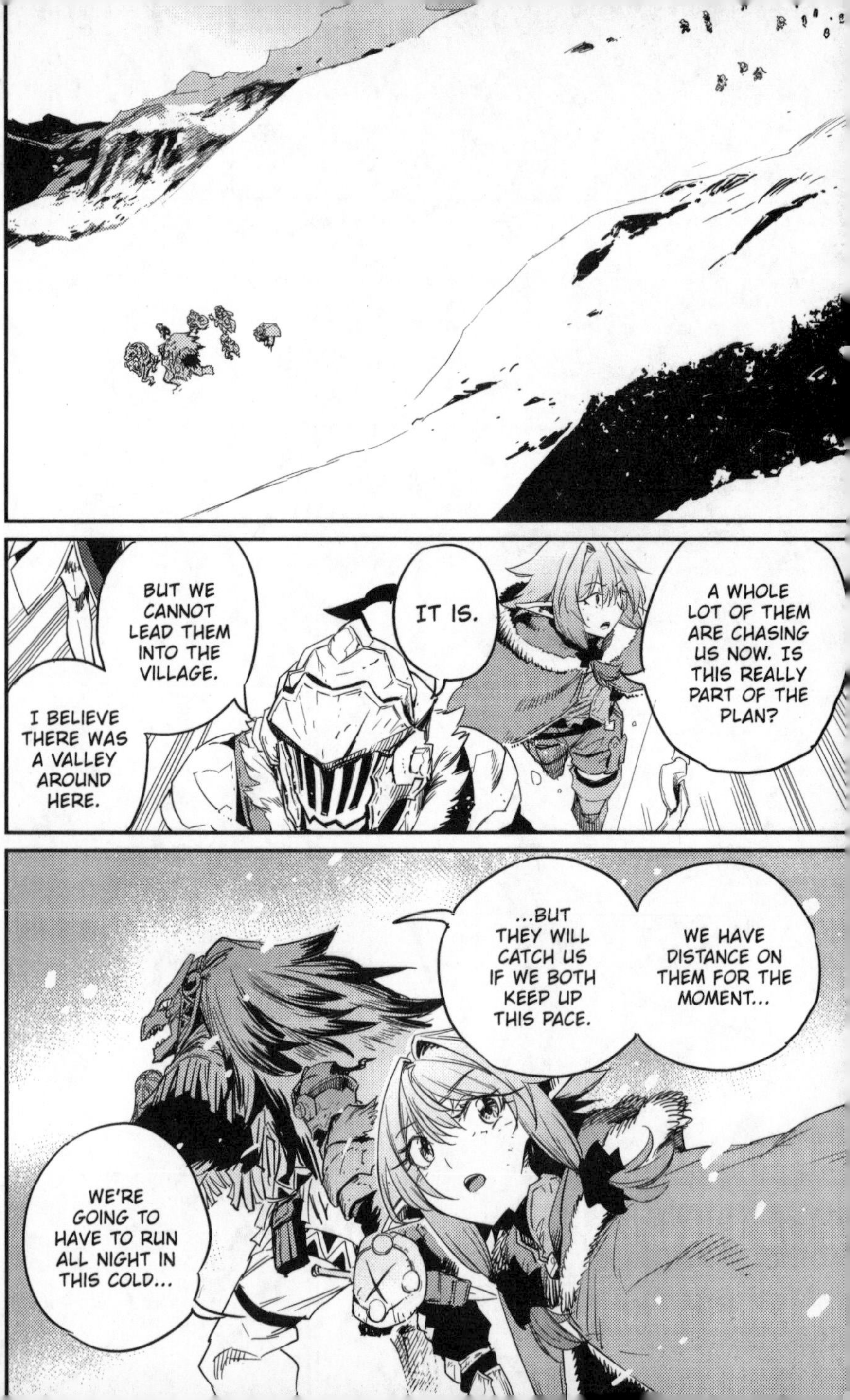
A WHOLE LOT OF THEM ARE CHASING US NOW. IS THIS REALLY PART OF THE PLAN?
IT IS.
BUT WE CANNOT LEAD THEM INTO THE VILLAGE.
I BELIEVE THERE WAS A VALLEY AROUND HERE.
WE HAVE DISTANCE ON THEM FOR THE MOMENT...
...BUT THEY WILL CATCH US IF WE BOTH KEEP UP THIS PACE.
WE'RE GOING TO HAVE TO RUN ALL NIGHT IN THIS COLD...

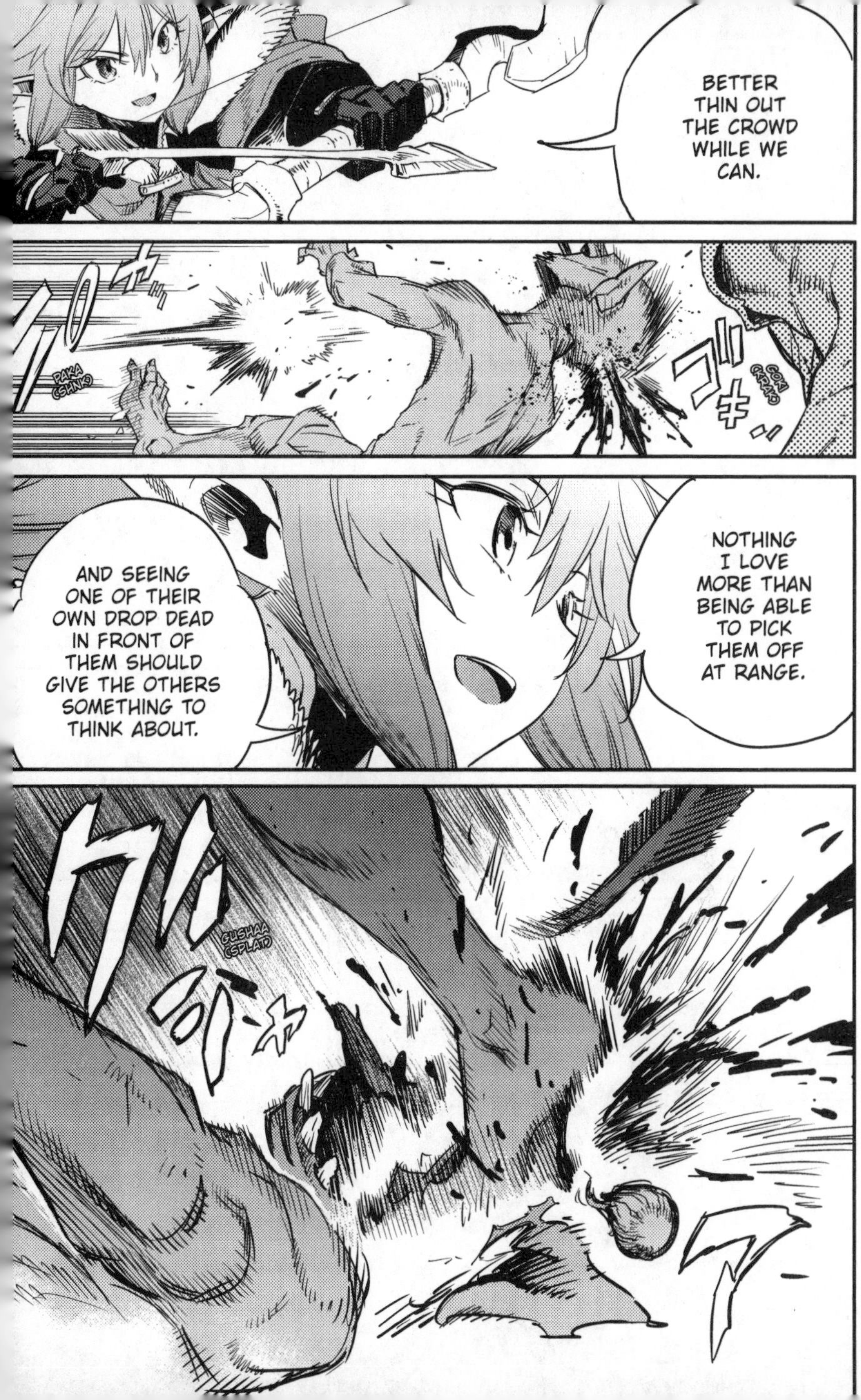
BETTER THIN OUT THE CROWD WHILE WE CAN.
GOKI (KRAK)
PAKA (SHNK)
NOTHING I LOVE MORE THAN BEING ABLE TO PICK THEM OFF AT RANGE.
AND SEEING ONE OF THEIR OWN DROP DEAD IN FRONT OF THEM SHOULD GIVE THE OTHERS SOMETHING TO THINK ABOUT.
GUSHAA (SPLAT)

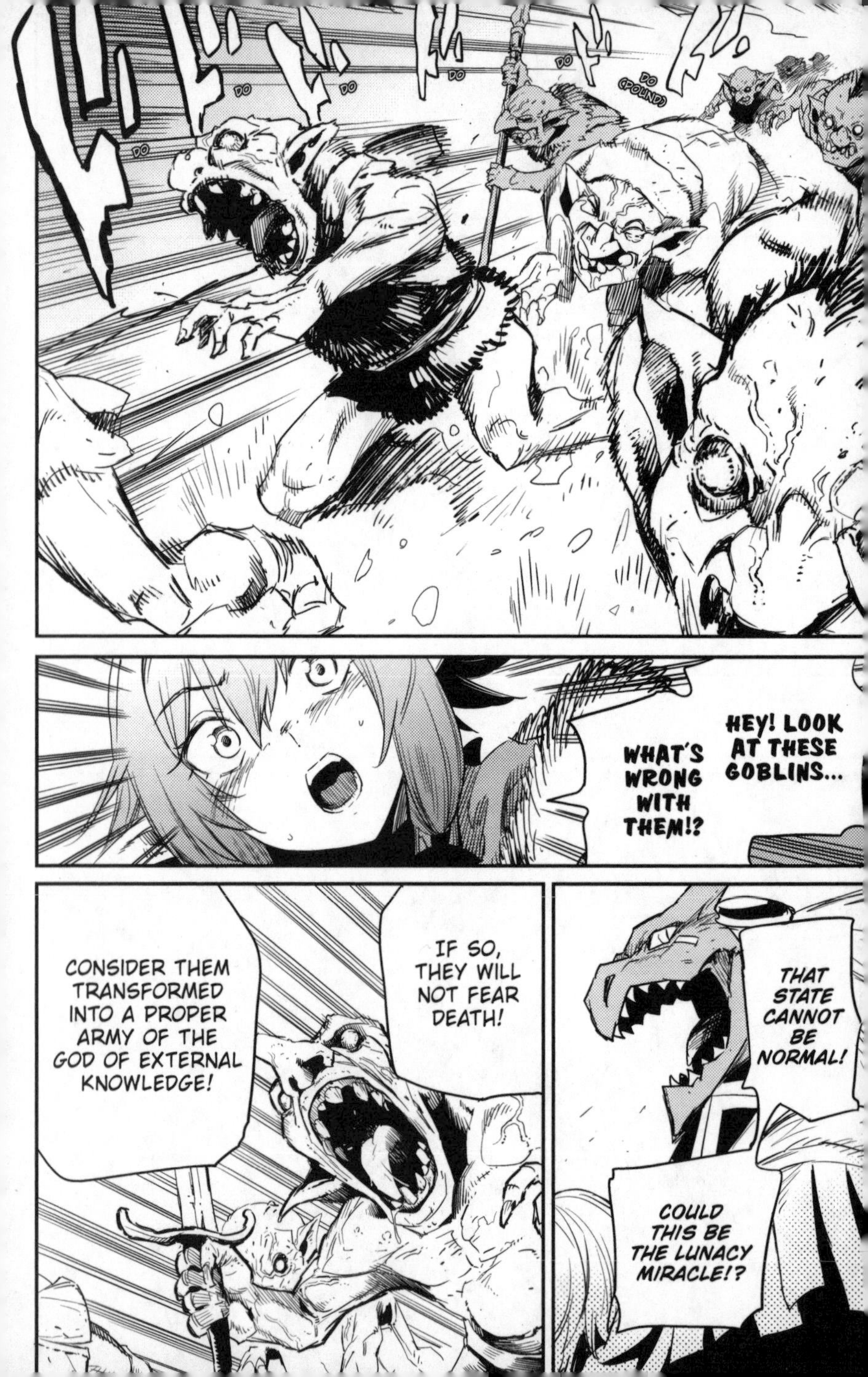
DO (POUND)
DO
DO
DO
DO
DO
HEY! LOOK AT THESE GOBLINS...
WHAT'S WRONG WITH THEM!?
THAT STATE CANNOT BE NORMAL!
COULD THIS BE THE LUNACY MIRACLE!?
IF SO, THEY WILL NOT FEAR DEATH!
CONSIDER THEM TRANSFORMED INTO A PROPER ARMY OF THE GOD OF EXTERNAL KNOWLEDGE!

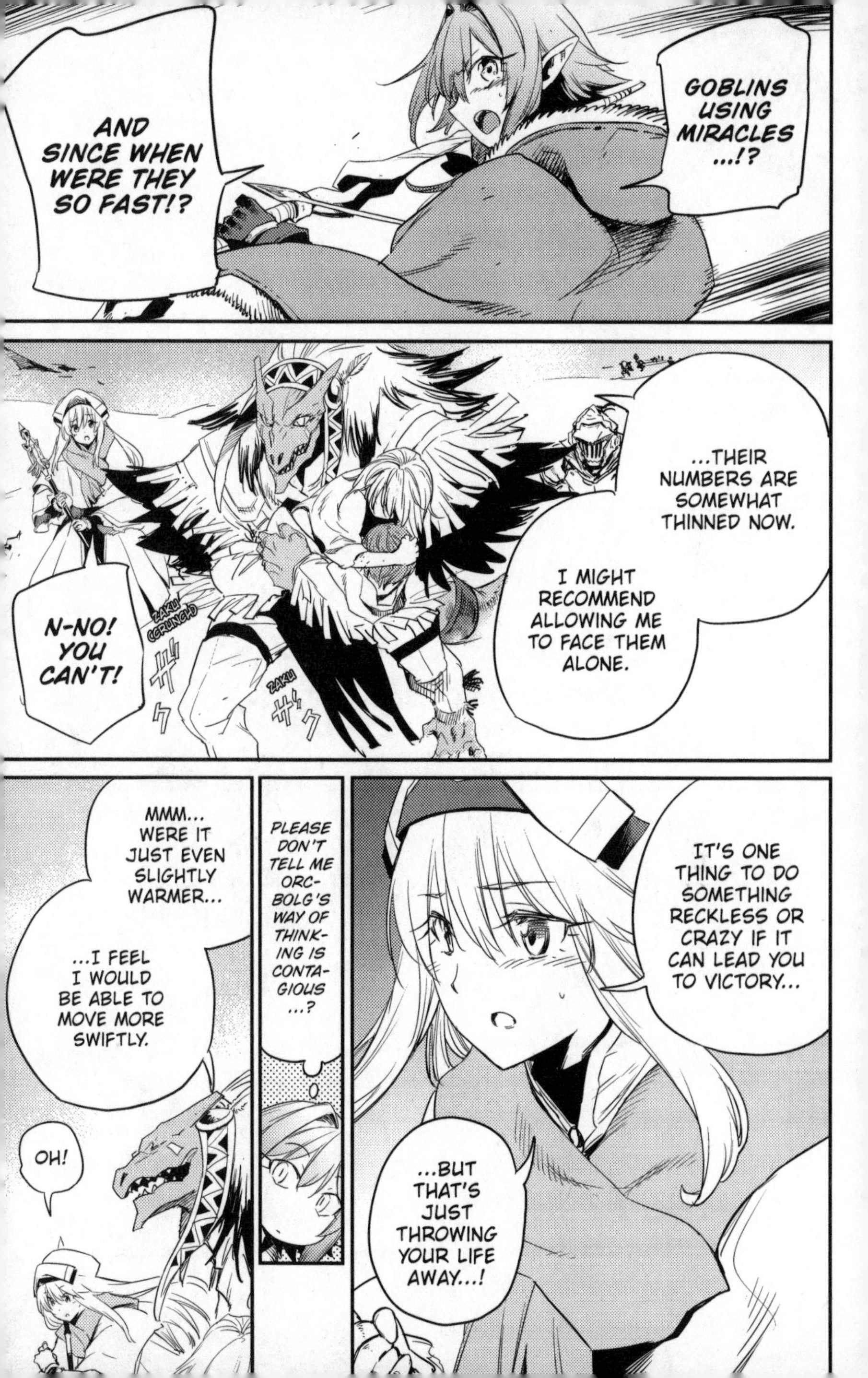
GOBLINS USING MIRACLES ...!?
AND SINCE WHEN WERE THEY SO FAST!?
...THEIR NUMBERS ARE SOMEWHAT THINNED NOW.
I MIGHT RECOMMEND ALLOWING ME TO FACE THEM ALONE.
ZAKU (CRUNCH)
ZAKU
N-NO! YOU CAN'T!
IT'S ONE THING TO DO SOMETHING RECKLESS OR CRAZY IF IT CAN LEAD YOU TO VICTORY...
...BUT THAT'S JUST THROWING YOUR LIFE AWAY...!
PLEASE DON'T TELL ME ORC-BOLG'S WAY OF THINKING IS CONTAGIOUS ...?
MMM... WERE IT JUST EVEN SLIGHTLY WARMER...
...I FEEL I WOULD BE ABLE TO MOVE MORE SWIFTLY.
OH!

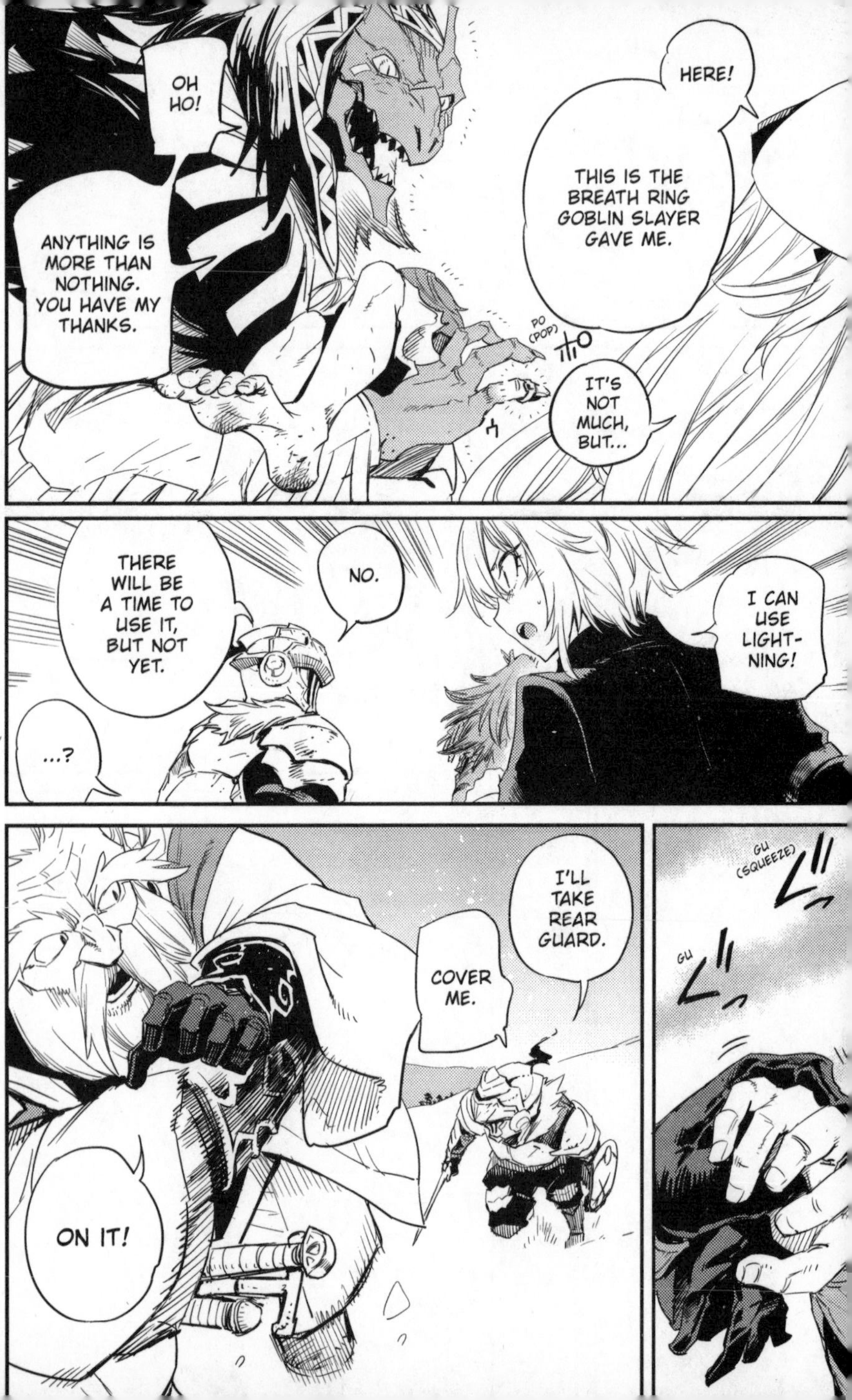
HERE!
THIS IS THE BREATH RING GOBLIN SLAYER GAVE ME.
PO (POP)
IT'S NOT MUCH, BUT...
OH HO!
ANYTHING IS MORE THAN NOTHING. YOU HAVE MY THANKS.
I CAN USE LIGHT-NING!
NO.
THERE WILL BE A TIME TO USE IT, BUT NOT YET.
...?
GU (SQUEEZE)
GU
I'LL TAKE REAR GUARD.
COVER ME.
ON IT!

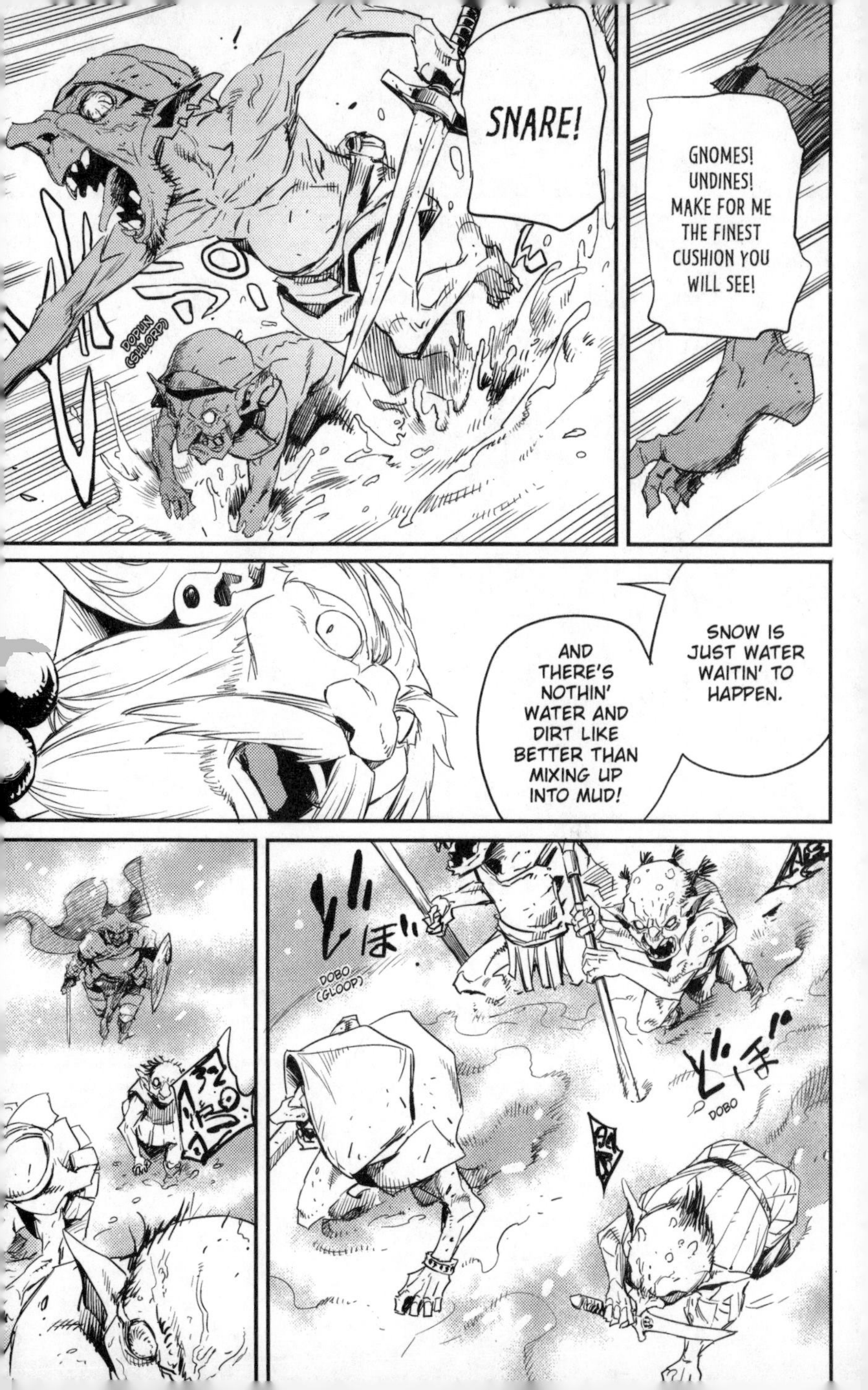
GNOMES! UNDINES! MAKE FOR ME THE FINEST CUSHION YOU WILL SEE!
SNARE!
DOPUN (SHLORP)
SNOW IS JUST WATER WAITIN' TO HAPPEN.
AND THERE'S NOTHIN' WATER AND DIRT LIKE BETTER THAN MIXING UP INTO MUD!
DOBO (GLOOP)
DOBO

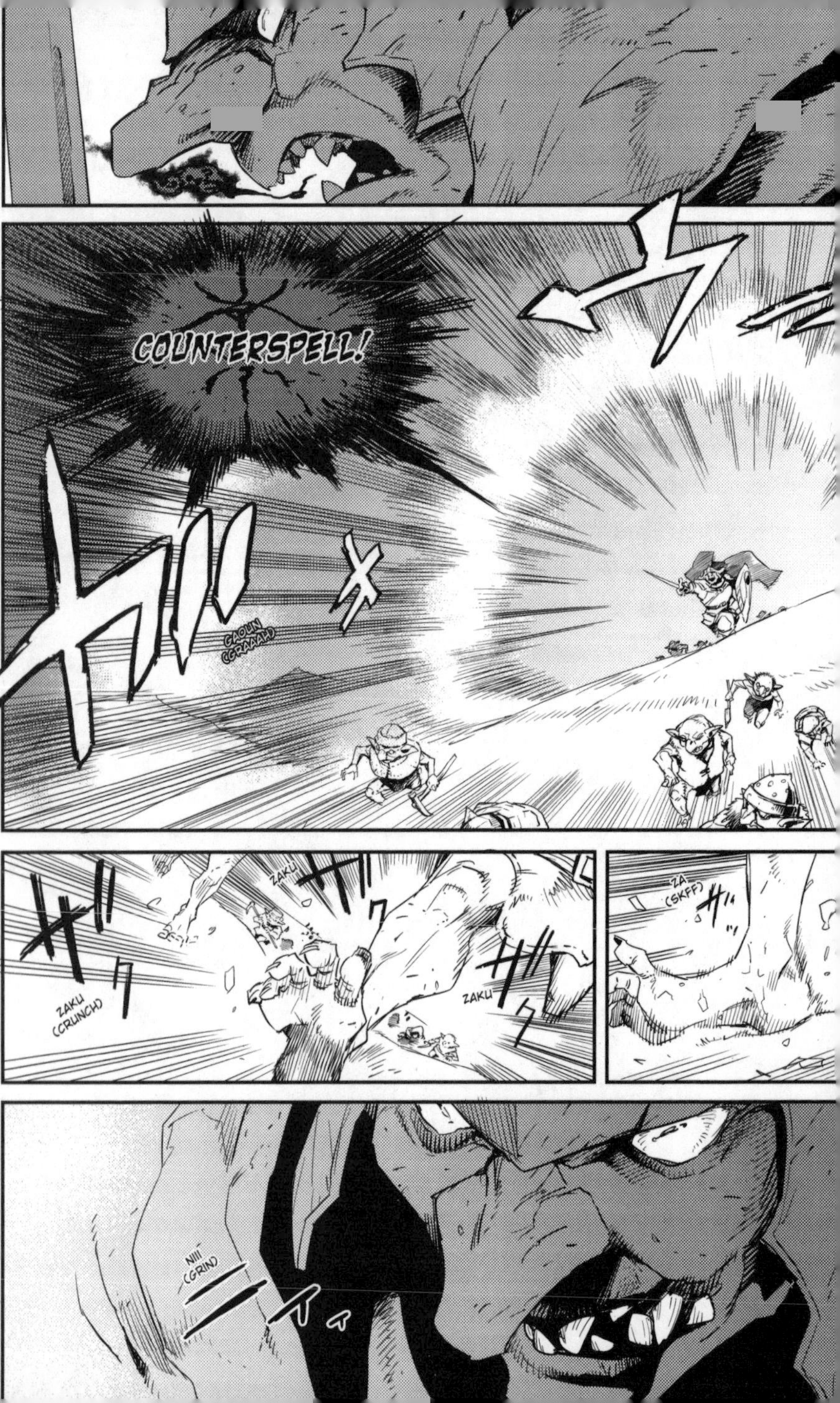
COUNTERSPELL!
GAOUN (GRAAAH)
ZA (SKFF)
ZAKU
ZAKU
ZAKU (CRUNCH)
NIII (GRIN)

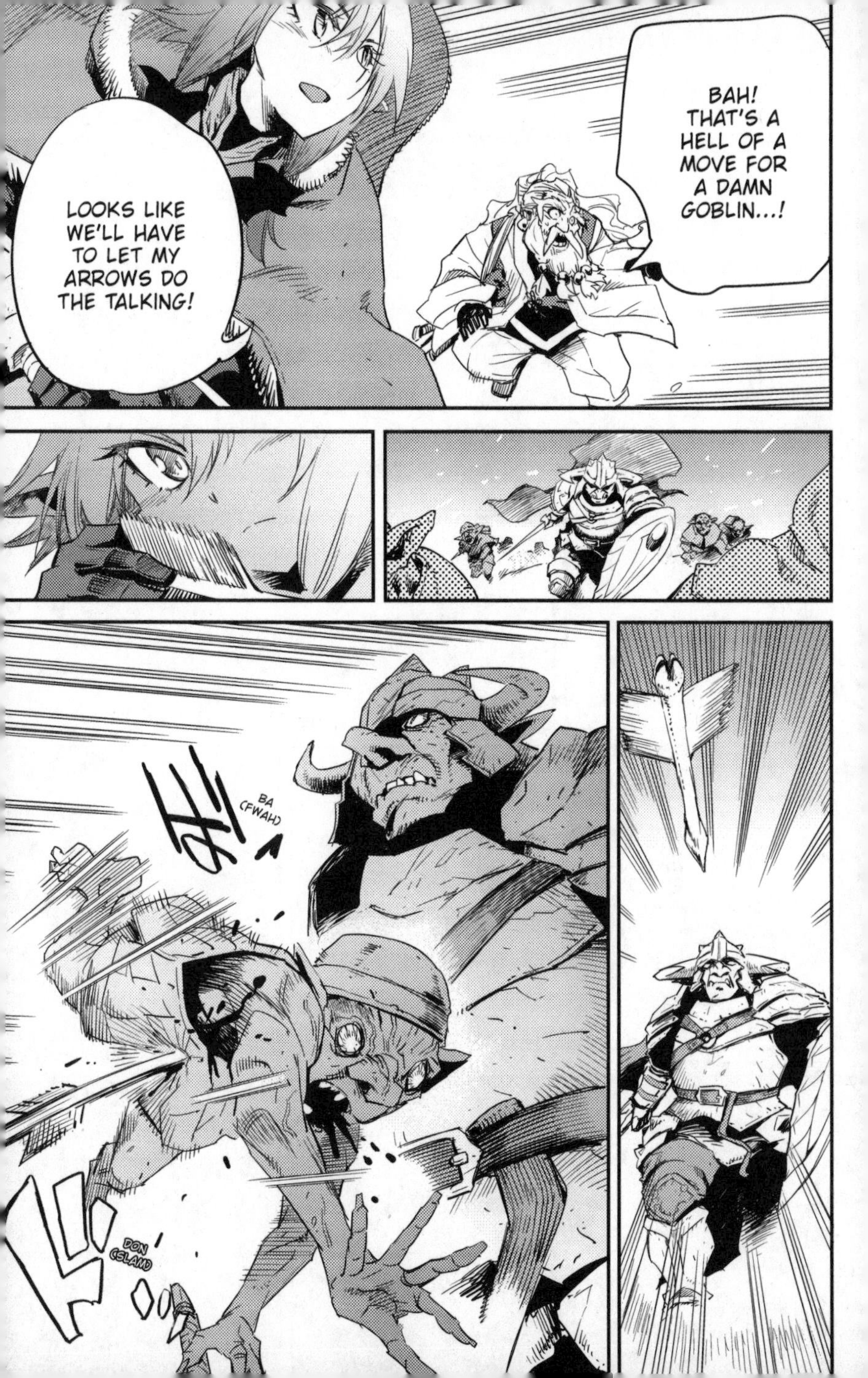
BAH! THAT'S A HELL OF A MOVE FOR A DAMN GOBLIN...!
LOOKS LIKE WE'LL HAVE TO LET MY ARROWS DO THE TALKING!
BA (FWAH)
DON (SLAM)

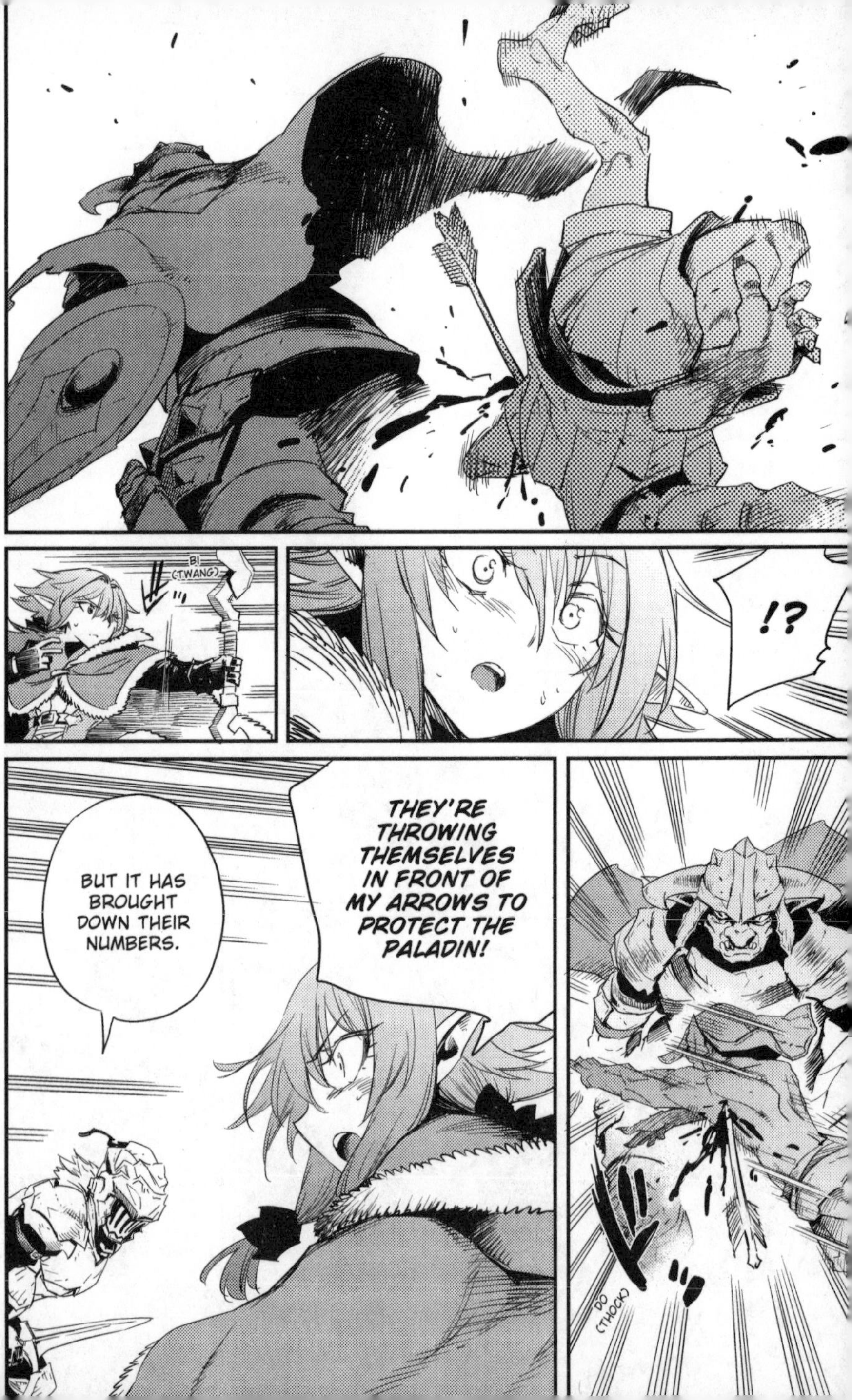
!?
BI (TWANG)
DO (THOCK)
THEY'RE THROWING THEMSELVES IN FRONT OF MY ARROWS TO PROTECT THE PALADIN!
BUT IT HAS BROUGHT DOWN THEIR NUMBERS.

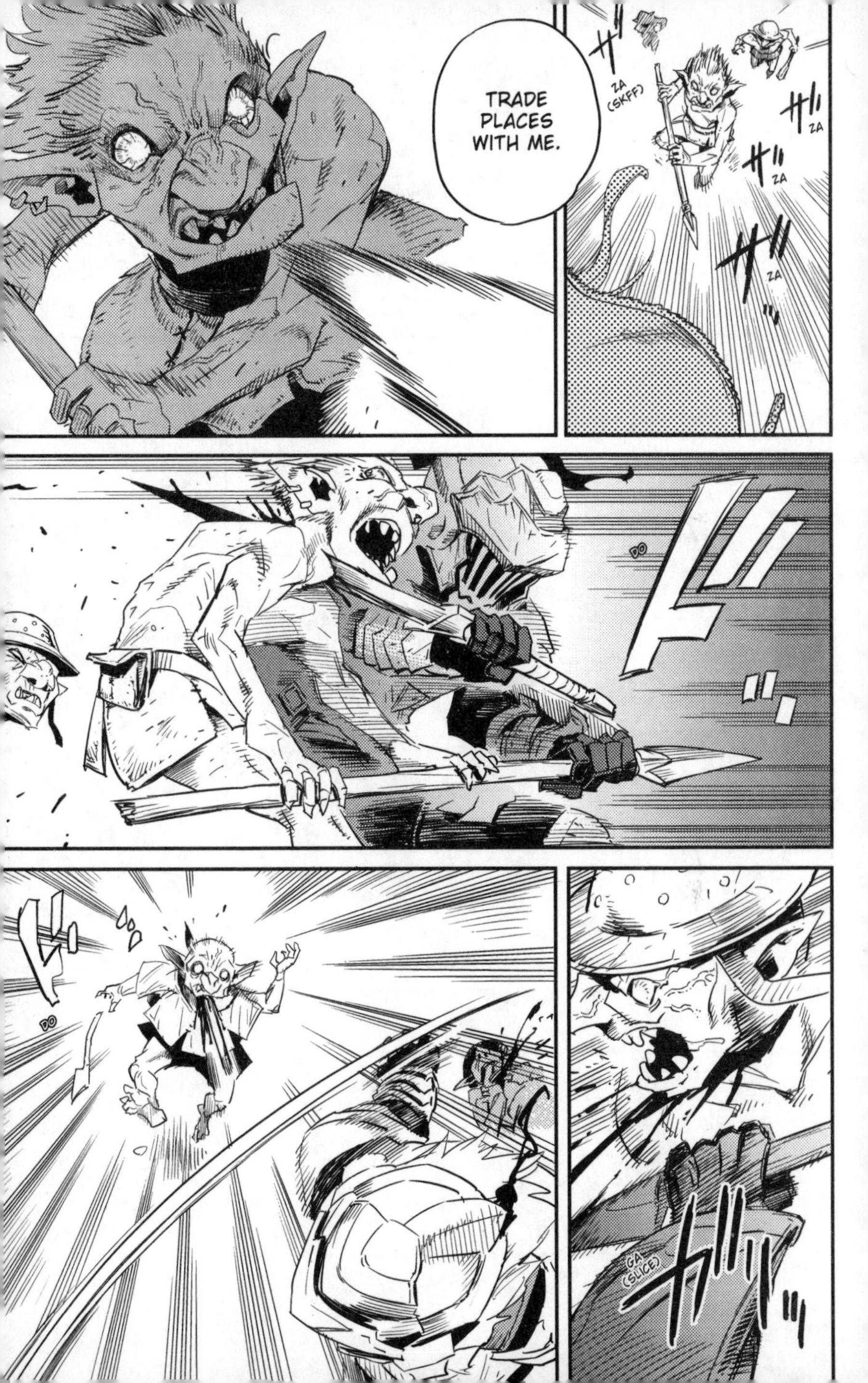
ZA (SKFF)
ZA
ZA
ZA
TRADE PLACES WITH ME.
DO
GA (SLICE)
DO

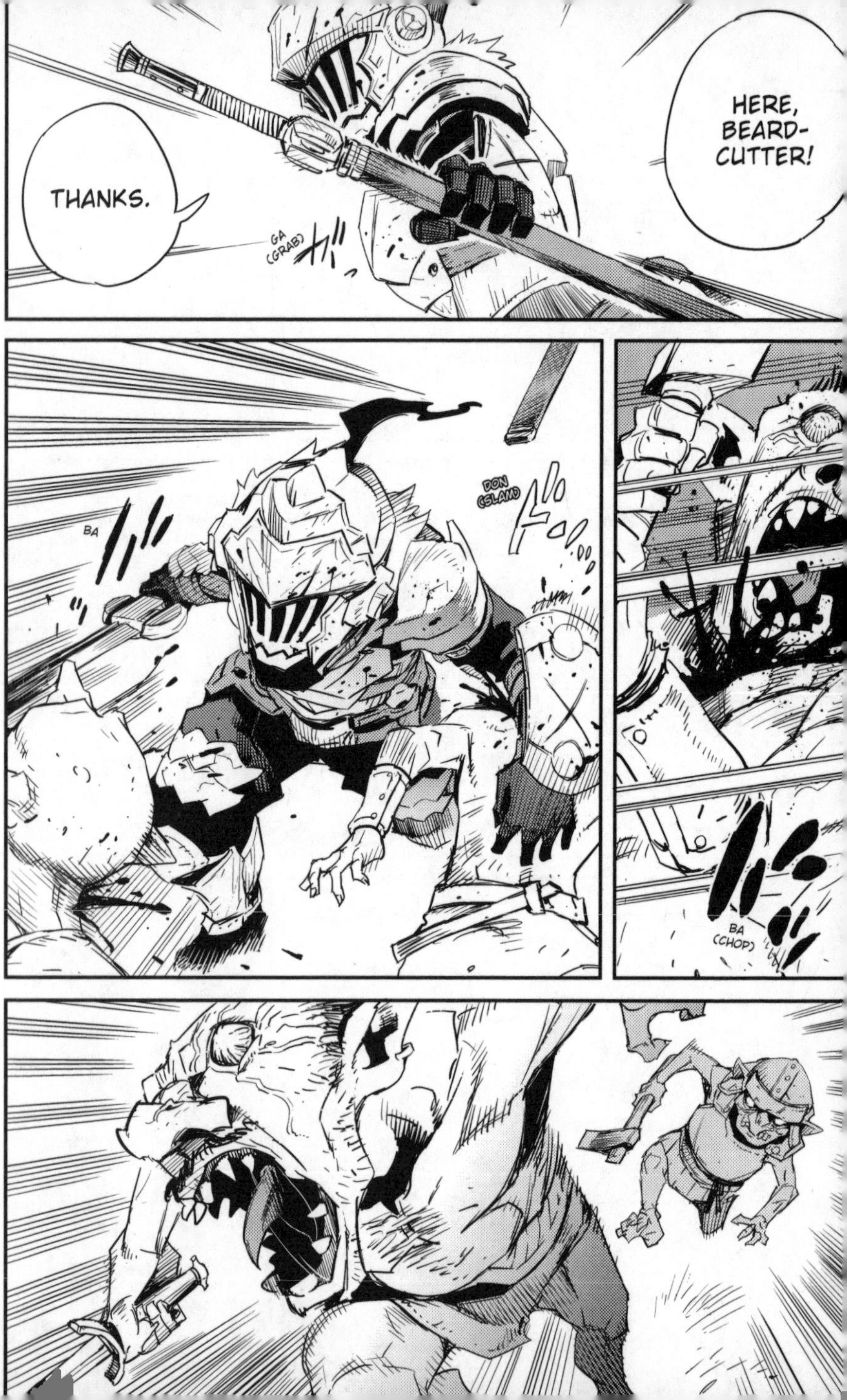
HERE, BEARD-CUTTER!
THANKS.
GA (GRAB)
BA (CHOP)
DON (SLAM)
BA

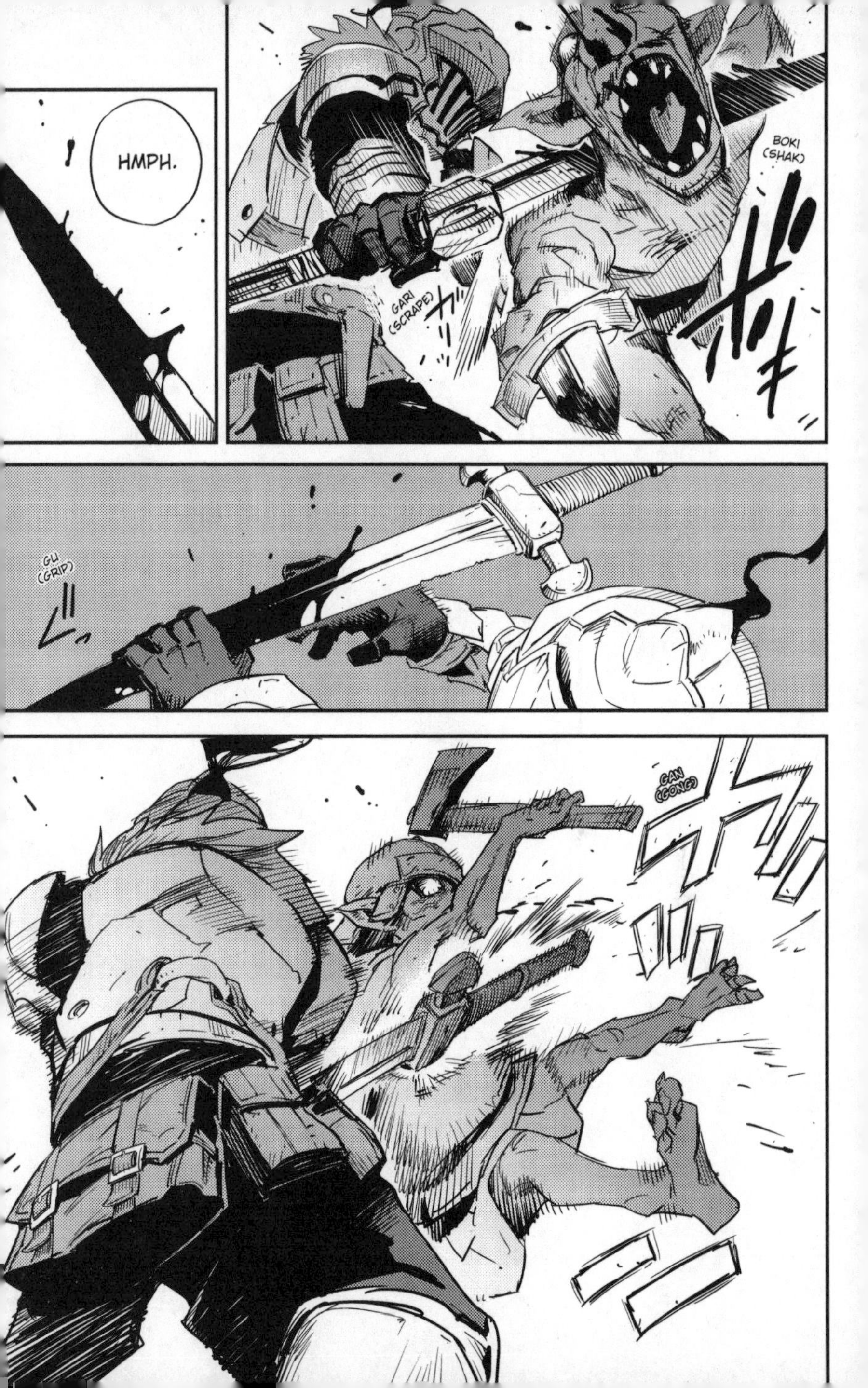
BOKI (SHAK)
GARI (SCRAPE)
HMPH.
GU (GRIP)
GAN (GONG)

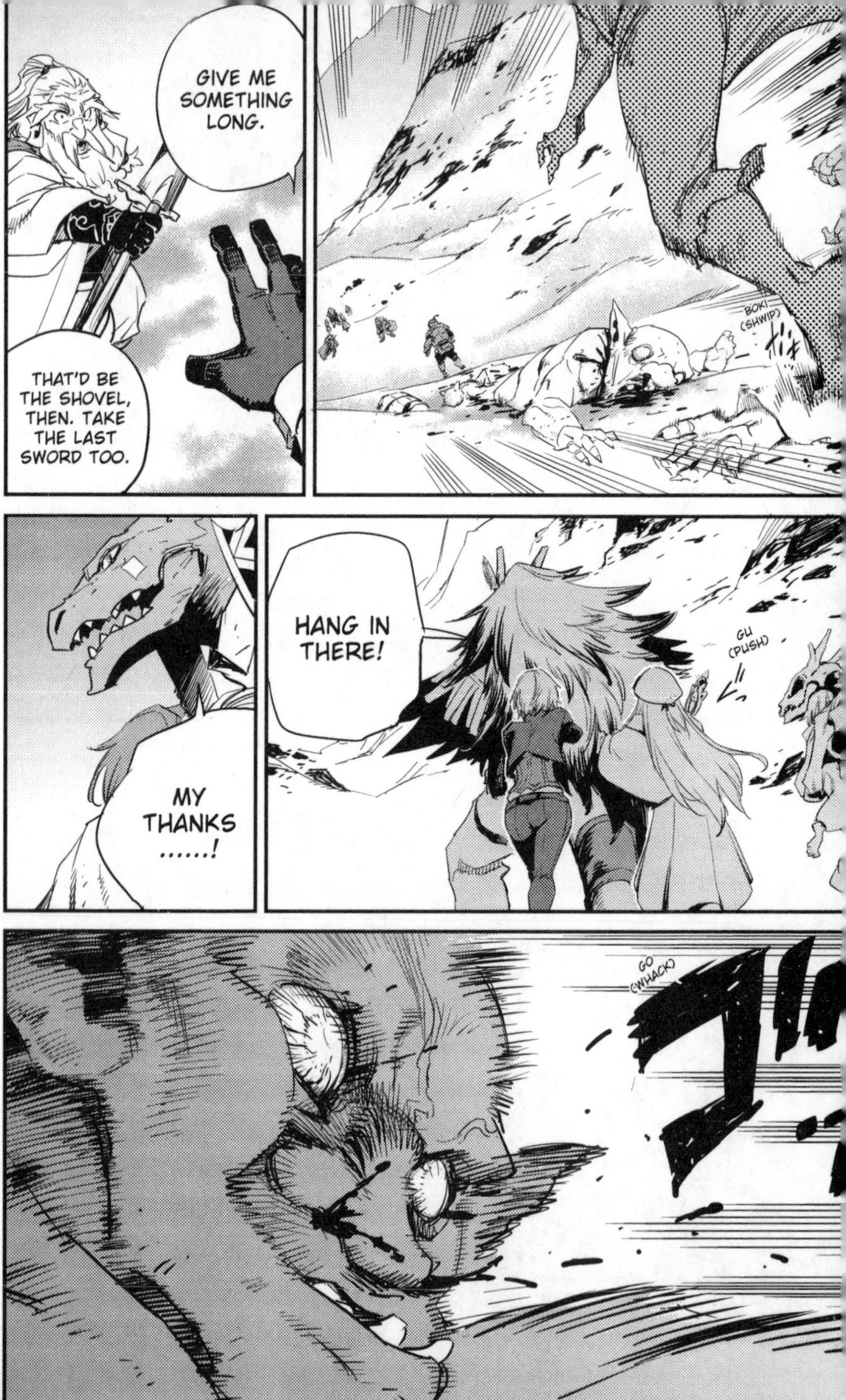
BOKI (SHWIP)
GIVE ME SOMETHING LONG.
THAT'D BE THE SHOVEL, THEN. TAKE THE LAST SWORD TOO.
GU (PUSH)
HANG IN THERE!
MY THANKS ......!
GO (WHACK)

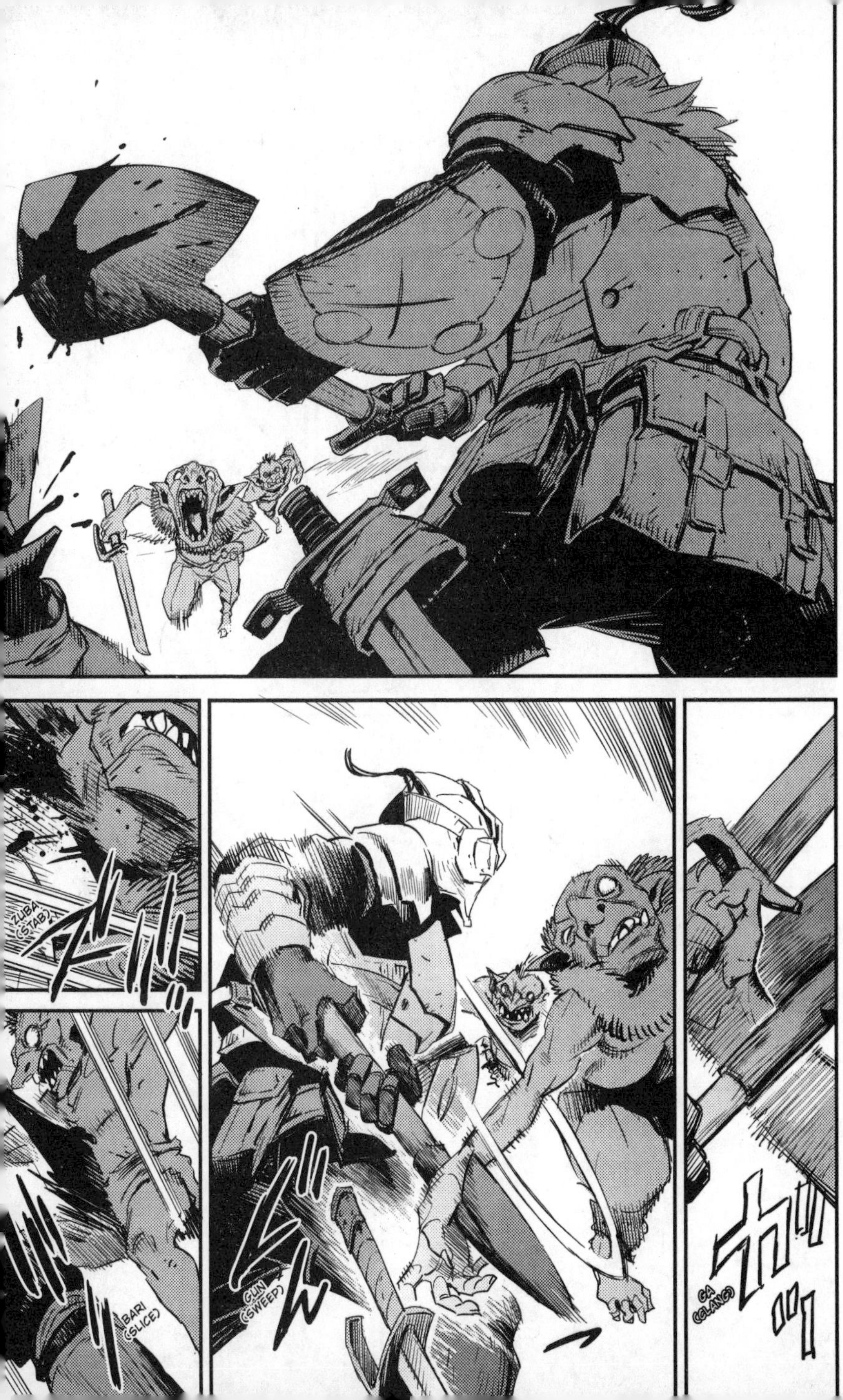
GA (CLANG)
GUN (SWEEP)
ZUBA (STAB)
BARI (SLICE)

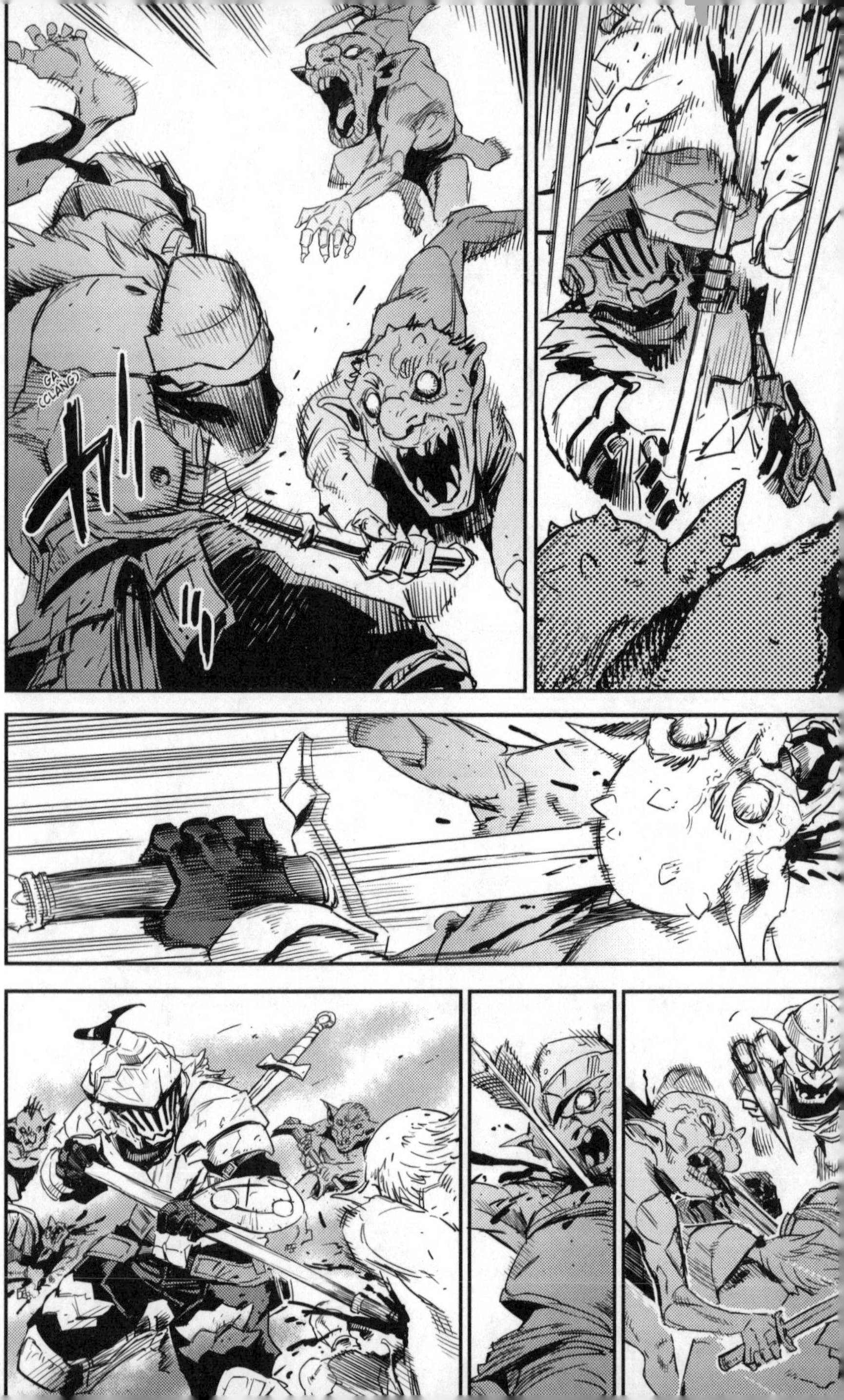
GA (CLANG)

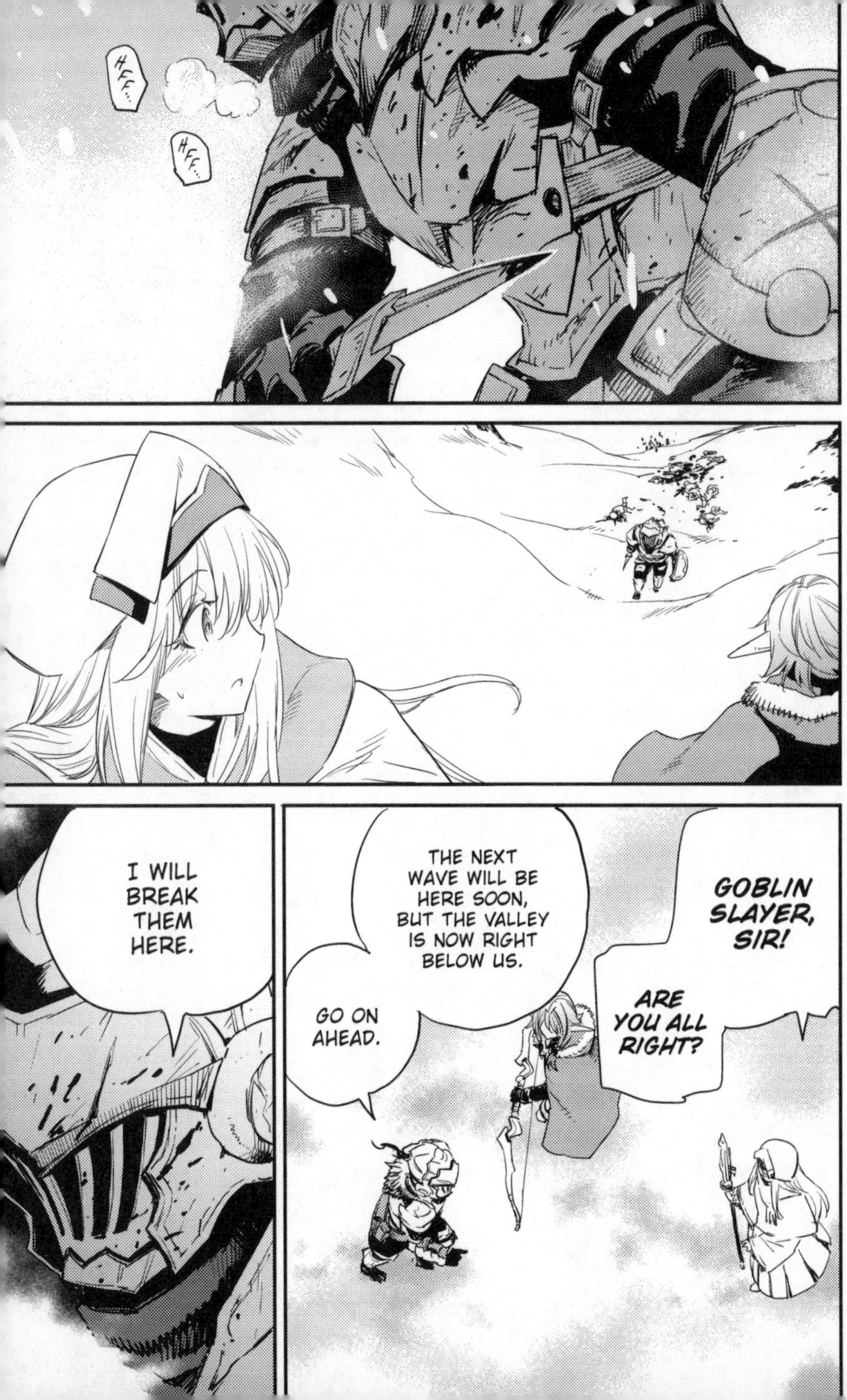
HFF...
HFF...
GOBLIN SLAYER, SIR!
ARE YOU ALL RIGHT?
THE NEXT WAVE WILL BE HERE SOON, BUT THE VALLEY IS NOW RIGHT BELOW US.
GO ON AHEAD.
I WILL BREAK THEM HERE.

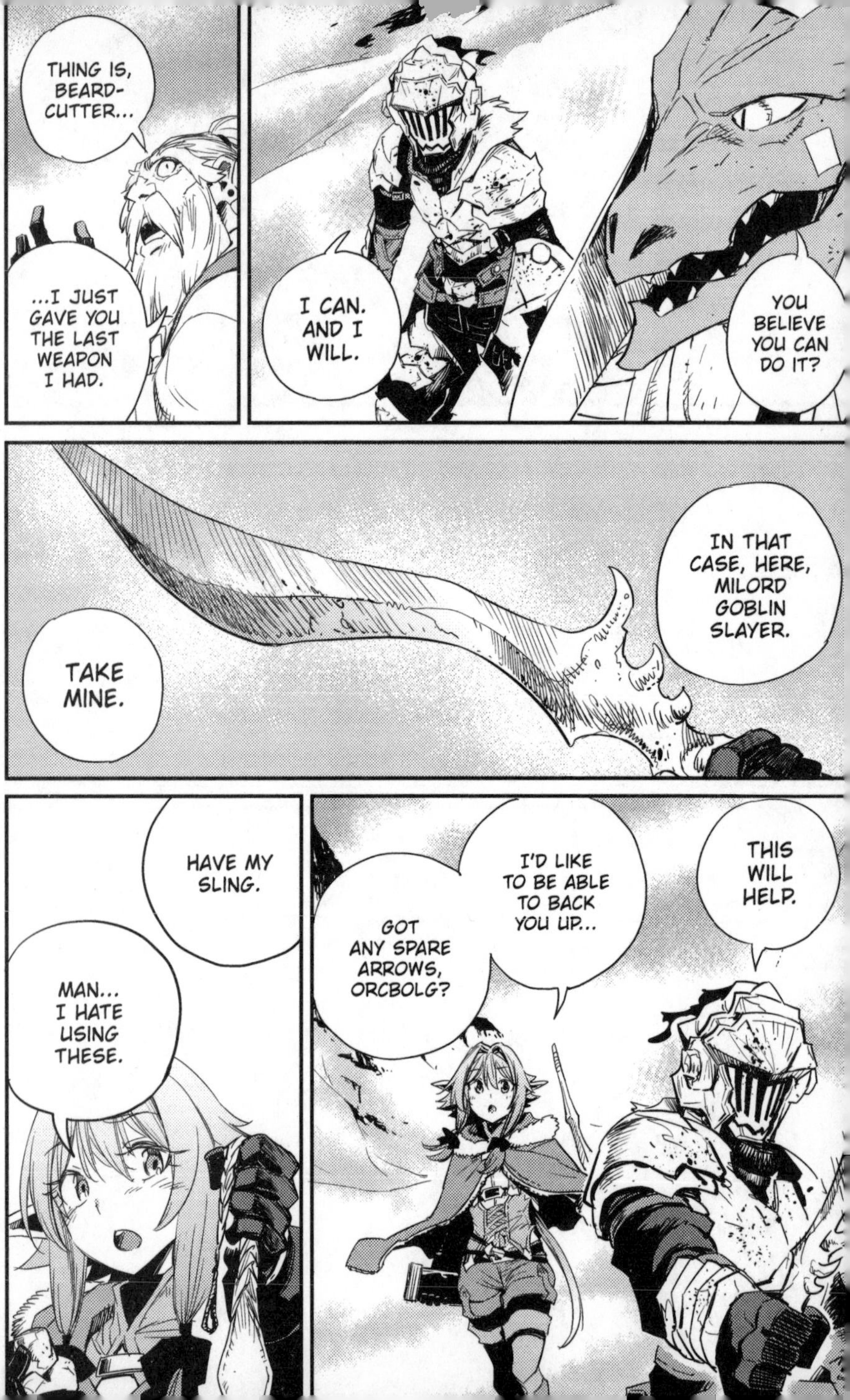
YOU BELIEVE YOU CAN DO IT?
I CAN. AND I WILL.
THING IS, BEARD-CUTTER...
...I JUST GAVE YOU THE LAST WEAPON I HAD.
IN THAT CASE, HERE, MILORD GOBLIN SLAYER.
TAKE MINE.
THIS WILL HELP.
I'D LIKE TO BE ABLE TO BACK YOU UP...
GOT ANY SPARE ARROWS, ORCBOLG?
HAVE MY SLING.
MAN... I HATE USING THESE.

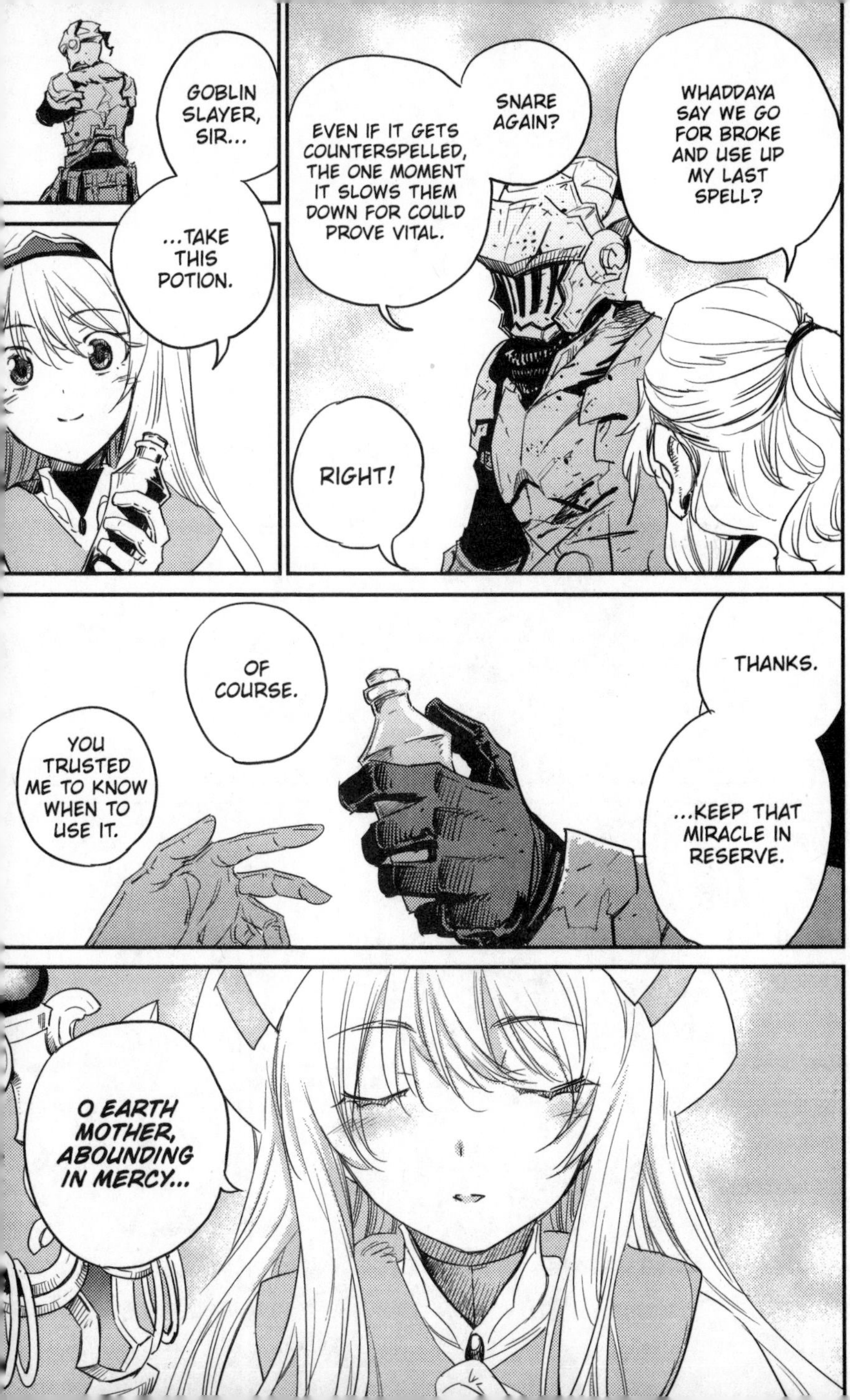
WHADDAYA SAY WE GO FOR BROKE AND USE UP MY LAST SPELL?
SNARE AGAIN?
EVEN IF IT GETS COUNTERSPELLED, THE ONE MOMENT IT SLOWS THEM DOWN FOR COULD PROVE VITAL.
RIGHT!
GOBLIN SLAYER, SIR...
...TAKE THIS POTION.
THANKS.
...KEEP THAT MIRACLE IN RESERVE.
OF COURSE.
YOU TRUSTED ME TO KNOW WHEN TO USE IT.
O EARTH MOTHER, ABOUNDING IN MERCY...

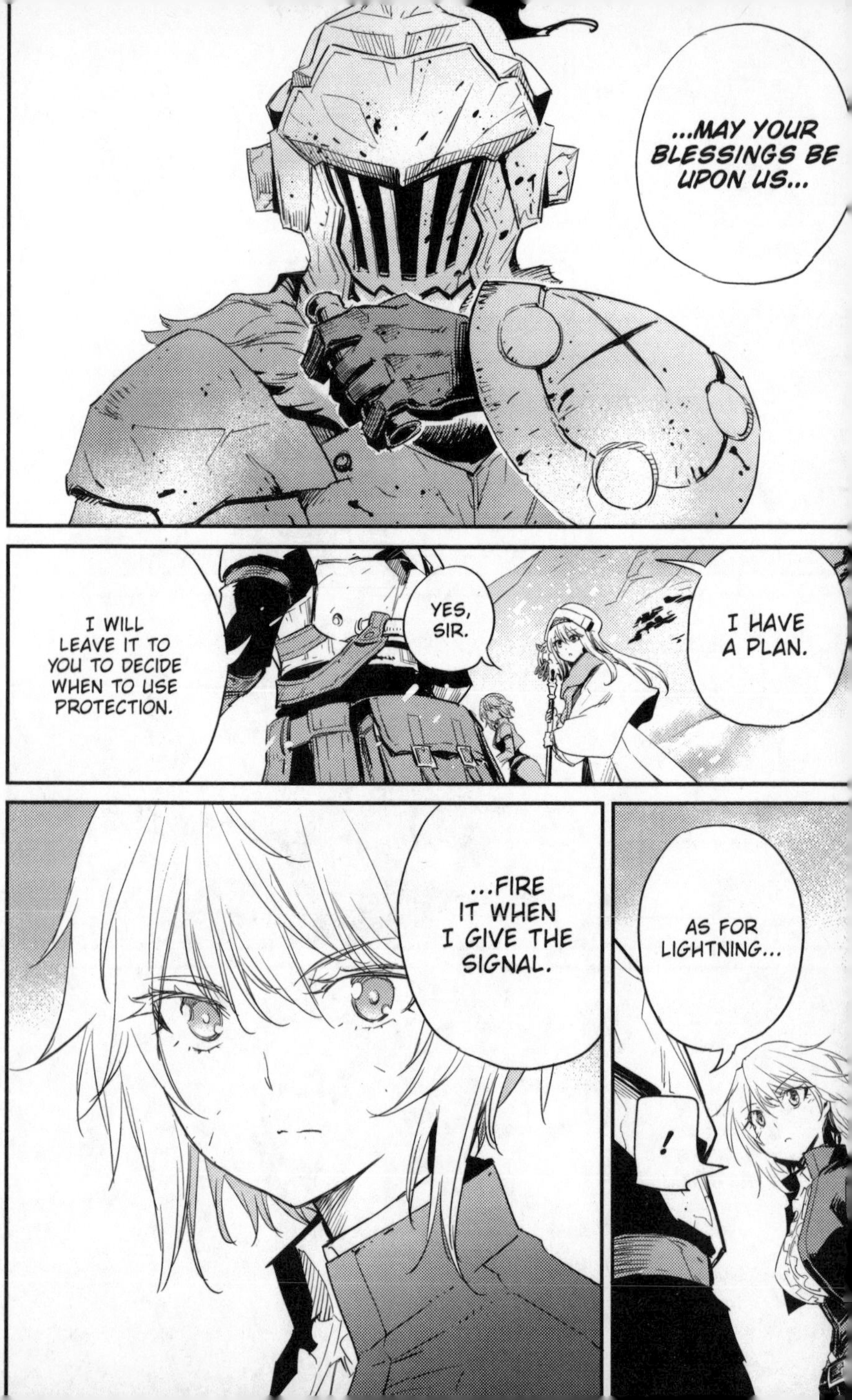
...MAY YOUR BLESSINGS BE UPON US...
I HAVE A PLAN.
YES, SIR.
I WILL LEAVE IT TO YOU TO DECIDE WHEN TO USE PROTECTION.
AS FOR LIGHTNING...
!
...FIRE IT WHEN I GIVE THE SIGNAL.

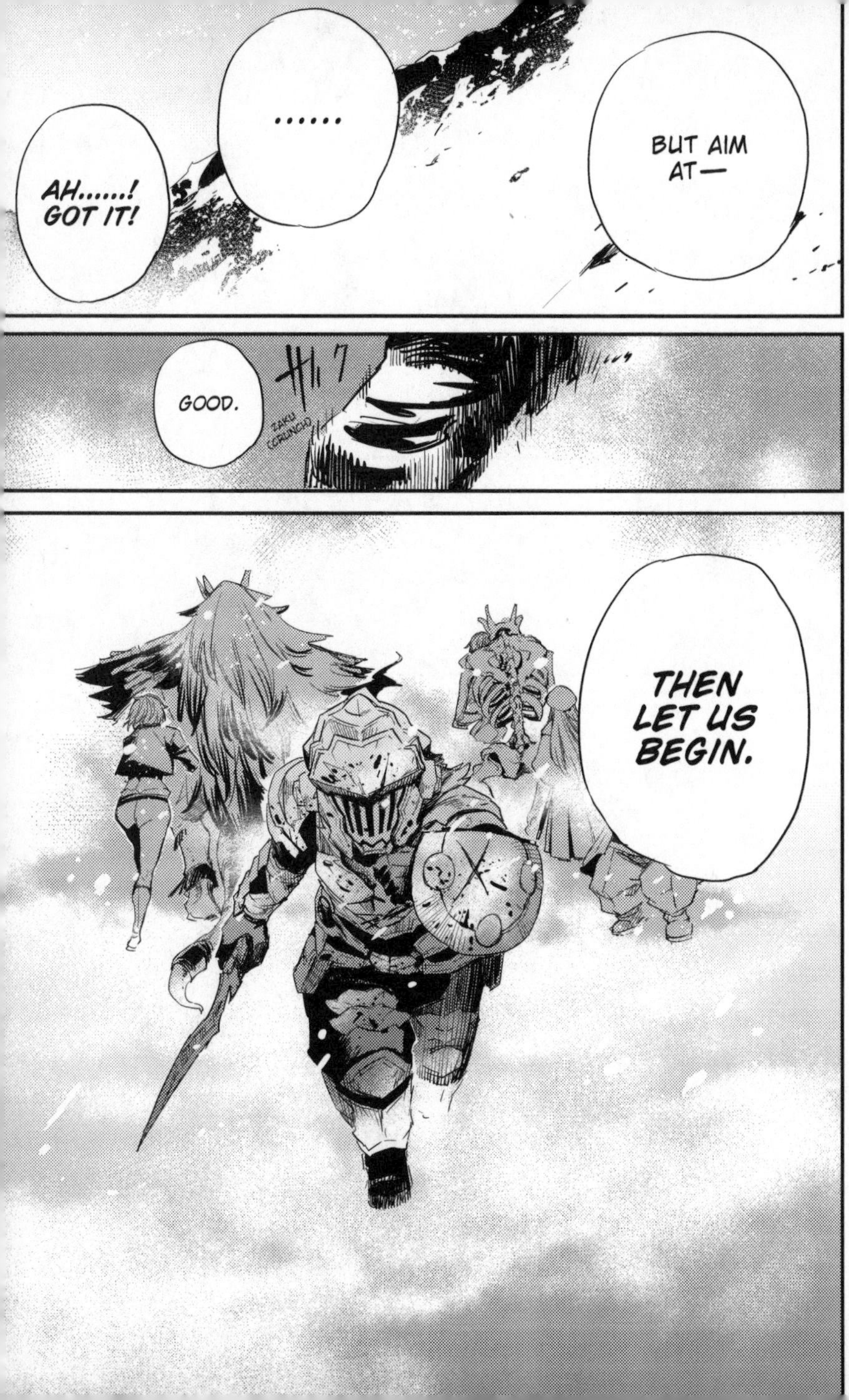
BUT AIM AT—
......
AH......! GOT IT!
ザクッ
ZAKU (CRUNCH)
GOOD.
THEN LET US BEGIN.

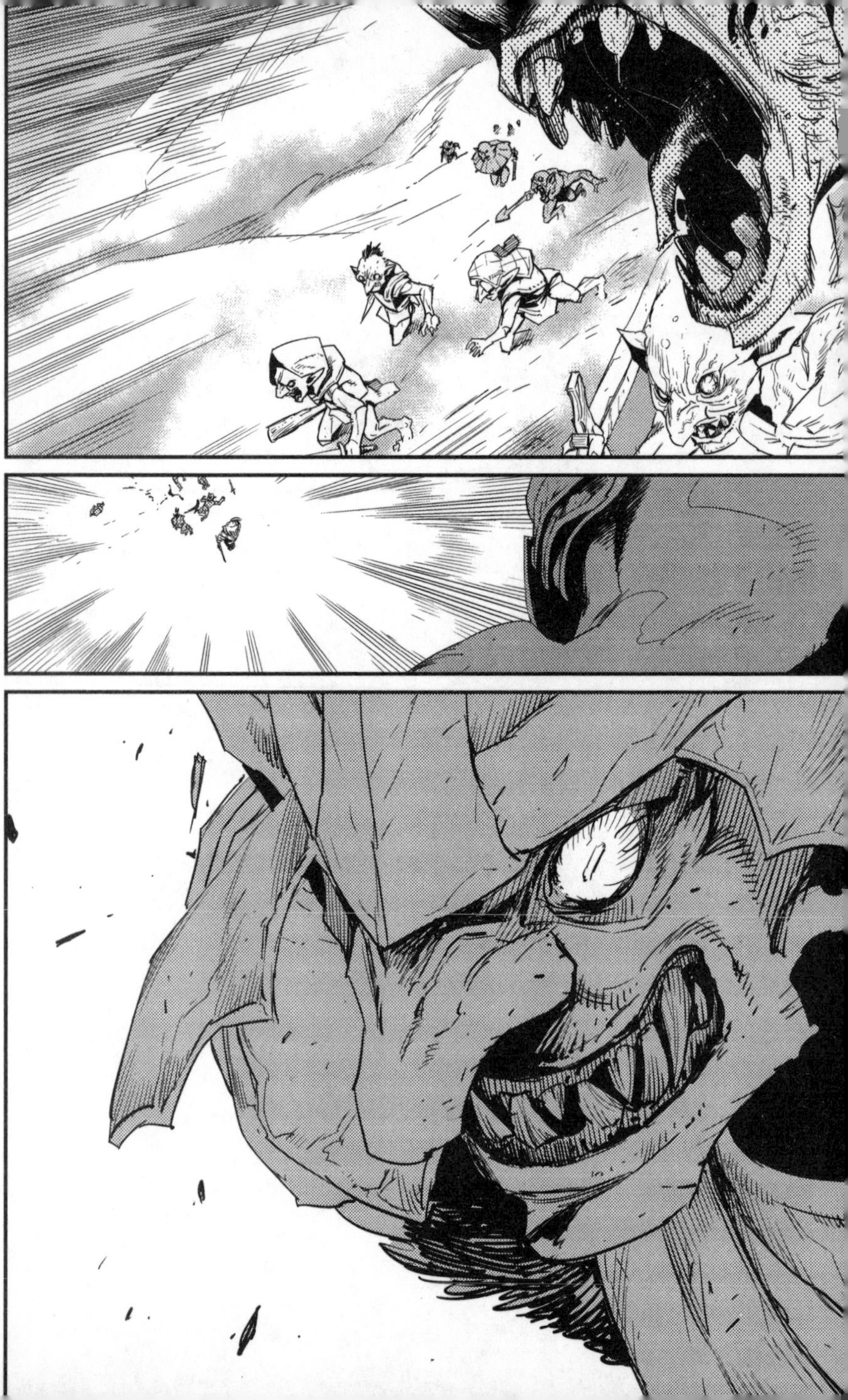

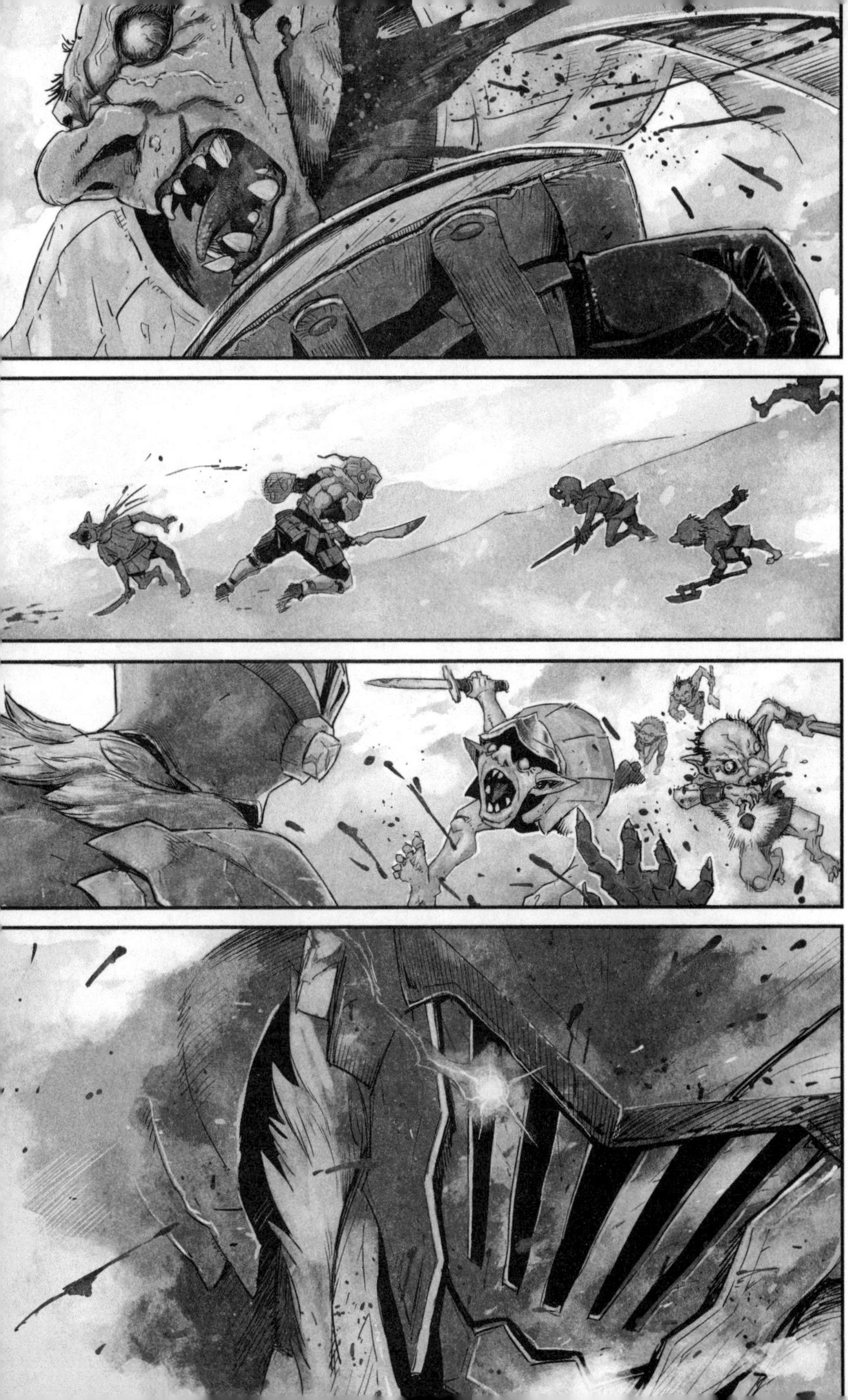

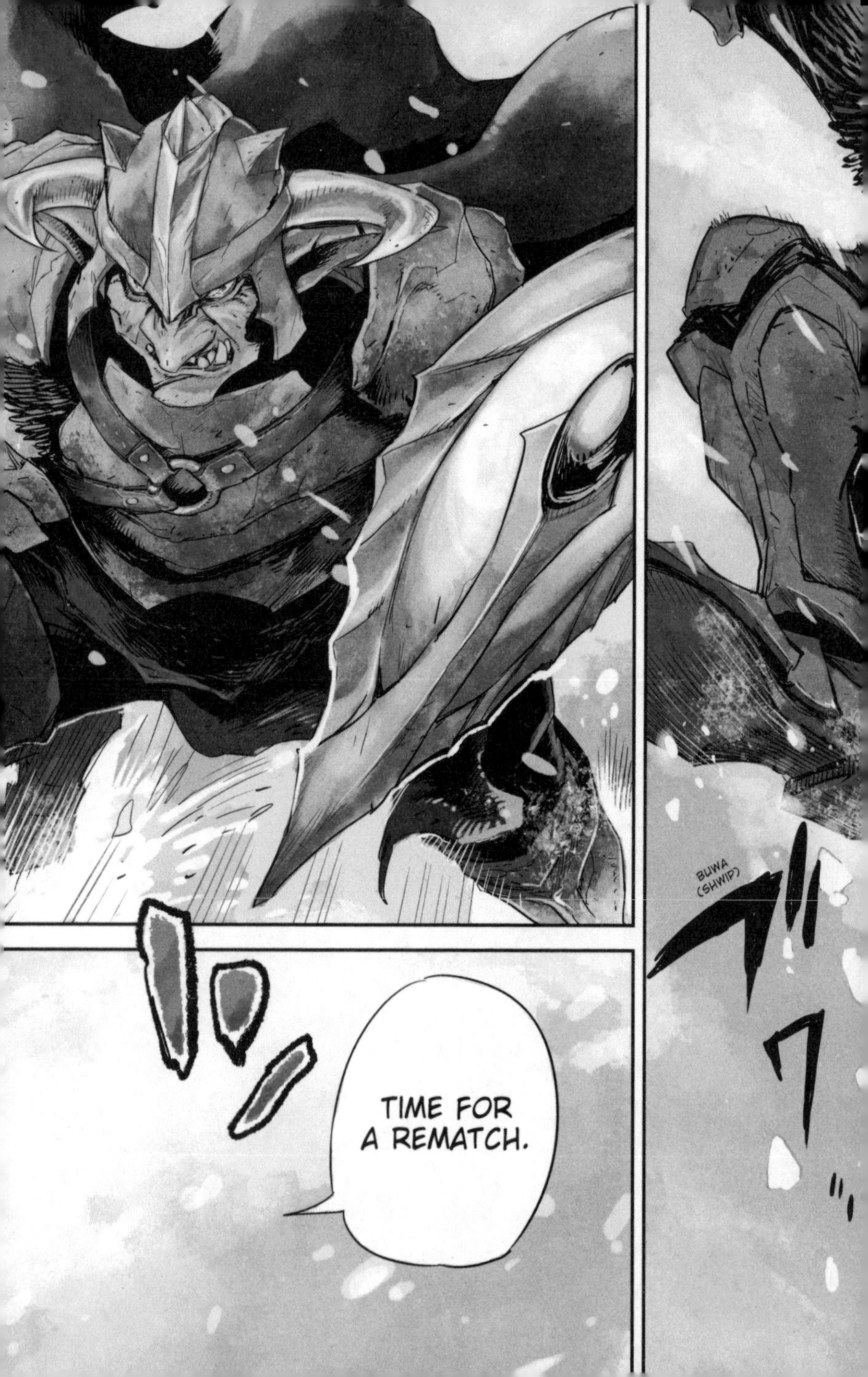
BUWA
(SHWIP)
TIME FOR A REMATCH.

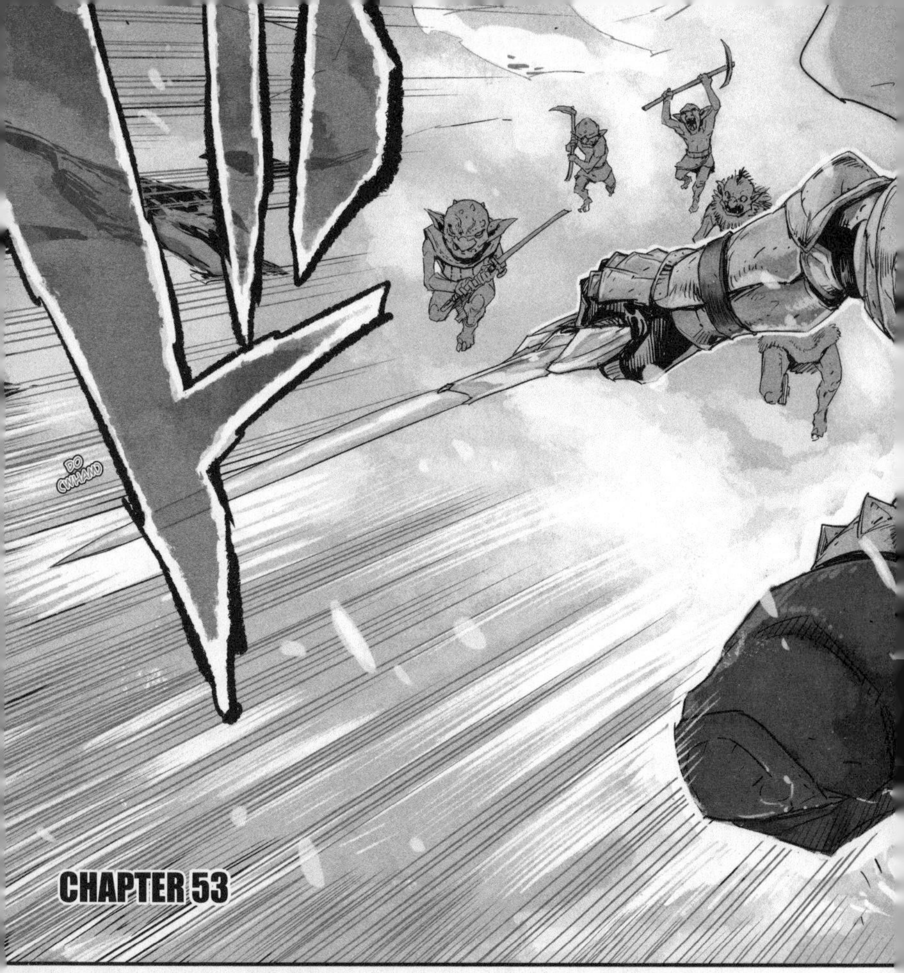
DO CWHAND
CHAPTER 53
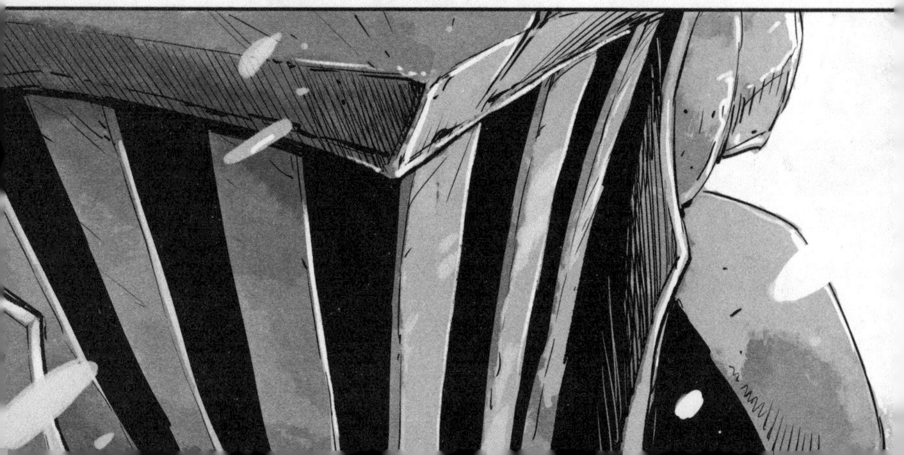

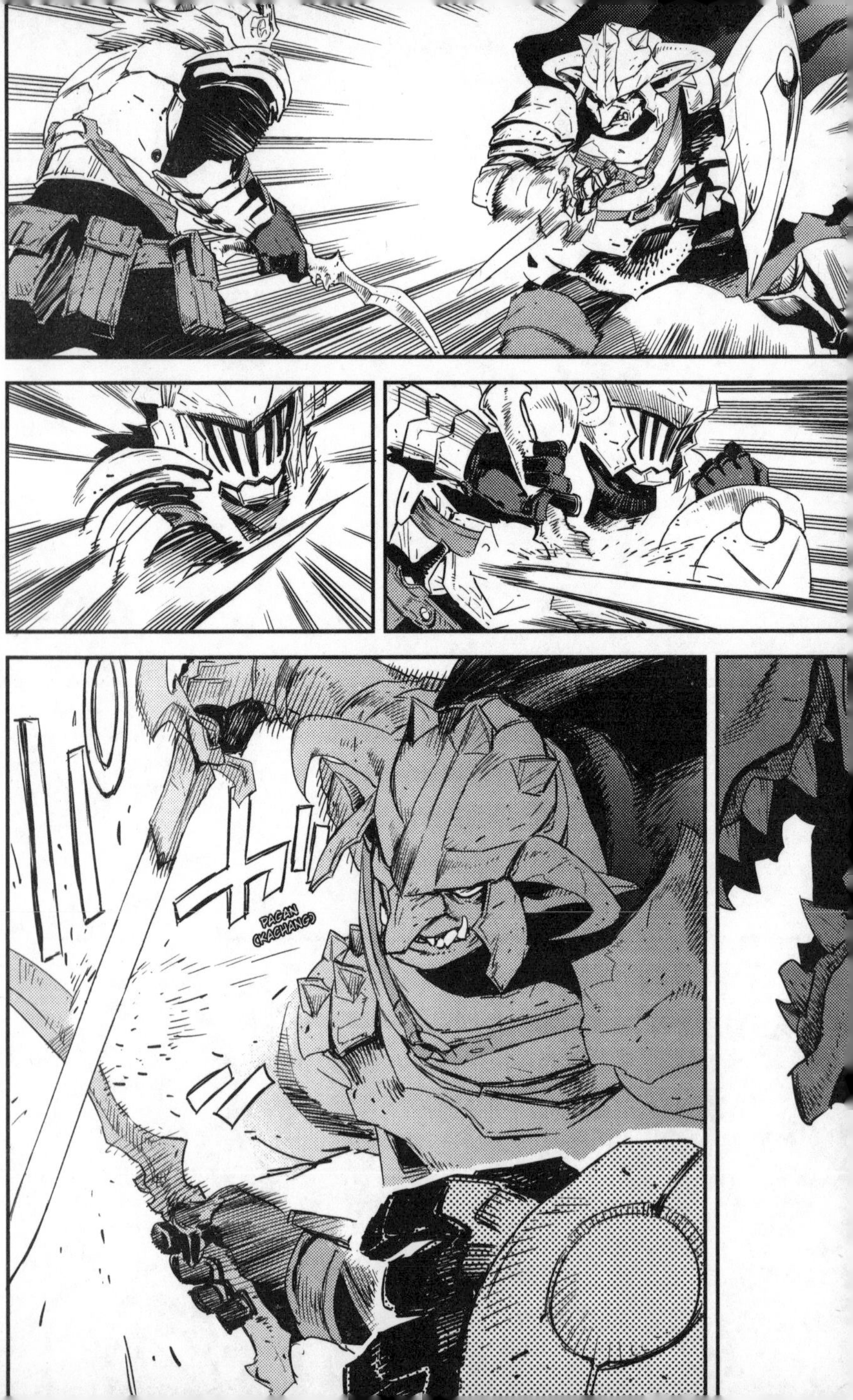
PAGAN
(KACHANG)

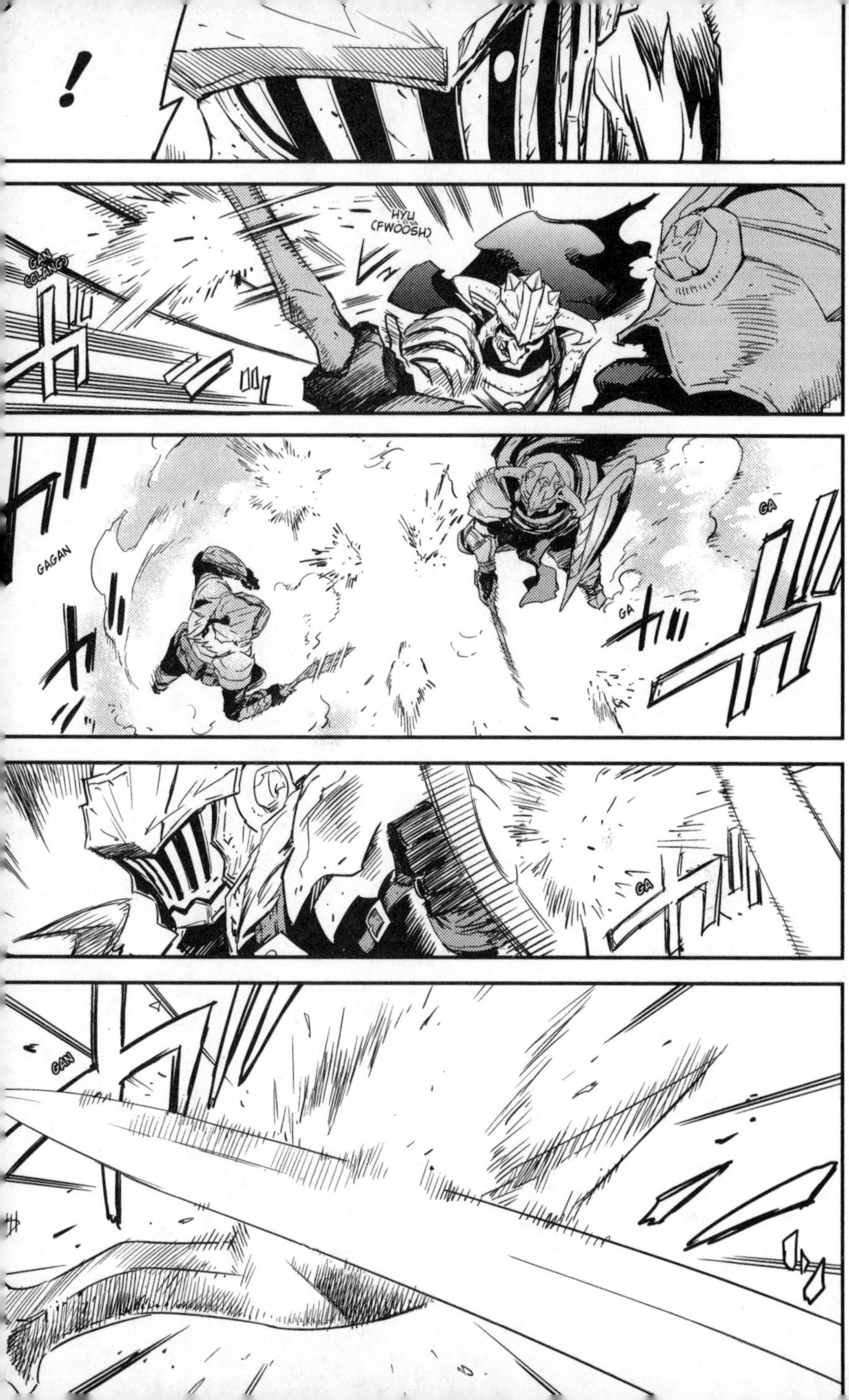
!
HYU
(FWOOSH)
GAN
(CLANG)
GA
GA
GAGAN
GA
GAN

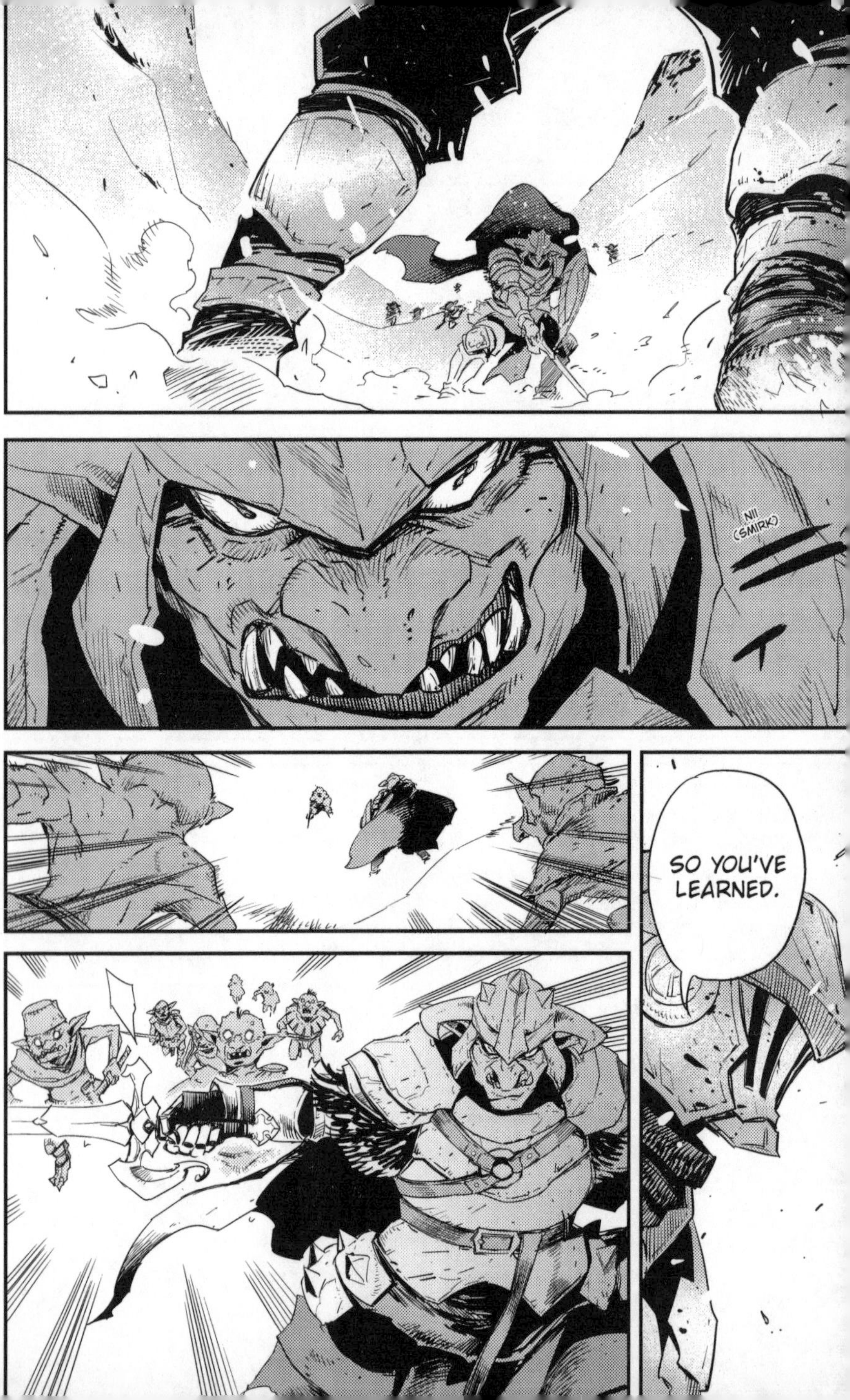
NII
(SMIRK)
SO YOU'VE LEARNED.

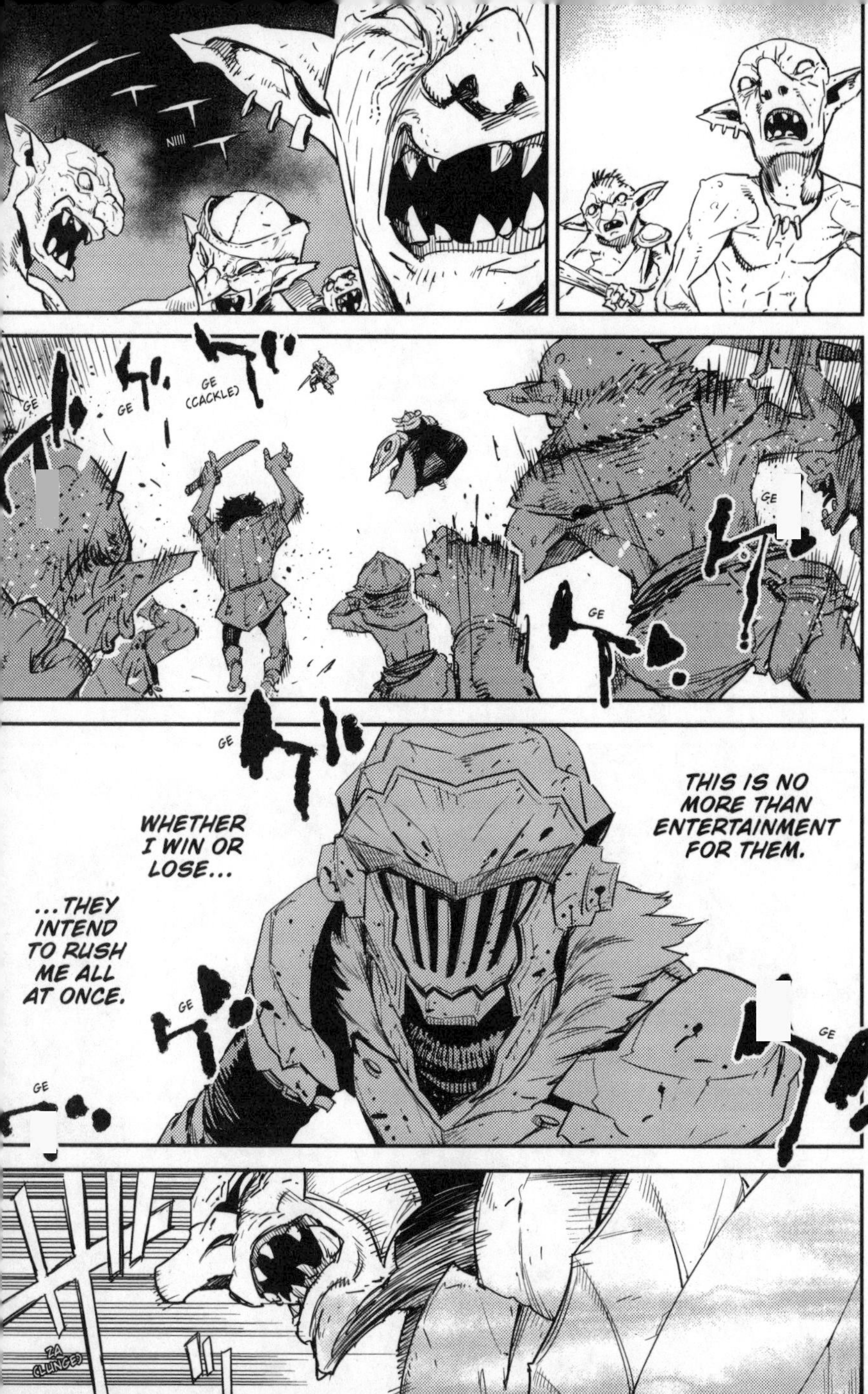
NIIII
GE
GE
GE
(CACKLE)
GE
GE
GE
THIS IS NO MORE THAN ENTERTAINMENT FOR THEM.
WHETHER I WIN OR LOSE...
...THEY INTEND TO RUSH ME ALL AT ONCE.
GE
GE
GE
ZA
(CLUNGED)

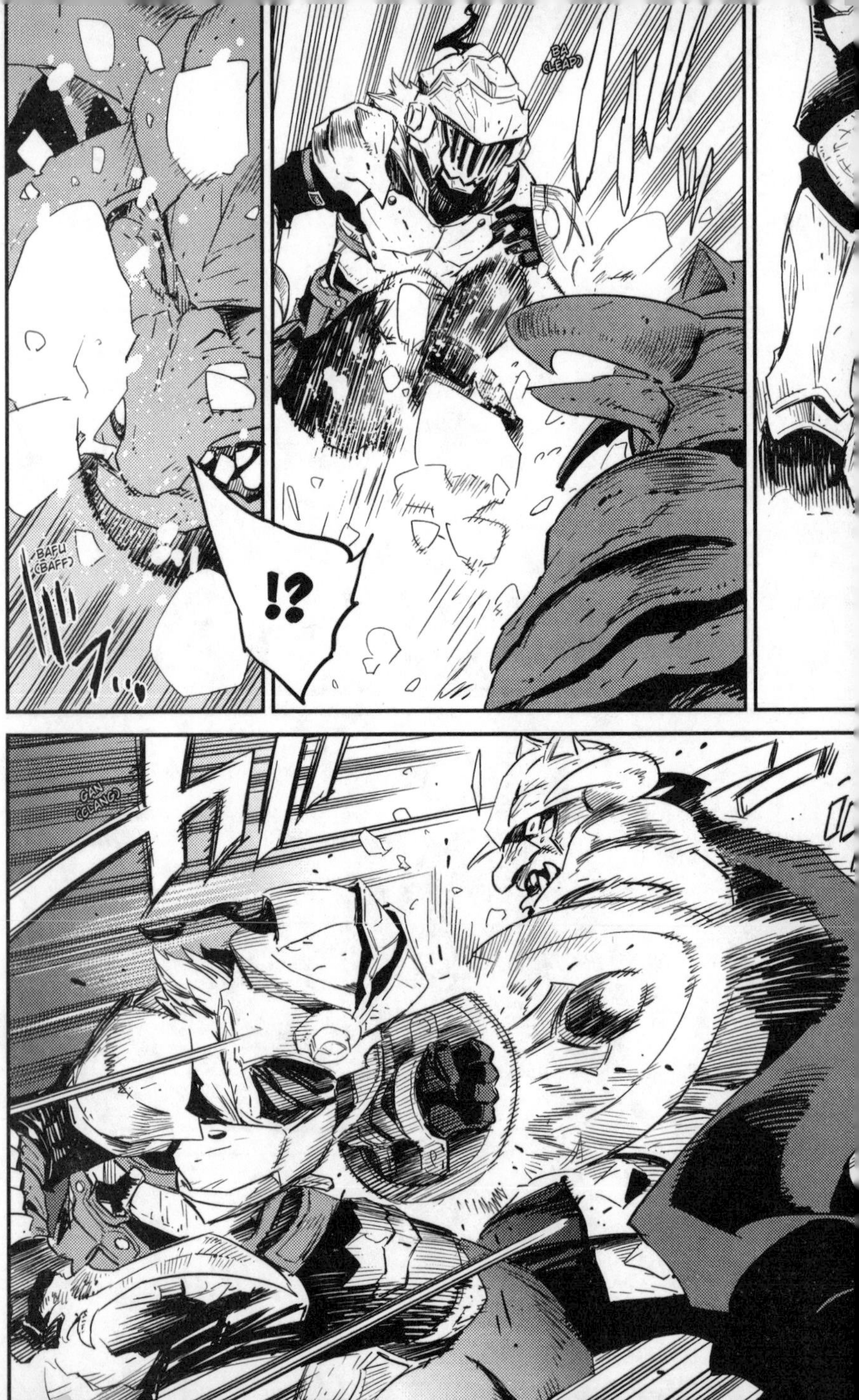
BA
(LEAP)
!?
BAFU
(BAFF)
GAN
(CLANG)

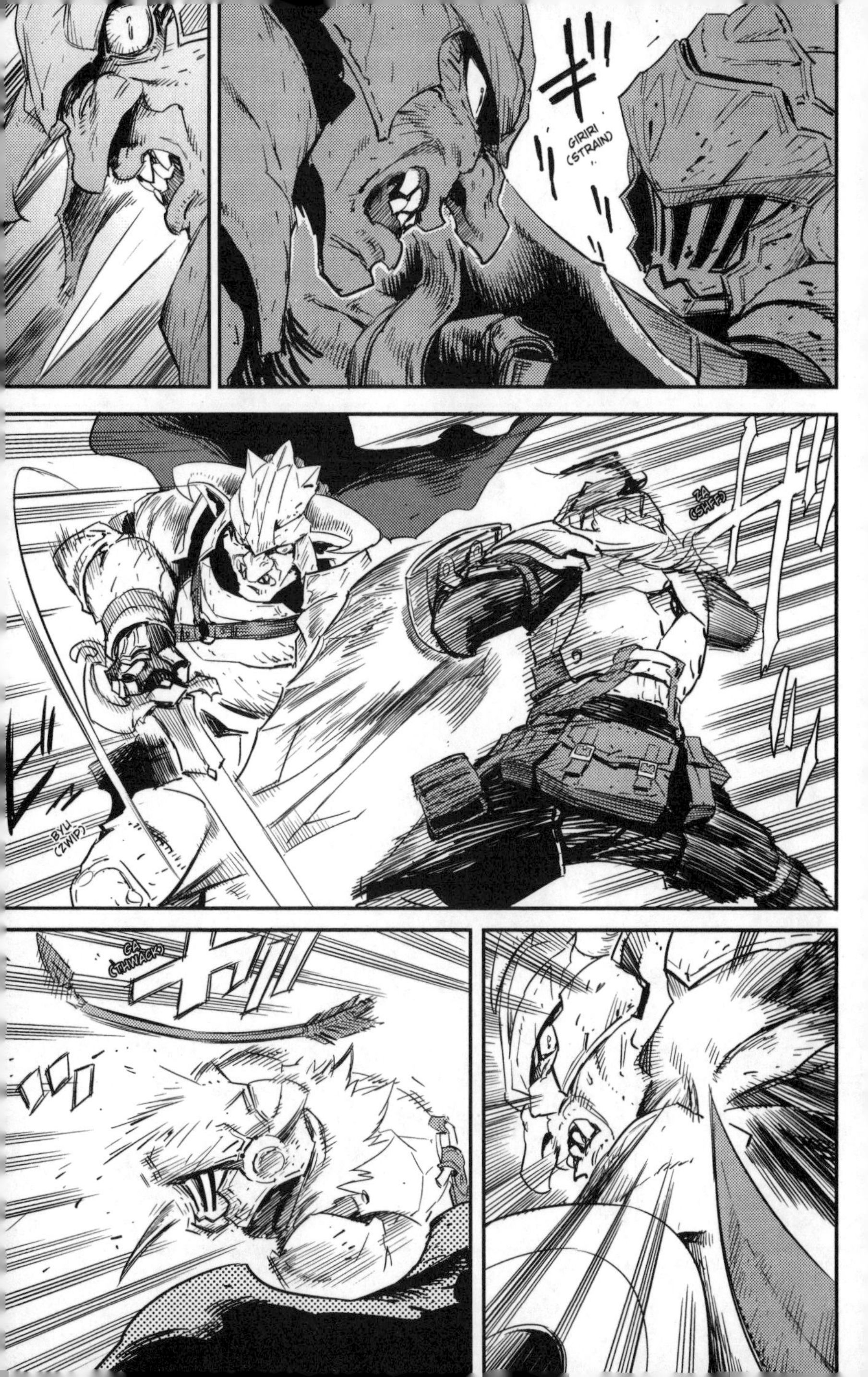
GIRIRI (STRAIN)
ZA (SHFF)
BYU (ZWIP)
GA (THWACK)

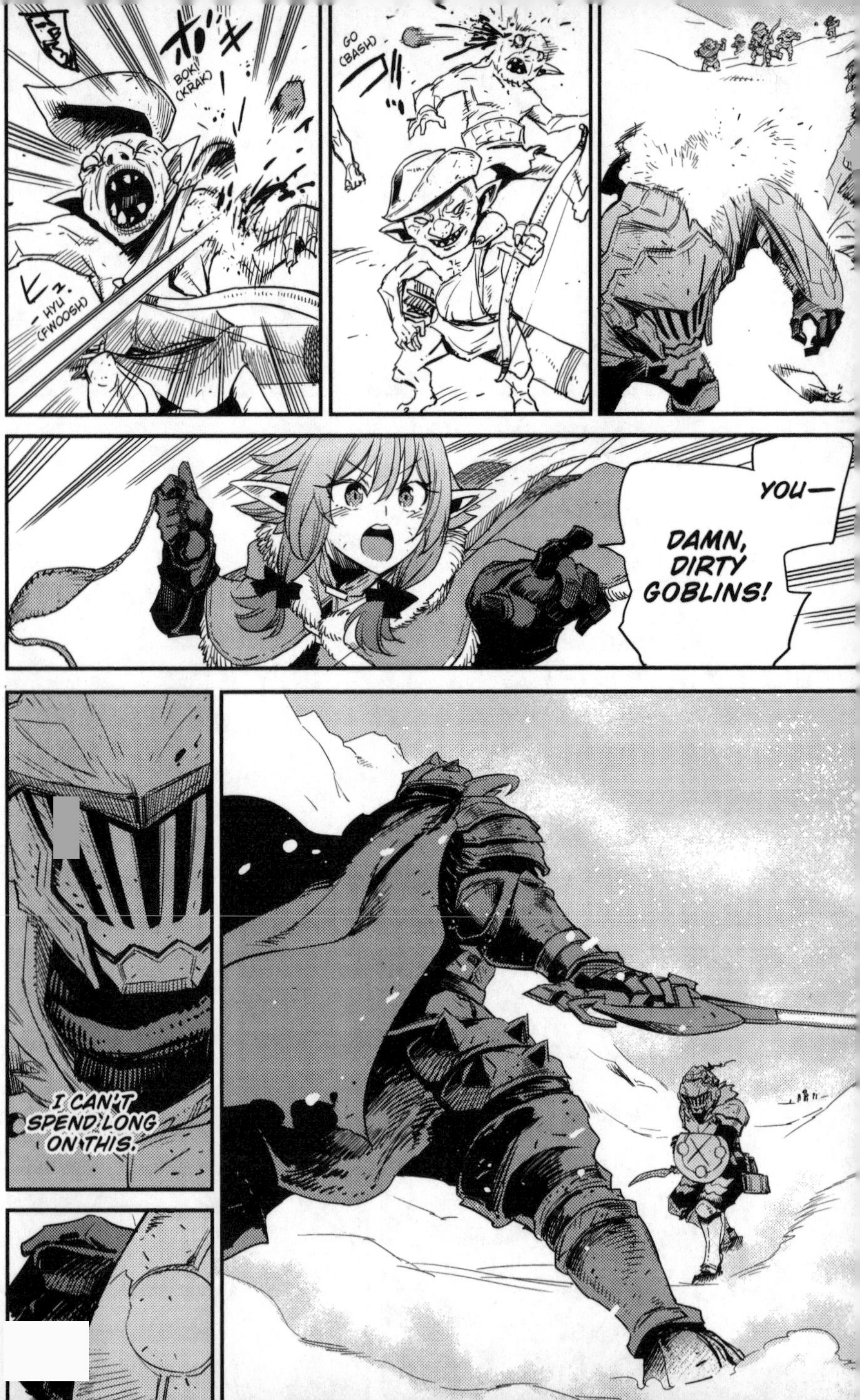
GO (BASH)
BOKI (KRAK)
HYU (FWOOSH)
YOU—
DAMN, DIRTY GOBLINS!
I CAN'T SPEND LONG ON THIS.

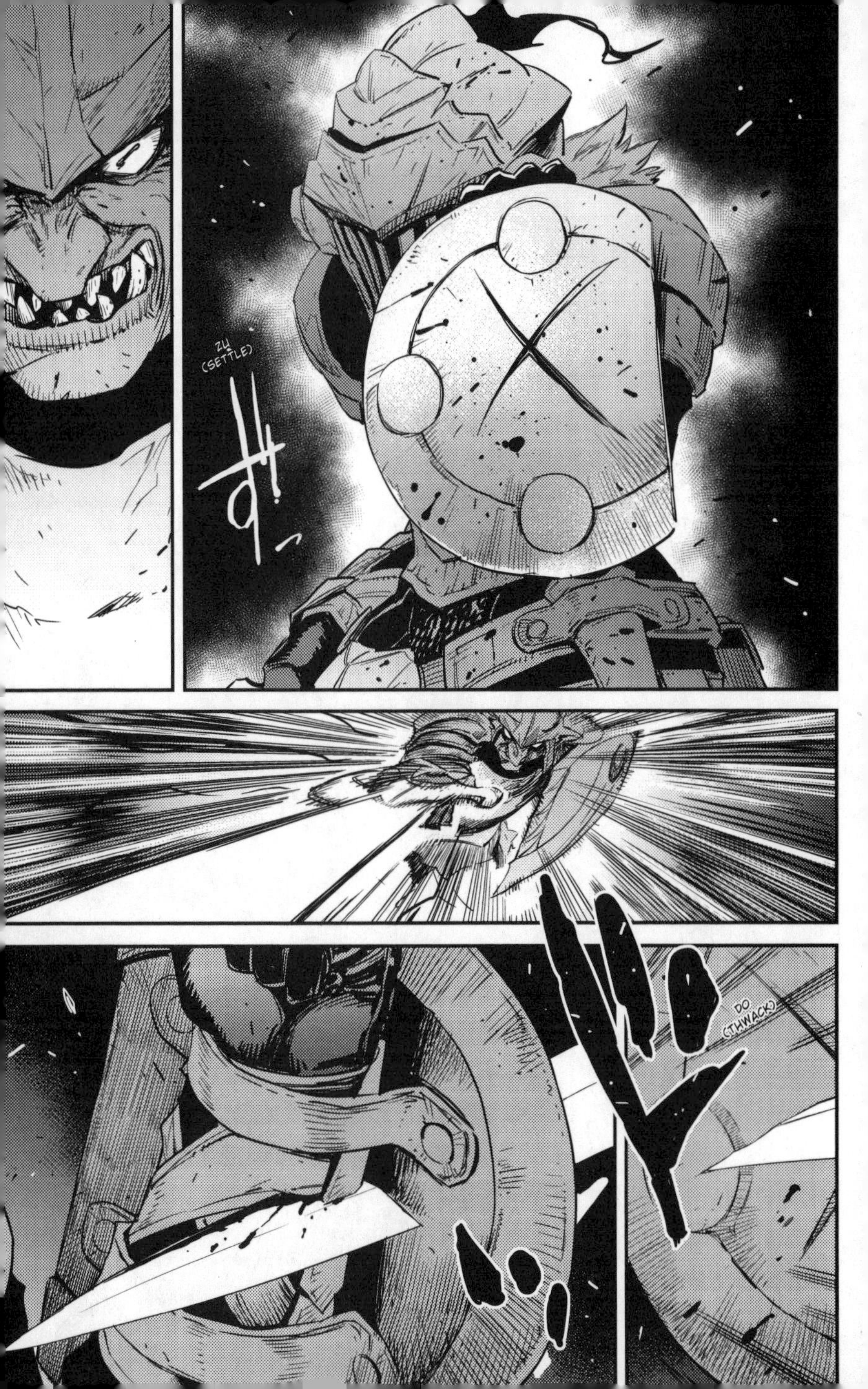
ZU
(SETTLE)
DO
(THWACK)

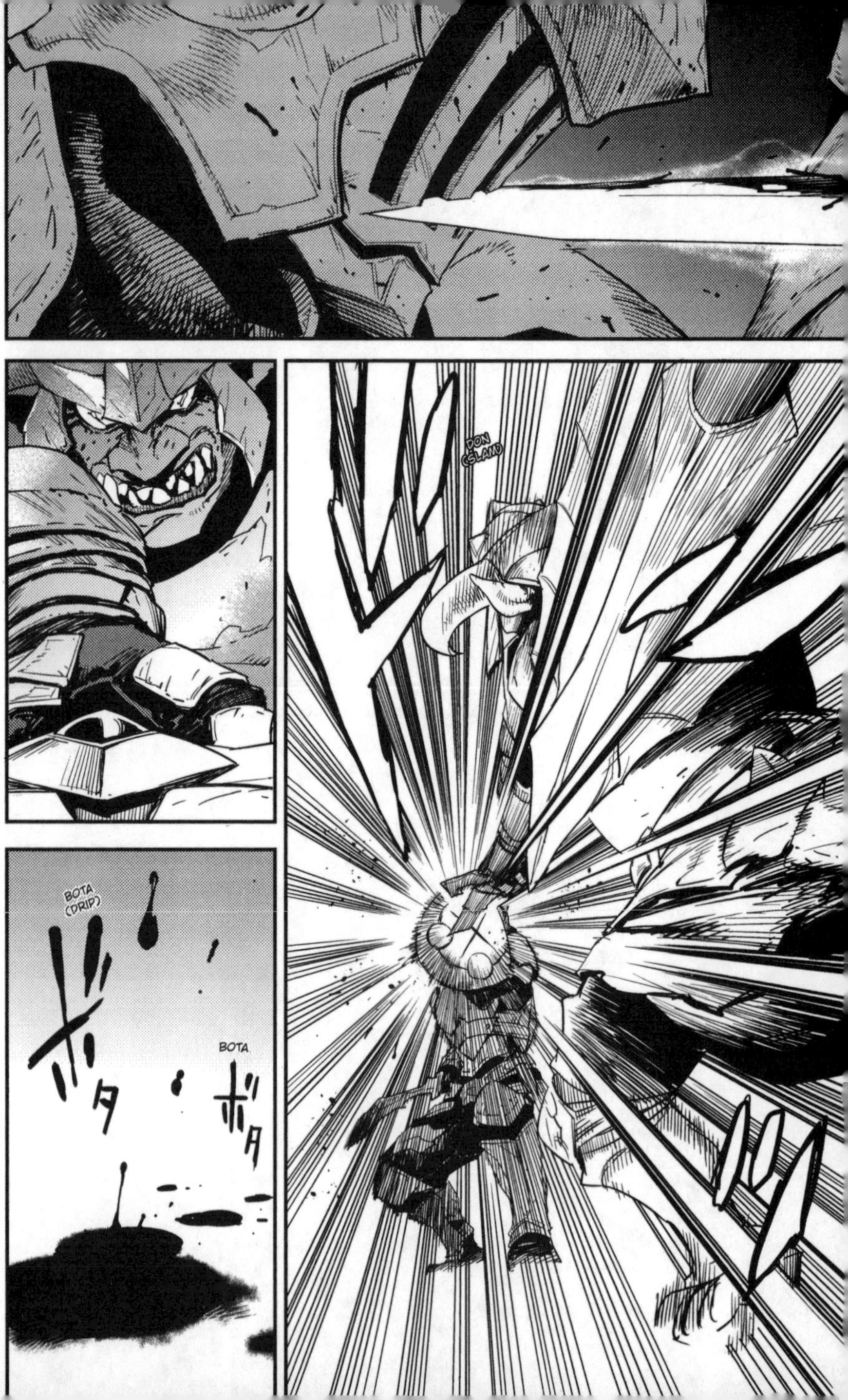
DON (SLAM)
BOTA (DRIP)
ボタ
BOTA
ボタ

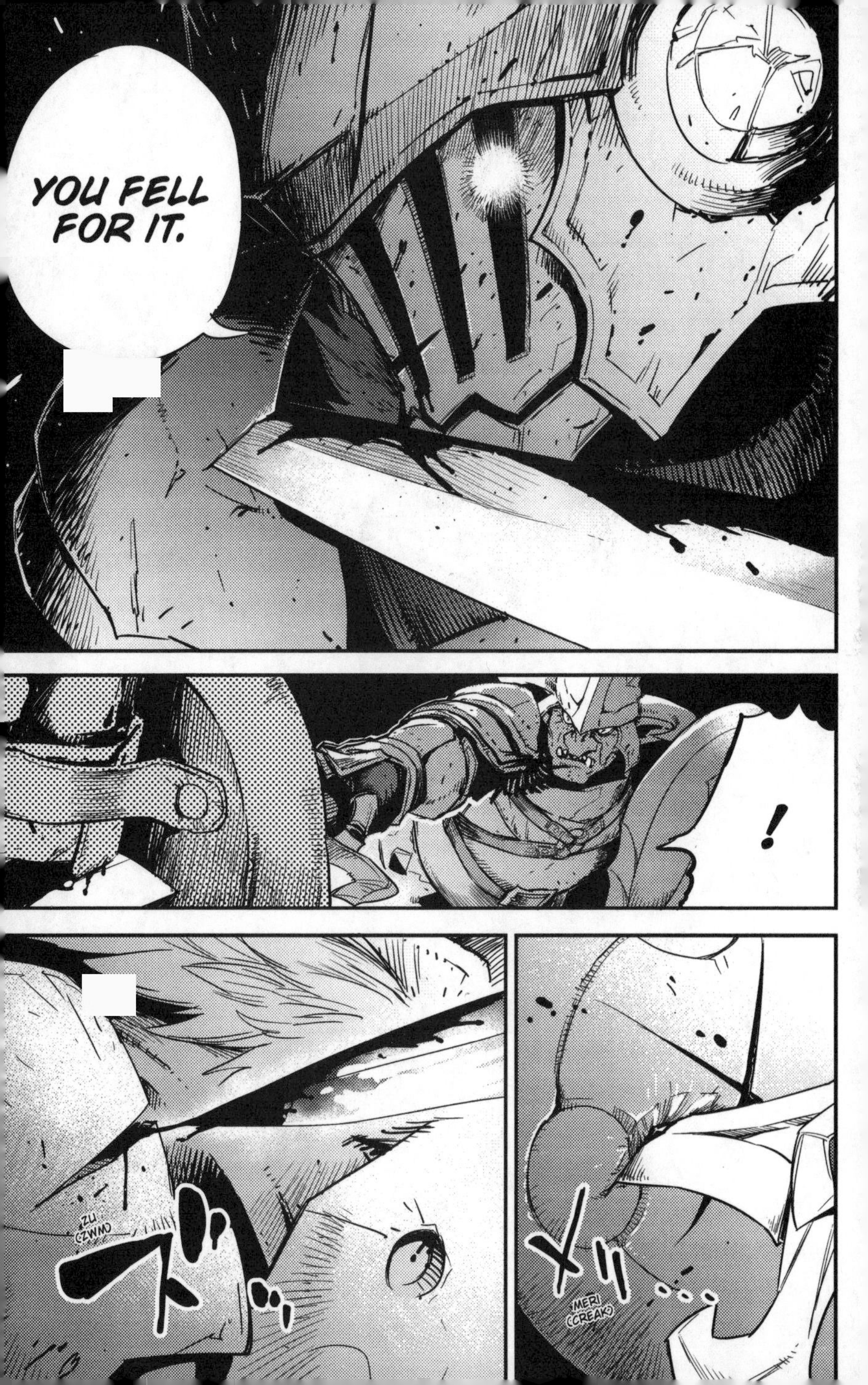
YOU FELL FOR IT.
!
ZU (ZWM)
MERI (CREAK)

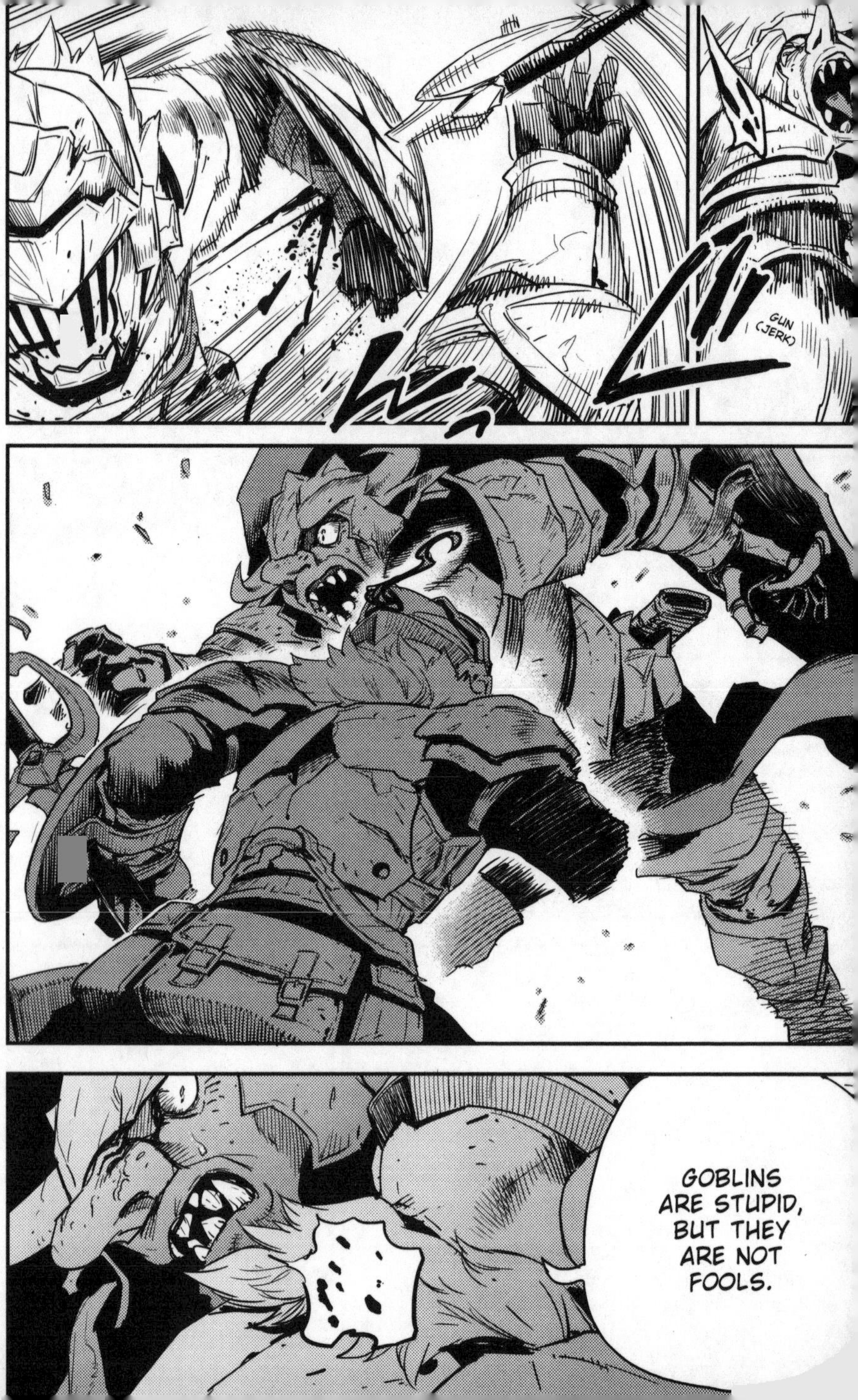
GUN (JERK)
GOBLINS ARE STUPID, BUT THEY ARE NOT FOOLS.

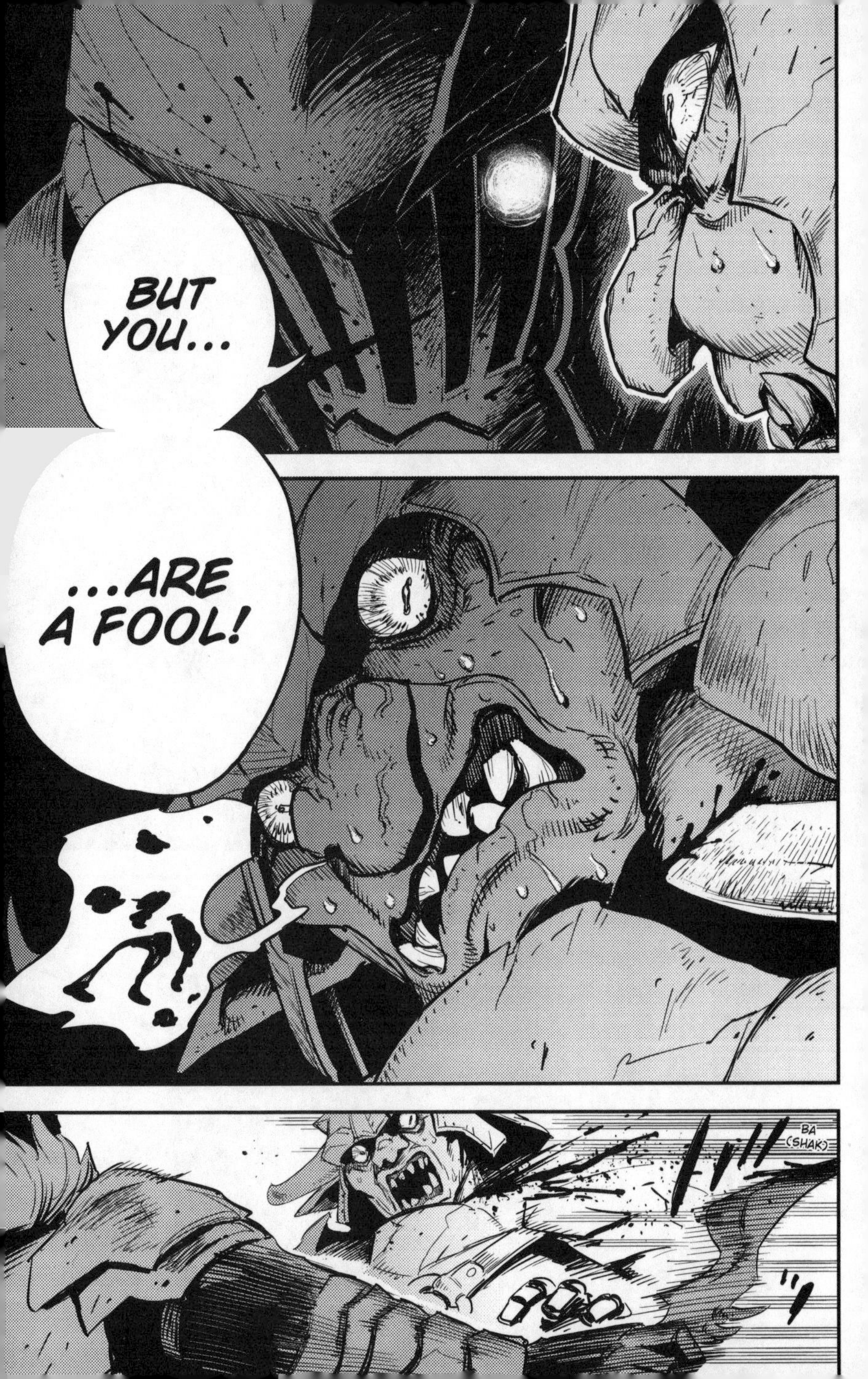
BUT YOU...
...ARE A FOOL!
BA (SHAK)

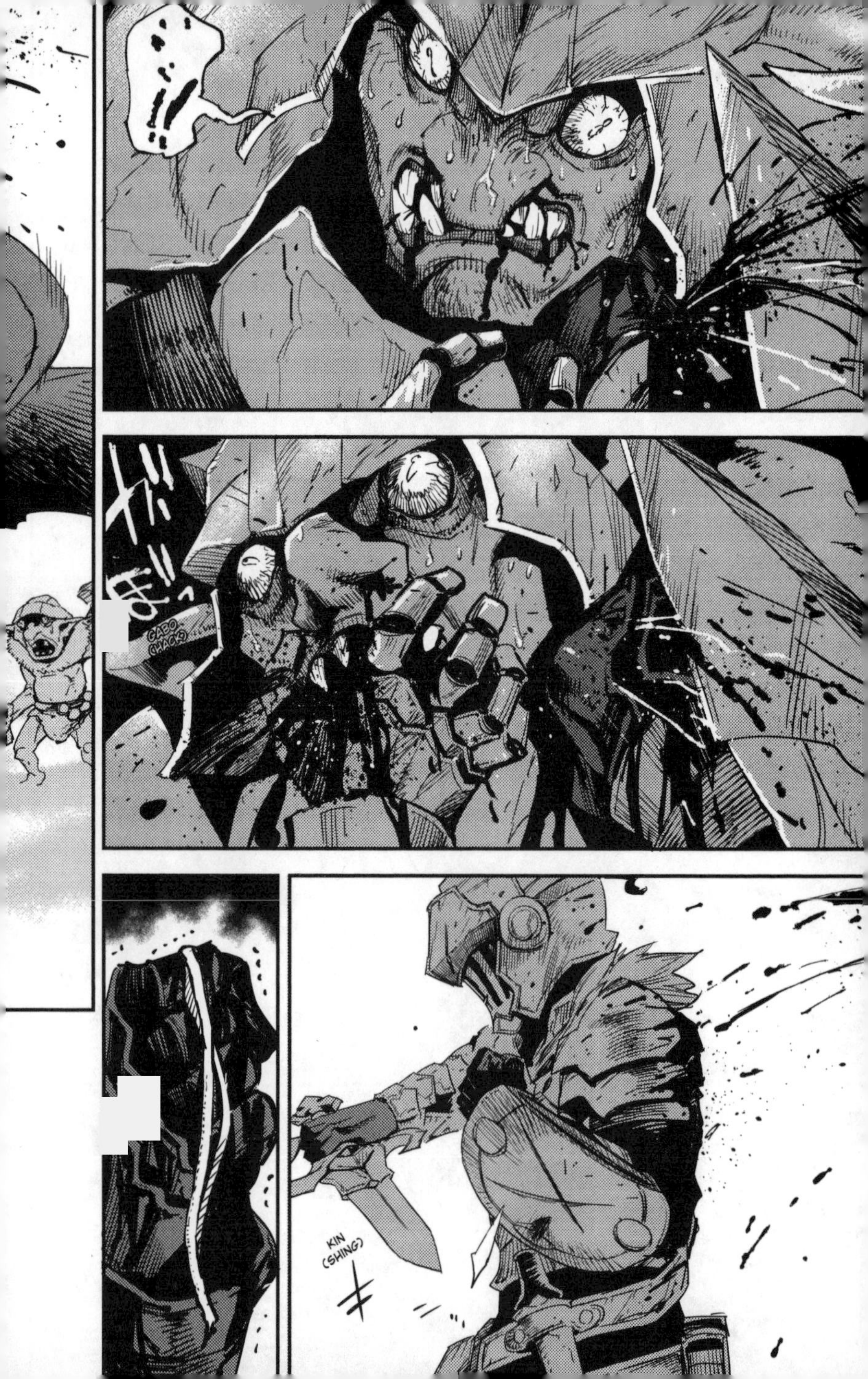
!!
GABO (CHACK)
KIN (SHING)

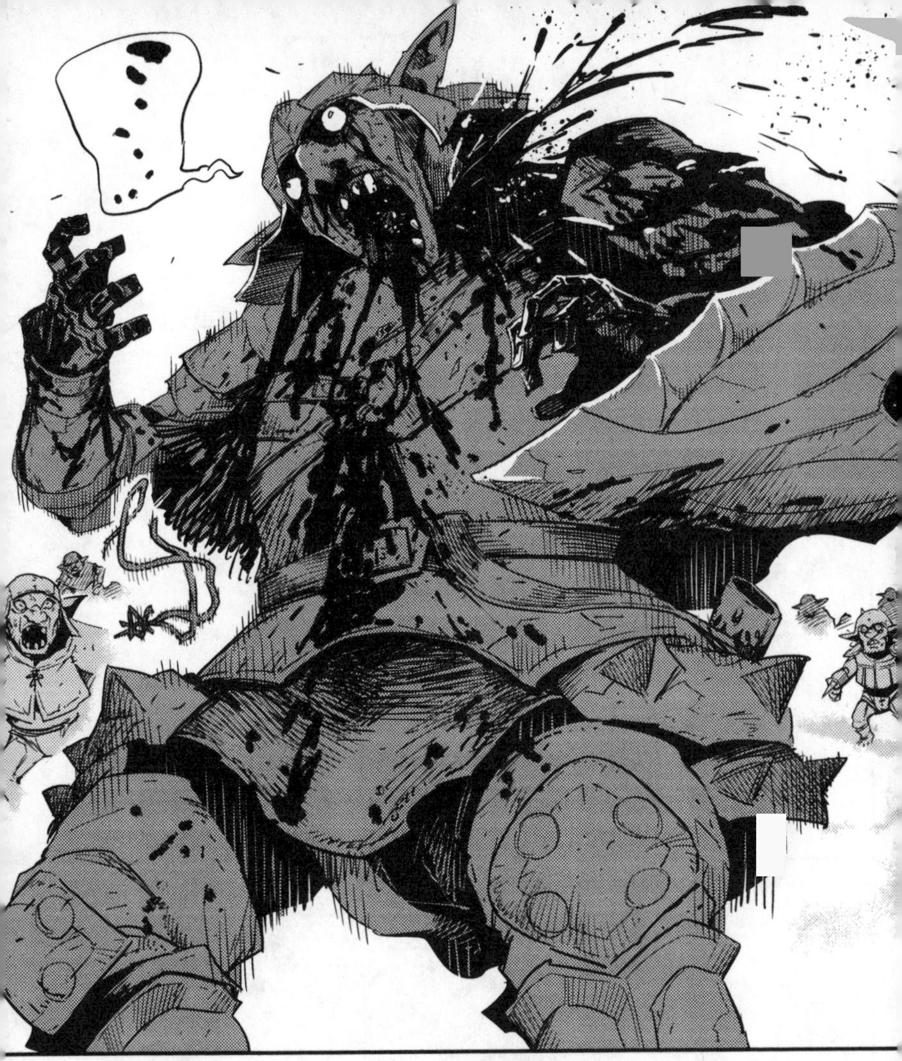
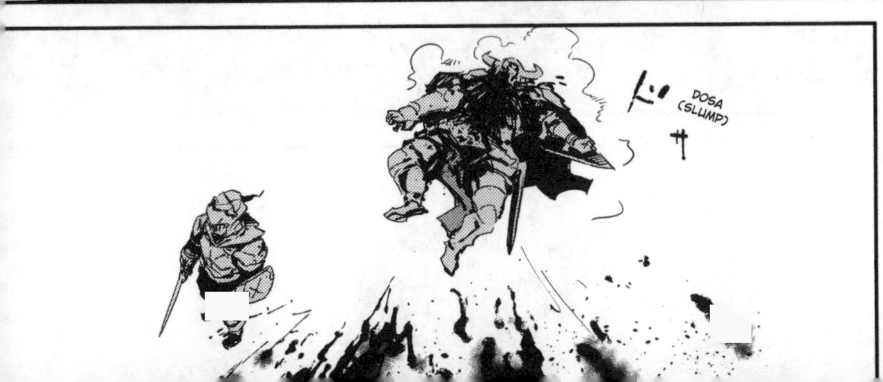
DOSA
(SLUMP)

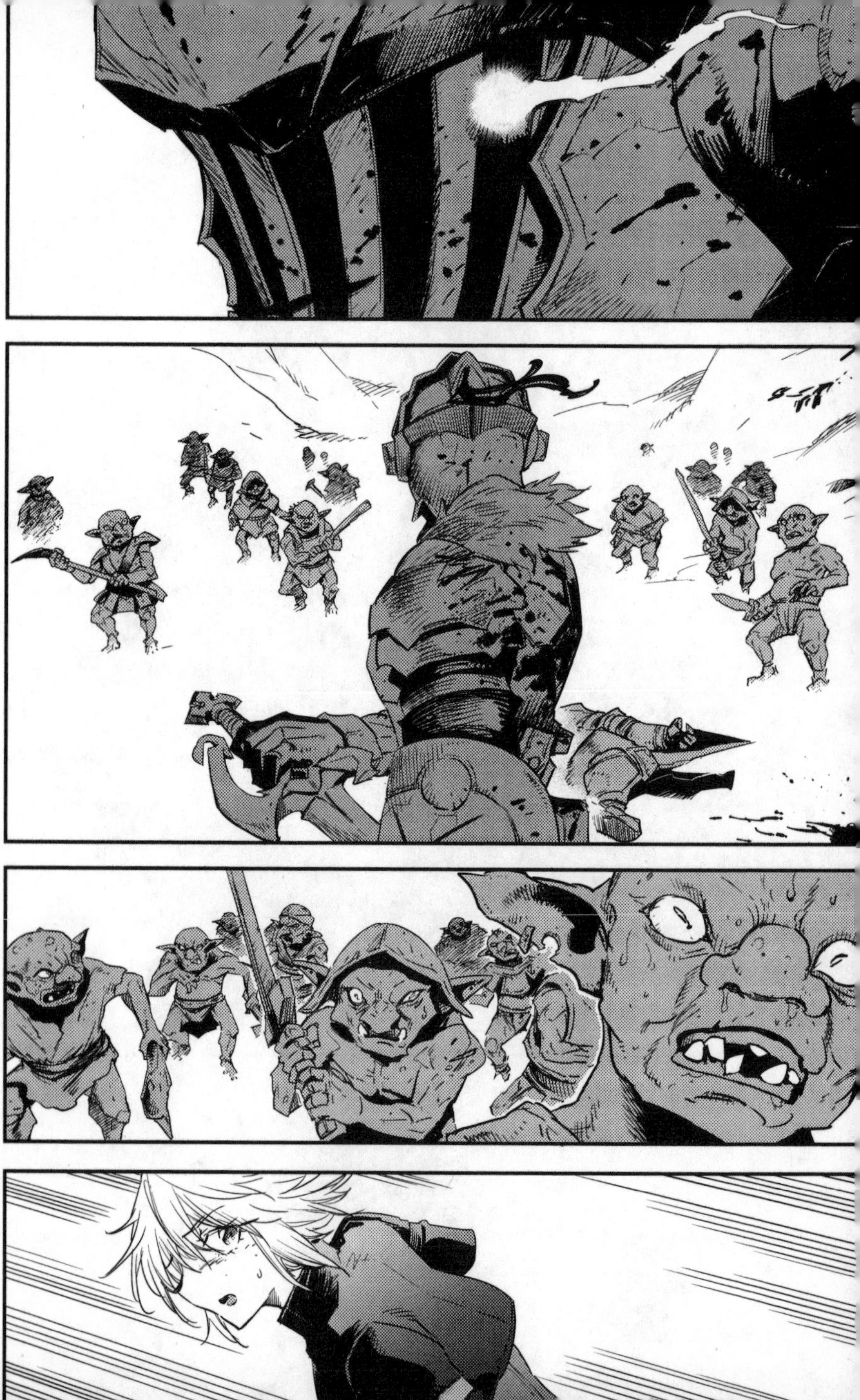

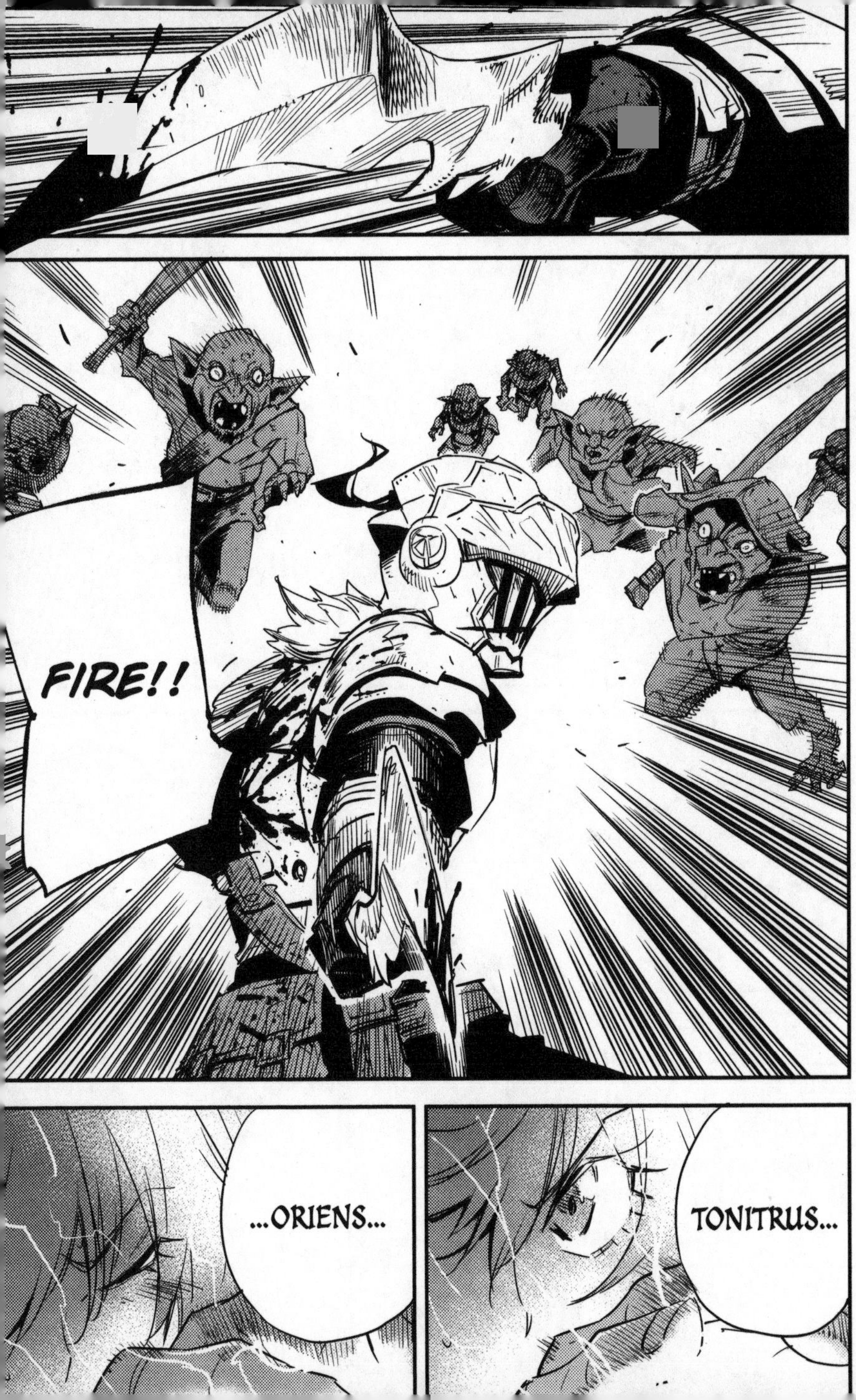
FIRE!!
TONITRUS...
...ORIENS...

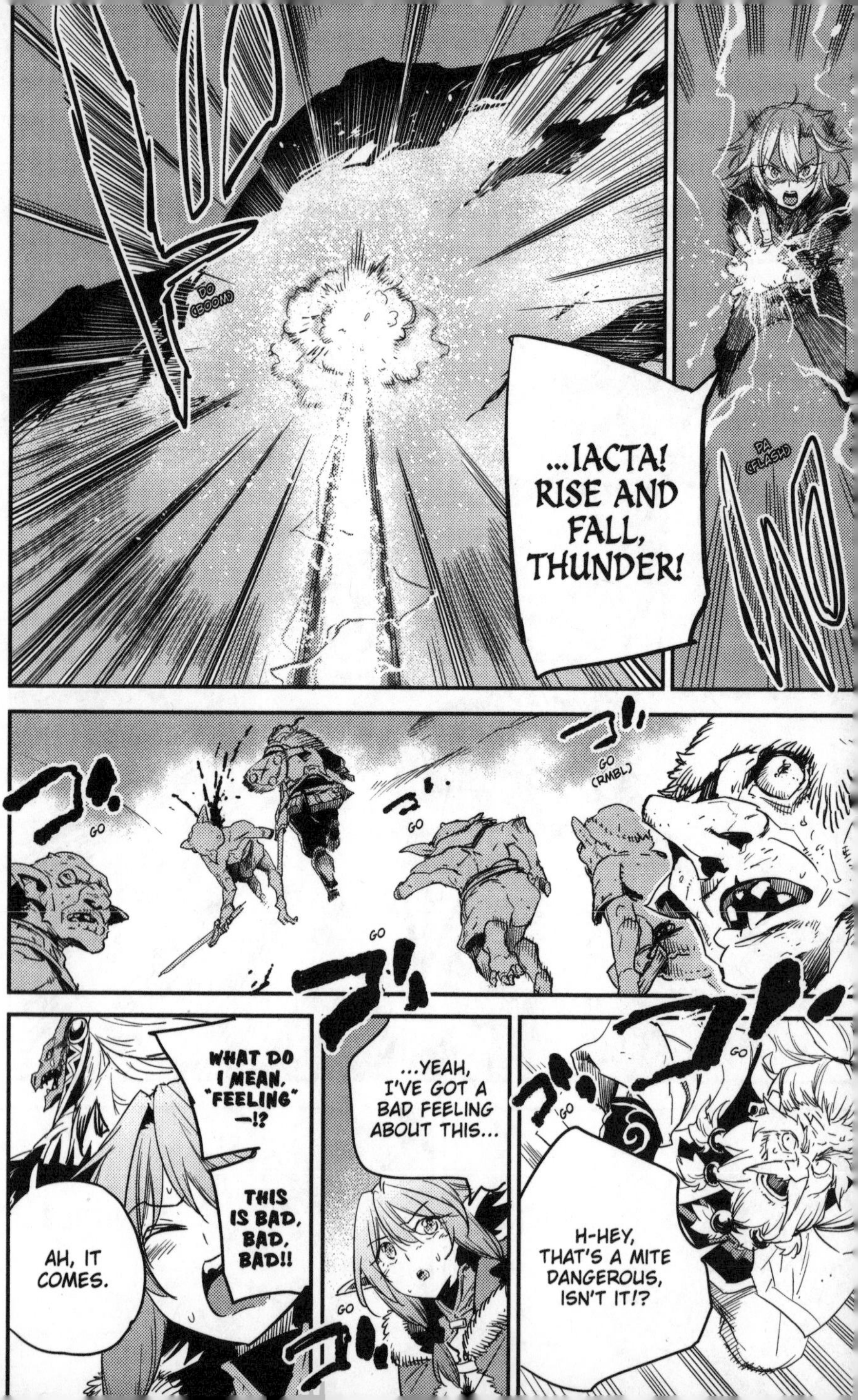
PA (FLASH)
...IACTA! RISE AND FALL, THUNDER!
DO (BOOM)
GO (RMBL)
GO
GO
GO
GO
GO
H-HEY, THAT'S A MITE DANGEROUS, ISN'T IT!?
...YEAH, I'VE GOT A BAD FEELING ABOUT THIS...
GO
WHAT DO I MEAN, "FEELING"—!?
THIS IS BAD, BAD, BAD!!
AH, IT COMES.

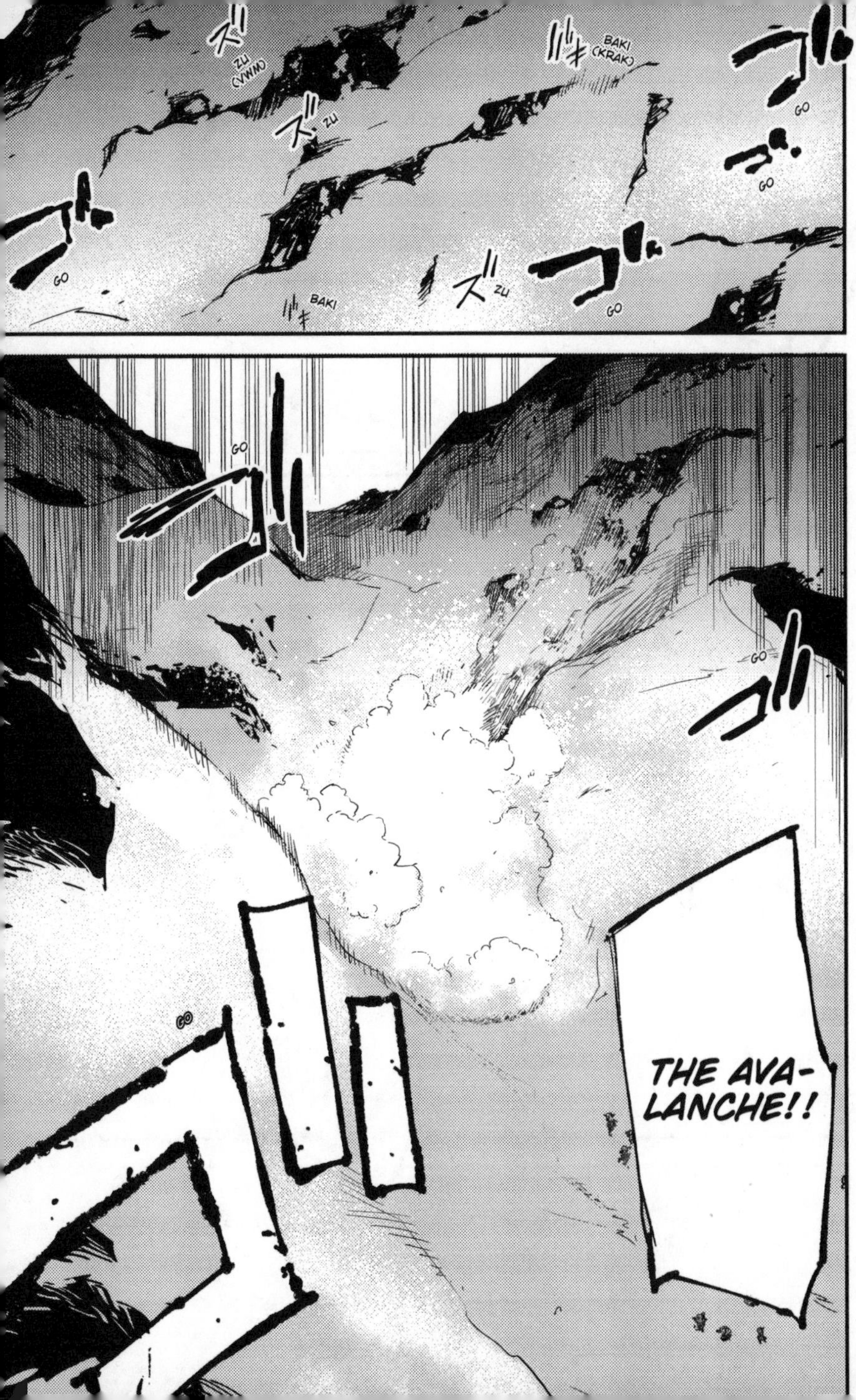

GO
GO
BAKI (KRAK)
ZU (VWM)
ZU
GO
ZU
BAKI
GO
GO
GO
THE AVA-
LANCHE!!
GO

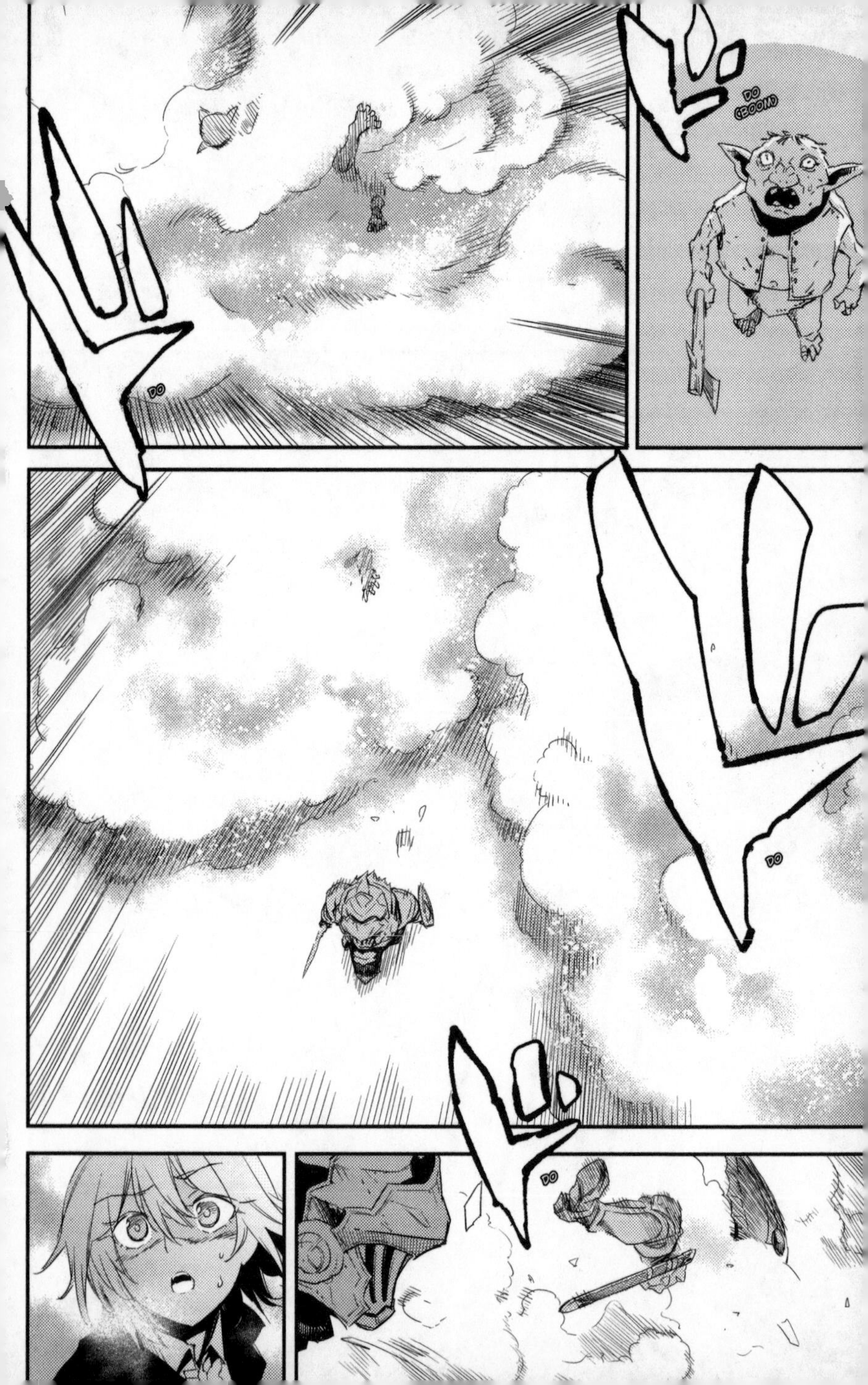
DO
(BOOM)
DO
DO
DO

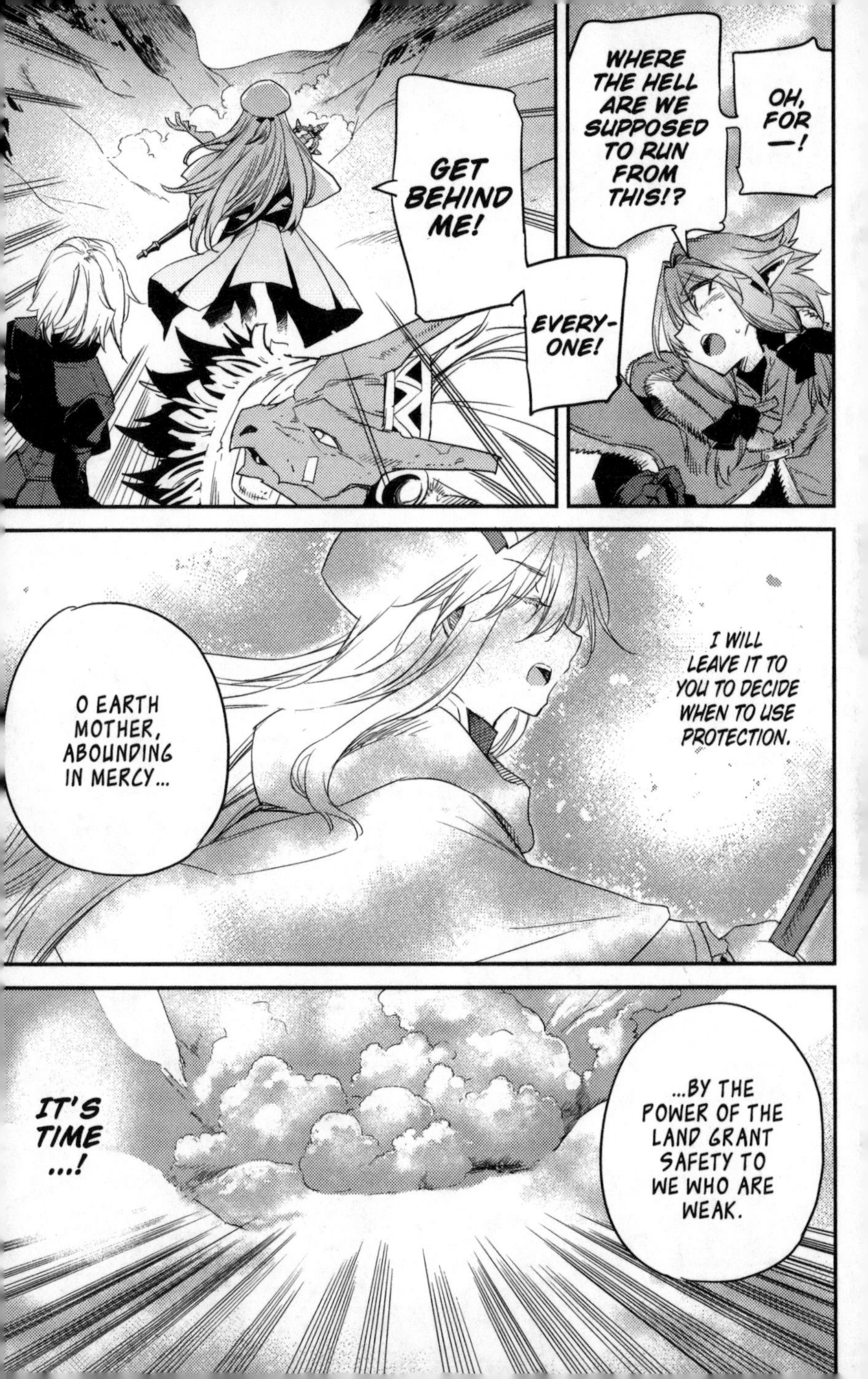
OH, FOR—!
WHERE THE HELL ARE WE SUPPOSED TO RUN FROM THIS!?
GET BEHIND ME!
EVERY-ONE!
I WILL LEAVE IT TO YOU TO DECIDE WHEN TO USE PROTECTION.
O EARTH MOTHER, ABOUNDING IN MERCY...
...BY THE POWER OF THE LAND GRANT SAFETY TO WE WHO ARE WEAK.
IT'S TIME...!

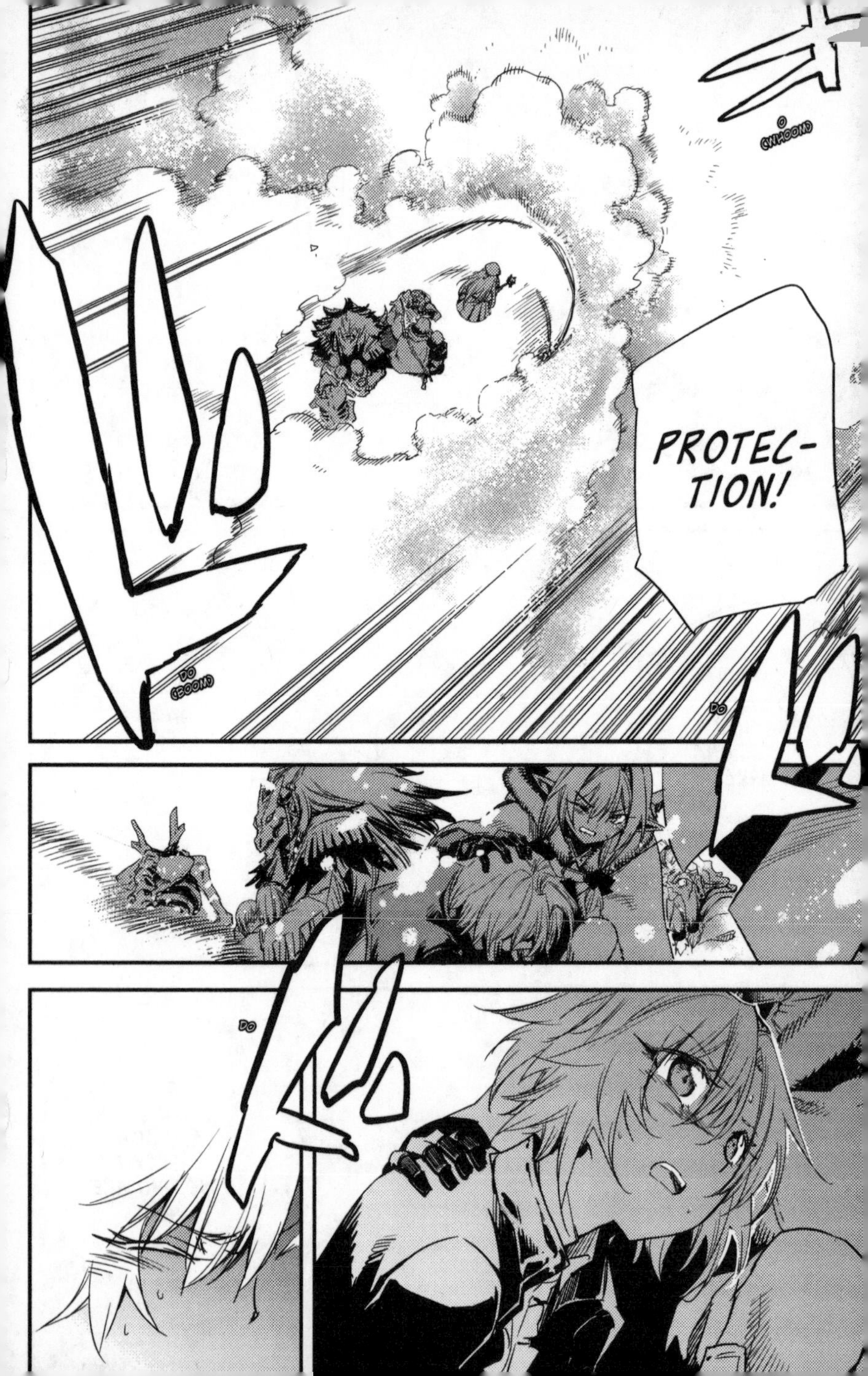
O
(WHOOM)
PROTEC-
TION!
DO
DO
(BOOM)
DO

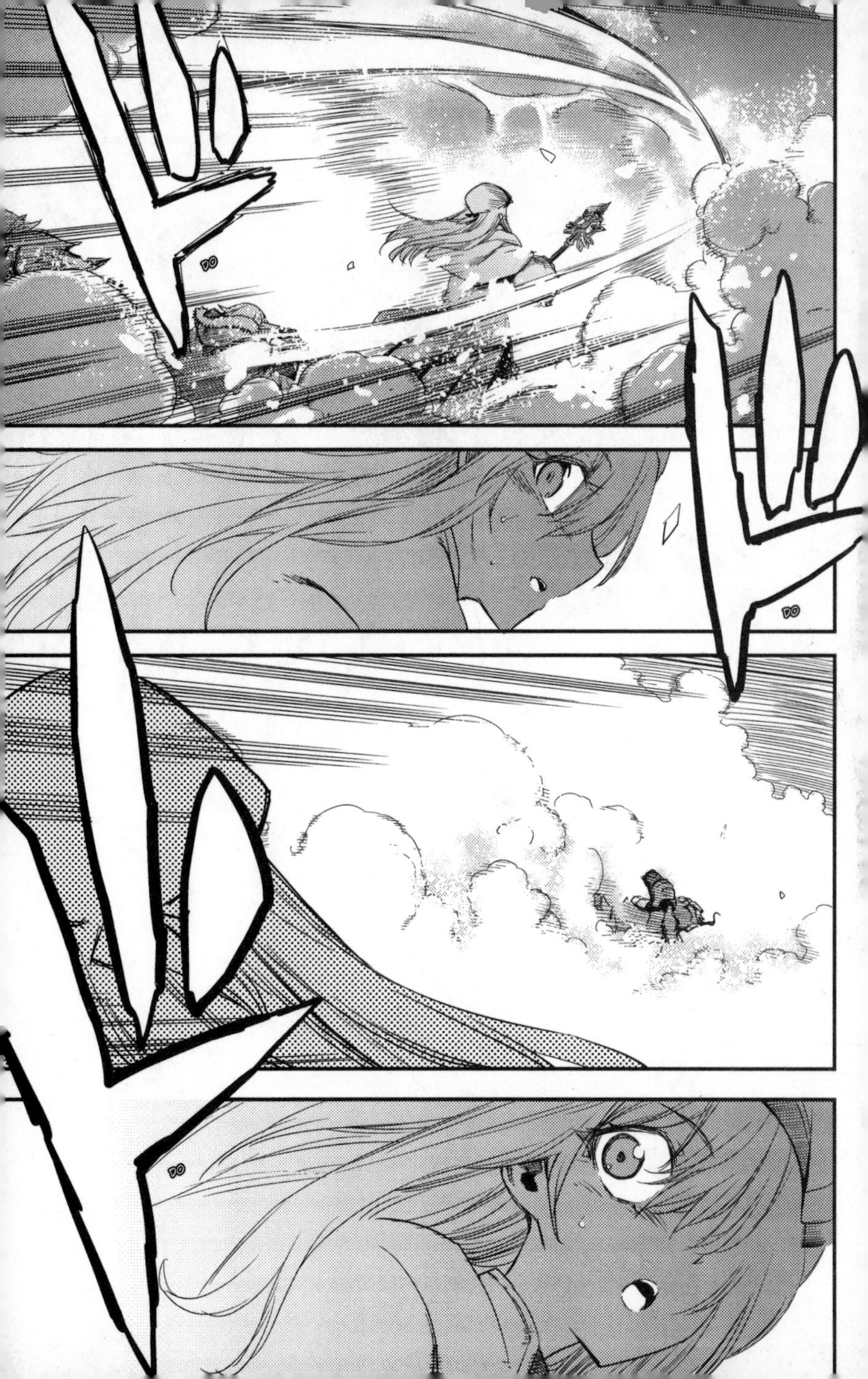
DO
DO
DO

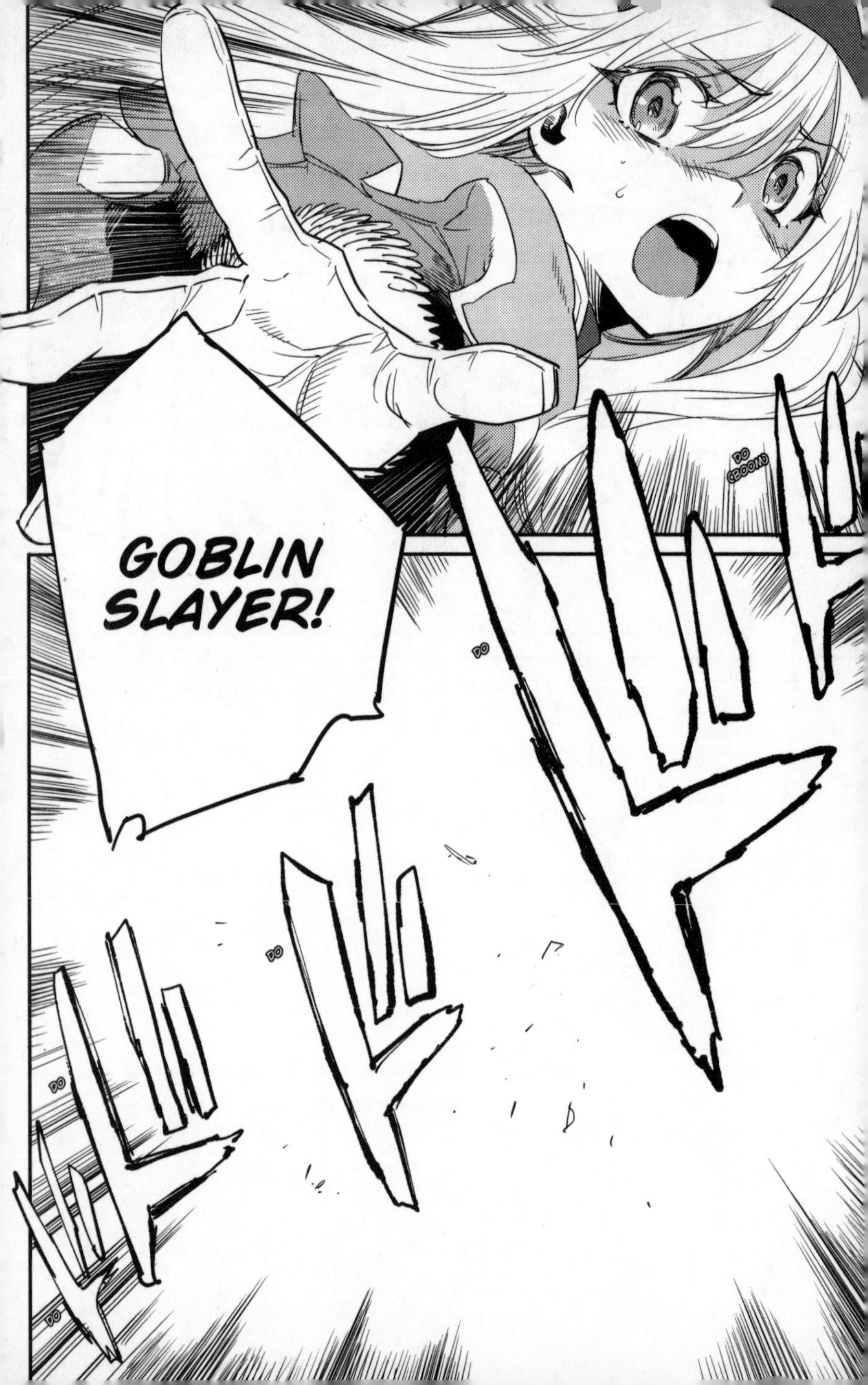
DO
(BOOM)
GOBLIN SLAYER!
DO
DO
DO
DO

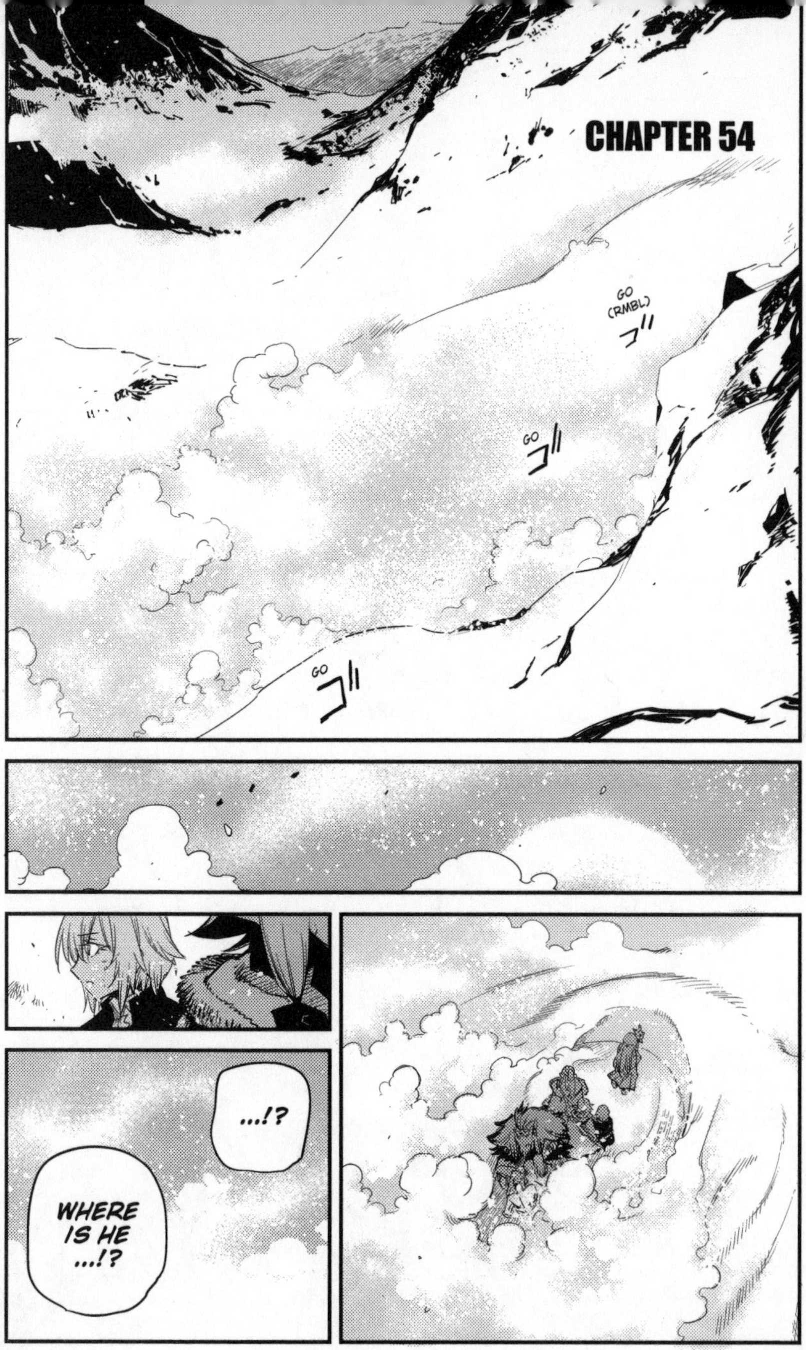
CHAPTER 54
GO (RMBL)
ゴ
GO
ゴ
GO
ゴ
...!?
WHERE IS HE ...!?

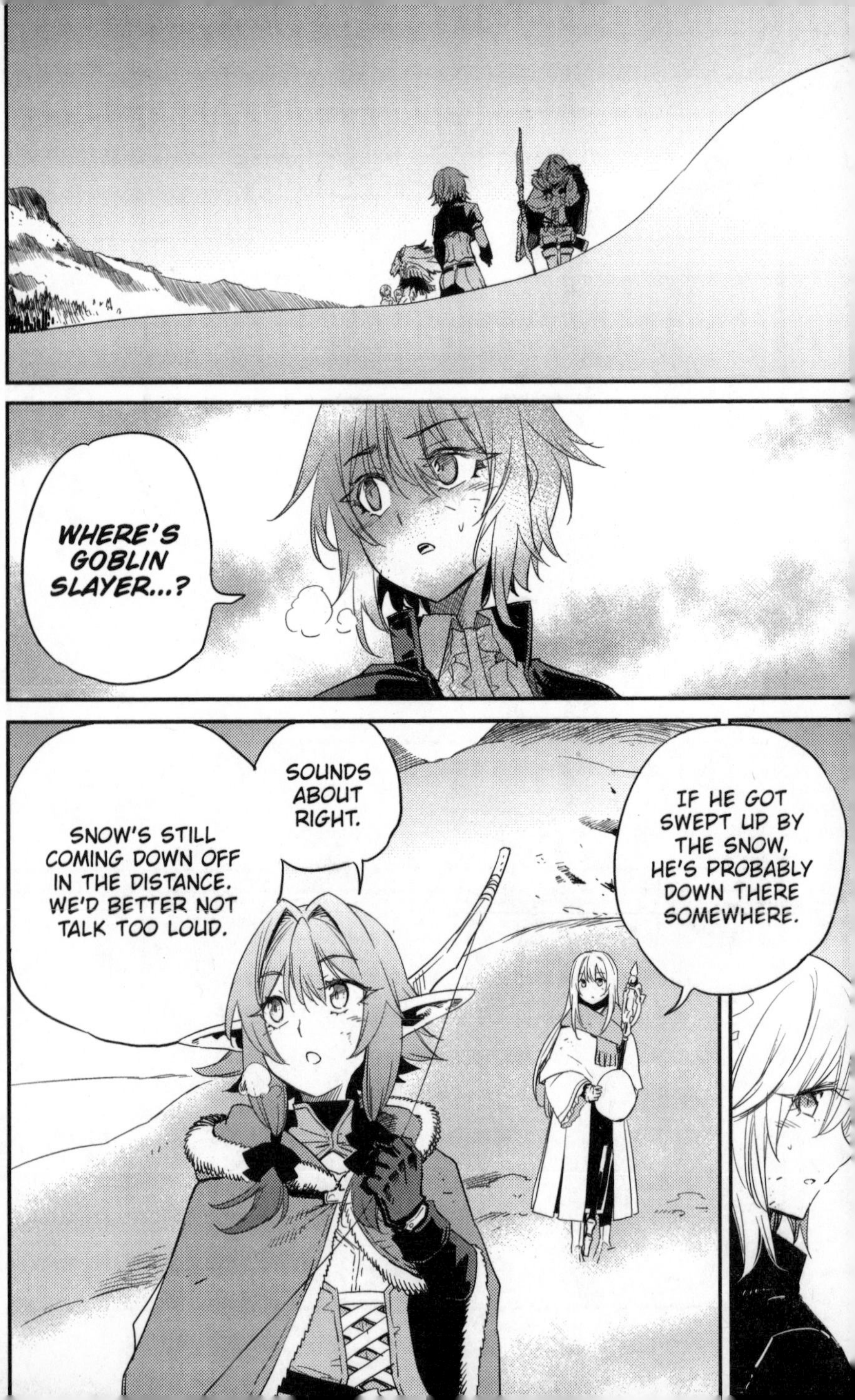
WHERE'S GOBLIN SLAYER...?
IF HE GOT SWEPT UP BY THE SNOW, HE'S PROBABLY DOWN THERE SOMEWHERE.
SOUNDS ABOUT RIGHT.
SNOW'S STILL COMING DOWN OFF IN THE DISTANCE. WE'D BETTER NOT TALK TOO LOUD.

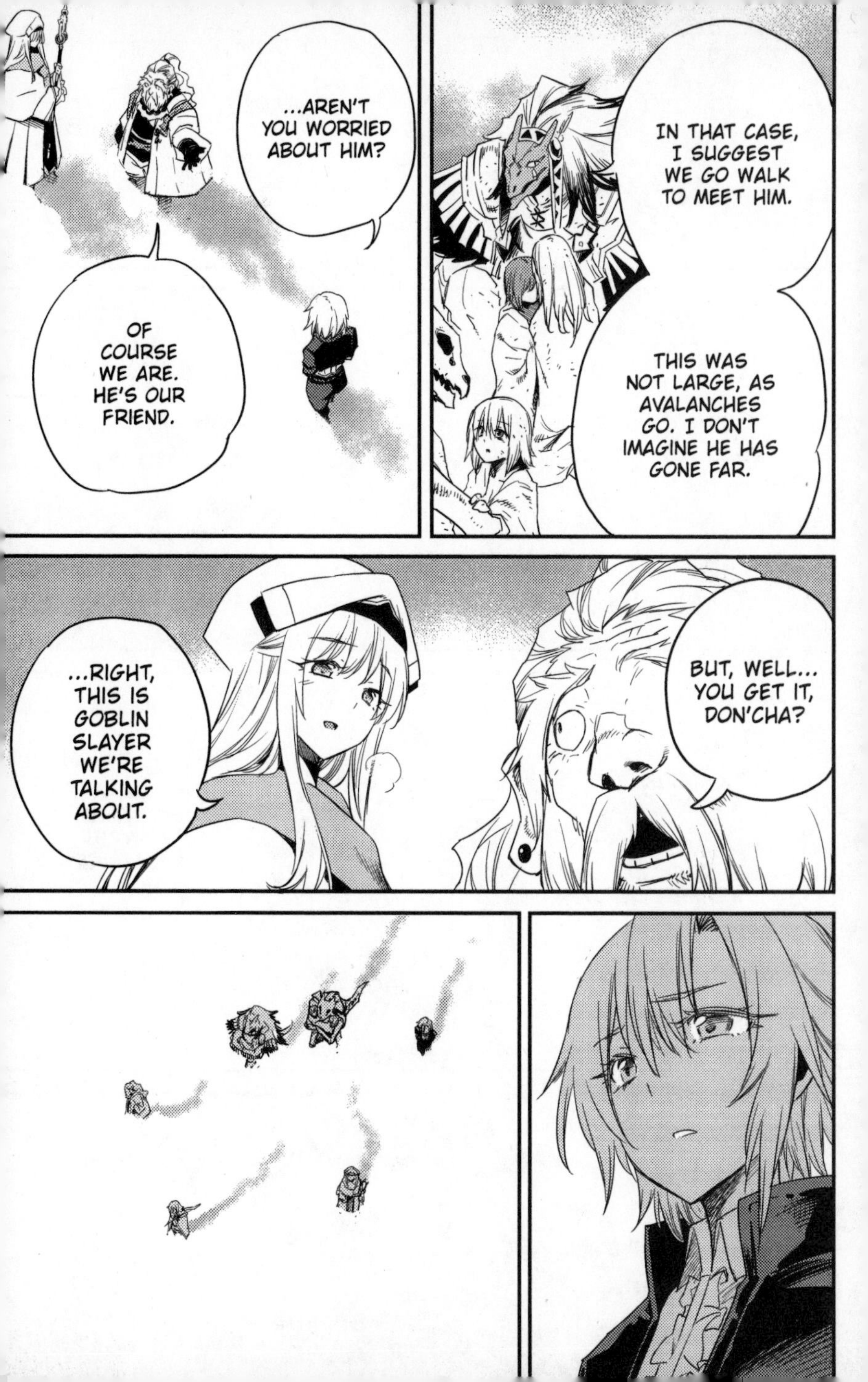
IN THAT CASE, I SUGGEST WE GO WALK TO MEET HIM.
THIS WAS NOT LARGE, AS AVALANCHES GO. I DON'T IMAGINE HE HAS GONE FAR.
...AREN'T YOU WORRIED ABOUT HIM?
OF COURSE WE ARE. HE'S OUR FRIEND.
BUT, WELL... YOU GET IT, DON'CHA?
...RIGHT, THIS IS GOBLIN SLAYER WE'RE TALKING ABOUT.

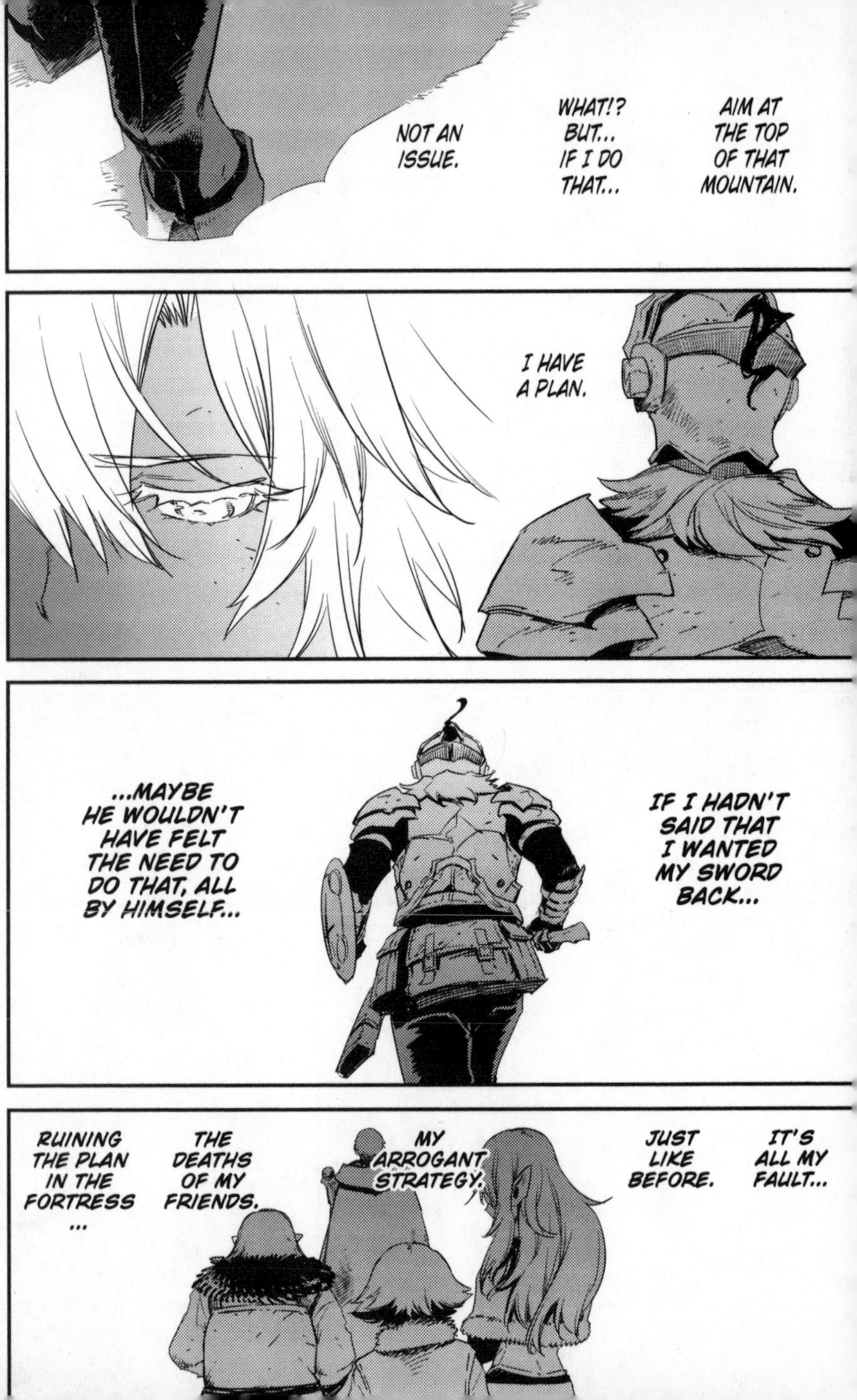
AIM AT THE TOP OF THAT MOUNTAIN.
WHAT!? BUT... IF I DO THAT...
NOT AN ISSUE.
I HAVE A PLAN.
IF I HADN'T SAID THAT I WANTED MY SWORD BACK...
...MAYBE HE WOULDN'T HAVE FELT THE NEED TO DO THAT, ALL BY HIMSELF...
IT'S ALL MY FAULT...
JUST LIKE BEFORE.
MY ARROGANT STRATEGY.
THE DEATHS OF MY FRIENDS.
RUINING THE PLAN IN THE FORTRESS...

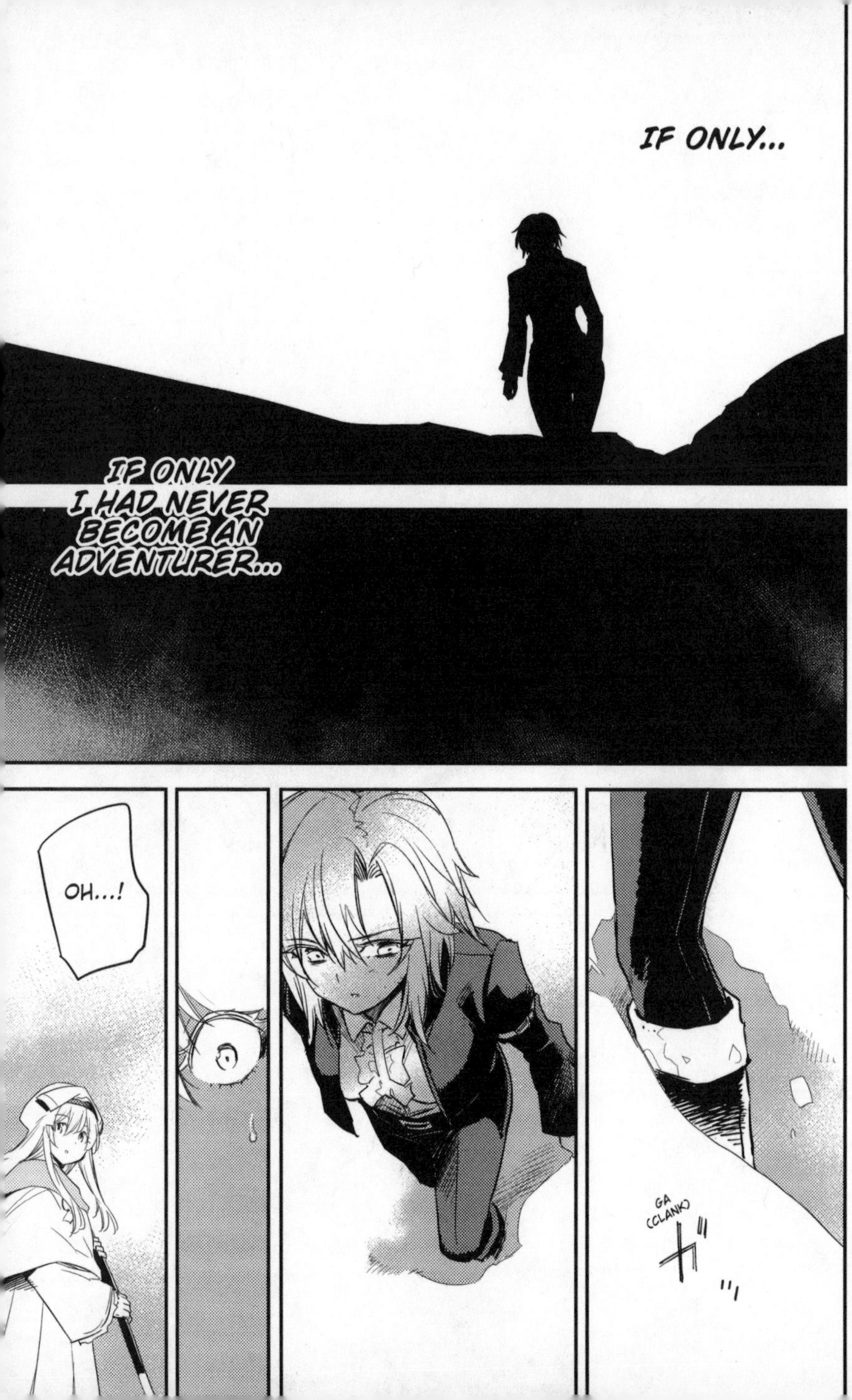
IF ONLY...
IF ONLY I HAD NEVER BECOME AN ADVENTURER...
GA (CLANK)
OH...!

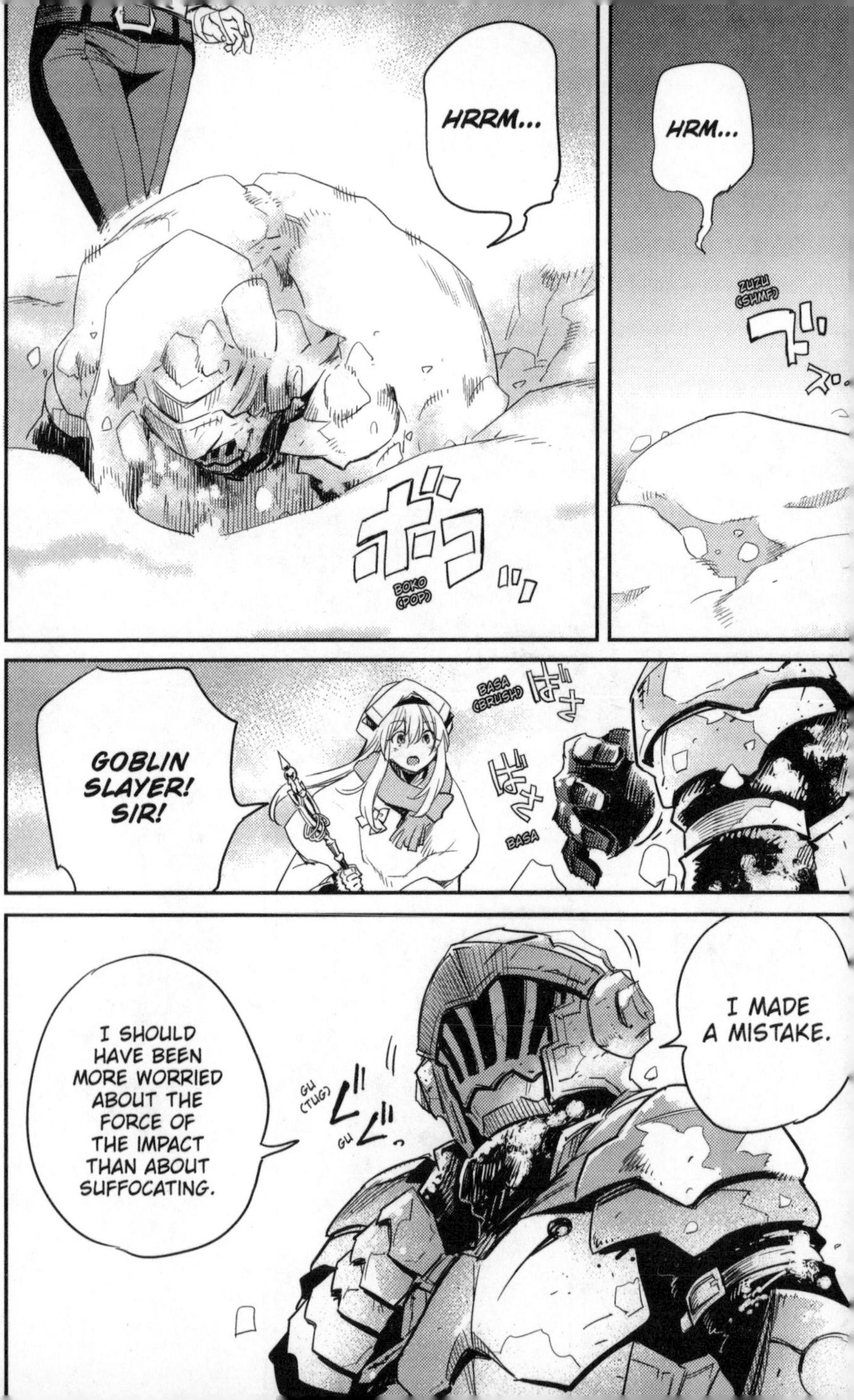
HRM...
ZUZU (SHMP)
HRRM...
BOKO (POP)
BASA (BRUSH)
BASA
GOBLIN SLAYER! SIR!
I MADE A MISTAKE.
GU (TUG)
GU
I SHOULD HAVE BEEN MORE WORRIED ABOUT THE FORCE OF THE IMPACT THAN ABOUT SUFFOCATING.

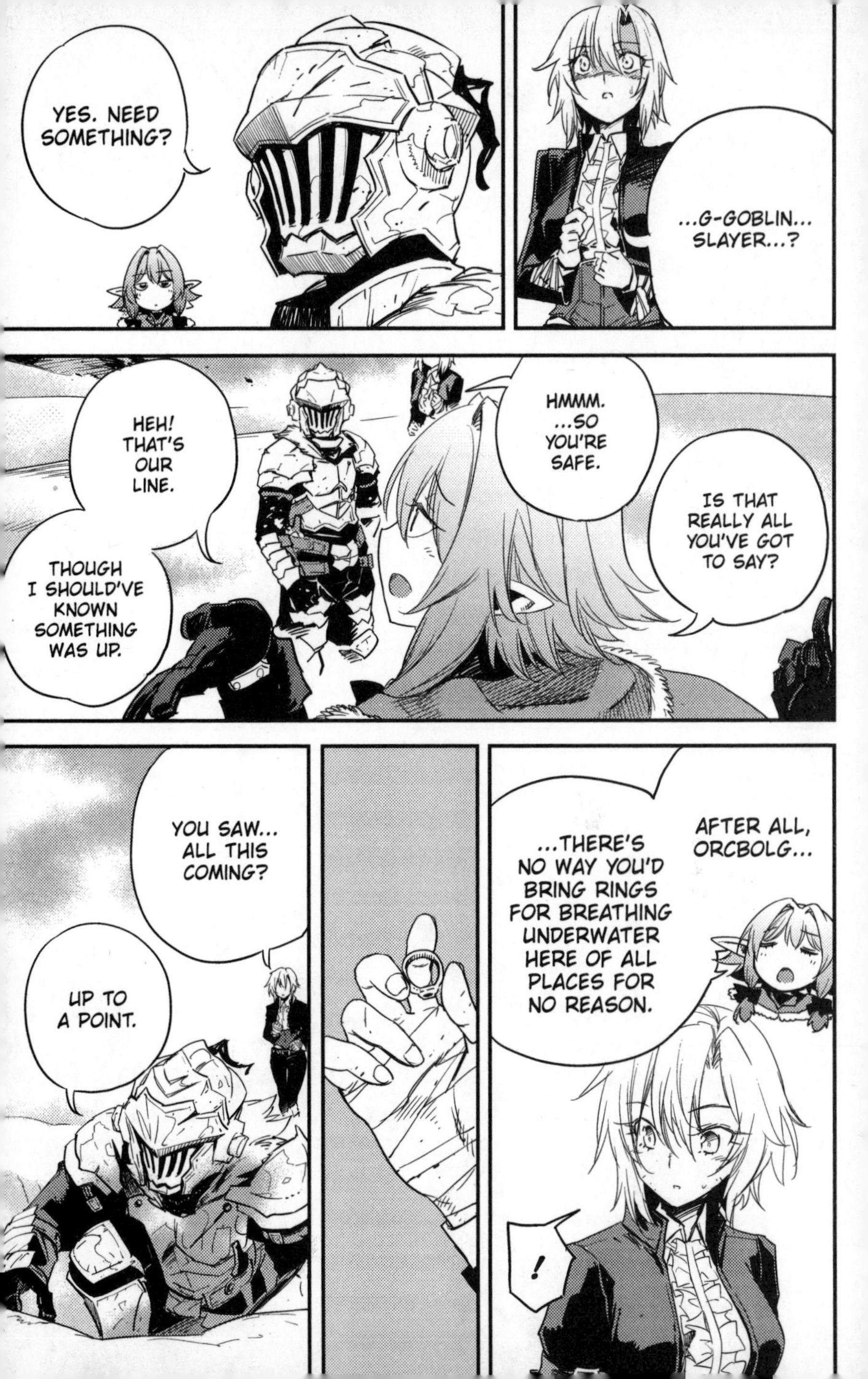
...G-GOBLIN... SLAYER...?
YES. NEED SOMETHING?
HMMM. ...SO YOU'RE SAFE.
IS THAT REALLY ALL YOU'VE GOT TO SAY?
HEH! THAT'S OUR LINE.
THOUGH I SHOULD'VE KNOWN SOMETHING WAS UP.
AFTER ALL, ORCBOLG...
...THERE'S NO WAY YOU'D BRING RINGS FOR BREATHING UNDERWATER HERE OF ALL PLACES FOR NO REASON.
!
YOU SAW... ALL THIS COMING?
UP TO A POINT.

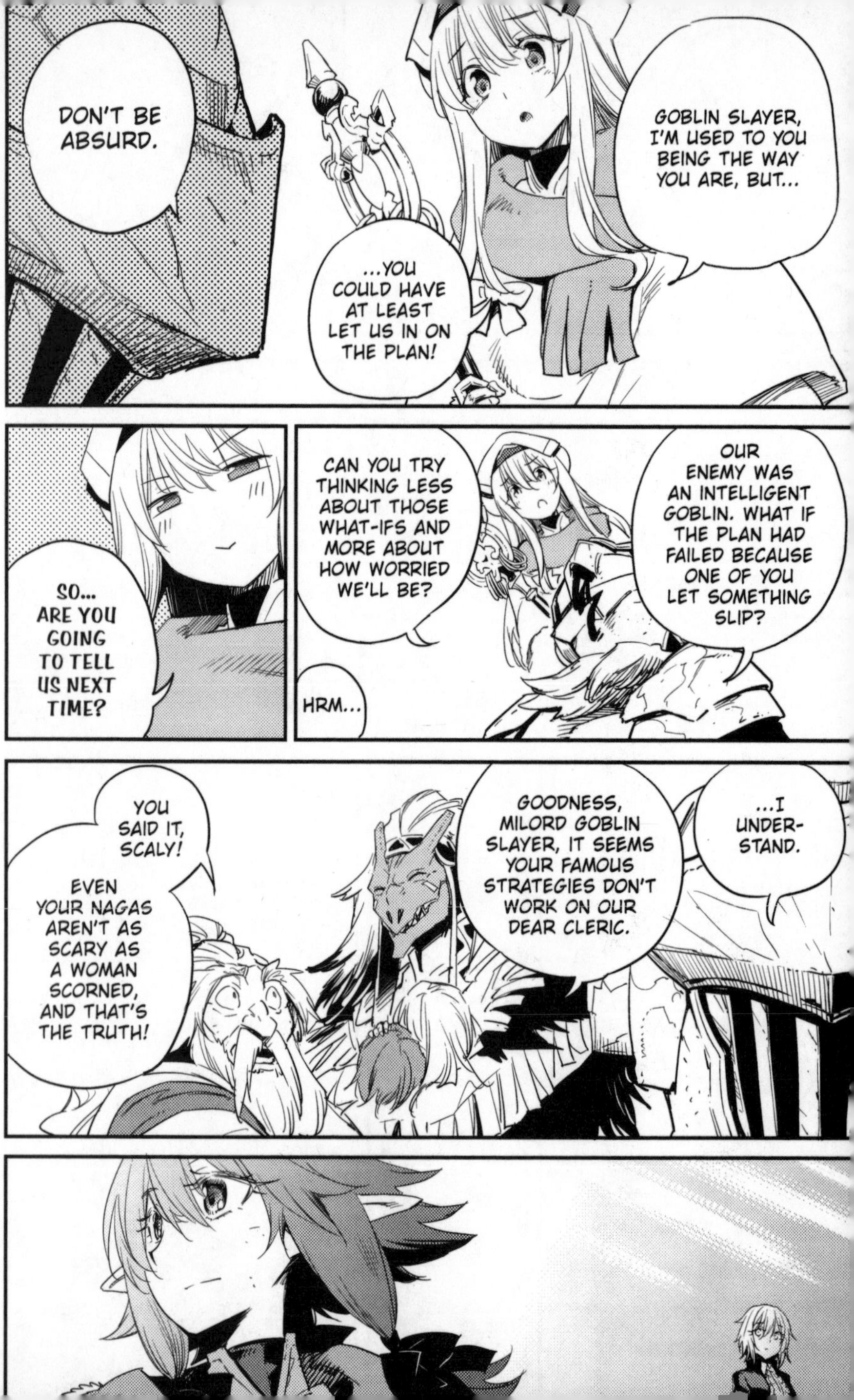
GOBLIN SLAYER, I'M USED TO YOU BEING THE WAY YOU ARE, BUT...
...YOU COULD HAVE AT LEAST LET US IN ON THE PLAN!
DON'T BE ABSURD.
OUR ENEMY WAS AN INTELLIGENT GOBLIN. WHAT IF THE PLAN HAD FAILED BECAUSE ONE OF YOU LET SOMETHING SLIP?
CAN YOU TRY THINKING LESS ABOUT THOSE WHAT-IFS AND MORE ABOUT HOW WORRIED WE'LL BE?
HRM...
SO... ARE YOU GOING TO TELL US NEXT TIME?
...I UNDER-STAND.
GOODNESS, MILORD GOBLIN SLAYER, IT SEEMS YOUR FAMOUS STRATEGIES DON'T WORK ON OUR DEAR CLERIC.
YOU SAID IT, SCALY!
EVEN YOUR NAGAS AREN'T AS SCARY AS A WOMAN SCORNED, AND THAT'S THE TRUTH!

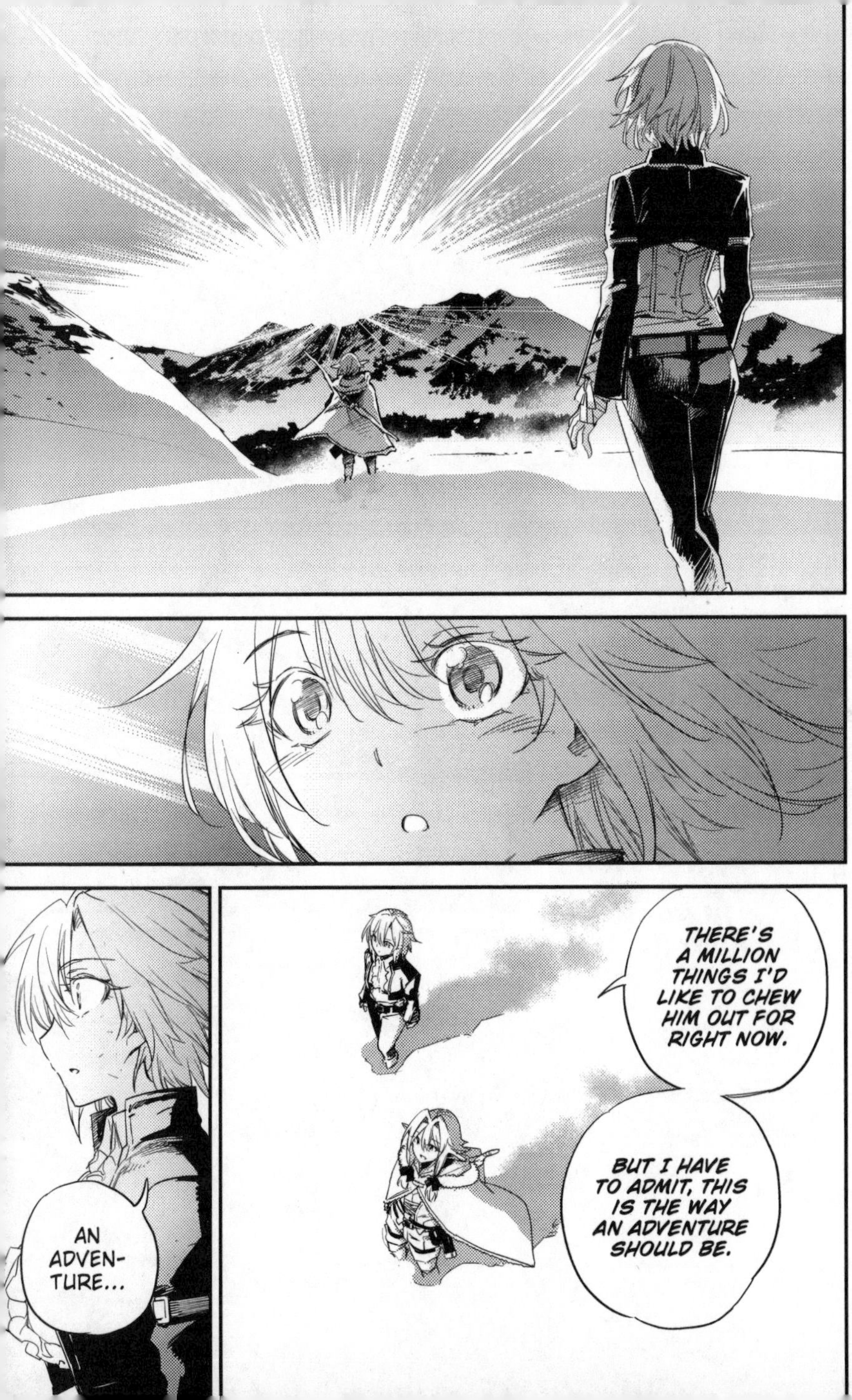
THERE'S A MILLION THINGS I'D LIKE TO CHEW HIM OUT FOR RIGHT NOW.
BUT I HAVE TO ADMIT, THIS IS THE WAY AN ADVENTURE SHOULD BE.
AN ADVEN-TURE...

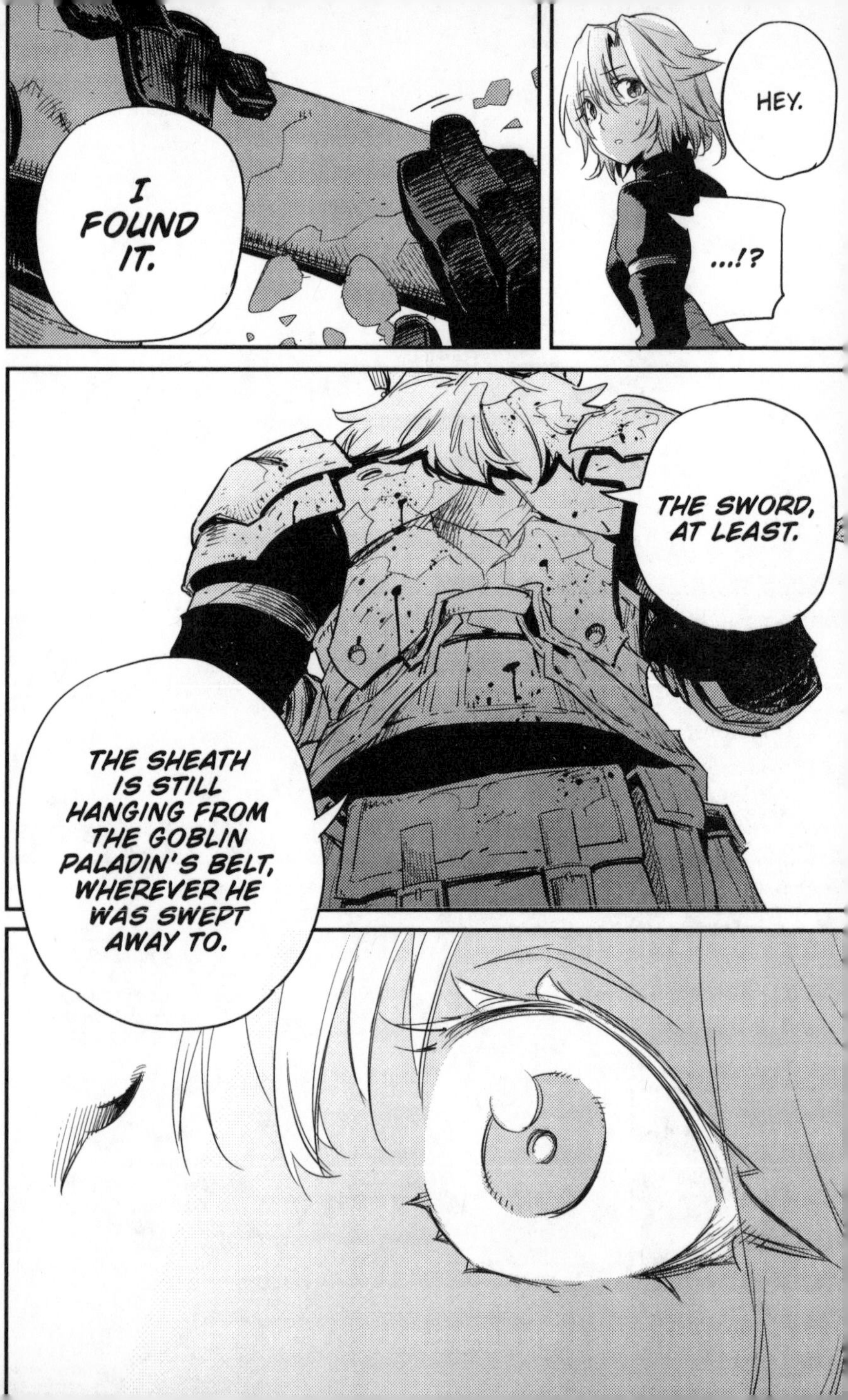
HEY.
...!?
I FOUND IT.
THE SWORD, AT LEAST.
THE SHEATH IS STILL HANGING FROM THE GOBLIN PALADIN'S BELT, WHEREVER HE WAS SWEPT AWAY TO.

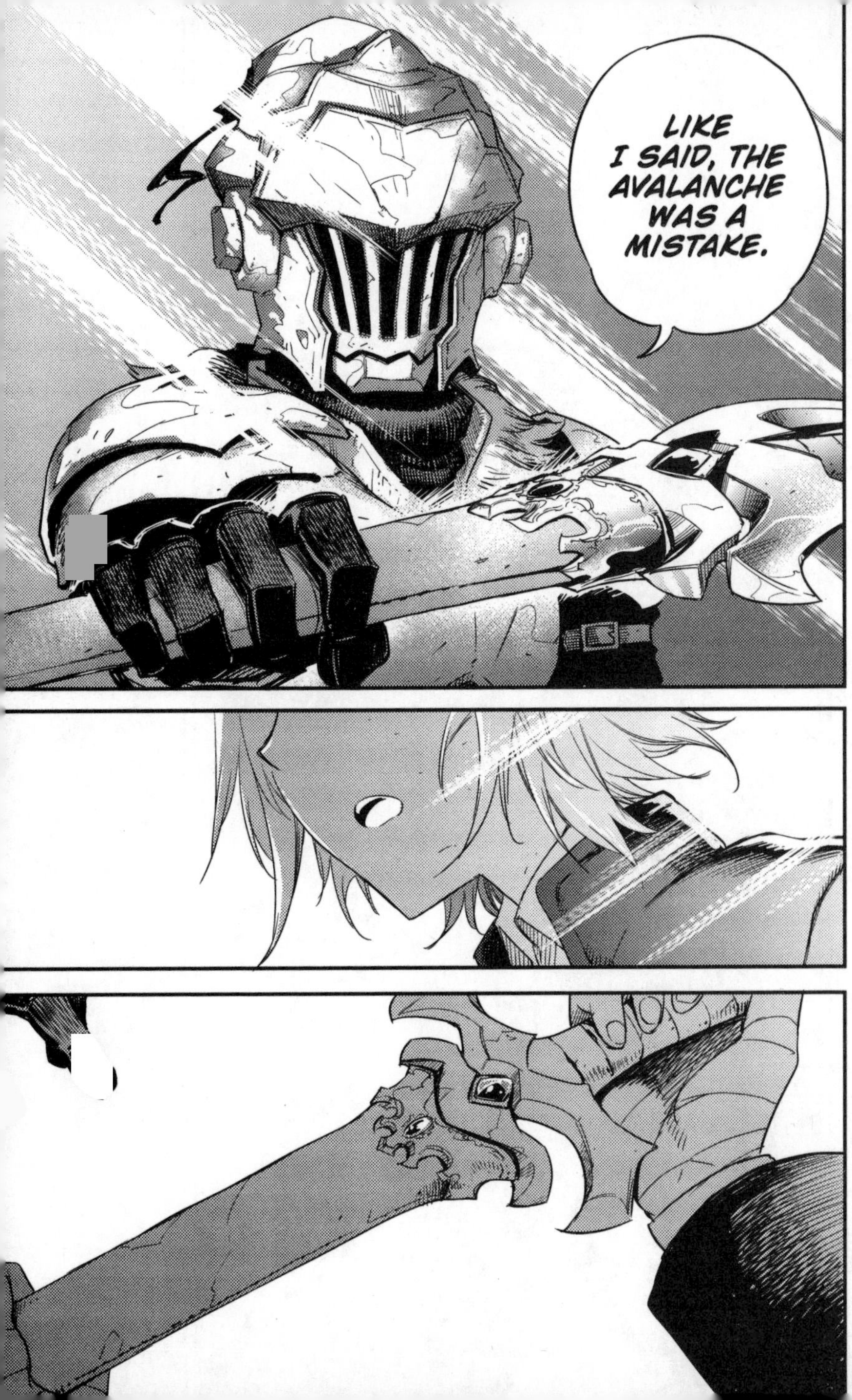
LIKE I SAID, THE AVALANCHE WAS A MISTAKE.

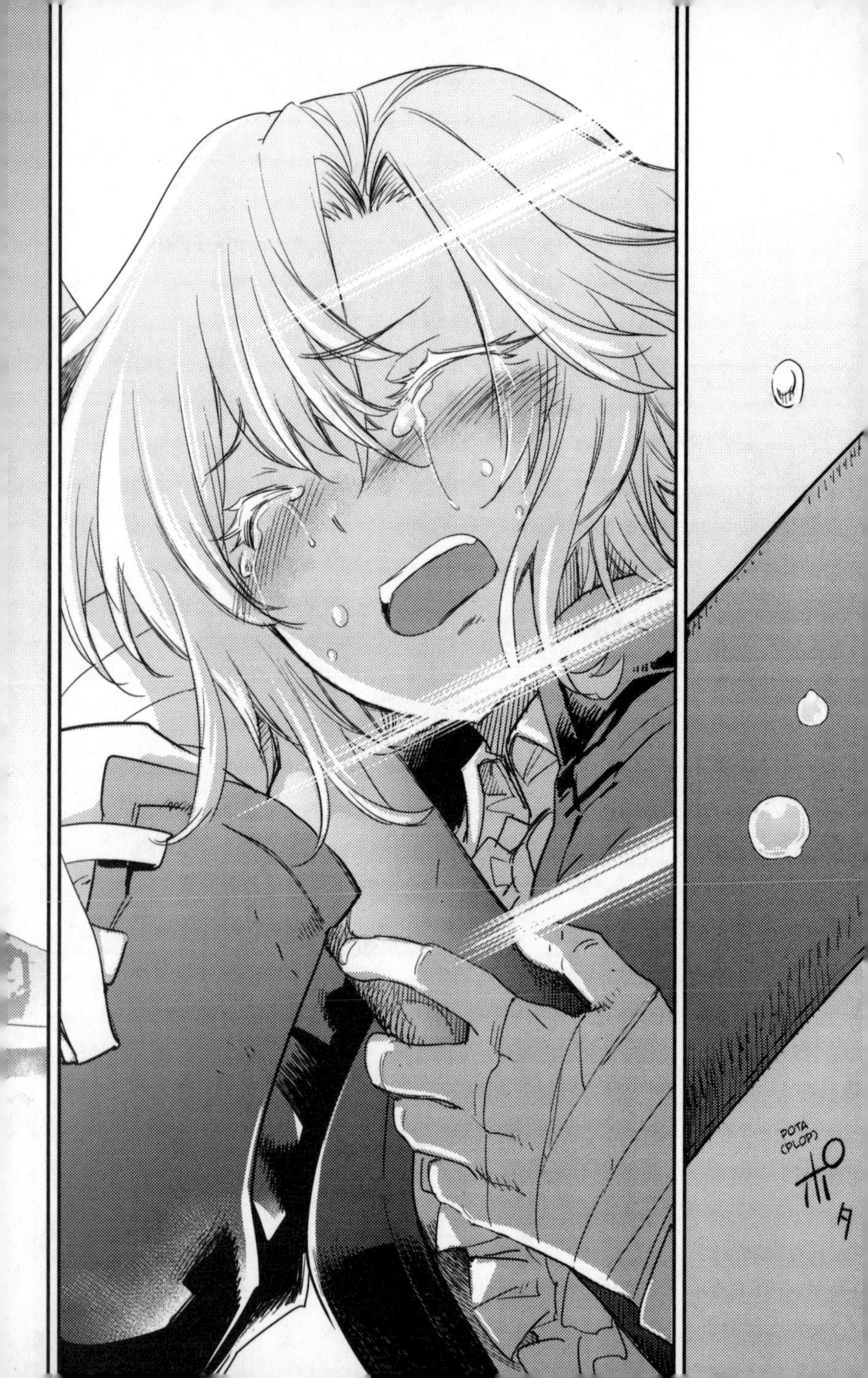
POTA
(PLOP)
ポタ

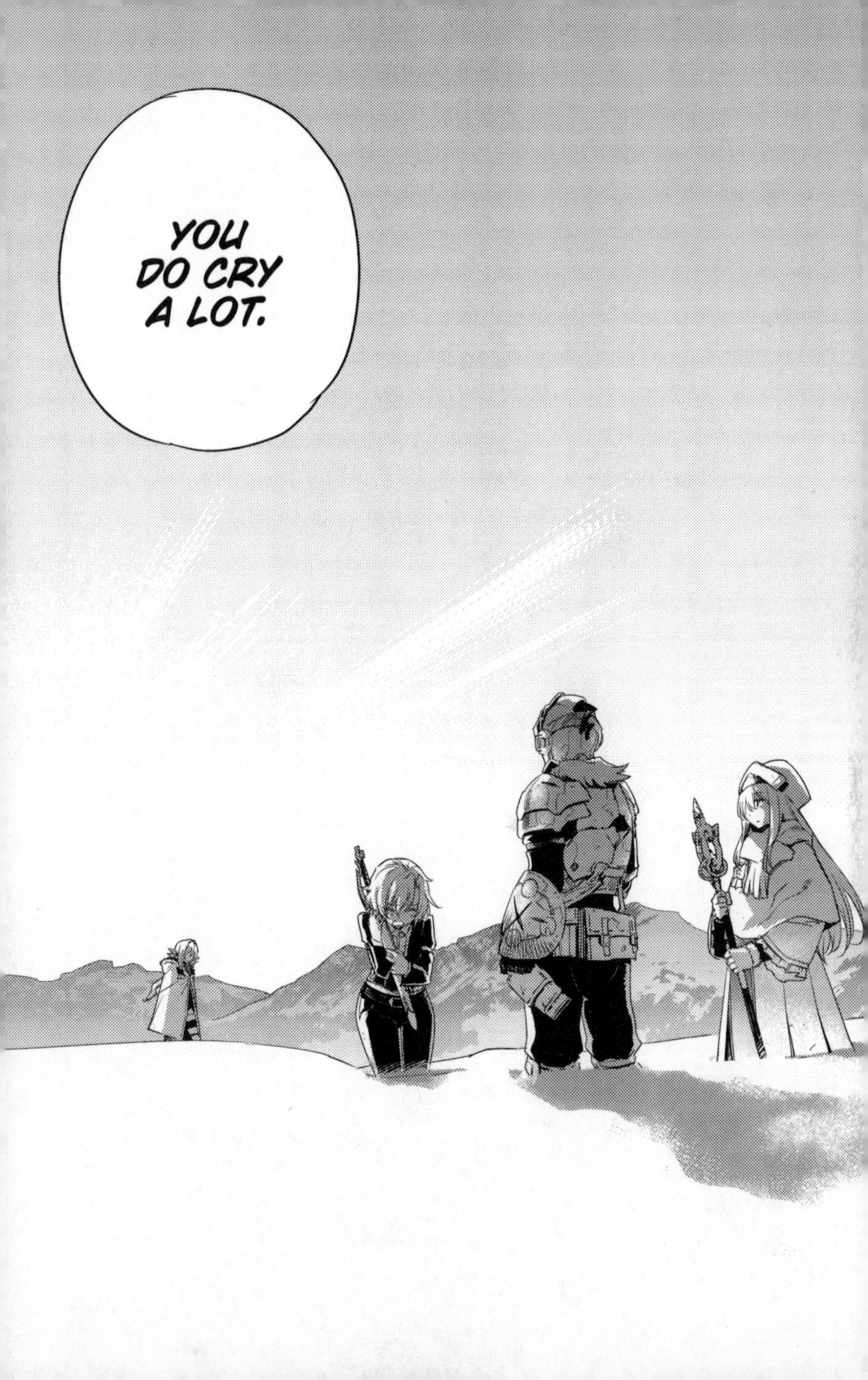
YOU DO CRY A LOT.

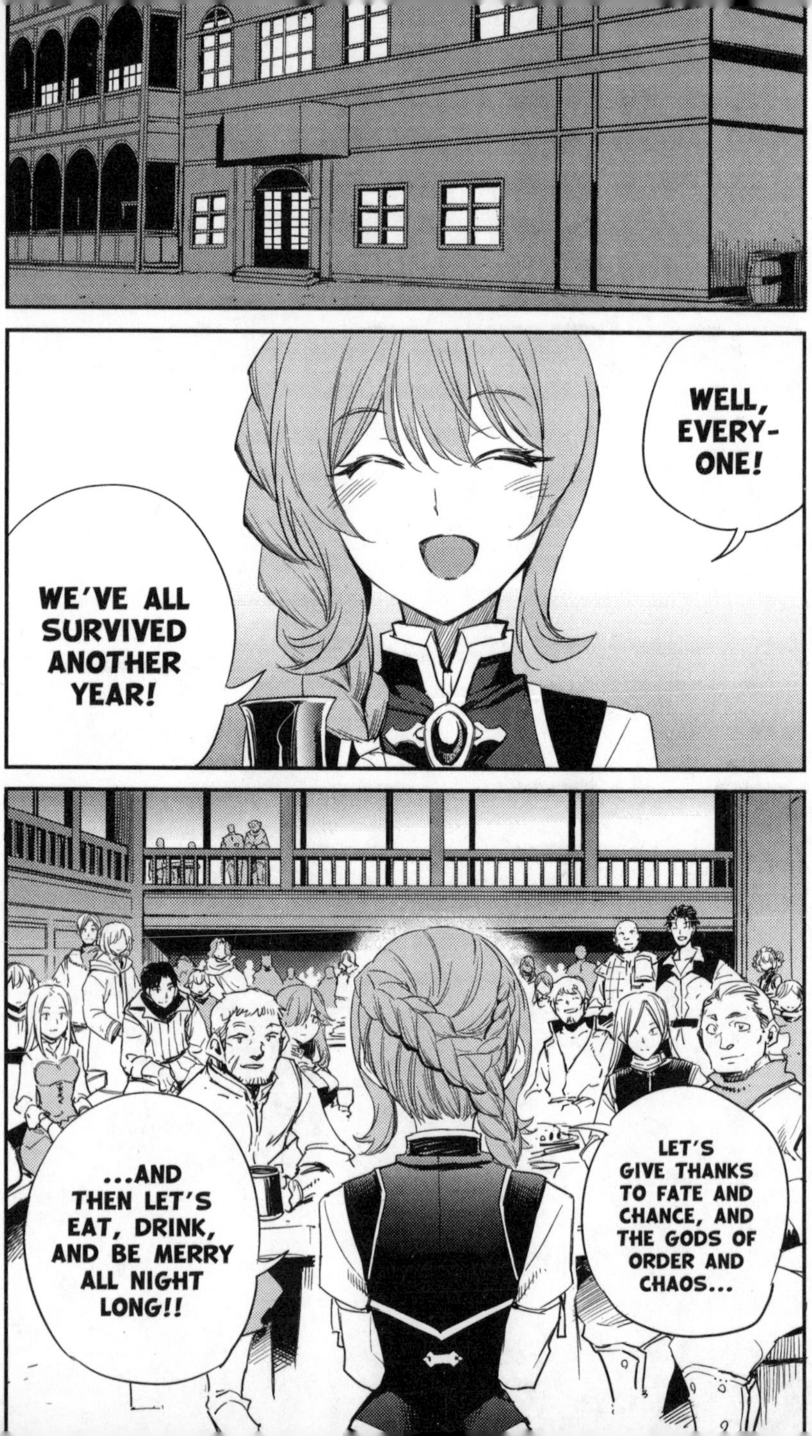
WELL, EVERY-ONE!
WE'VE ALL SURVIVED ANOTHER YEAR!
LET'S GIVE THANKS TO FATE AND CHANCE, AND THE GODS OF ORDER AND CHAOS...
...AND THEN LET'S EAT, DRINK, AND BE MERRY ALL NIGHT LONG!!

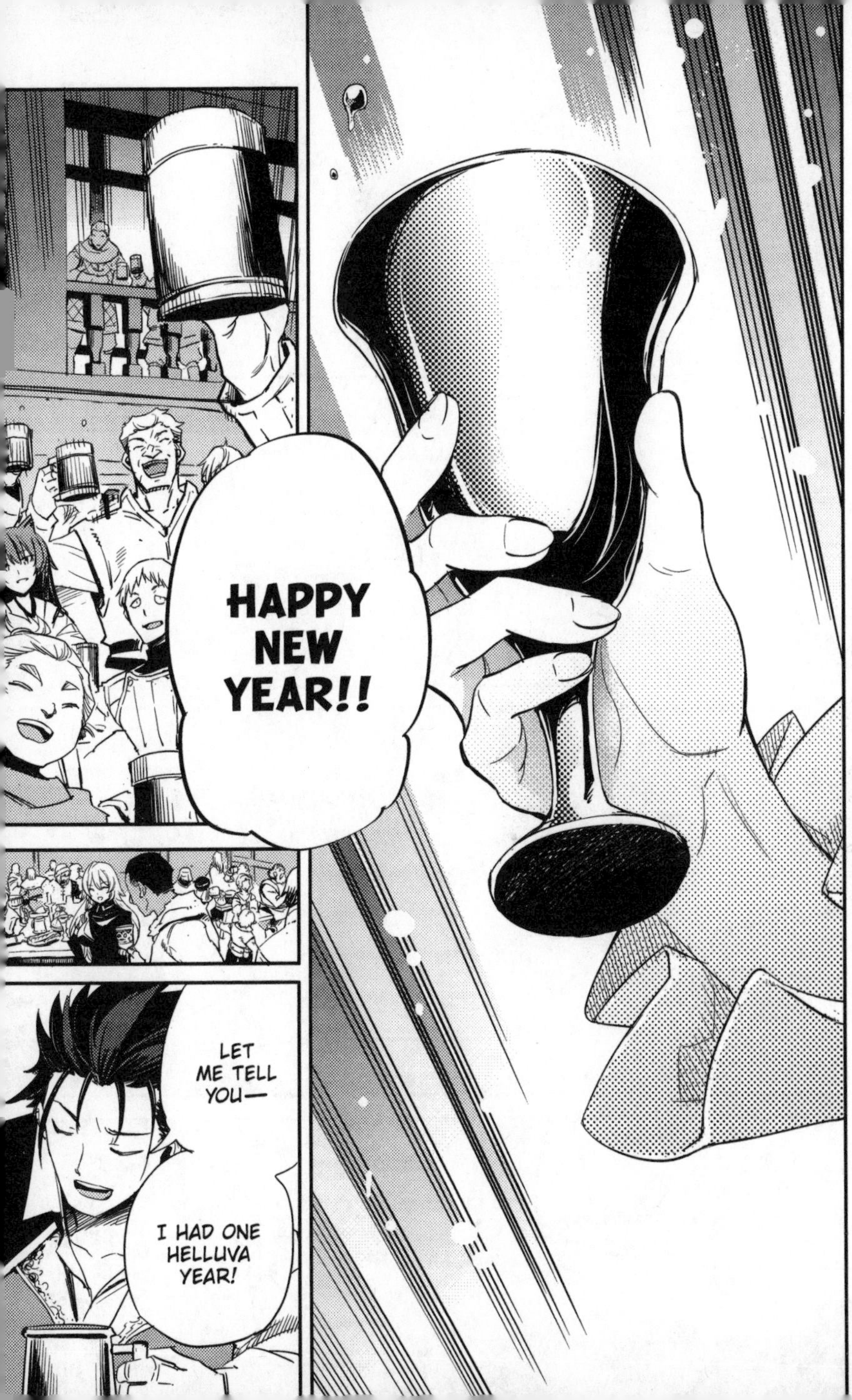
HAPPY NEW YEAR!!
LET ME TELL YOU—
I HAD ONE HELLUVA YEAR!

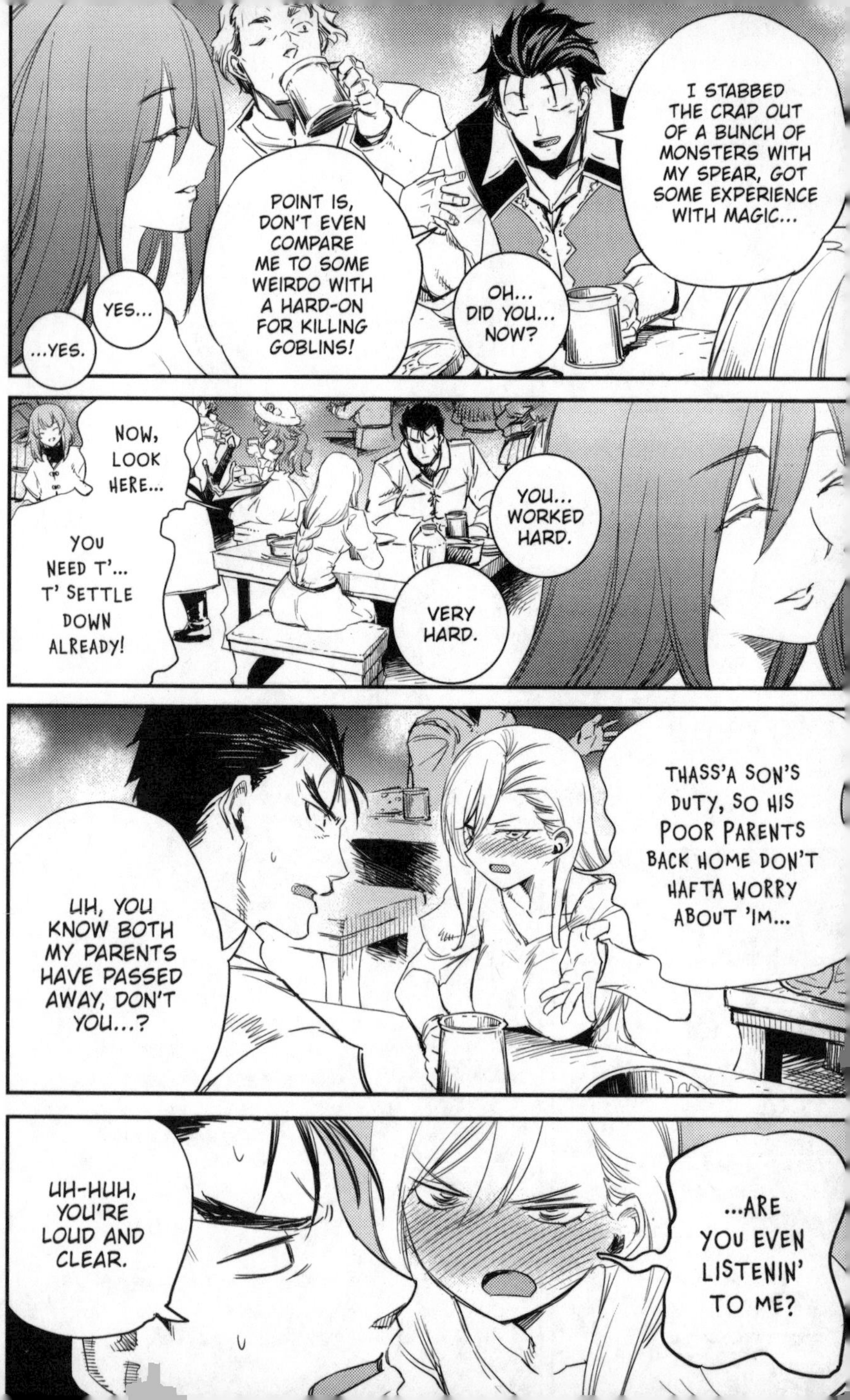
I STABBED THE CRAP OUT OF A BUNCH OF MONSTERS WITH MY SPEAR, GOT SOME EXPERIENCE WITH MAGIC...
OH... DID YOU... NOW?
POINT IS, DON'T EVEN COMPARE ME TO SOME WEIRDO WITH A HARD-ON FOR KILLING GOBLINS!
YES...
...YES.
YOU... WORKED HARD.
VERY HARD.
NOW, LOOK HERE...
YOU NEED T'... T' SETTLE DOWN ALREADY!
THASS'A SON'S DUTY, SO HIS POOR PARENTS BACK HOME DON'T HAFTA WORRY ABOUT 'IM...
UH, YOU KNOW BOTH MY PARENTS HAVE PASSED AWAY, DON'T YOU...?
...ARE YOU EVEN LISTENIN' TO ME?
UH-HUH, YOU'RE LOUD AND CLEAR.

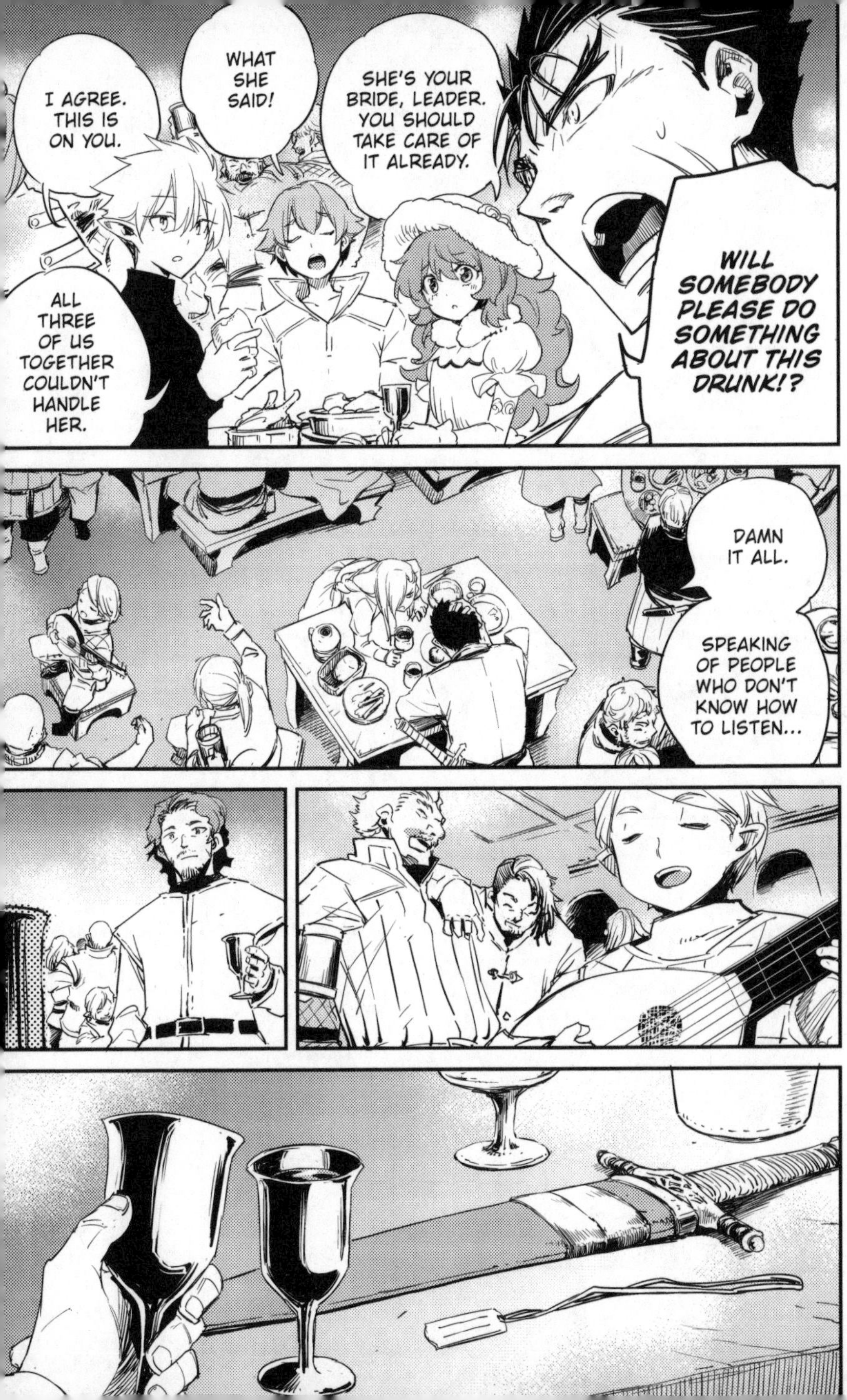
WILL SOMEBODY PLEASE DO SOMETHING ABOUT THIS DRUNK!?
SHE'S YOUR BRIDE, LEADER. YOU SHOULD TAKE CARE OF IT ALREADY.
WHAT SHE SAID!
I AGREE. THIS IS ON YOU.
ALL THREE OF US TOGETHER COULDN'T HANDLE HER.
DAMN IT ALL.
SPEAKING OF PEOPLE WHO DON'T KNOW HOW TO LISTEN...

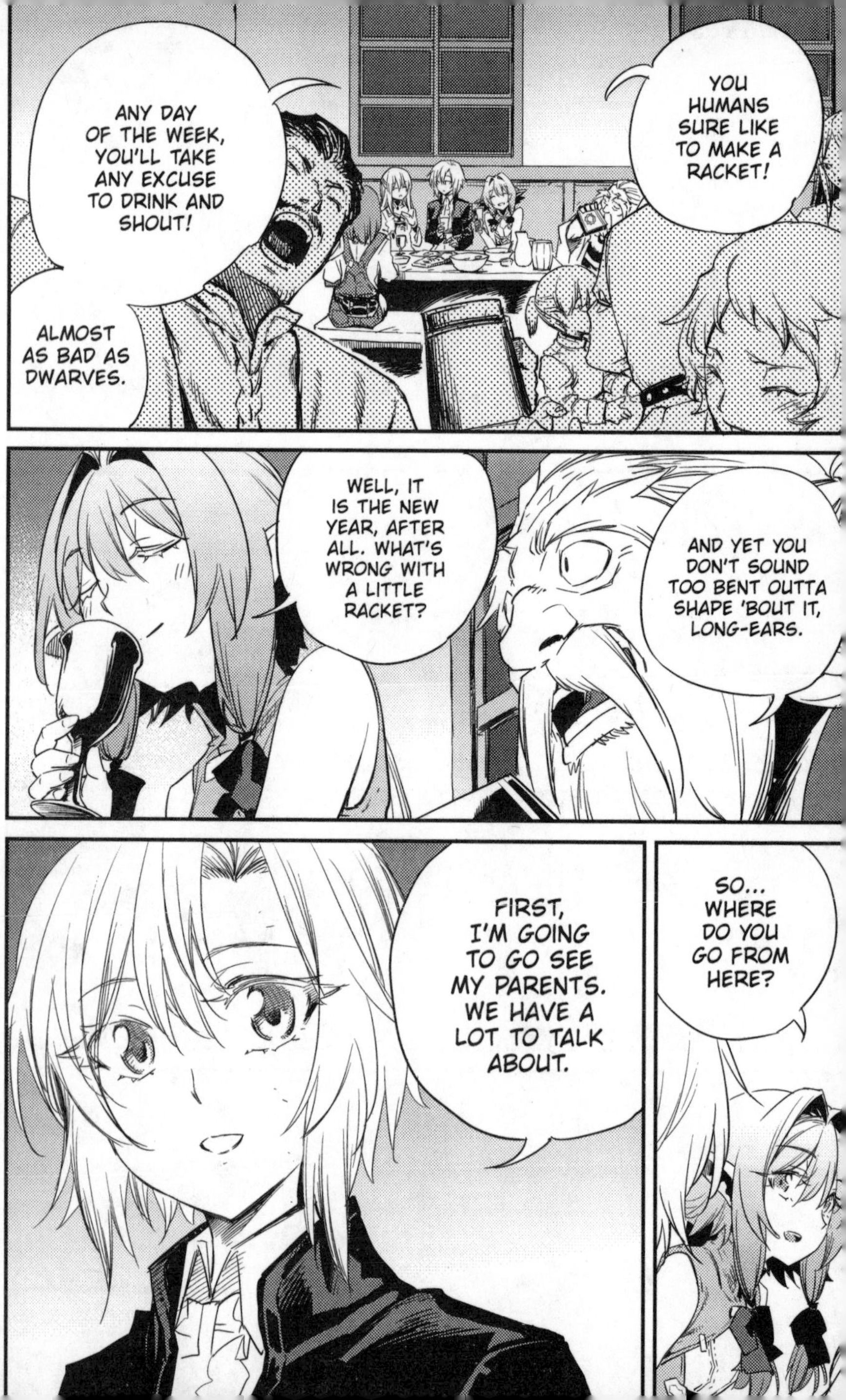
YOU HUMANS SURE LIKE TO MAKE A RACKET!
ANY DAY OF THE WEEK, YOU'LL TAKE ANY EXCUSE TO DRINK AND SHOUT!
ALMOST AS BAD AS DWARVES.
AND YET YOU DON'T SOUND TOO BENT OUTTA SHAPE 'BOUT IT, LONG-EARS.
WELL, IT IS THE NEW YEAR, AFTER ALL. WHAT'S WRONG WITH A LITTLE RACKET?
SO... WHERE DO YOU GO FROM HERE?
FIRST, I'M GOING TO GO SEE MY PARENTS. WE HAVE A LOT TO TALK ABOUT.

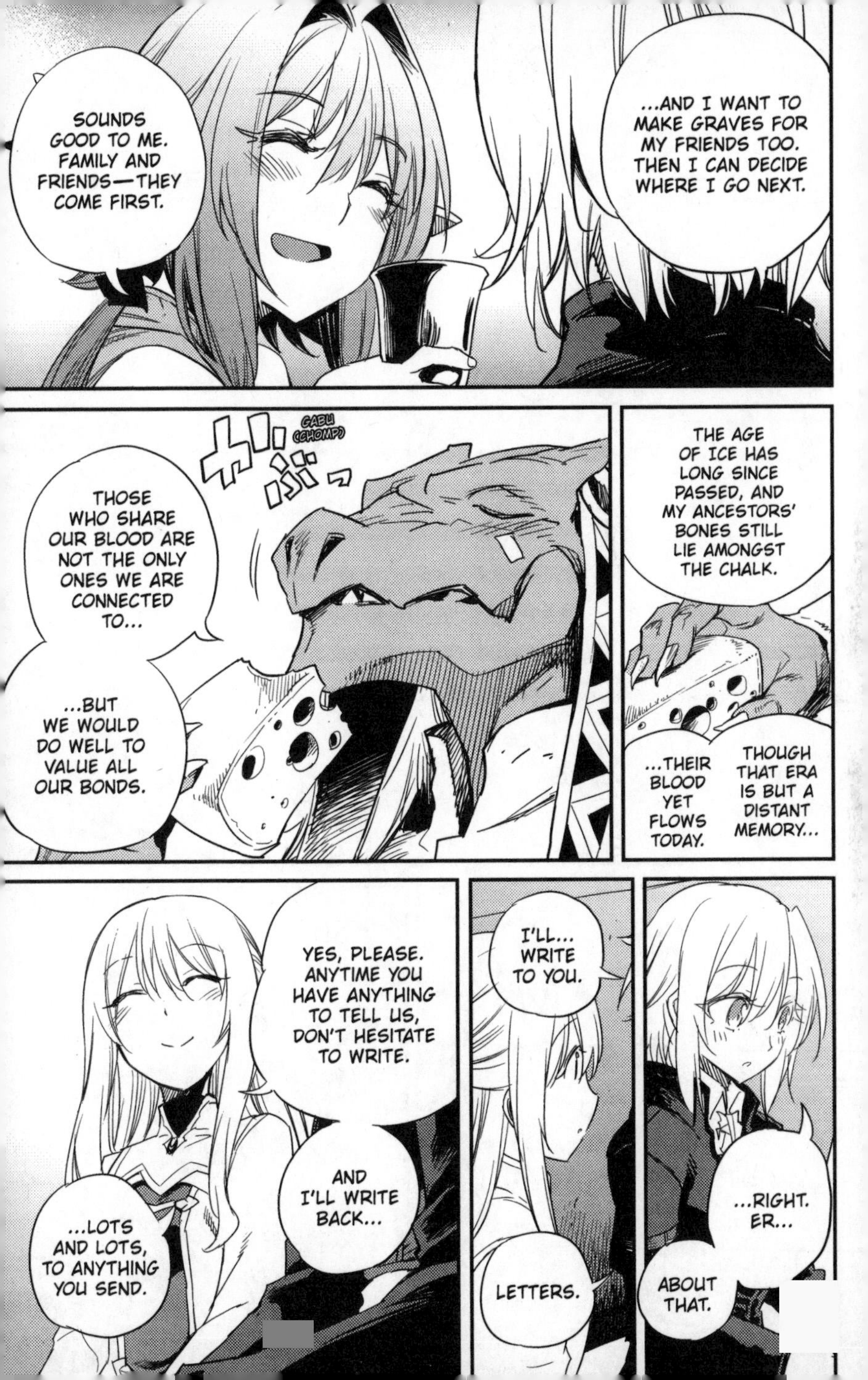
...AND I WANT TO MAKE GRAVES FOR MY FRIENDS TOO. THEN I CAN DECIDE WHERE I GO NEXT.
SOUNDS GOOD TO ME. FAMILY AND FRIENDS—THEY COME FIRST.
THE AGE OF ICE HAS LONG SINCE PASSED, AND MY ANCESTORS' BONES STILL LIE AMONGST THE CHALK.
THOUGH THAT ERA IS BUT A DISTANT MEMORY...
...THEIR BLOOD YET FLOWS TODAY.
GABU (CHOMP)
THOSE WHO SHARE OUR BLOOD ARE NOT THE ONLY ONES WE ARE CONNECTED TO...
...BUT WE WOULD DO WELL TO VALUE ALL OUR BONDS.
...RIGHT. ER...
ABOUT THAT.
I'LL... WRITE TO YOU.
LETTERS.
YES, PLEASE. ANYTIME YOU HAVE ANYTHING TO TELL US, DON'T HESITATE TO WRITE.
AND I'LL WRITE BACK...
...LOTS AND LOTS, TO ANYTHING YOU SEND.

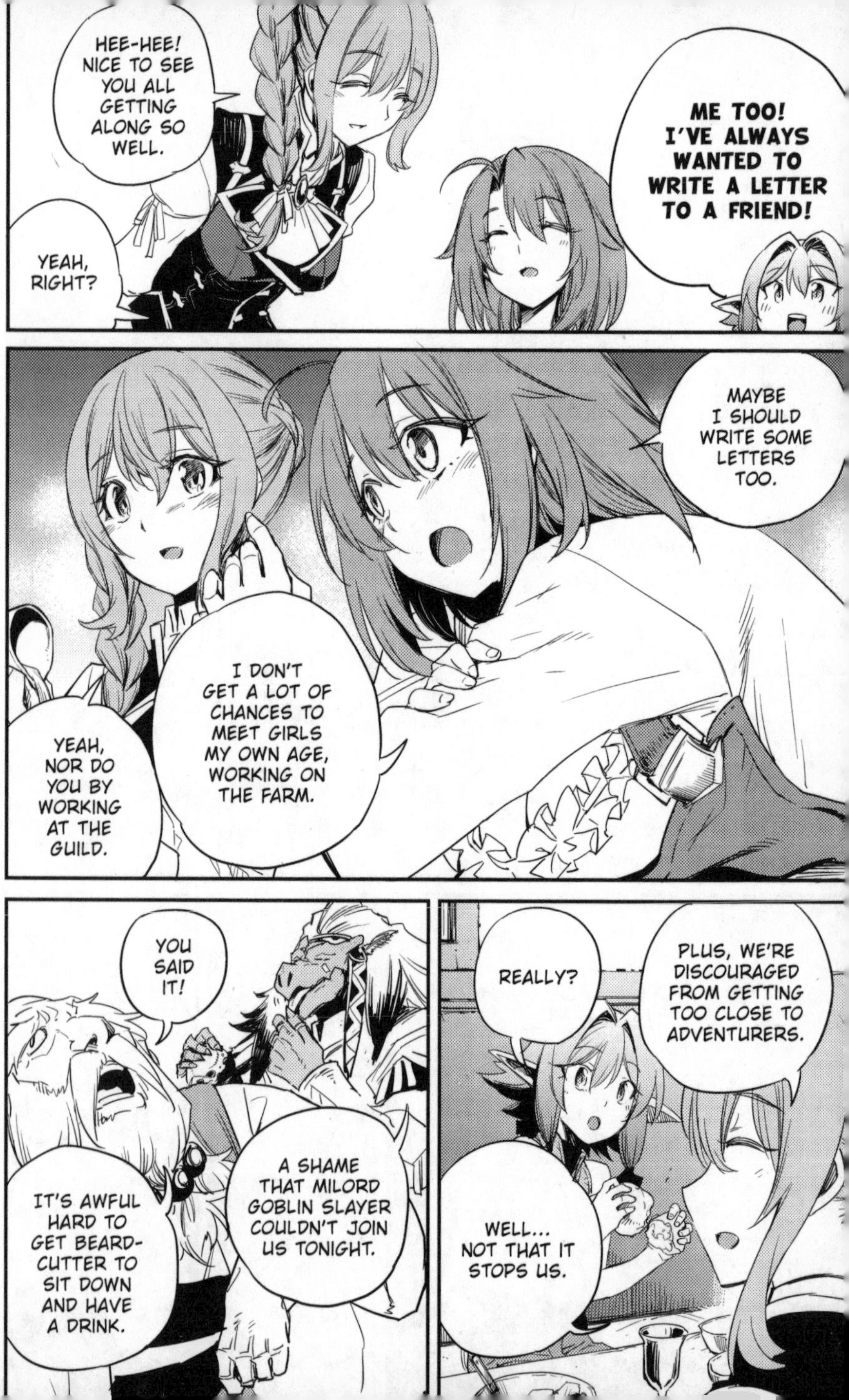

ME TOO! I'VE ALWAYS WANTED TO WRITE A LETTER TO A FRIEND!
HEE-HEE! NICE TO SEE YOU ALL GETTING ALONG SO WELL.
YEAH, RIGHT?
MAYBE I SHOULD WRITE SOME LETTERS TOO.
I DON'T GET A LOT OF CHANCES TO MEET GIRLS MY OWN AGE, WORKING ON THE FARM.
YEAH, NOR DO YOU BY WORKING AT THE GUILD.
PLUS, WE'RE DISCOURAGED FROM GETTING TOO CLOSE TO ADVENTURERS.
REALLY?
WELL... NOT THAT IT STOPS US.
YOU SAID IT!
A SHAME THAT MILORD GOBLIN SLAYER COULDN'T JOIN US TONIGHT.
IT'S AWFUL HARD TO GET BEARD-CUTTER TO SIT DOWN AND HAVE A DRINK.

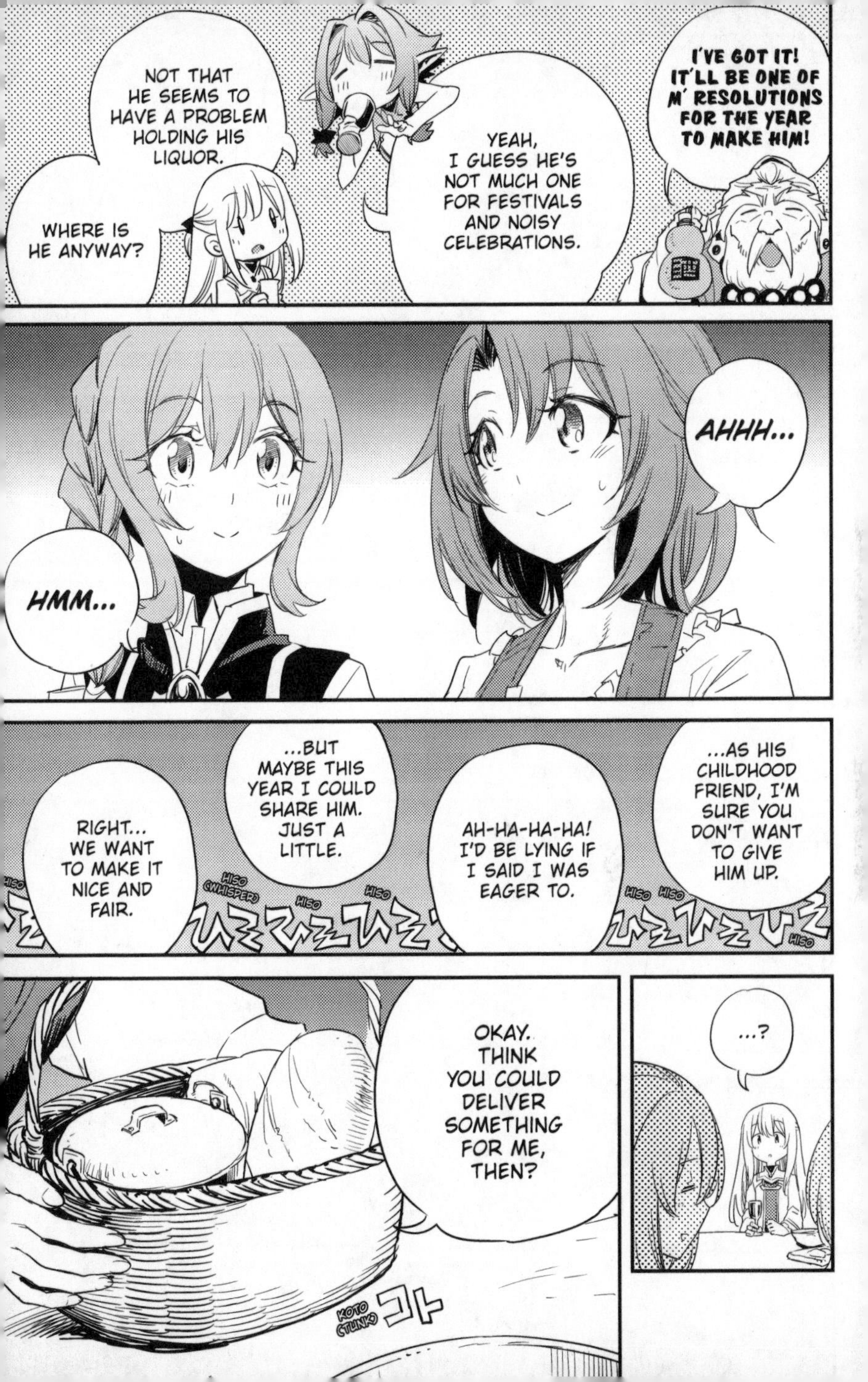
I'VE GOT IT! IT'LL BE ONE OF M' RESOLUTIONS FOR THE YEAR TO MAKE HIM!
YEAH, I GUESS HE'S NOT MUCH ONE FOR FESTIVALS AND NOISY CELEBRATIONS.
NOT THAT HE SEEMS TO HAVE A PROBLEM HOLDING HIS LIQUOR.
WHERE IS HE ANYWAY?
AHHH...
HMM...
...AS HIS CHILDHOOD FRIEND, I'M SURE YOU DON'T WANT TO GIVE HIM UP.
HISO HISO
HISO
AH-HA-HA-HA! I'D BE LYING IF I SAID I WAS EAGER TO.
...BUT MAYBE THIS YEAR I COULD SHARE HIM. JUST A LITTLE.
HISO
HISO (WHISPER)
RIGHT... WE WANT TO MAKE IT NICE AND FAIR.
HISO
...?
OKAY. THINK YOU COULD DELIVER SOMETHING FOR ME, THEN?
KOTO (TUNK)

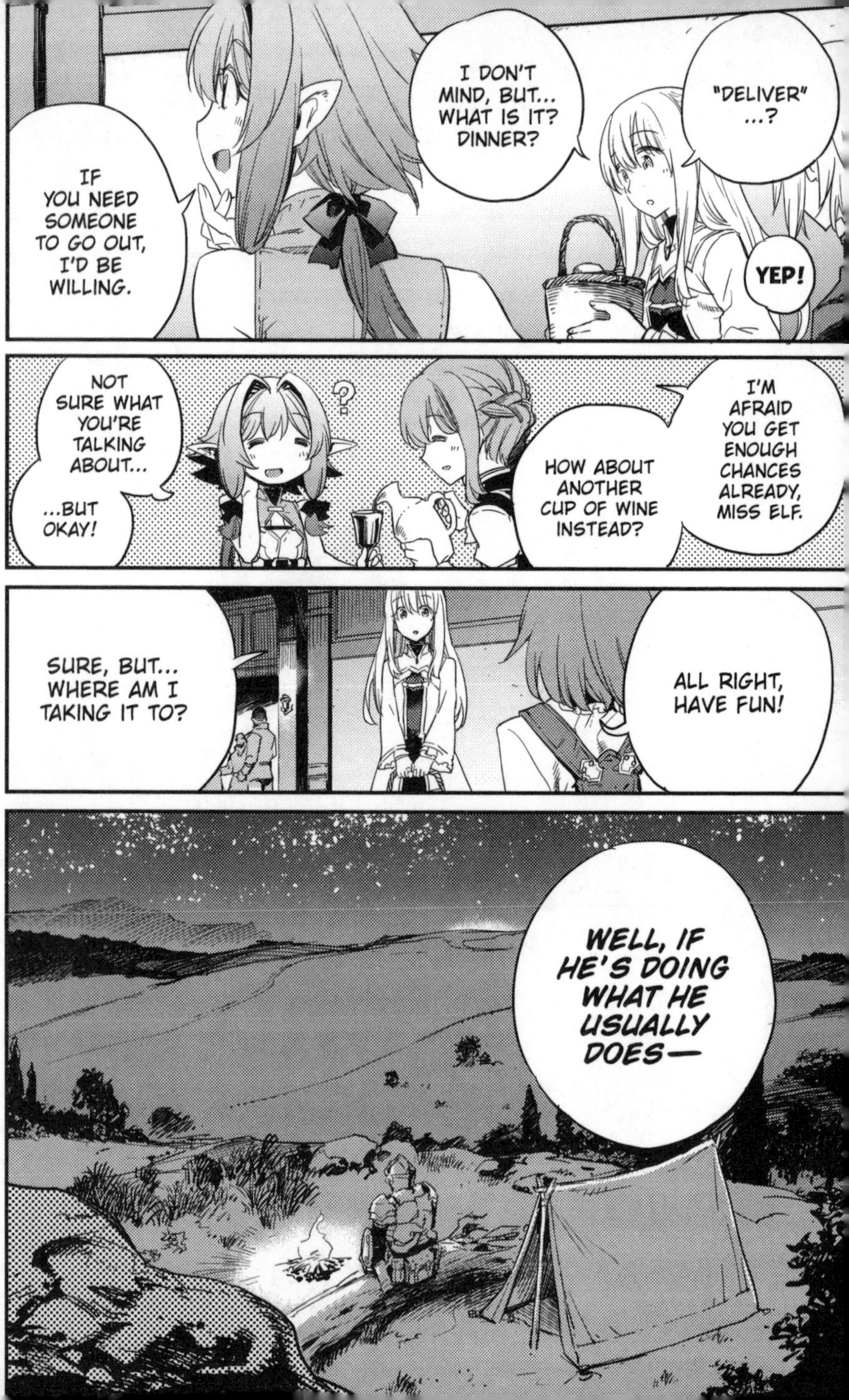
"DELIVER" ...?
I DON'T MIND, BUT... WHAT IS IT? DINNER?
YEP!
IF YOU NEED SOMEONE TO GO OUT, I'D BE WILLING.
I'M AFRAID YOU GET ENOUGH CHANCES ALREADY, MISS ELF.
HOW ABOUT ANOTHER CUP OF WINE INSTEAD?
NOT SURE WHAT YOU'RE TALKING ABOUT...
...BUT OKAY!
ALL RIGHT, HAVE FUN!
SURE, BUT... WHERE AM I TAKING IT TO?
WELL, IF HE'S DOING WHAT HE USUALLY DOES—

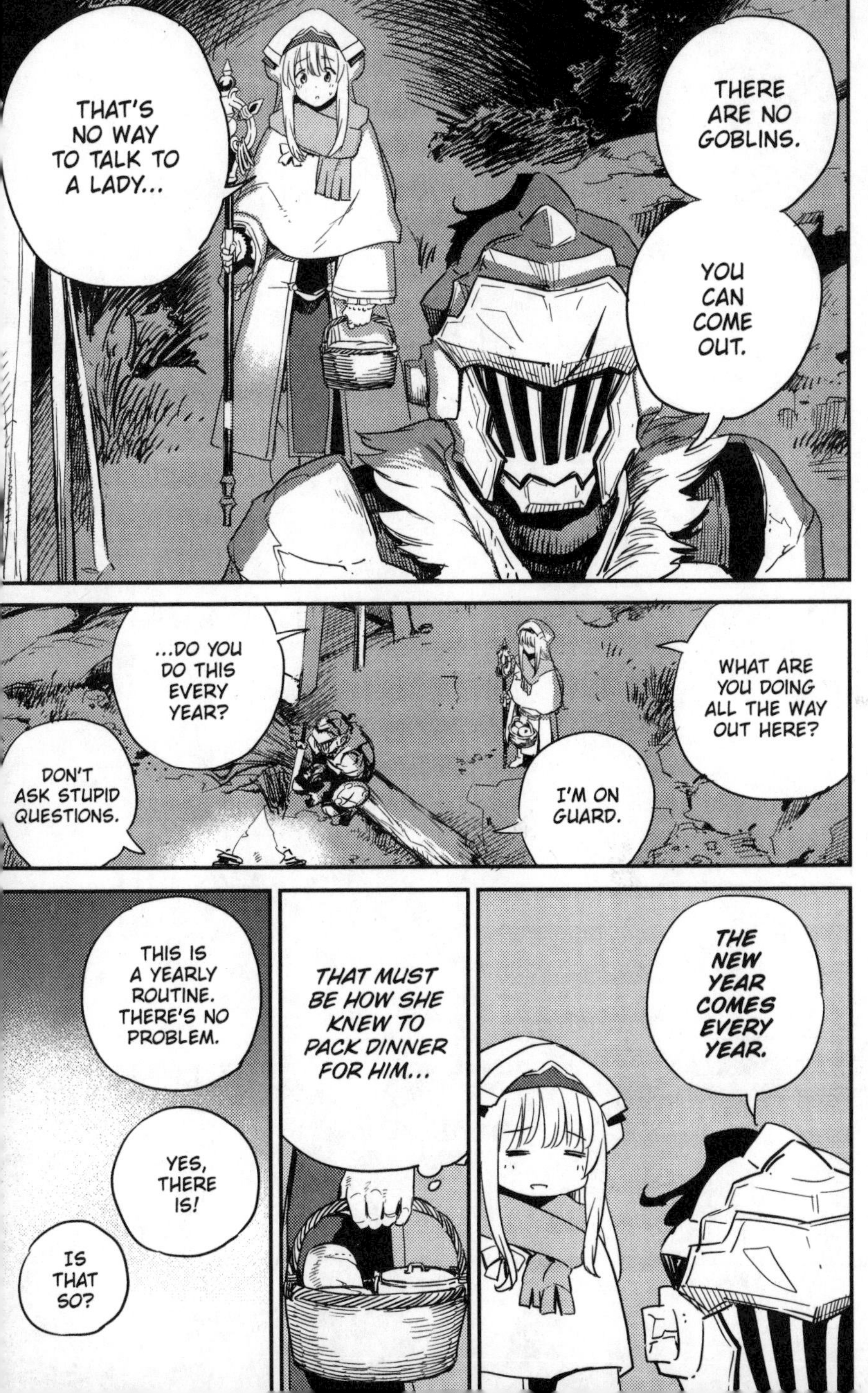
THERE ARE NO GOBLINS.
YOU CAN COME OUT.
THAT'S NO WAY TO TALK TO A LADY...
WHAT ARE YOU DOING ALL THE WAY OUT HERE?
I'M ON GUARD.
...DO YOU DO THIS EVERY YEAR?
DON'T ASK STUPID QUESTIONS.
THE NEW YEAR COMES EVERY YEAR.
THAT MUST BE HOW SHE KNEW TO PACK DINNER FOR HIM...
THIS IS A YEARLY ROUTINE. THERE'S NO PROBLEM.
YES, THERE IS!
IS THAT SO?

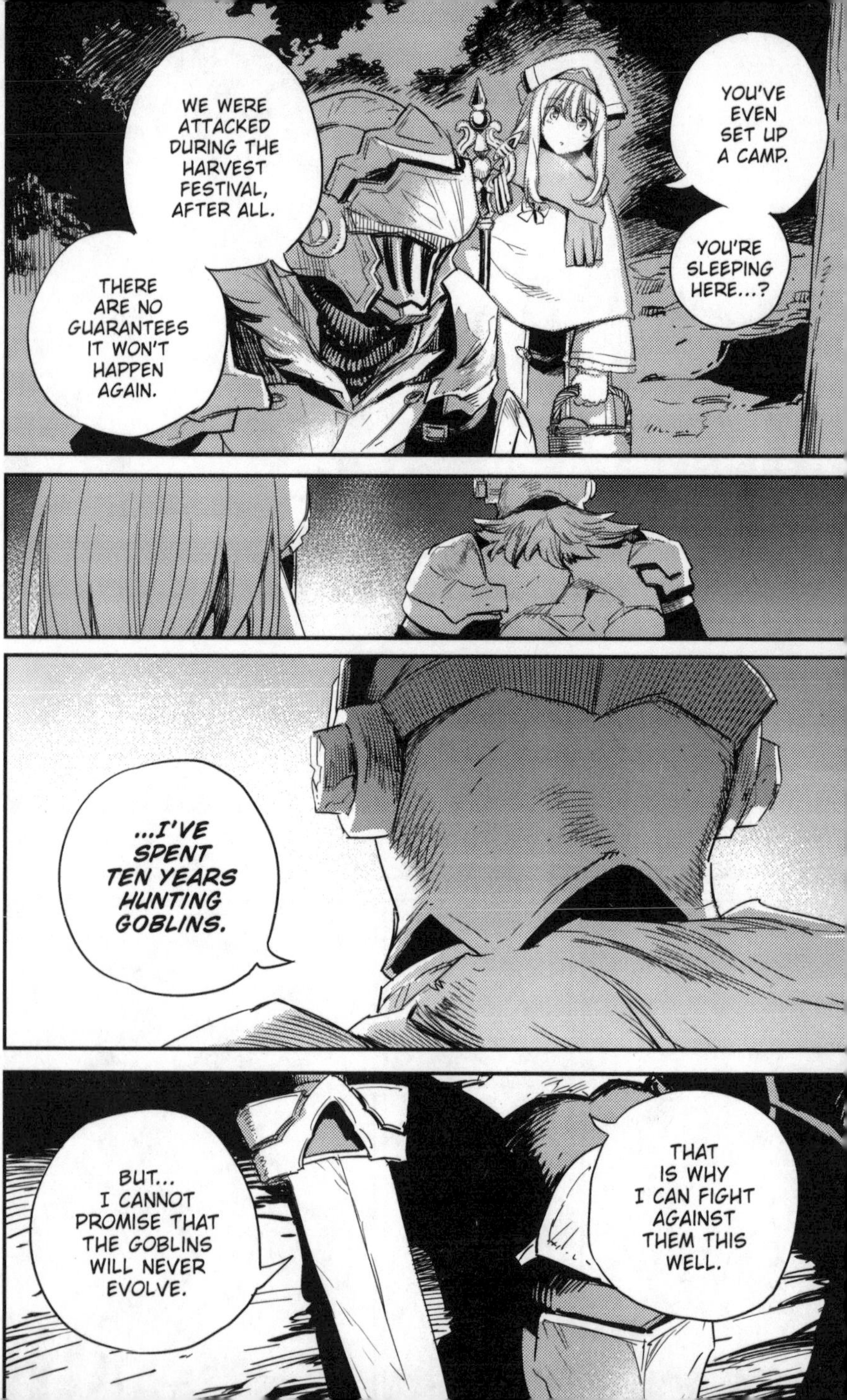
YOU'VE EVEN SET UP A CAMP.
YOU'RE SLEEPING HERE...?
WE WERE ATTACKED DURING THE HARVEST FESTIVAL, AFTER ALL.
THERE ARE NO GUARANTEES IT WON'T HAPPEN AGAIN.
...I'VE SPENT TEN YEARS HUNTING GOBLINS.
THAT IS WHY I CAN FIGHT AGAINST THEM THIS WELL.
BUT... I CANNOT PROMISE THAT THE GOBLINS WILL NEVER EVOLVE.

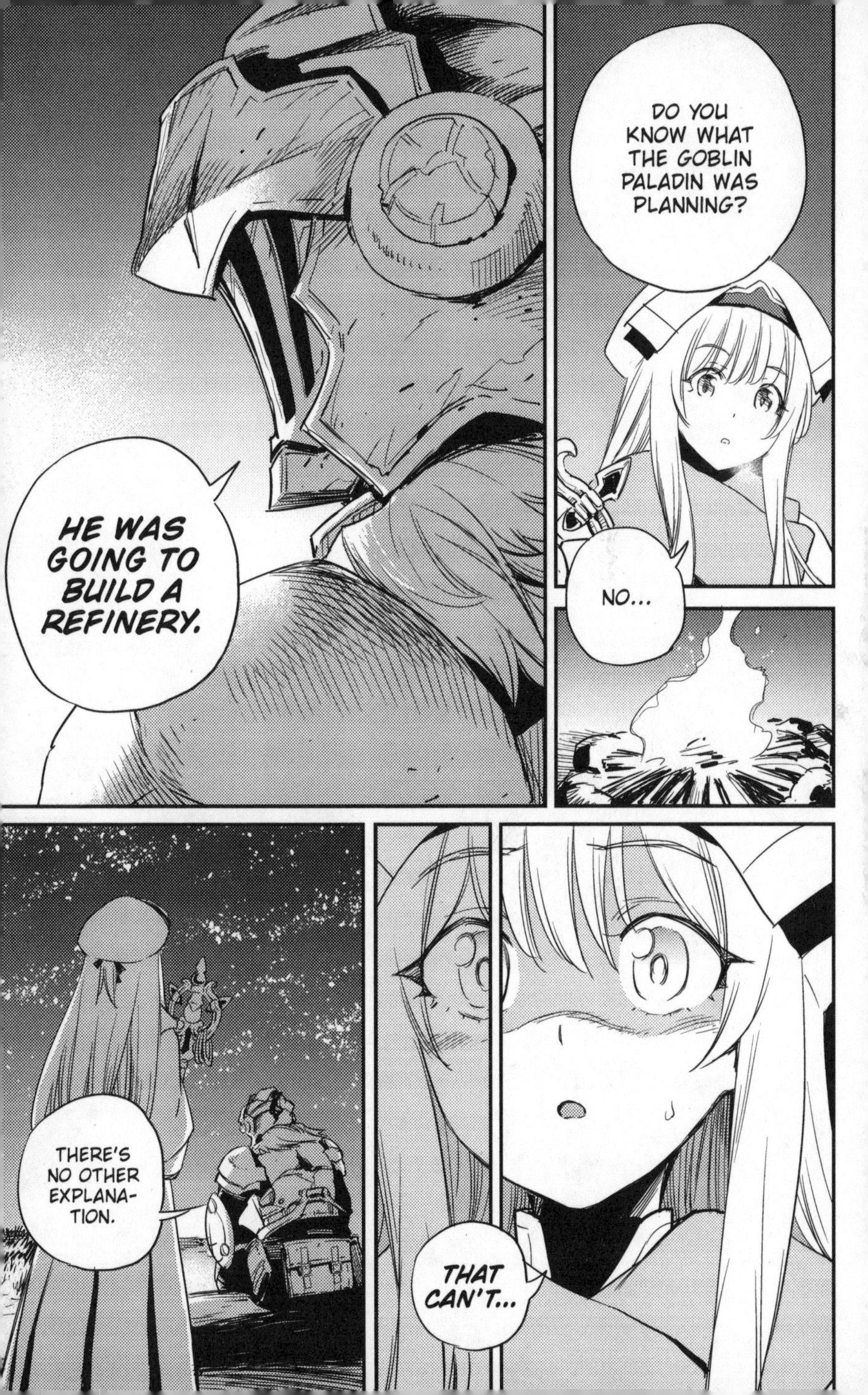
DO YOU KNOW WHAT THE GOBLIN PALADIN WAS PLANNING?
NO...
HE WAS GOING TO BUILD A REFINERY.
THAT CAN'T...
THERE'S NO OTHER EXPLANATION.

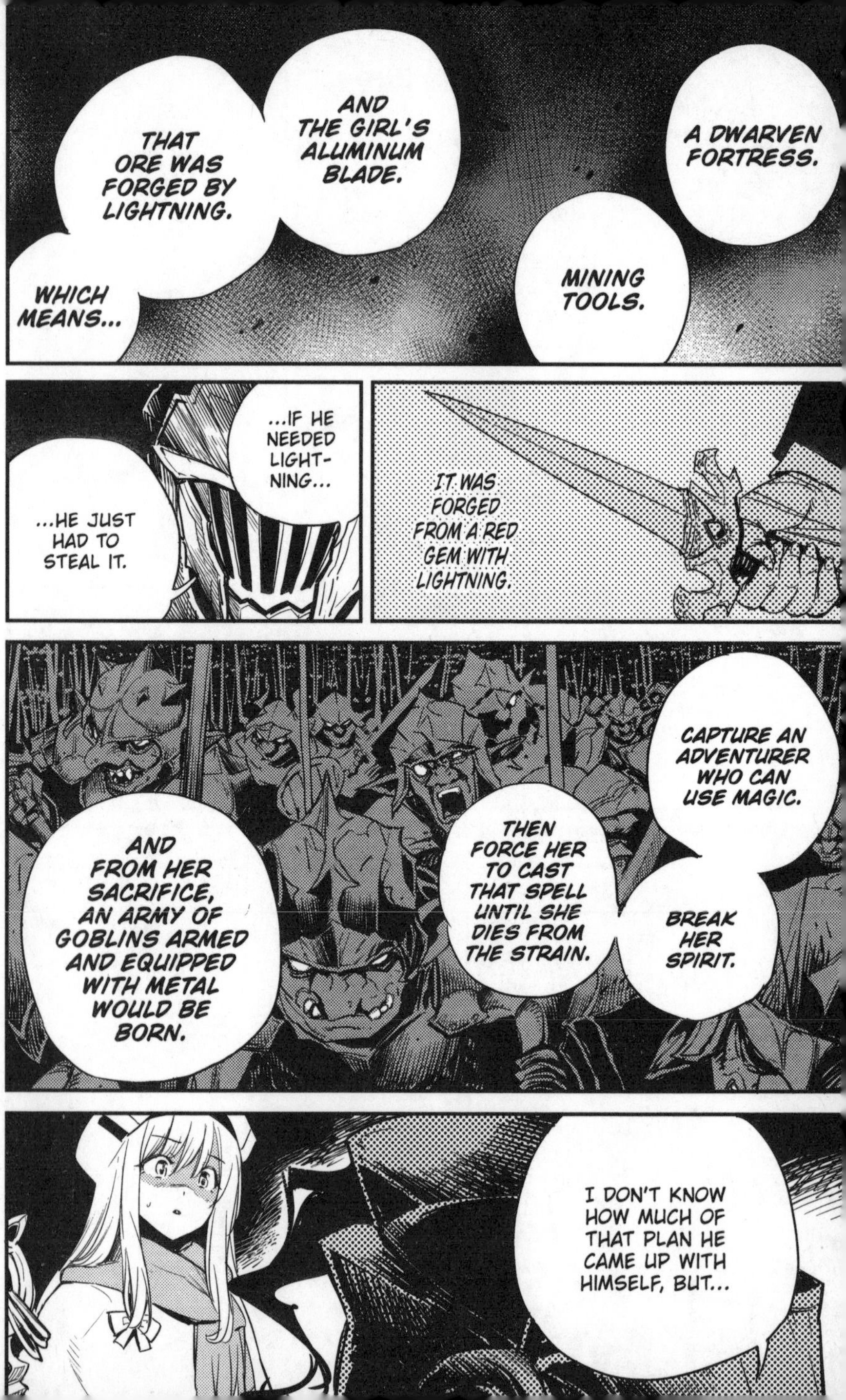
A DWARVEN FORTRESS.
MINING TOOLS.
AND THE GIRL'S ALUMINUM BLADE.
THAT ORE WAS FORGED BY LIGHTNING.
WHICH MEANS...
IT WAS FORGED FROM A RED GEM WITH LIGHTNING.
...IF HE NEEDED LIGHT-NING...
...HE JUST HAD TO STEAL IT.
CAPTURE AN ADVENTURER WHO CAN USE MAGIC.
BREAK HER SPIRIT.
THEN FORCE HER TO CAST THAT SPELL UNTIL SHE DIES FROM THE STRAIN.
AND FROM HER SACRIFICE, AN ARMY OF GOBLINS ARMED AND EQUIPPED WITH METAL WOULD BE BORN.
I DON'T KNOW HOW MUCH OF THAT PLAN HE CAME UP WITH HIMSELF, BUT...

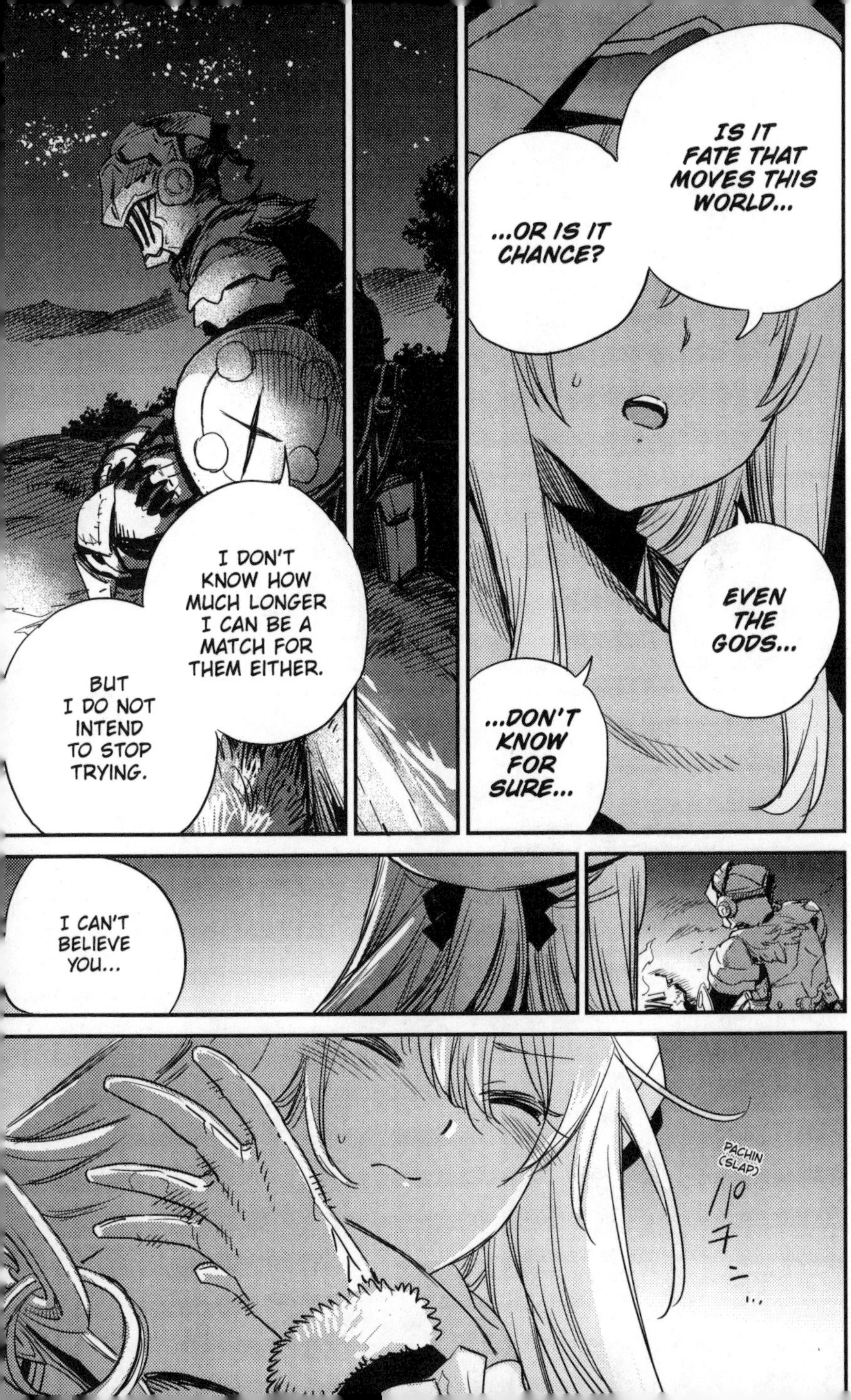
IS IT FATE THAT MOVES THIS WORLD...
...OR IS IT CHANCE?
EVEN THE GODS...
...DON'T KNOW FOR SURE...
I DON'T KNOW HOW MUCH LONGER I CAN BE A MATCH FOR THEM EITHER.
BUT I DO NOT INTEND TO STOP TRYING.
I CAN'T BELIEVE YOU...
PACHIN (SLAP)
パチン

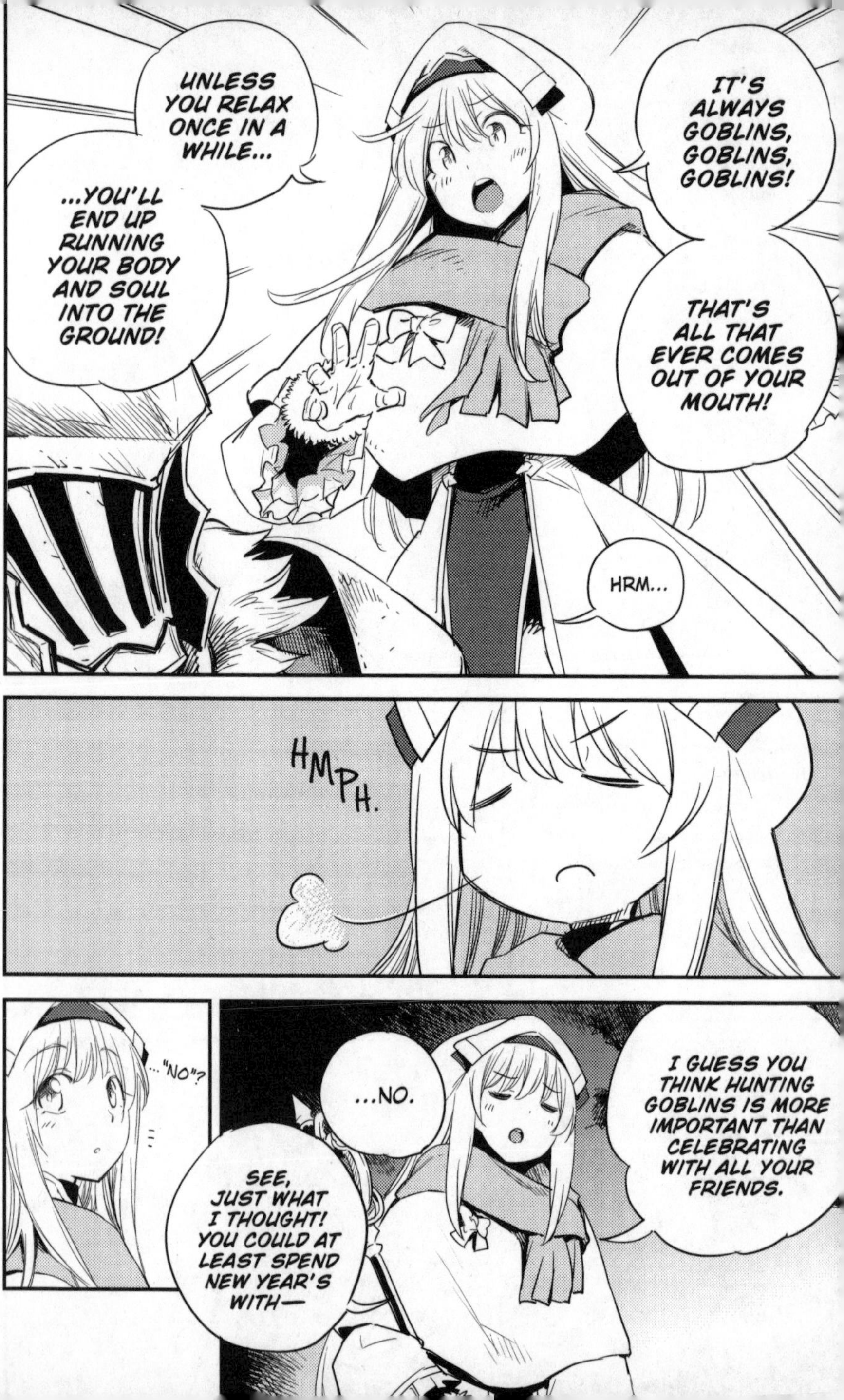
IT'S ALWAYS GOBLINS, GOBLINS, GOBLINS!
THAT'S ALL THAT EVER COMES OUT OF YOUR MOUTH!
UNLESS YOU RELAX ONCE IN A WHILE...
...YOU'LL END UP RUNNING YOUR BODY AND SOUL INTO THE GROUND!
HRM...
HMPH.
I GUESS YOU THINK HUNTING GOBLINS IS MORE IMPORTANT THAN CELEBRATING WITH ALL YOUR FRIENDS.
...NO.
SEE, JUST WHAT I THOUGHT! YOU COULD AT LEAST SPEND NEW YEAR'S WITH—
..."NO"?

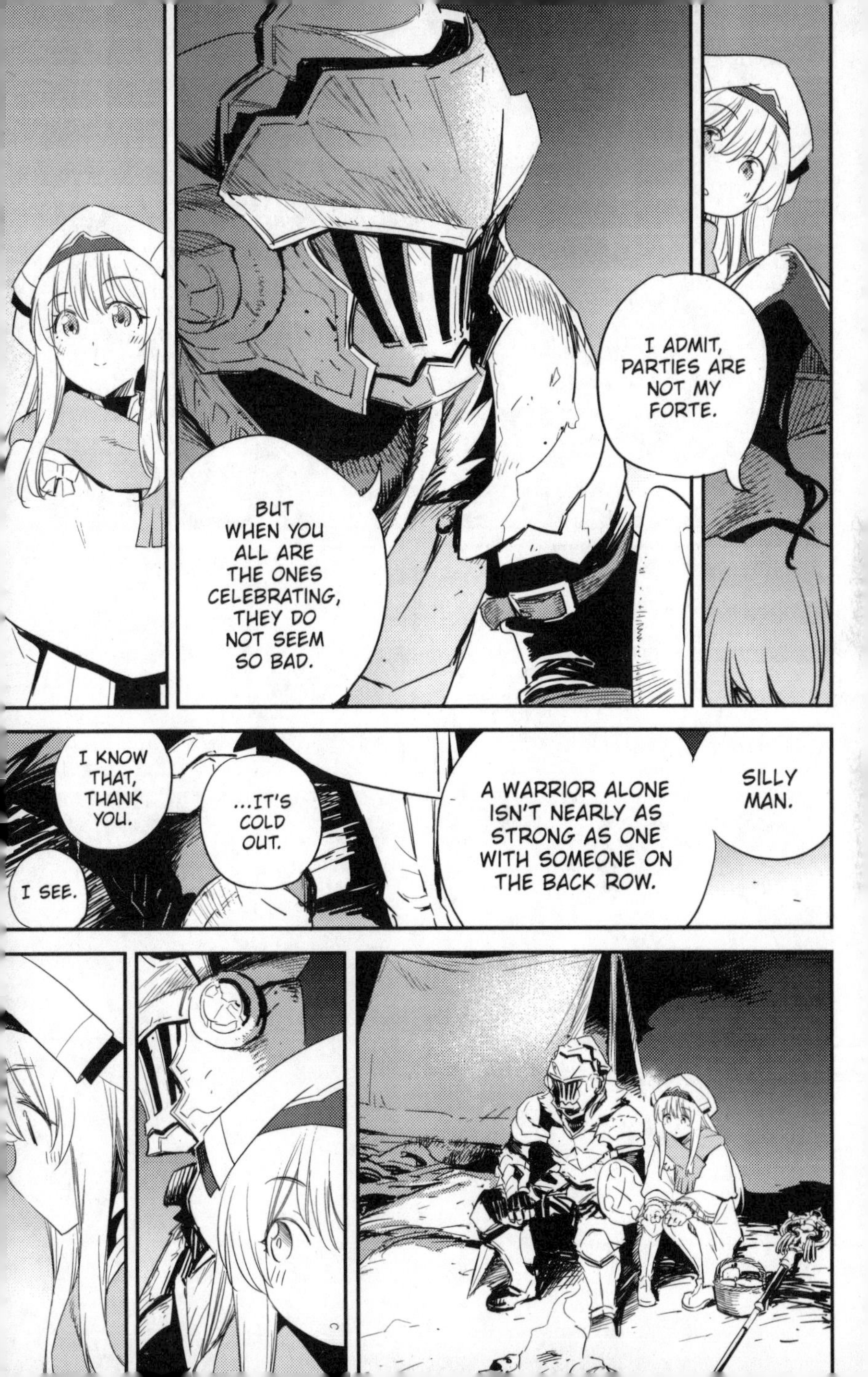
I ADMIT, PARTIES ARE NOT MY FORTE.
BUT WHEN YOU ALL ARE THE ONES CELEBRATING, THEY DO NOT SEEM SO BAD.
SILLY MAN.
A WARRIOR ALONE ISN'T NEARLY AS STRONG AS ONE WITH SOMEONE ON THE BACK ROW.
...IT'S COLD OUT.
I KNOW THAT, THANK YOU.
I SEE.

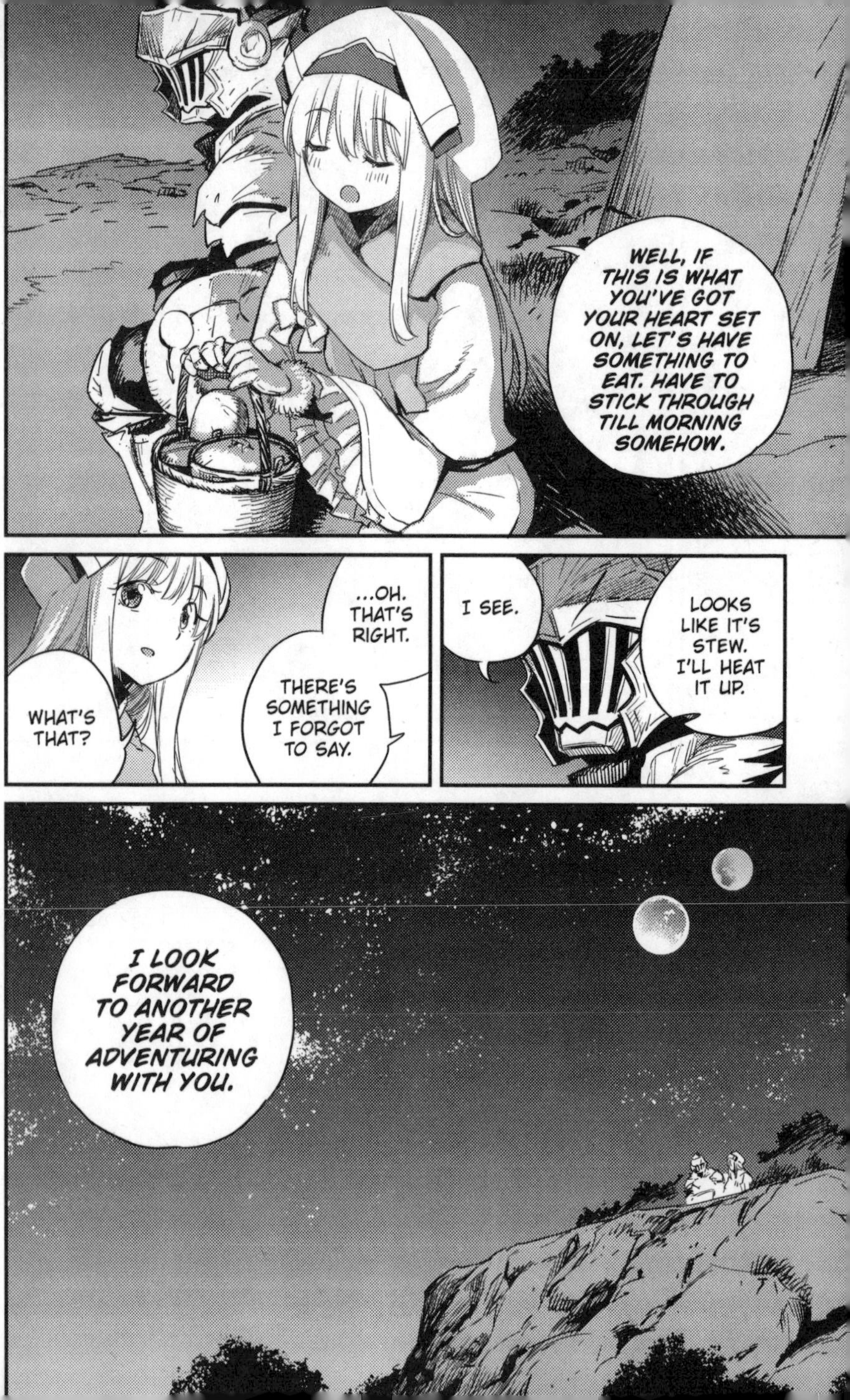
WELL, IF THIS IS WHAT YOU'VE GOT YOUR HEART SET ON, LET'S HAVE SOMETHING TO EAT. HAVE TO STICK THROUGH TILL MORNING SOMEHOW.
LOOKS LIKE IT'S STEW. I'LL HEAT IT UP.
I SEE.
...OH. THAT'S RIGHT.
THERE'S SOMETHING I FORGOT TO SAY.
WHAT'S THAT?
I LOOK FORWARD TO ANOTHER YEAR OF ADVENTURING WITH YOU.

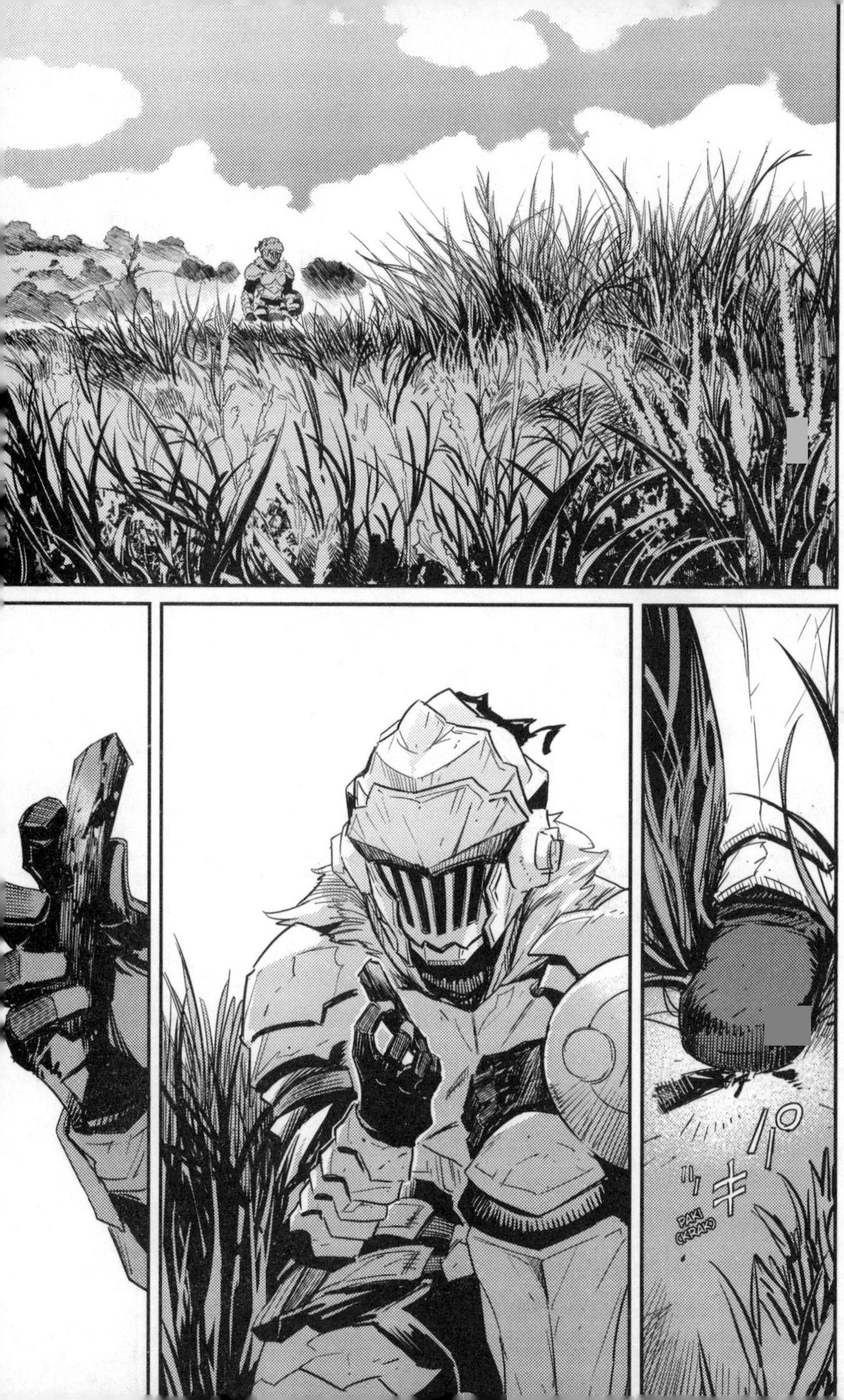
パキッ
PAKI
(KRAK)

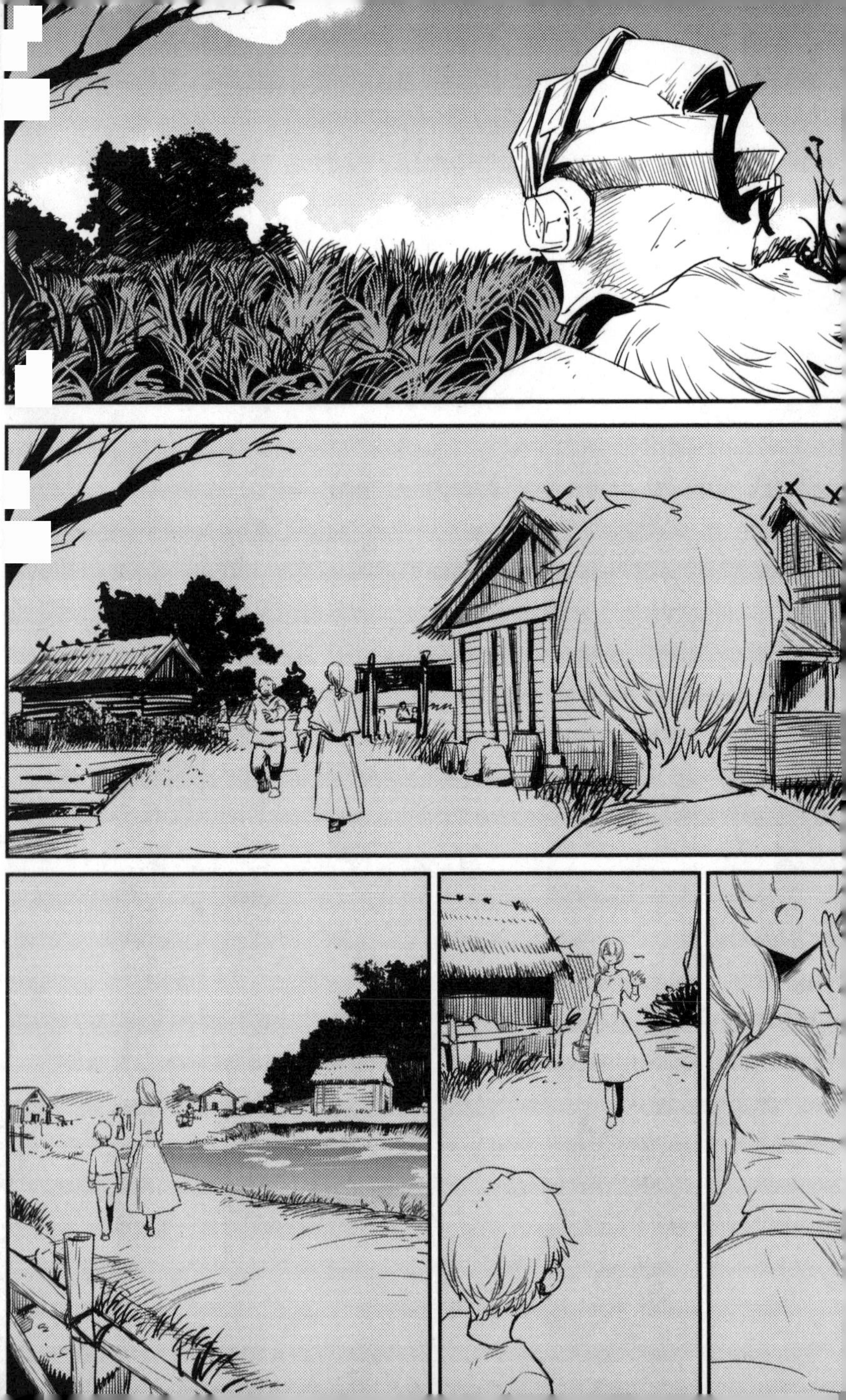

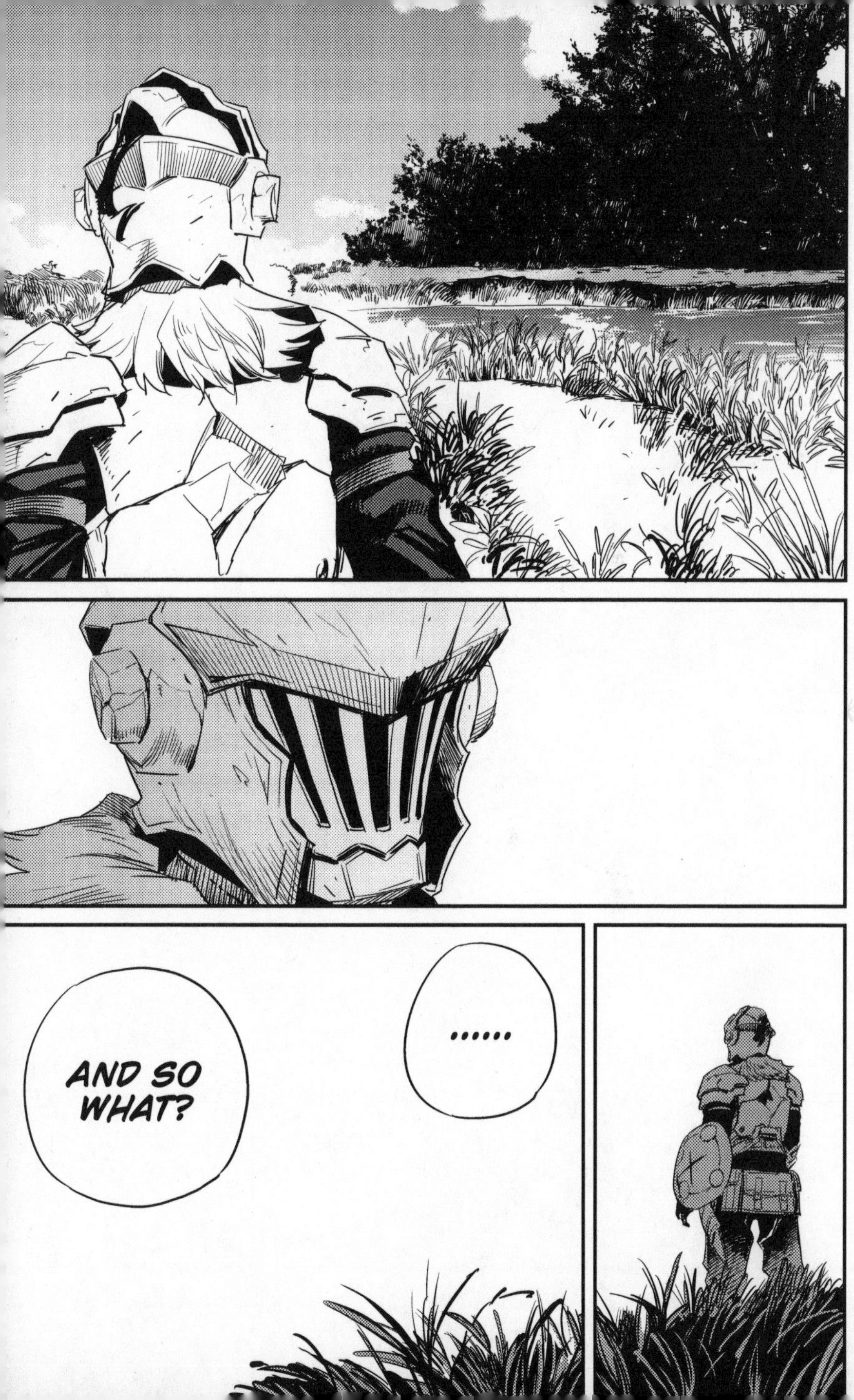
......
AND SO WHAT?

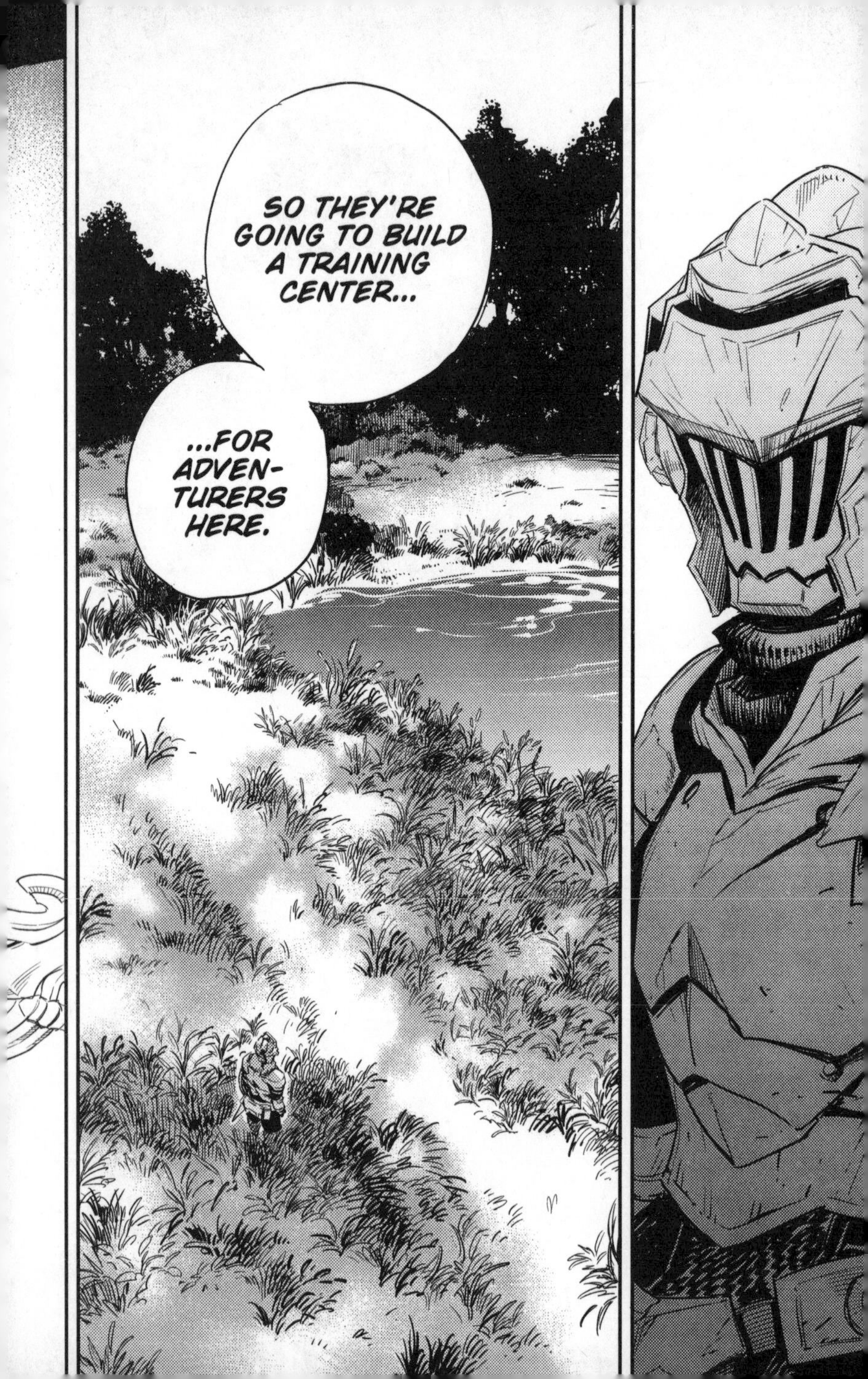
SO THEY'RE GOING TO BUILD A TRAINING CENTER...
...FOR ADVENTURERS HERE.

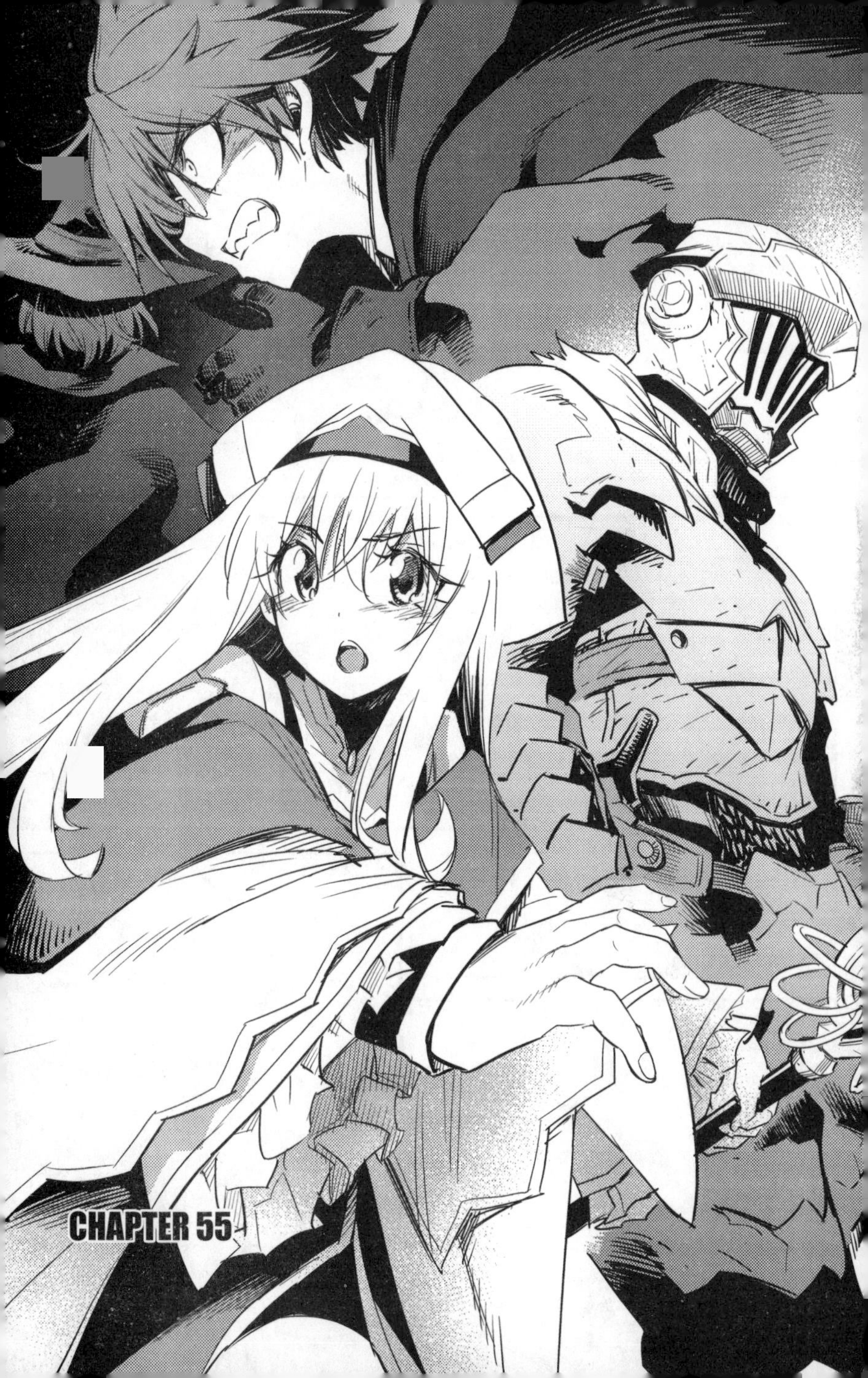
CHAPTER 55

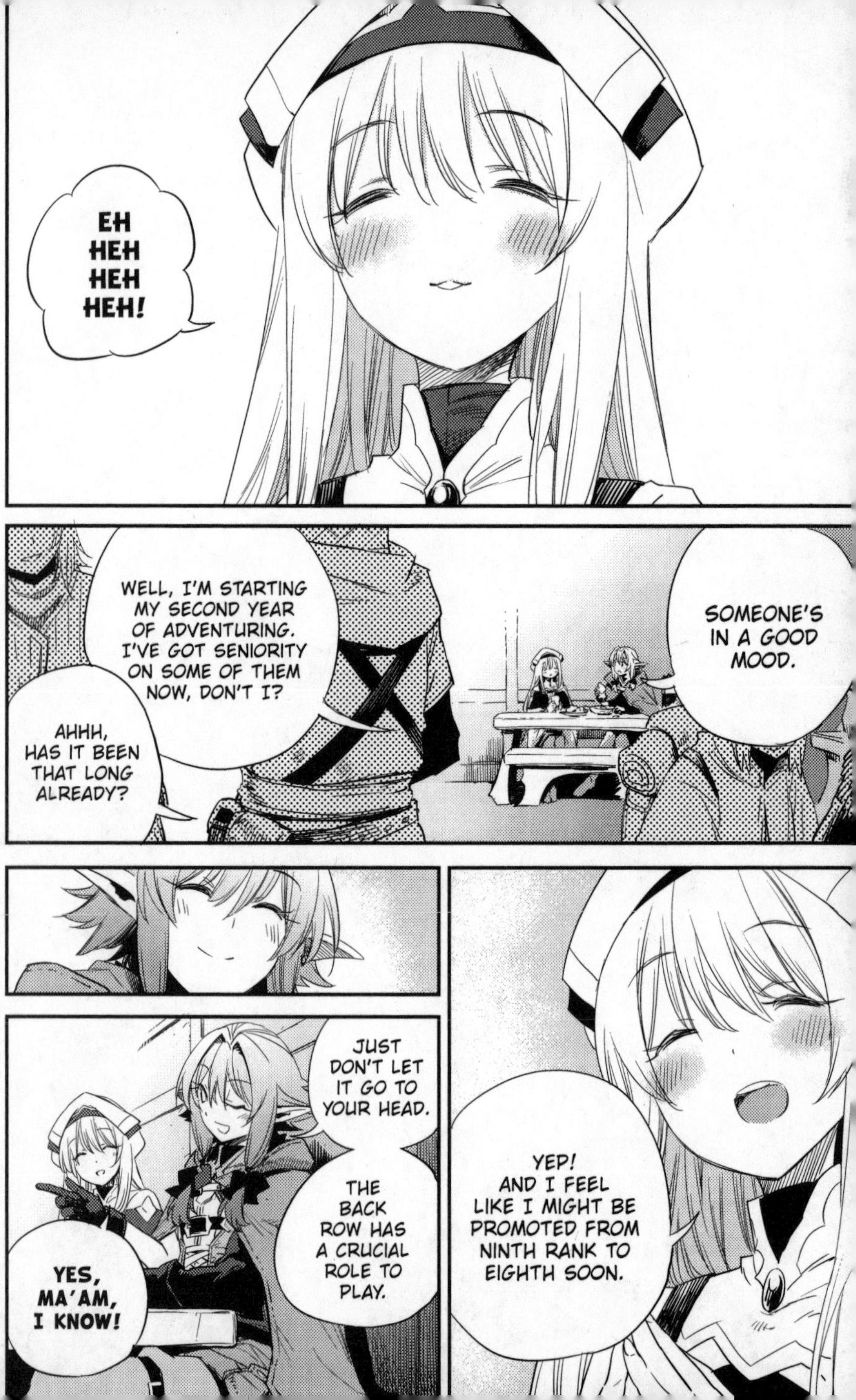
EH HEH HEH HEH!
SOMEONE'S IN A GOOD MOOD.
WELL, I'M STARTING MY SECOND YEAR OF ADVENTURING. I'VE GOT SENIORITY ON SOME OF THEM NOW, DON'T I?
AHHH, HAS IT BEEN THAT LONG ALREADY?
YEP! AND I FEEL LIKE I MIGHT BE PROMOTED FROM NINTH RANK TO EIGHTH SOON.
JUST DON'T LET IT GO TO YOUR HEAD.
THE BACK ROW HAS A CRUCIAL ROLE TO PLAY.
YES, MA'AM, I KNOW!

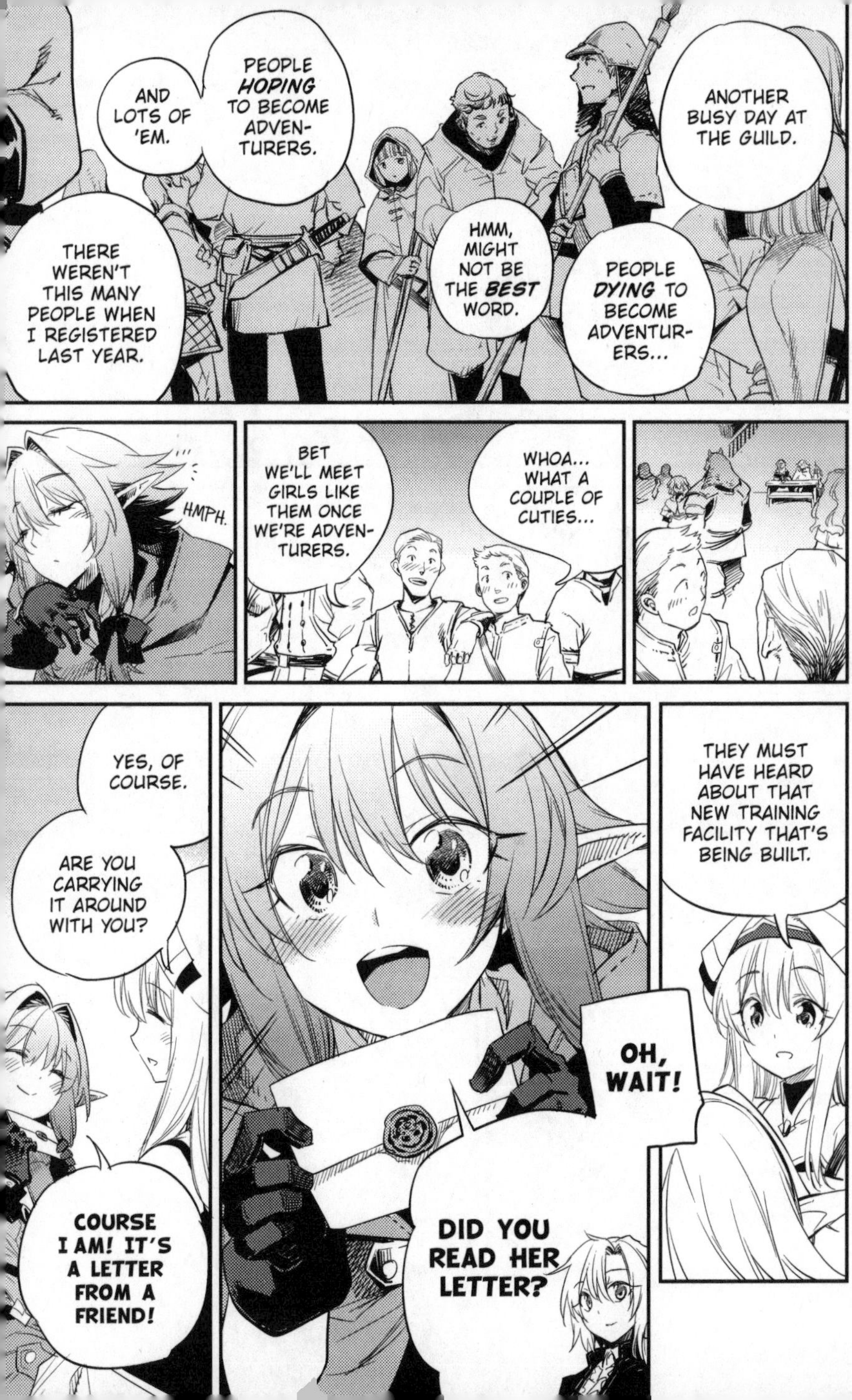

ANOTHER BUSY DAY AT THE GUILD.
PEOPLE DYING TO BECOME ADVENTURERS...
HMM, MIGHT NOT BE THE BEST WORD.
PEOPLE HOPING TO BECOME ADVENTURERS.
AND LOTS OF 'EM.
THERE WEREN'T THIS MANY PEOPLE WHEN I REGISTERED LAST YEAR.
WHOA... WHAT A COUPLE OF CUTIES...
BET WE'LL MEET GIRLS LIKE THEM ONCE WE'RE ADVENTURERS.
HMPH.
THEY MUST HAVE HEARD ABOUT THAT NEW TRAINING FACILITY THAT'S BEING BUILT.
OH, WAIT!
DID YOU READ HER LETTER?
YES, OF COURSE.
ARE YOU CARRYING IT AROUND WITH YOU?
COURSE I AM! IT'S A LETTER FROM A FRIEND!

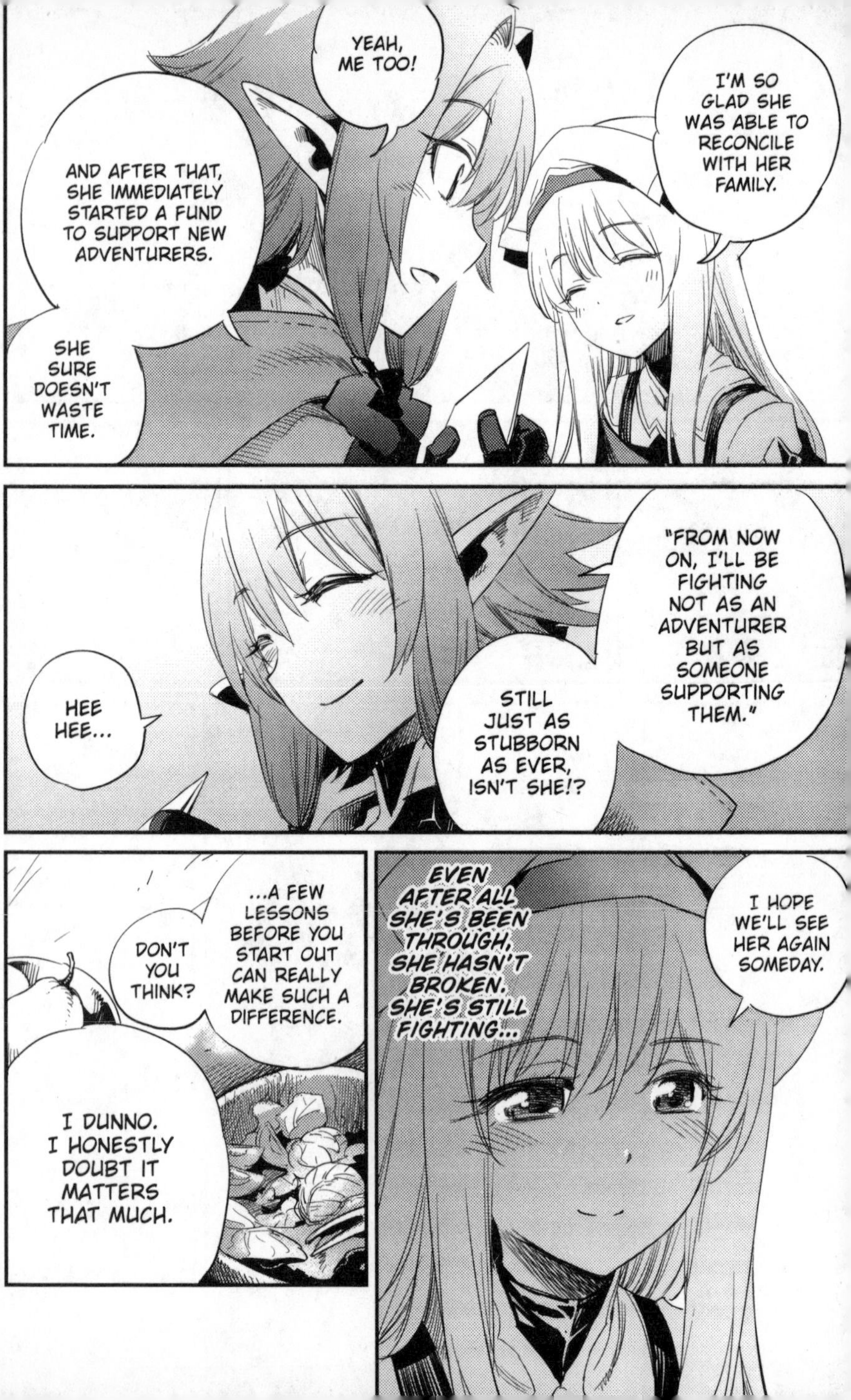
I'M SO GLAD SHE WAS ABLE TO RECONCILE WITH HER FAMILY.
YEAH, ME TOO!
AND AFTER THAT, SHE IMMEDIATELY STARTED A FUND TO SUPPORT NEW ADVENTURERS.
SHE SURE DOESN'T WASTE TIME.
"FROM NOW ON, I'LL BE FIGHTING NOT AS AN ADVENTURER BUT AS SOMEONE SUPPORTING THEM."
STILL JUST AS STUBBORN AS EVER, ISN'T SHE!?
HEE HEE...
I HOPE WE'LL SEE HER AGAIN SOMEDAY.
EVEN AFTER ALL SHE'S BEEN THROUGH, SHE HASN'T BROKEN. SHE'S STILL FIGHTING...
...A FEW LESSONS BEFORE YOU START OUT CAN REALLY MAKE SUCH A DIFFERENCE.
DON'T YOU THINK?
I DUNNO. I HONESTLY DOUBT IT MATTERS THAT MUCH.

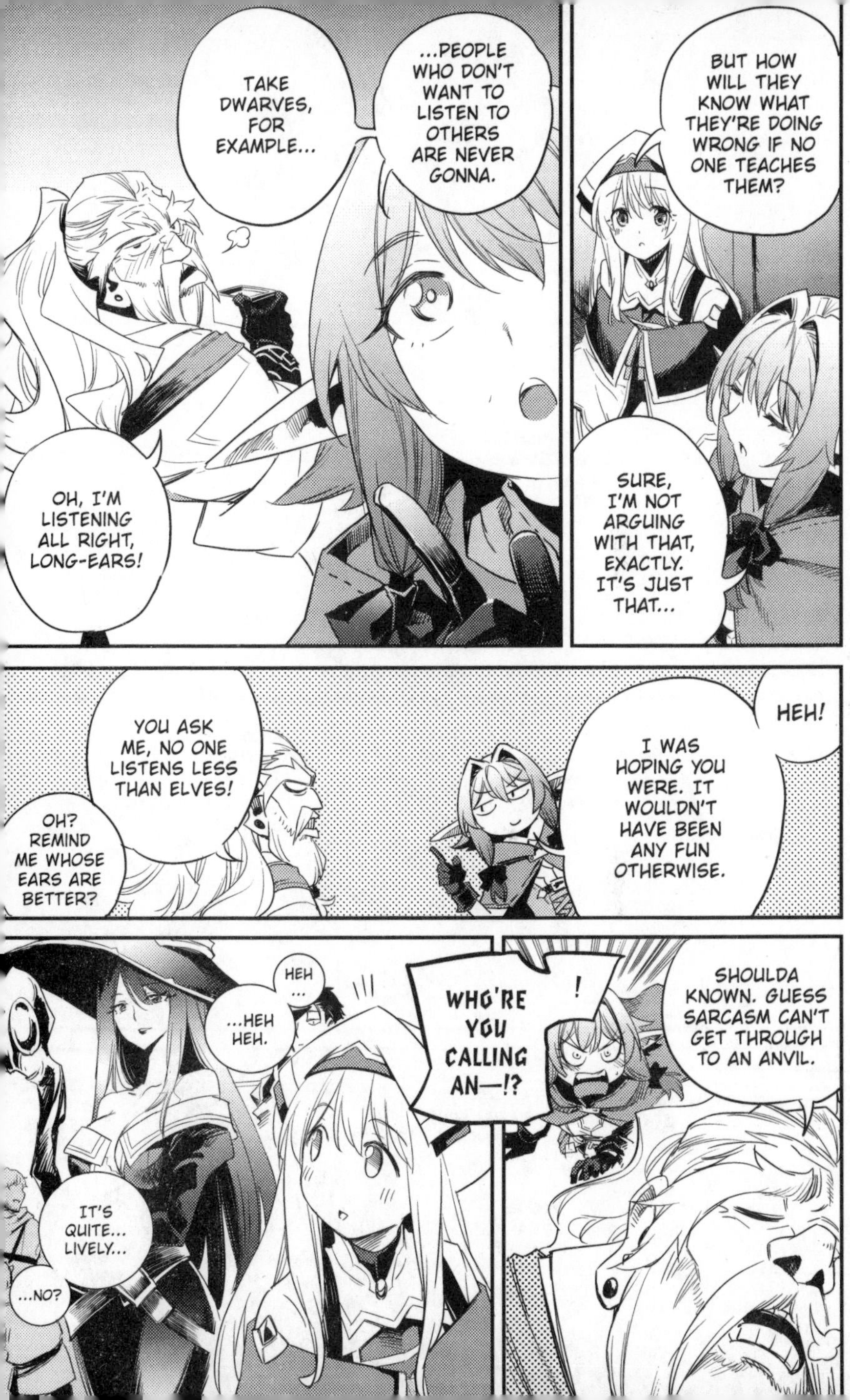
BUT HOW WILL THEY KNOW WHAT THEY'RE DOING WRONG IF NO ONE TEACHES THEM?
SURE, I'M NOT ARGUING WITH THAT, EXACTLY. IT'S JUST THAT...
...PEOPLE WHO DON'T WANT TO LISTEN TO OTHERS ARE NEVER GONNA.
TAKE DWARVES, FOR EXAMPLE...
OH, I'M LISTENING ALL RIGHT, LONG-EARS!
HEH!
I WAS HOPING YOU WERE. IT WOULDN'T HAVE BEEN ANY FUN OTHERWISE.
YOU ASK ME, NO ONE LISTENS LESS THAN ELVES!
OH? REMIND ME WHOSE EARS ARE BETTER?
SHOULDA KNOWN. GUESS SARCASM CAN'T GET THROUGH TO AN ANVIL.
!
WHO'RE YOU CALLING AN—!?
HEH ...
...HEH HEH.
IT'S QUITE... LIVELY...
...NO?

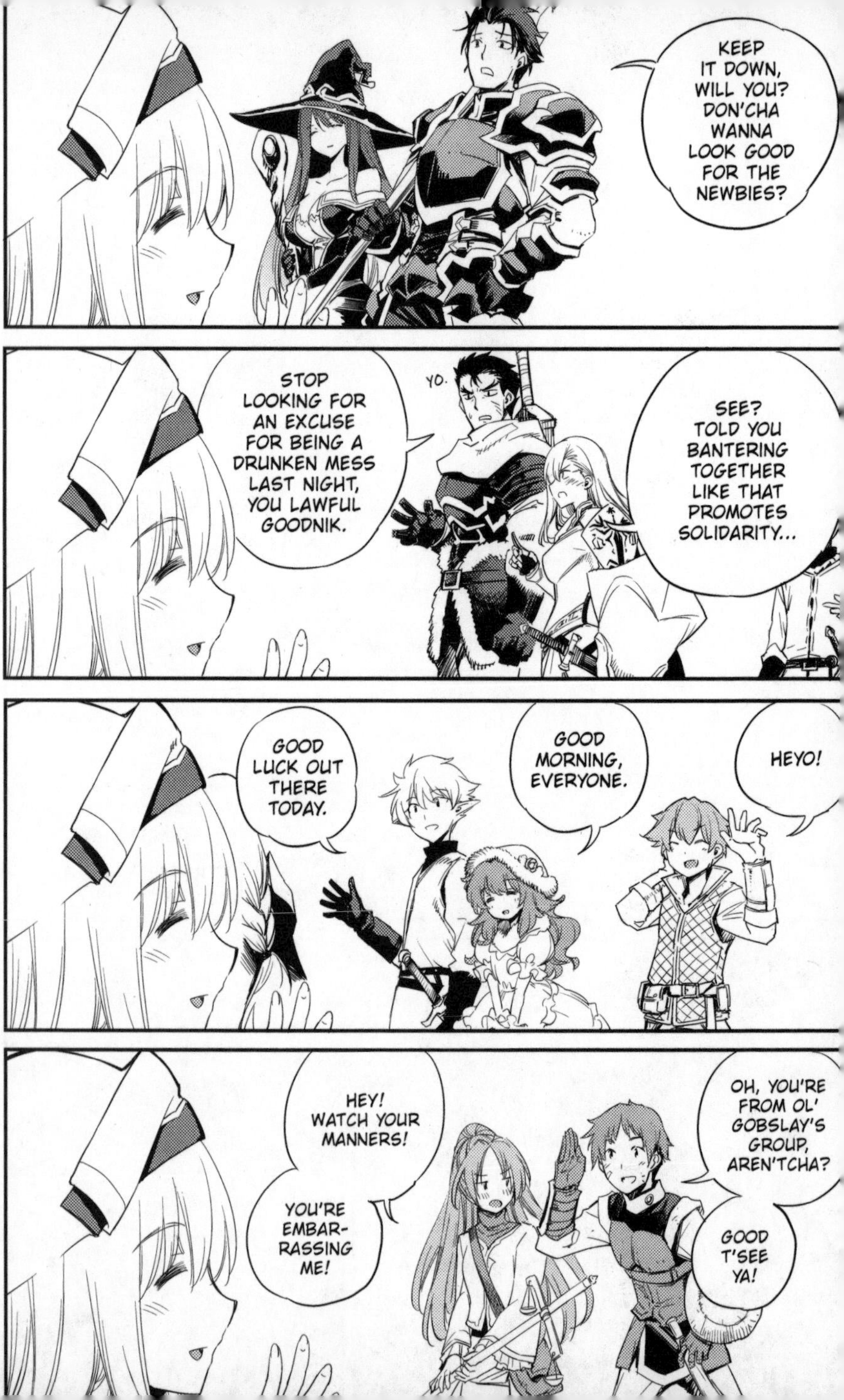
KEEP IT DOWN, WILL YOU? DON'CHA WANNA LOOK GOOD FOR THE NEWBIES?
SEE? TOLD YOU BANTERING TOGETHER LIKE THAT PROMOTES SOLIDARITY...
YO.
STOP LOOKING FOR AN EXCUSE FOR BEING A DRUNKEN MESS LAST NIGHT, YOU LAWFUL GOODNIK.
HEYO!
GOOD MORNING, EVERYONE.
GOOD LUCK OUT THERE TODAY.
OH, YOU'RE FROM OL' GOBSLAY'S GROUP, AREN'TCHA?
GOOD T'SEE YA!
HEY! WATCH YOUR MANNERS!
YOU'RE EMBAR-RASSING ME!

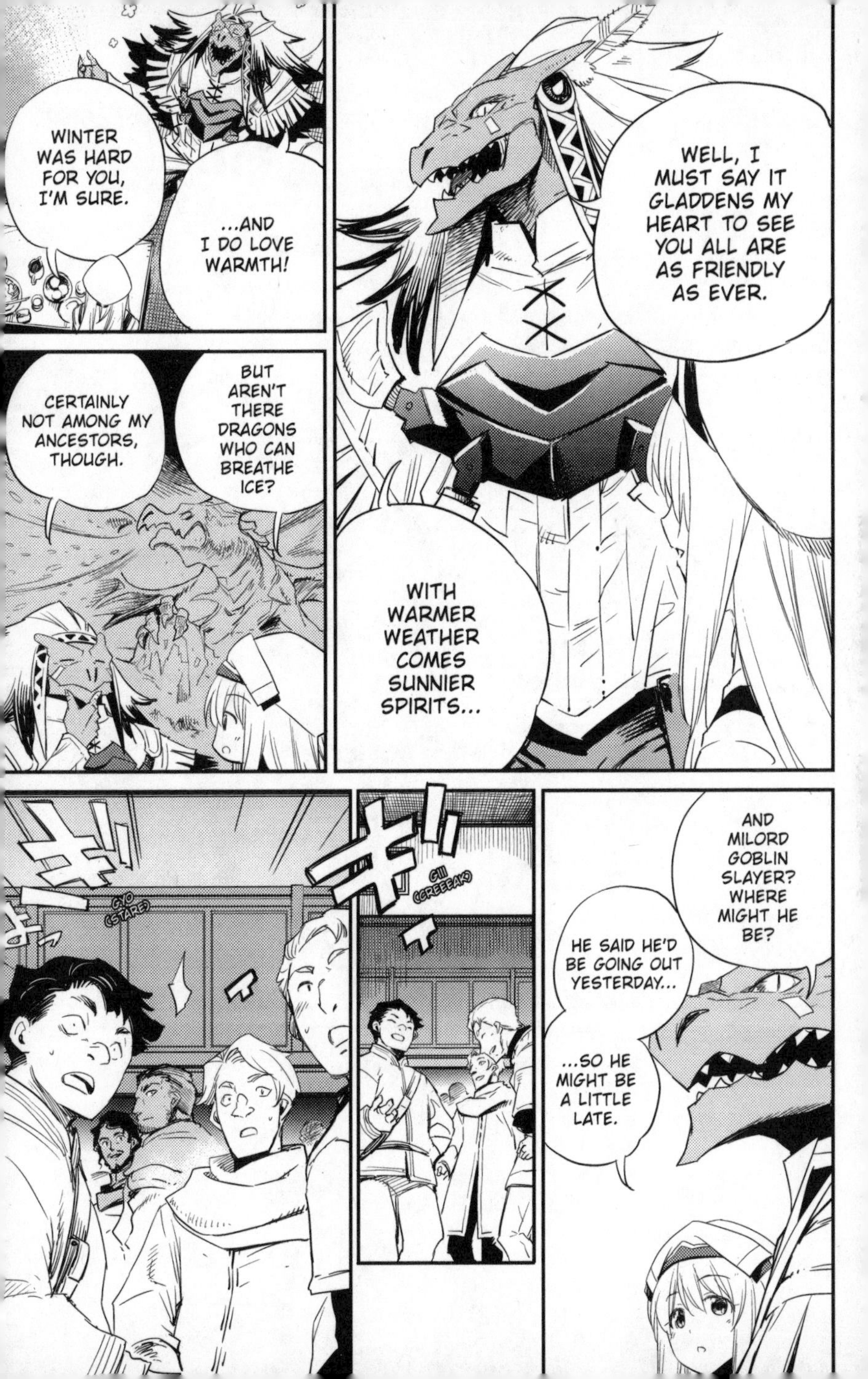
WELL, I MUST SAY IT GLADDENS MY HEART TO SEE YOU ALL ARE AS FRIENDLY AS EVER.
WITH WARMER WEATHER COMES SUNNIER SPIRITS...
WINTER WAS HARD FOR YOU, I'M SURE.
...AND I DO LOVE WARMTH!
BUT AREN'T THERE DRAGONS WHO CAN BREATHE ICE?
CERTAINLY NOT AMONG MY ANCESTORS, THOUGH.
AND MILORD GOBLIN SLAYER? WHERE MIGHT HE BE?
HE SAID HE'D BE GOING OUT YESTERDAY...
...SO HE MIGHT BE A LITTLE LATE.
GIII (CREEEAK)
GYO (STARE)

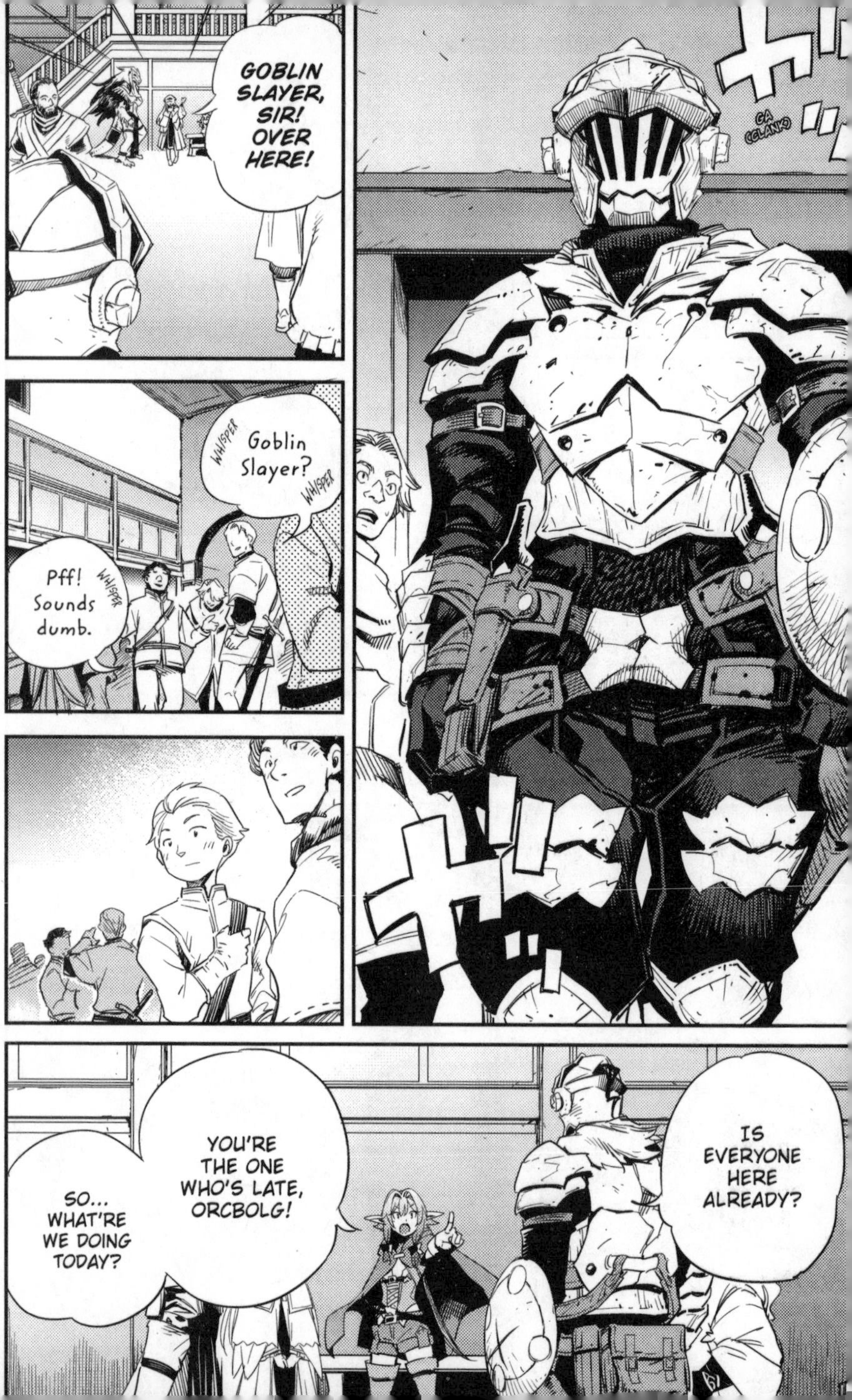
GA (CLANK)
GOBLIN SLAYER, SIR! OVER HERE!
WHISPER
Goblin Slayer?
WHISPER
WHISPER
Pff! Sounds dumb.
IS EVERYONE HERE ALREADY?
YOU'RE THE ONE WHO'S LATE, ORCBOLG!
SO... WHAT'RE WE DOING TODAY?

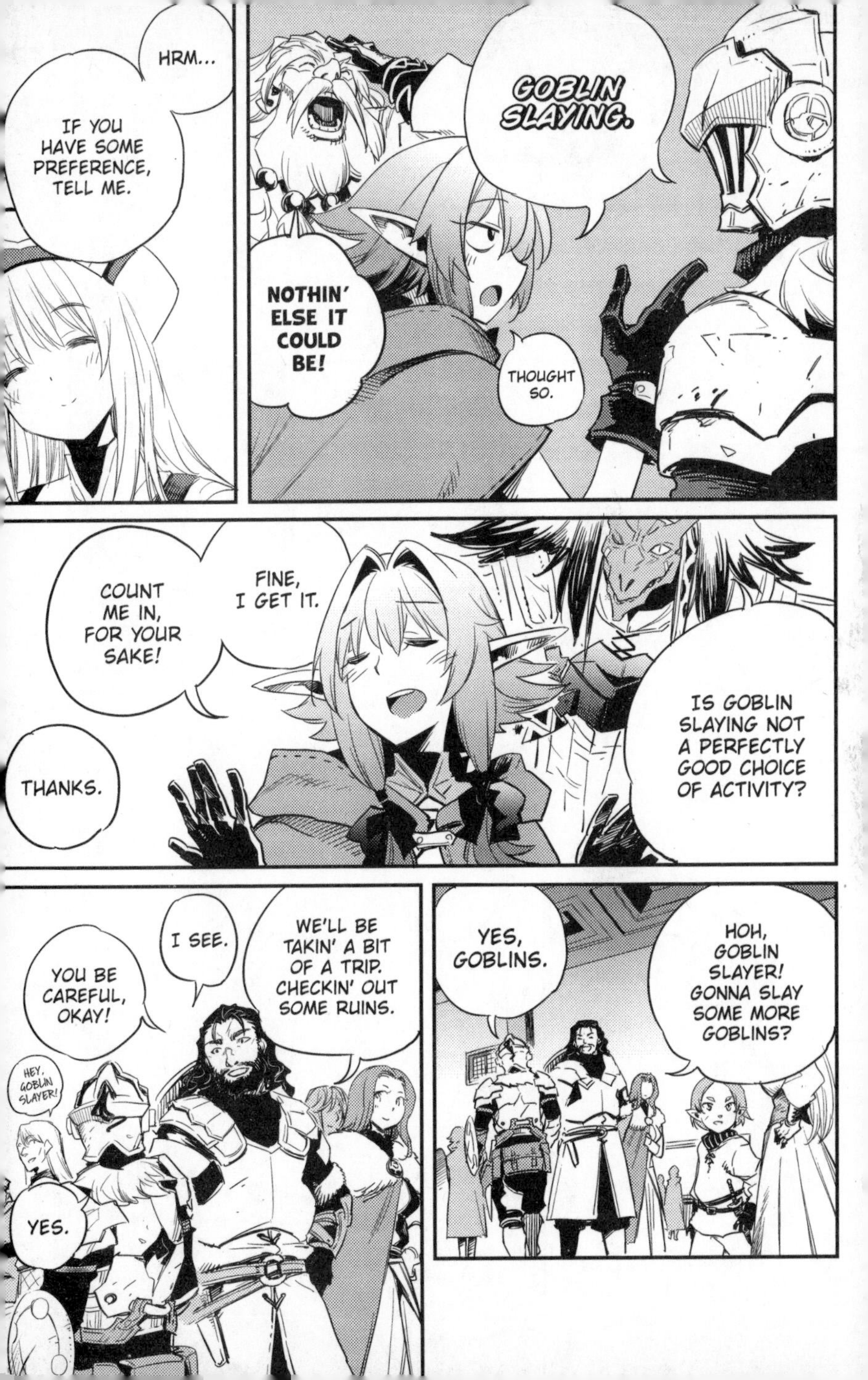
GOBLIN SLAYING.
NOTHIN' ELSE IT COULD BE!
THOUGHT SO.
HRM...
IF YOU HAVE SOME PREFERENCE, TELL ME.
IS GOBLIN SLAYING NOT A PERFECTLY GOOD CHOICE OF ACTIVITY?
FINE, I GET IT.
COUNT ME IN, FOR YOUR SAKE!
THANKS.
HOH, GOBLIN SLAYER! GONNA SLAY SOME MORE GOBLINS?
YES, GOBLINS.
WE'LL BE TAKIN' A BIT OF A TRIP. CHECKIN' OUT SOME RUINS.
I SEE.
YOU BE CAREFUL, OKAY!
HEY, GOBLIN SLAYER!
YES.

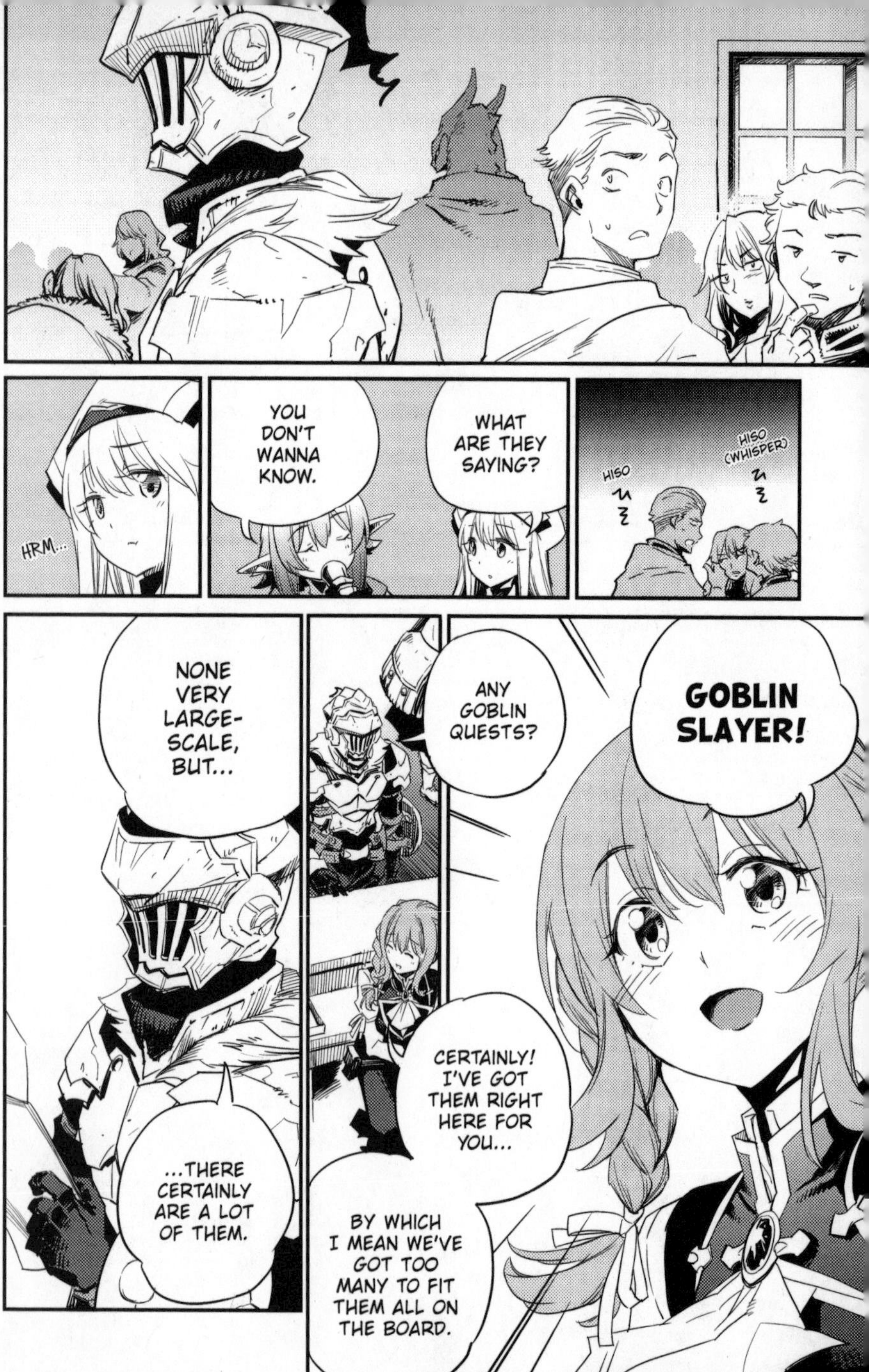
HISO (WHISPER)
HISO
WHAT ARE THEY SAYING?
YOU DON'T WANNA KNOW.
HRM...
GOBLIN SLAYER!
ANY GOBLIN QUESTS?
CERTAINLY! I'VE GOT THEM RIGHT HERE FOR YOU...
BY WHICH I MEAN WE'VE GOT TOO MANY TO FIT THEM ALL ON THE BOARD.
NONE VERY LARGE-SCALE, BUT...
...THERE CERTAINLY ARE A LOT OF THEM.

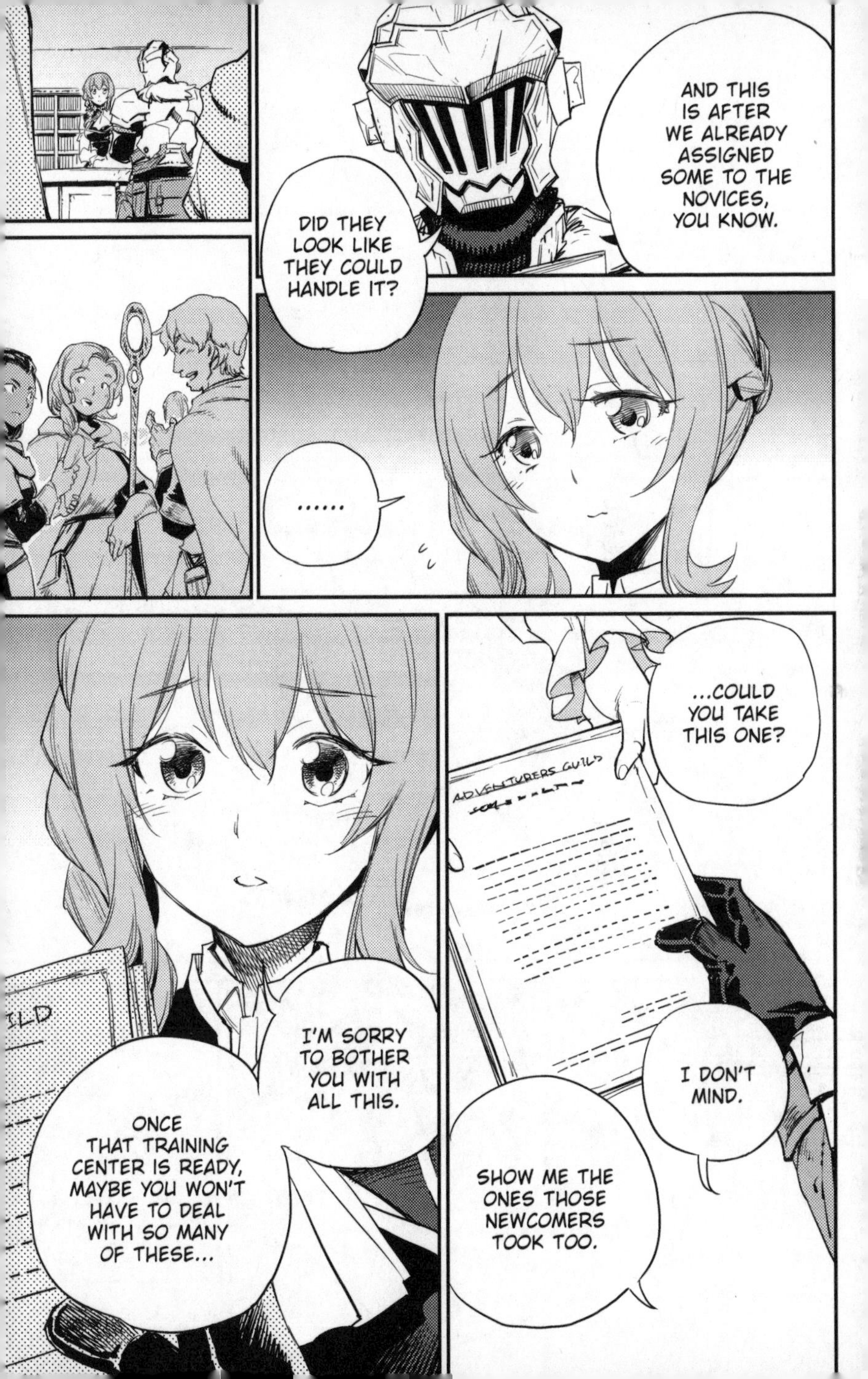
AND THIS IS AFTER WE ALREADY ASSIGNED SOME TO THE NOVICES, YOU KNOW.
DID THEY LOOK LIKE THEY COULD HANDLE IT?
......
...COULD YOU TAKE THIS ONE?
ADVENTURERS GUILD
I DON'T MIND.
SHOW ME THE ONES THOSE NEWCOMERS TOOK TOO.
I'M SORRY TO BOTHER YOU WITH ALL THIS.
ONCE THAT TRAINING CENTER IS READY, MAYBE YOU WON'T HAVE TO DEAL WITH SO MANY OF THESE...

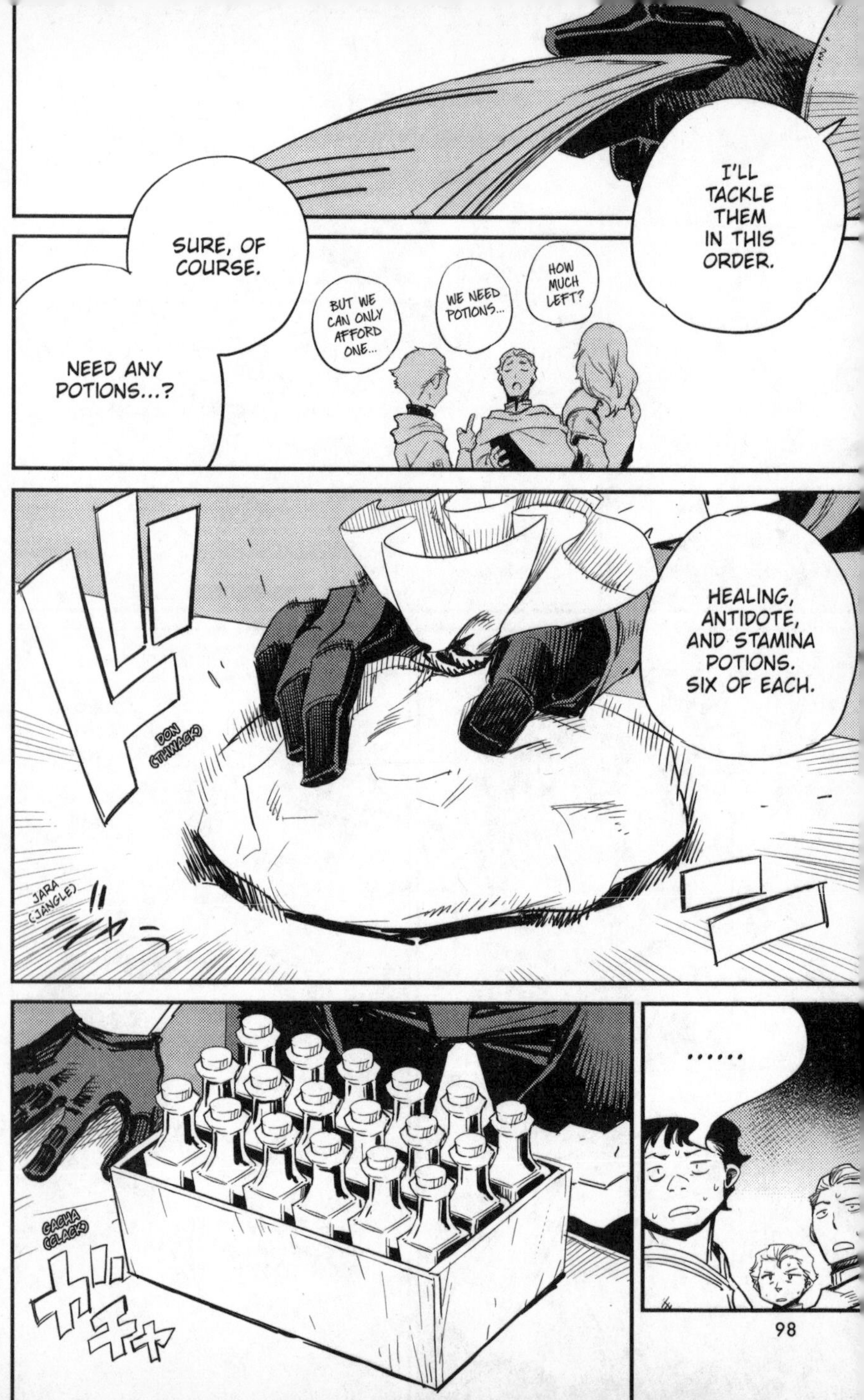
I'LL TACKLE THEM IN THIS ORDER.
SURE, OF COURSE.
NEED ANY POTIONS...?
HOW MUCH LEFT?
WE NEED POTIONS...
BUT WE CAN ONLY AFFORD ONE...
HEALING, ANTIDOTE, AND STAMINA POTIONS. SIX OF EACH.
DON (THWACK)
JARA (JANGLE)
......
GACHA (CLACK)

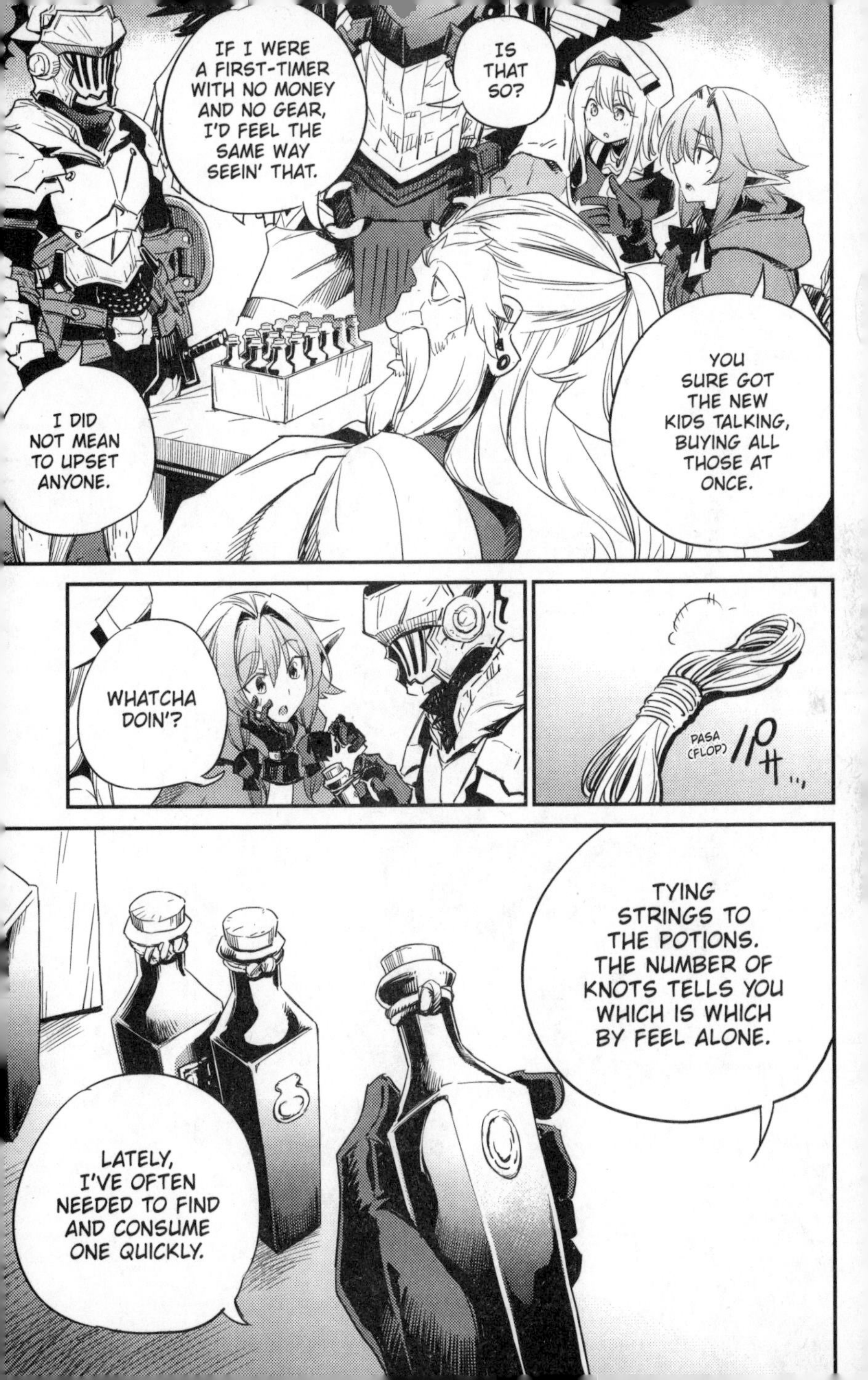
YOU SURE GOT THE NEW KIDS TALKING, BUYING ALL THOSE AT ONCE.
I DID NOT MEAN TO UPSET ANYONE.
IF I WERE A FIRST-TIMER WITH NO MONEY AND NO GEAR, I'D FEEL THE SAME WAY SEEIN' THAT.
IS THAT SO?
PASA (FLOP)
WHATCHA DOIN'?
TYING STRINGS TO THE POTIONS. THE NUMBER OF KNOTS TELLS YOU WHICH IS WHICH BY FEEL ALONE.
LATELY, I'VE OFTEN NEEDED TO FIND AND CONSUME ONE QUICKLY.

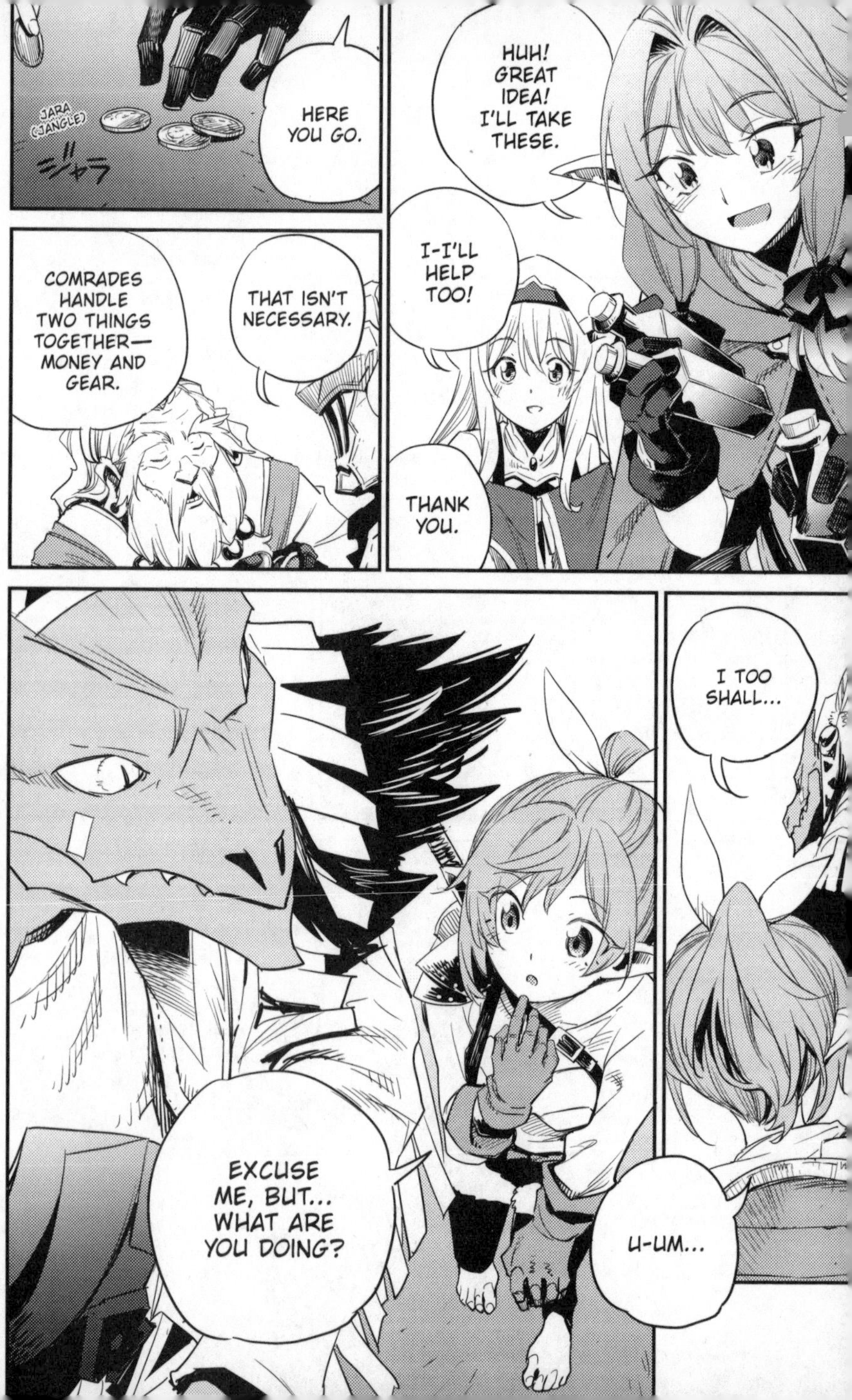
HUH! GREAT IDEA! I'LL TAKE THESE.
I-I'LL HELP TOO!
THANK YOU.
HERE YOU GO.
JARA (JANGLE)
ジャラ
THAT ISN'T NECESSARY.
COMRADES HANDLE TWO THINGS TOGETHER—MONEY AND GEAR.
I TOO SHALL...
U-UM...
EXCUSE ME, BUT... WHAT ARE YOU DOING?

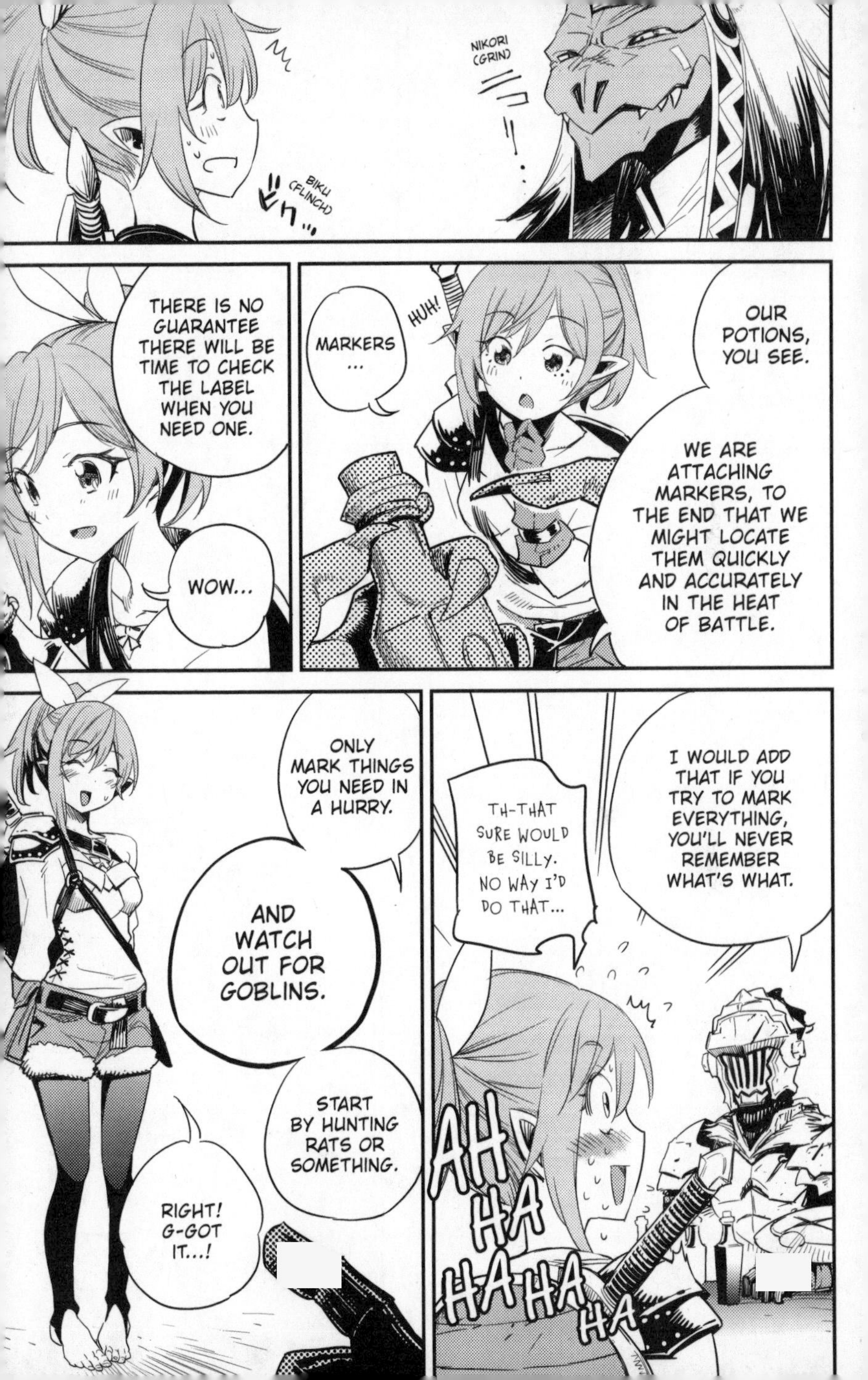
NIKORI (GRIN)
BIKU (FLINCH)
OUR POTIONS, YOU SEE.
WE ARE ATTACHING MARKERS, TO THE END THAT WE MIGHT LOCATE THEM QUICKLY AND ACCURATELY IN THE HEAT OF BATTLE.
HUH!
MARKERS ...
THERE IS NO GUARANTEE THERE WILL BE TIME TO CHECK THE LABEL WHEN YOU NEED ONE.
WOW...
I WOULD ADD THAT IF YOU TRY TO MARK EVERYTHING, YOU'LL NEVER REMEMBER WHAT'S WHAT.
TH-THAT SURE WOULD BE SILLY. NO WAY I'D DO THAT...
AH HA HA HA HA
ONLY MARK THINGS YOU NEED IN A HURRY.
AND WATCH OUT FOR GOBLINS.
START BY HUNTING RATS OR SOMETHING.
RIGHT! G-GOT IT...!

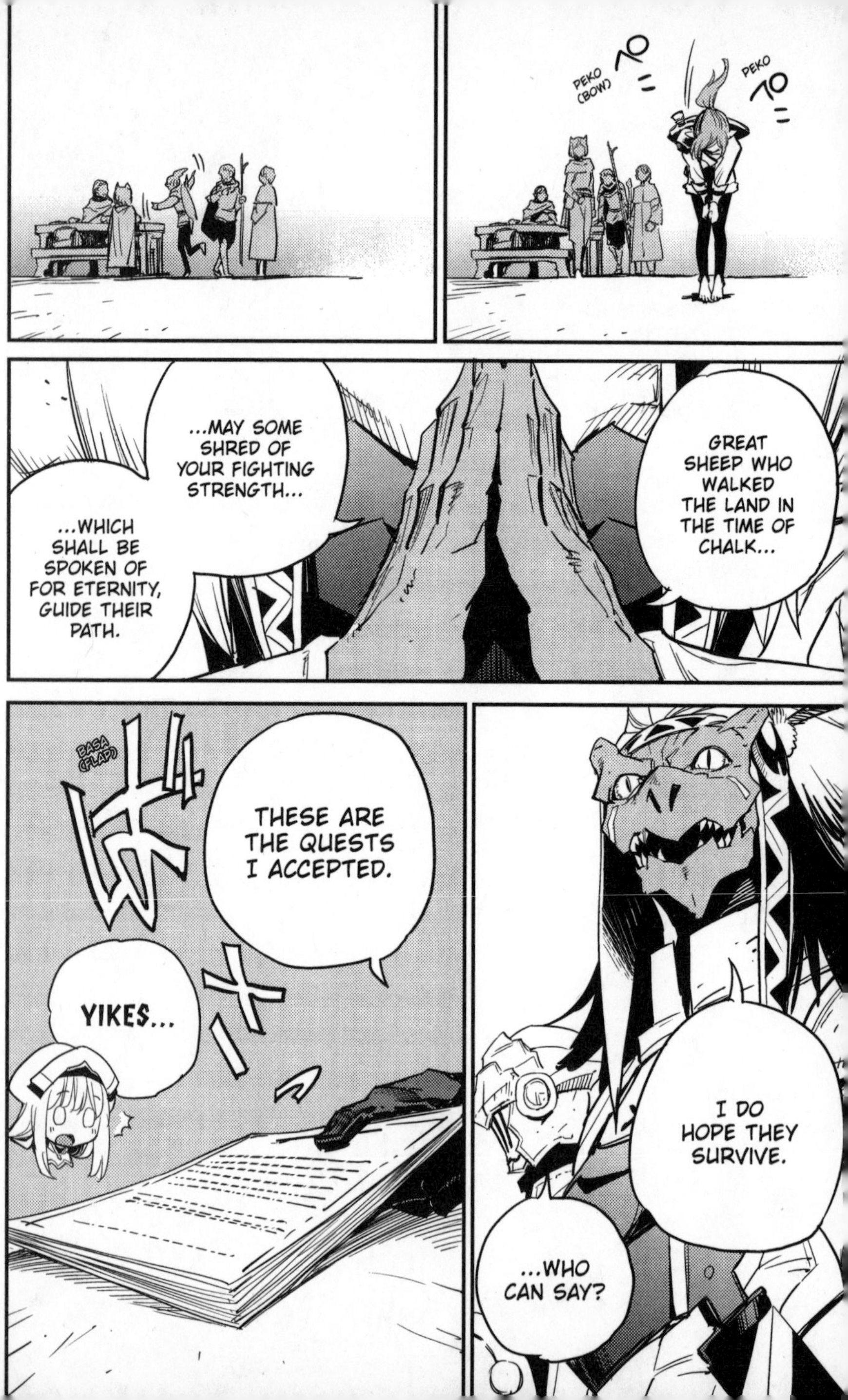
PEKO
PEKO (BOW)
GREAT SHEEP WHO WALKED THE LAND IN THE TIME OF CHALK...
...MAY SOME SHRED OF YOUR FIGHTING STRENGTH...
...WHICH SHALL BE SPOKEN OF FOR ETERNITY, GUIDE THEIR PATH.
I DO HOPE THEY SURVIVE.
...WHO CAN SAY?
BASA (FLAP)
THESE ARE THE QUESTS I ACCEPTED.
YIKES...

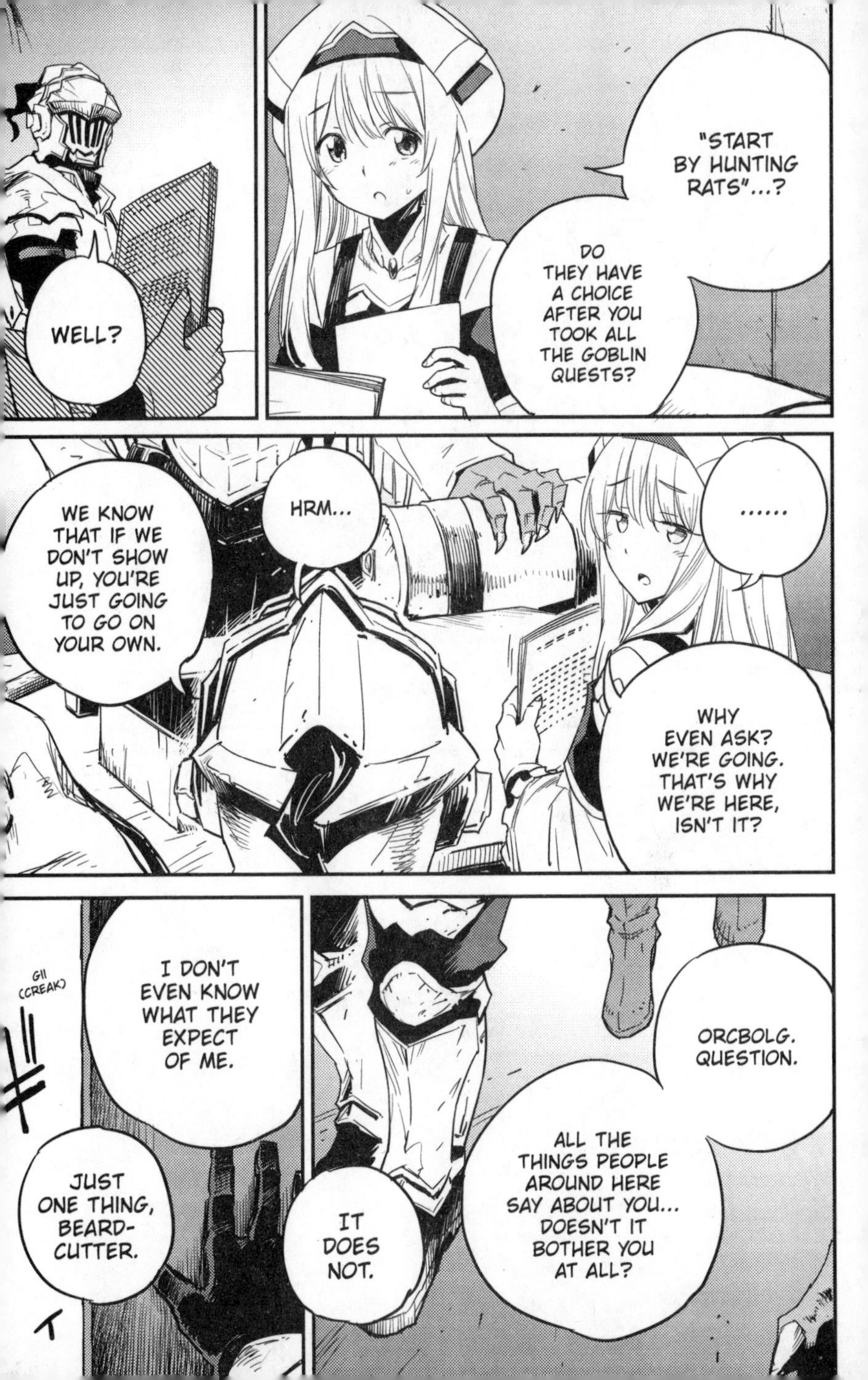
"START BY HUNTING RATS"...?
DO THEY HAVE A CHOICE AFTER YOU TOOK ALL THE GOBLIN QUESTS?
WELL?
......
WHY EVEN ASK? WE'RE GOING. THAT'S WHY WE'RE HERE, ISN'T IT?
HRM...
WE KNOW THAT IF WE DON'T SHOW UP, YOU'RE JUST GOING TO GO ON YOUR OWN.
ORCBOLG. QUESTION.
ALL THE THINGS PEOPLE AROUND HERE SAY ABOUT YOU... DOESN'T IT BOTHER YOU AT ALL?
IT DOES NOT.
I DON'T EVEN KNOW WHAT THEY EXPECT OF ME.
GII (CREAK)
JUST ONE THING, BEARD-CUTTER.

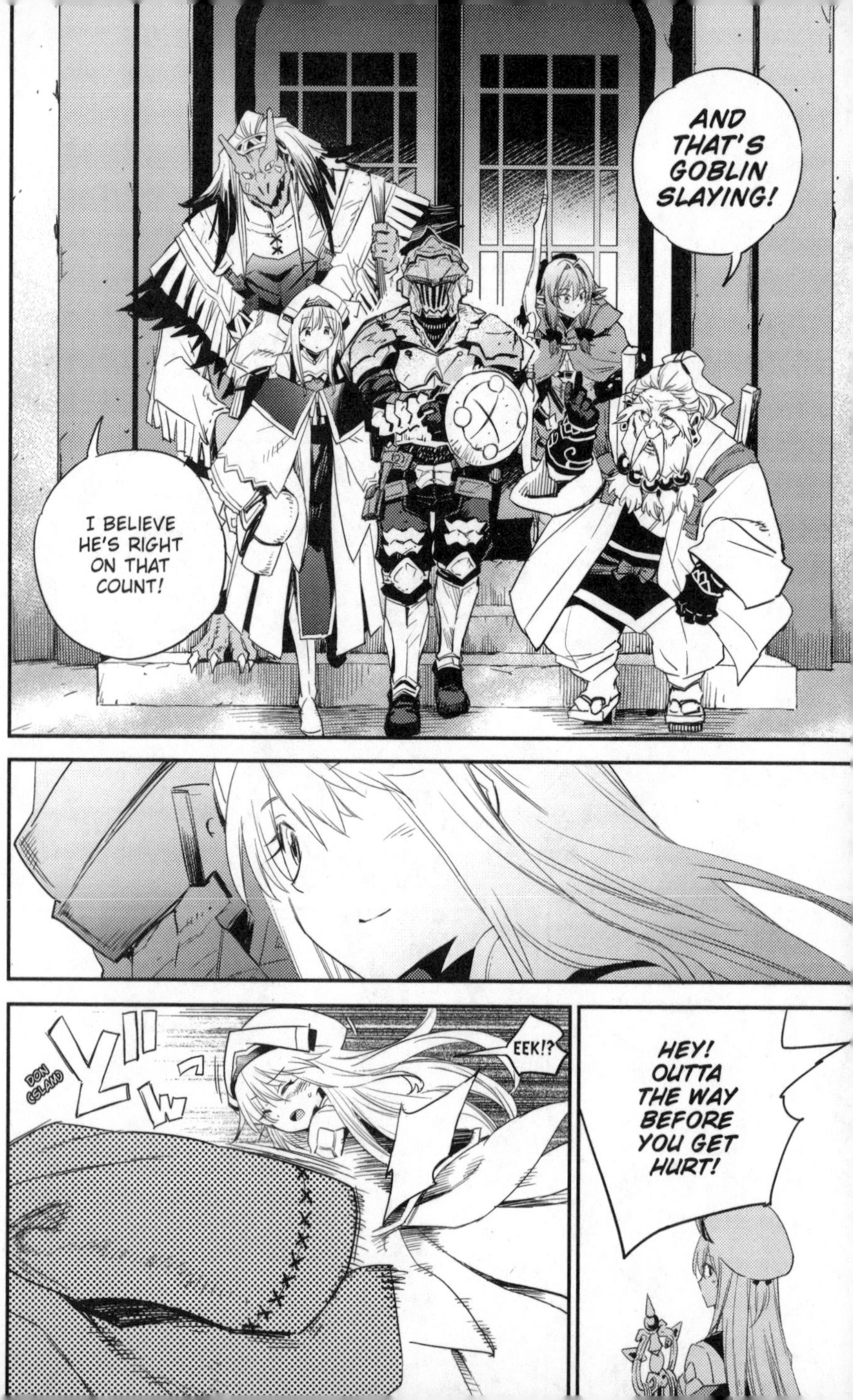
AND THAT'S GOBLIN SLAYING!
I BELIEVE HE'S RIGHT ON THAT COUNT!
HEY! OUTTA THE WAY BEFORE YOU GET HURT!
EEK!?
DON (SLAM)

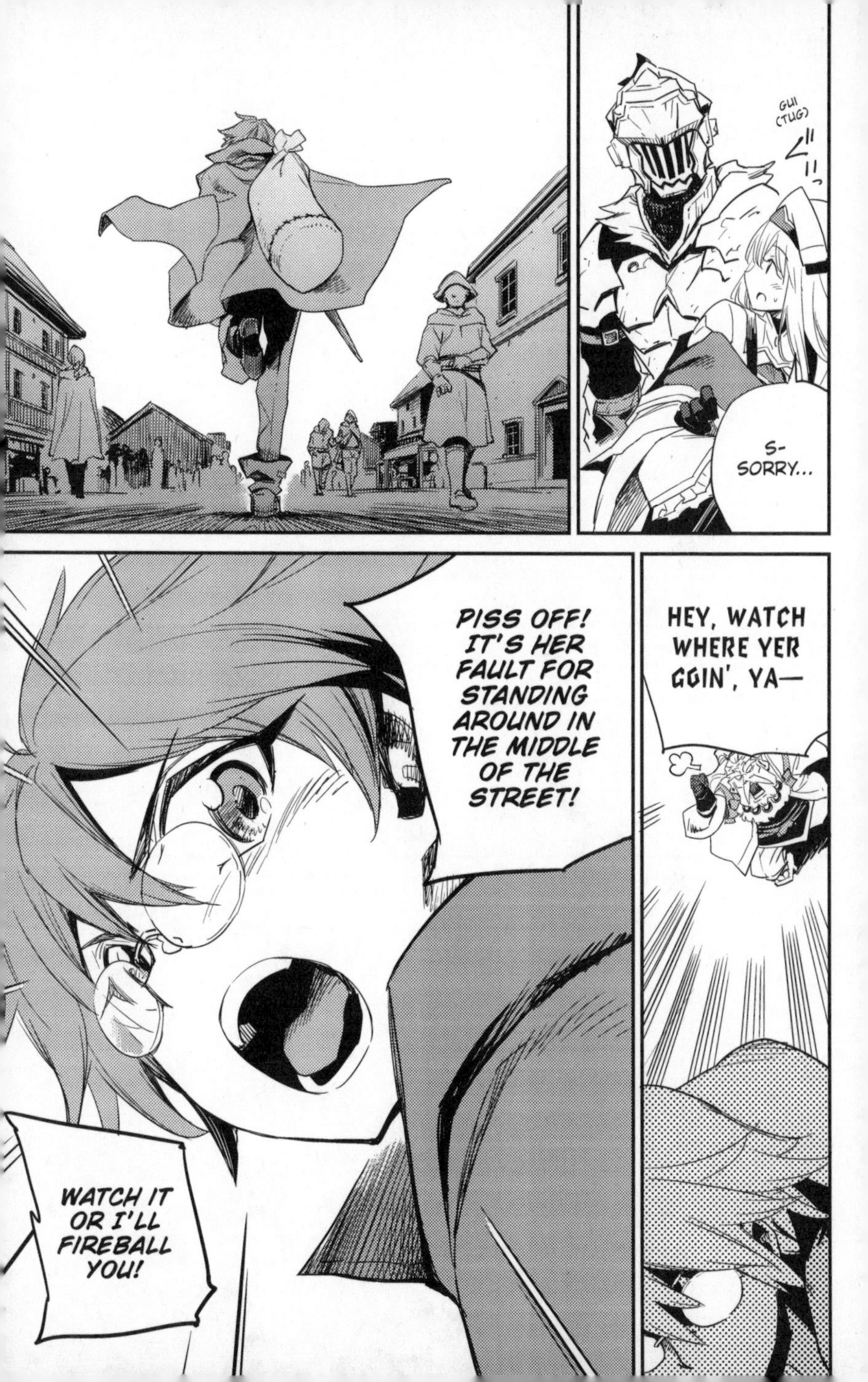
GUI (TUG)
S-SORRY...
HEY, WATCH WHERE YER GOIN', YA—
PISS OFF! IT'S HER FAULT FOR STANDING AROUND IN THE MIDDLE OF THE STREET!
WATCH IT OR I'LL FIREBALL YOU!

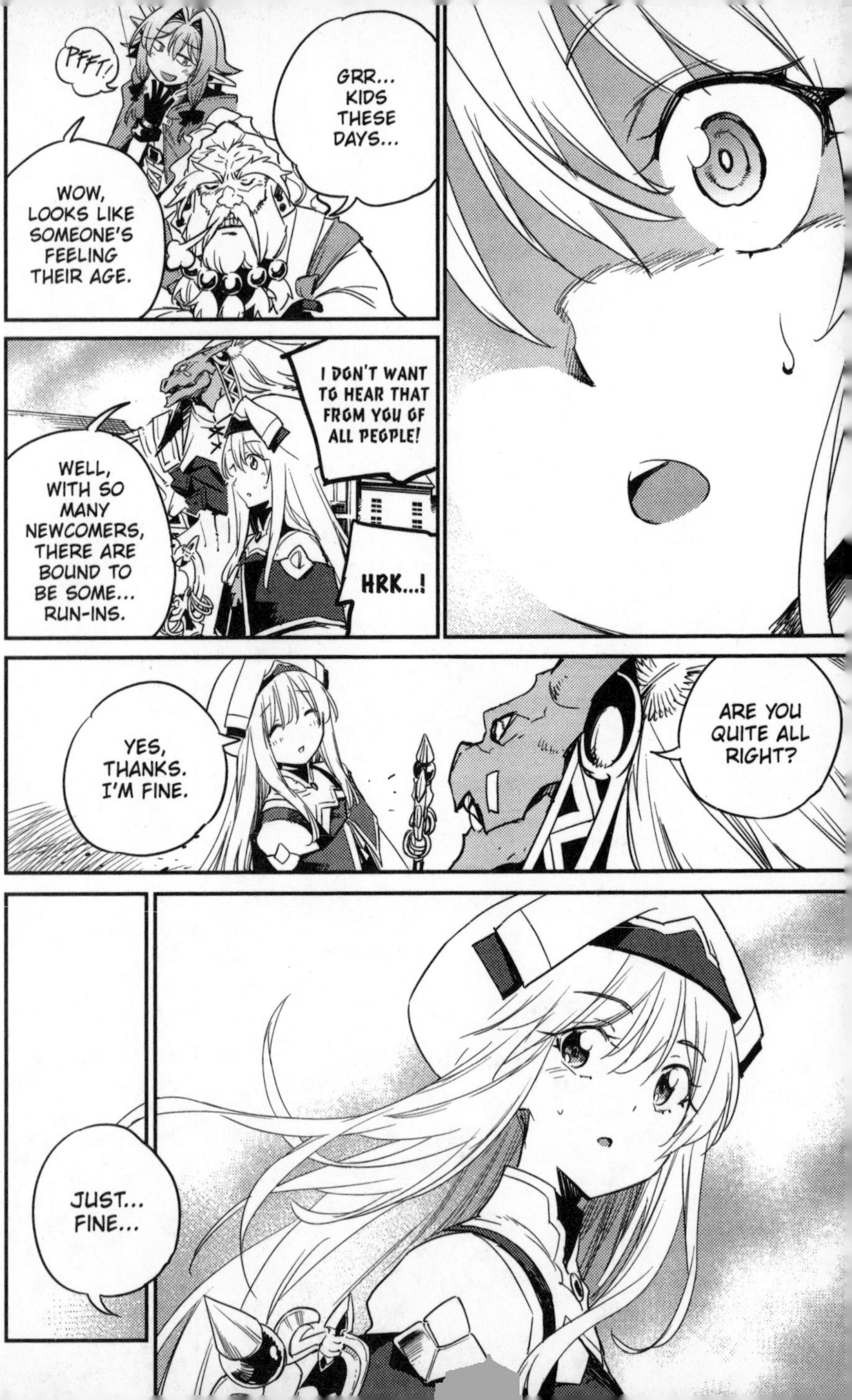
GRR... KIDS THESE DAYS...
PFFT!
WOW, LOOKS LIKE SOMEONE'S FEELING THEIR AGE.
I DON'T WANT TO HEAR THAT FROM YOU OF ALL PEOPLE!
WELL, WITH SO MANY NEWCOMERS, THERE ARE BOUND TO BE SOME... RUN-INS.
HRK...!
ARE YOU QUITE ALL RIGHT?
YES, THANKS. I'M FINE.
JUST... FINE...

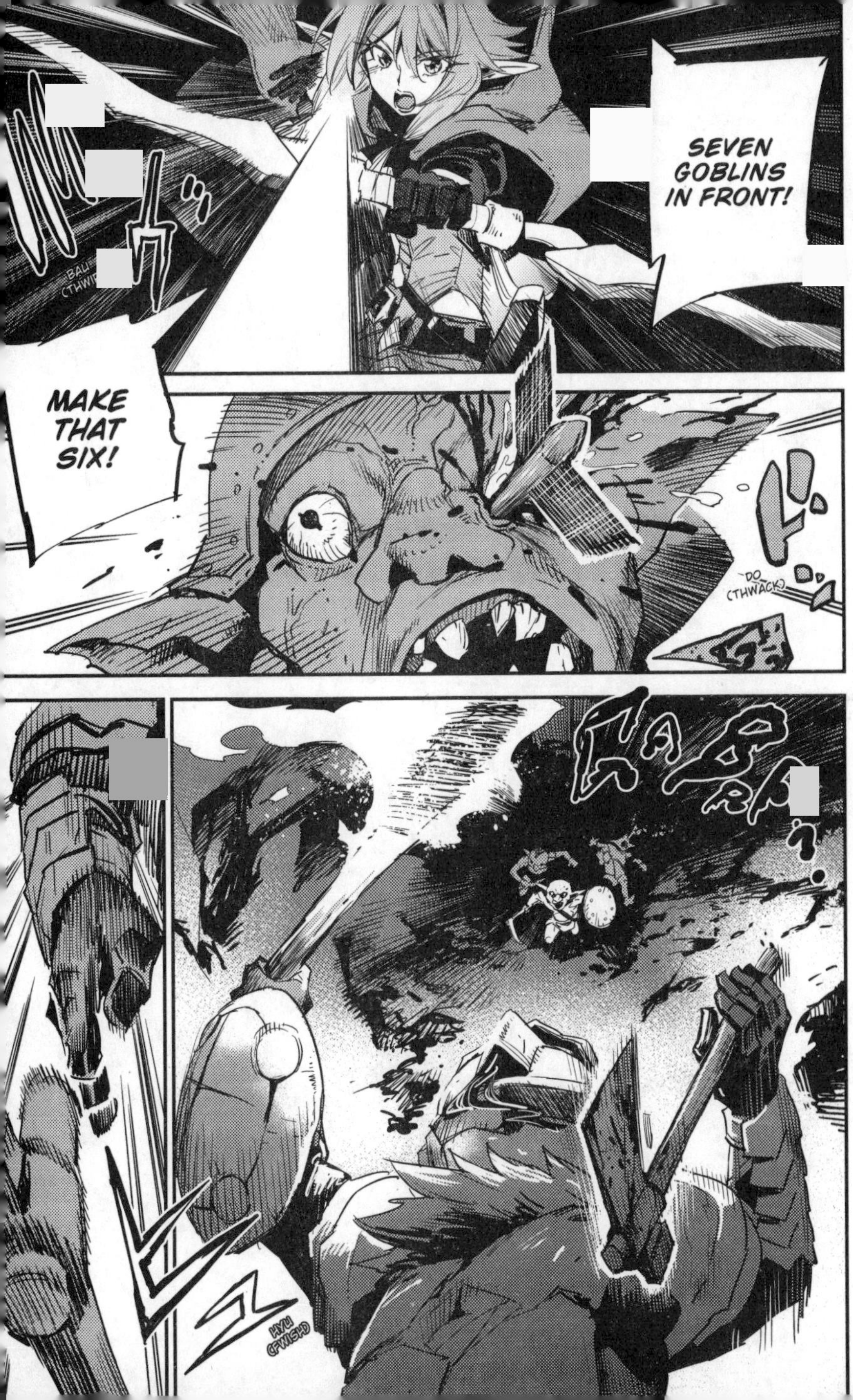
SEVEN GOBLINS IN FRONT!
BAU (THWI
MAKE THAT SIX!
DO (THWACK)
HYU (FWISH)

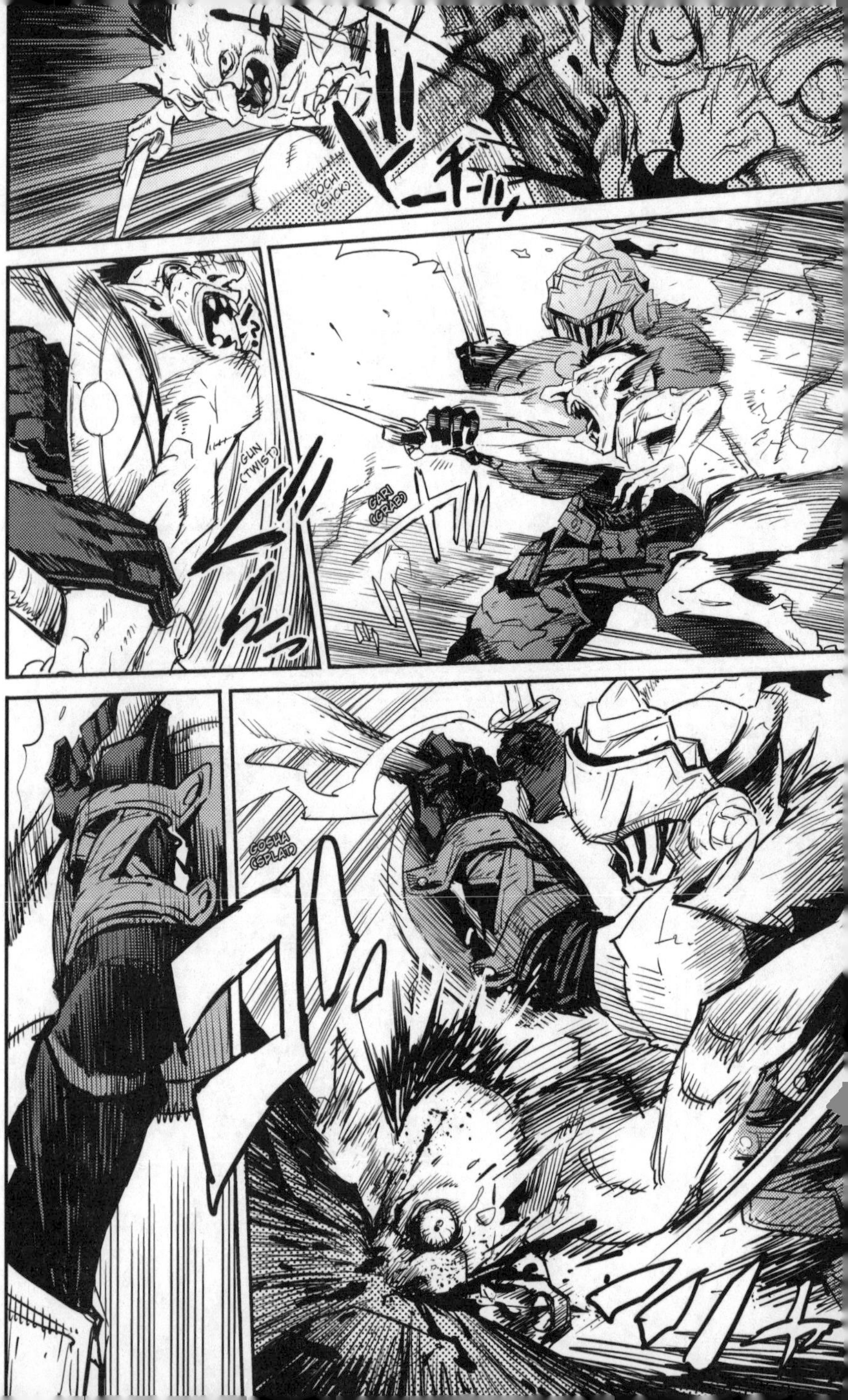
DOCHI (SHCK)
GARI (GRAB)
GUN (TWIST)
GOSHA (SPLAT)

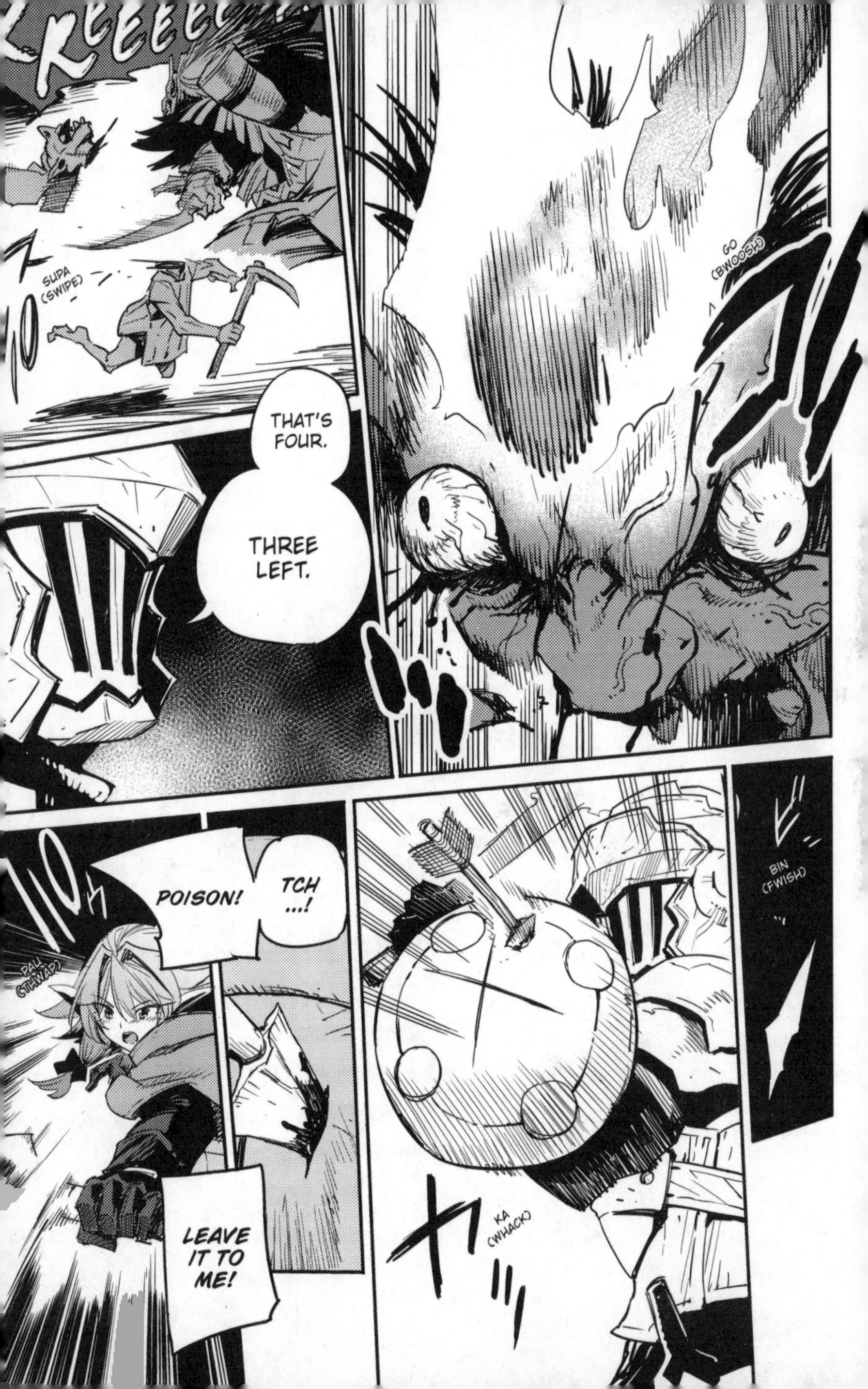
GO
(BWOOSH)
SUPA
(SWIPE)
THAT'S FOUR.
THREE LEFT.
BIN
(FWISH)
KA
(WHACK)
TCH ...!
POISON!
PAU
(THWAP)
LEAVE IT TO ME!

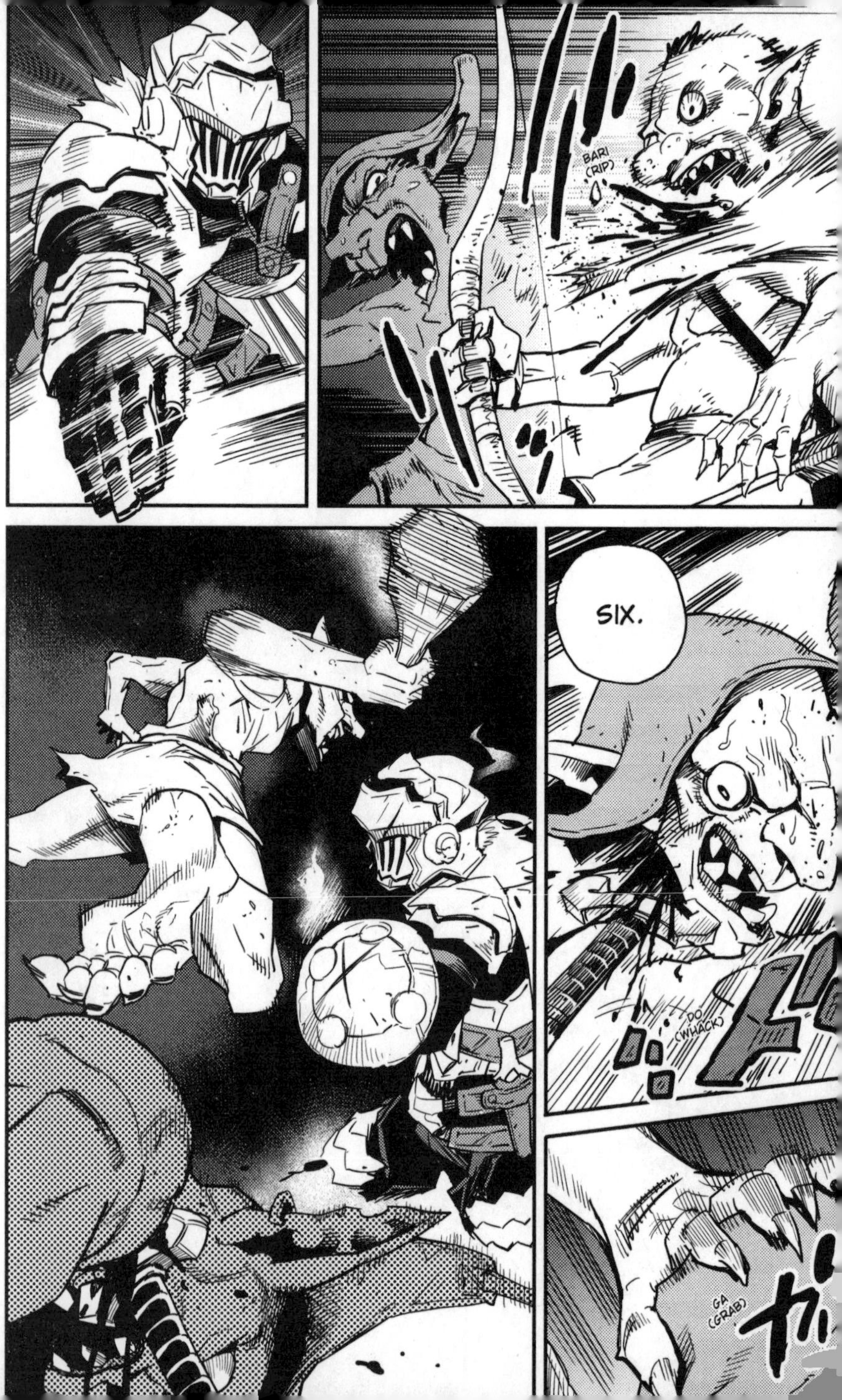
BARI (RIP)
SIX.
DO (WHACK)
GA (GRAB)

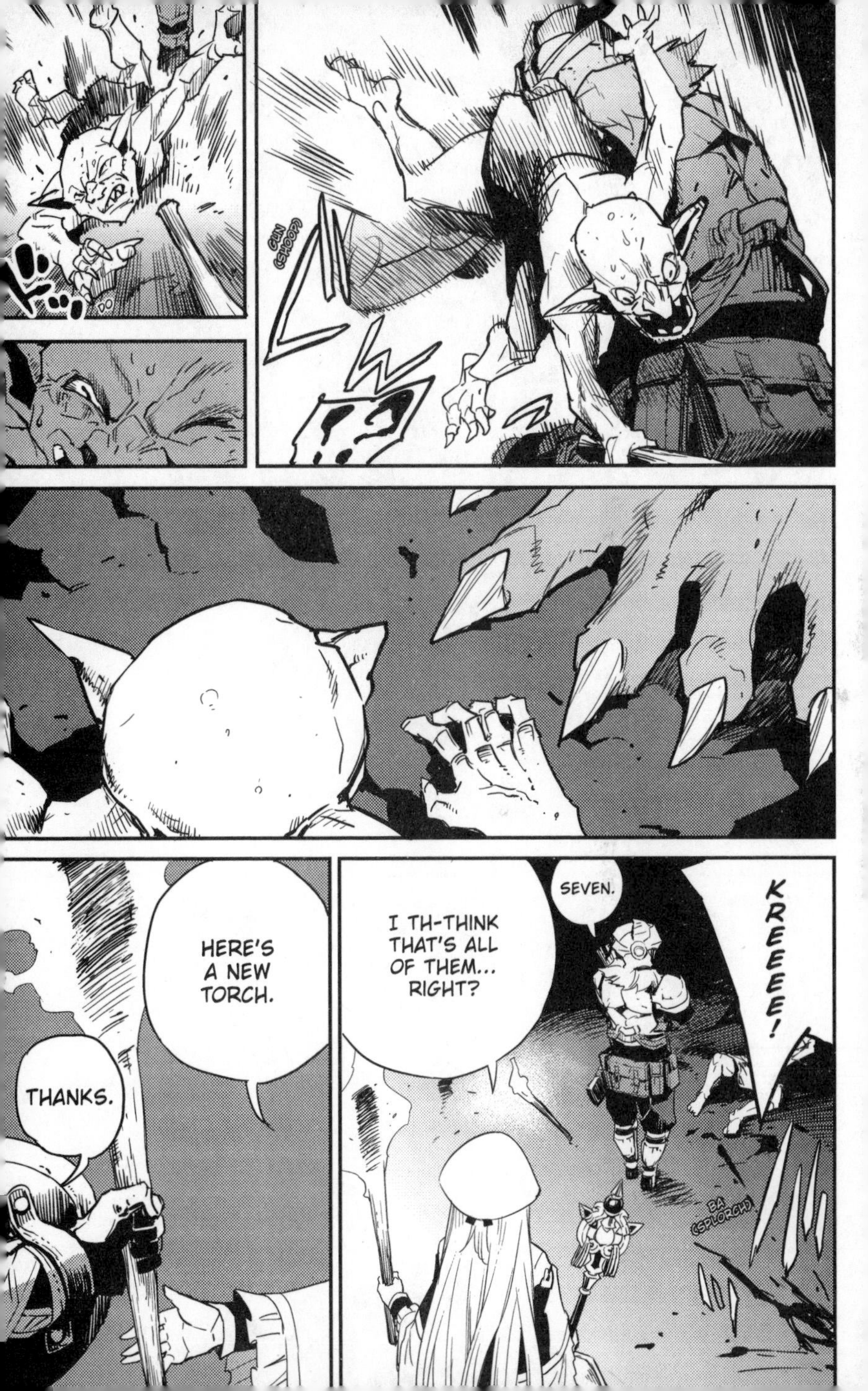
GUN
(SHOOP)
DO
KREEEE!
SEVEN.
I TH-THINK THAT'S ALL OF THEM... RIGHT?
BA
(SPLORCH)
HERE'S A NEW TORCH.
THANKS.

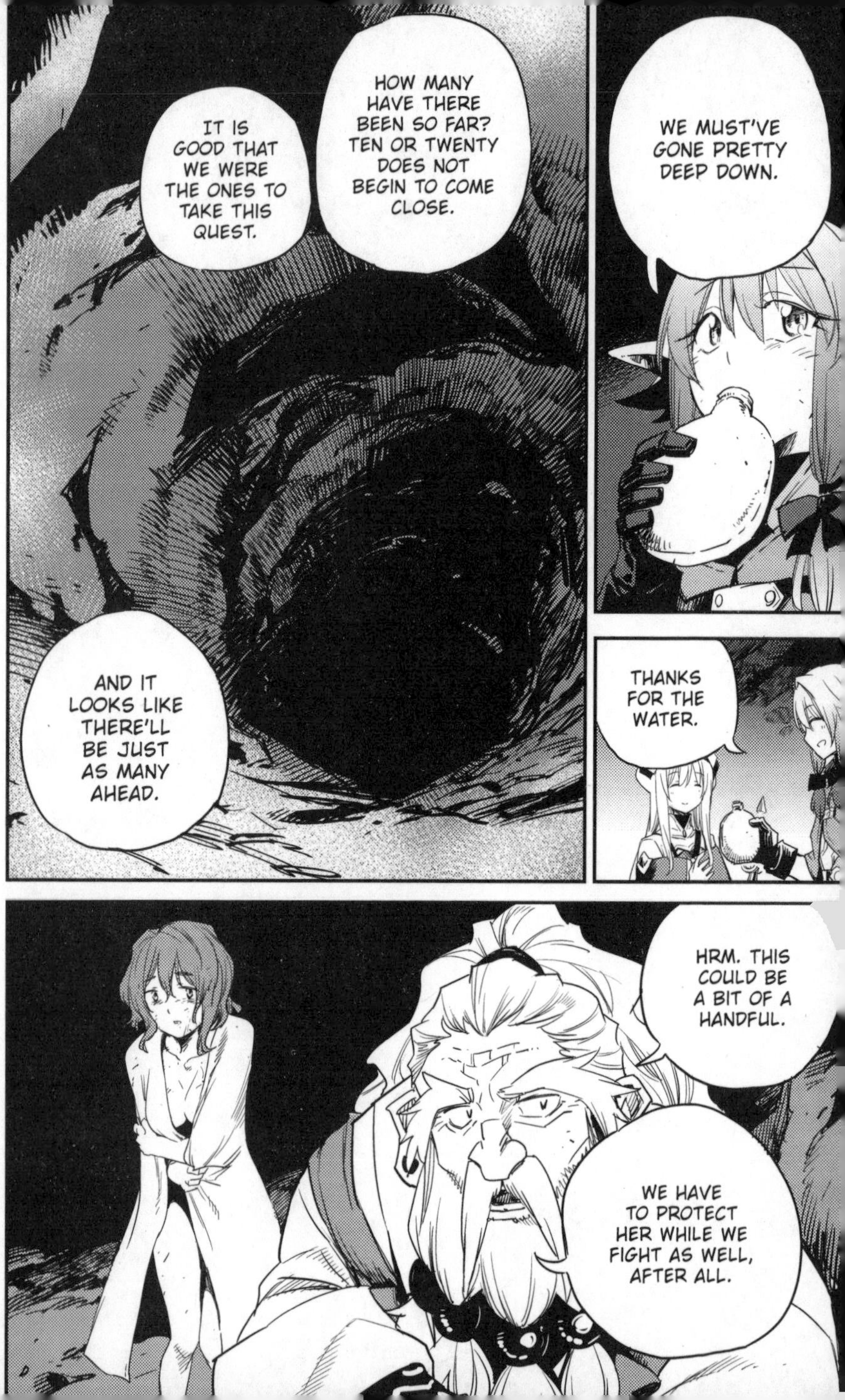
WE MUST'VE GONE PRETTY DEEP DOWN.
THANKS FOR THE WATER.
HOW MANY HAVE THERE BEEN SO FAR? TEN OR TWENTY DOES NOT BEGIN TO COME CLOSE.
IT IS GOOD THAT WE WERE THE ONES TO TAKE THIS QUEST.
AND IT LOOKS LIKE THERE'LL BE JUST AS MANY AHEAD.
HRM. THIS COULD BE A BIT OF A HANDFUL.
WE HAVE TO PROTECT HER WHILE WE FIGHT AS WELL, AFTER ALL.

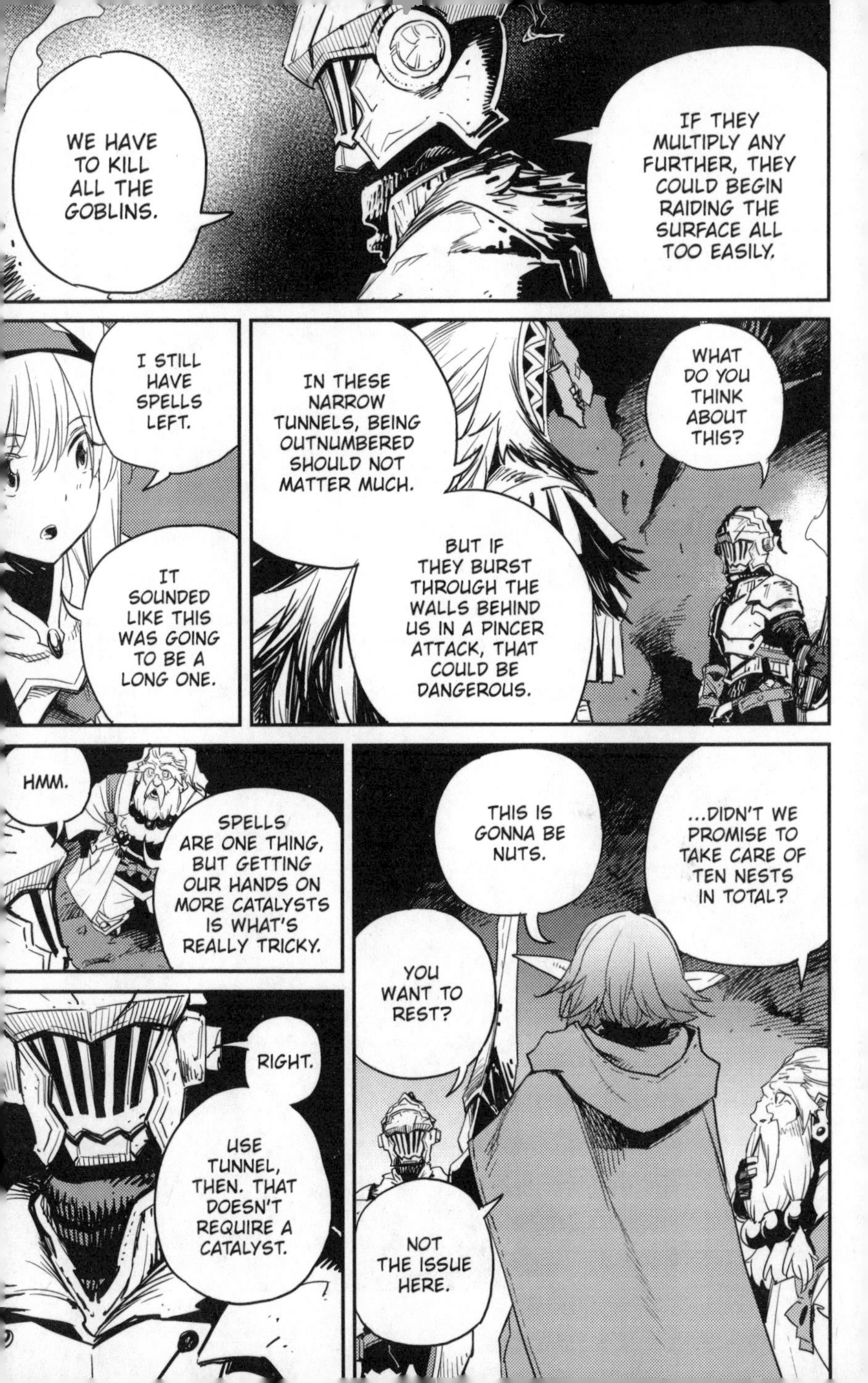
IF THEY MULTIPLY ANY FURTHER, THEY COULD BEGIN RAIDING THE SURFACE ALL TOO EASILY.
WE HAVE TO KILL ALL THE GOBLINS.
WHAT DO YOU THINK ABOUT THIS?
IN THESE NARROW TUNNELS, BEING OUTNUMBERED SHOULD NOT MATTER MUCH.
BUT IF THEY BURST THROUGH THE WALLS BEHIND US IN A PINCER ATTACK, THAT COULD BE DANGEROUS.
I STILL HAVE SPELLS LEFT.
IT SOUNDED LIKE THIS WAS GOING TO BE A LONG ONE.
...DIDN'T WE PROMISE TO TAKE CARE OF TEN NESTS IN TOTAL?
THIS IS GONNA BE NUTS.
YOU WANT TO REST?
NOT THE ISSUE HERE.
HMM.
SPELLS ARE ONE THING, BUT GETTING OUR HANDS ON MORE CATALYSTS IS WHAT'S REALLY TRICKY.
RIGHT.
USE TUNNEL, THEN. THAT DOESN'T REQUIRE A CATALYST.

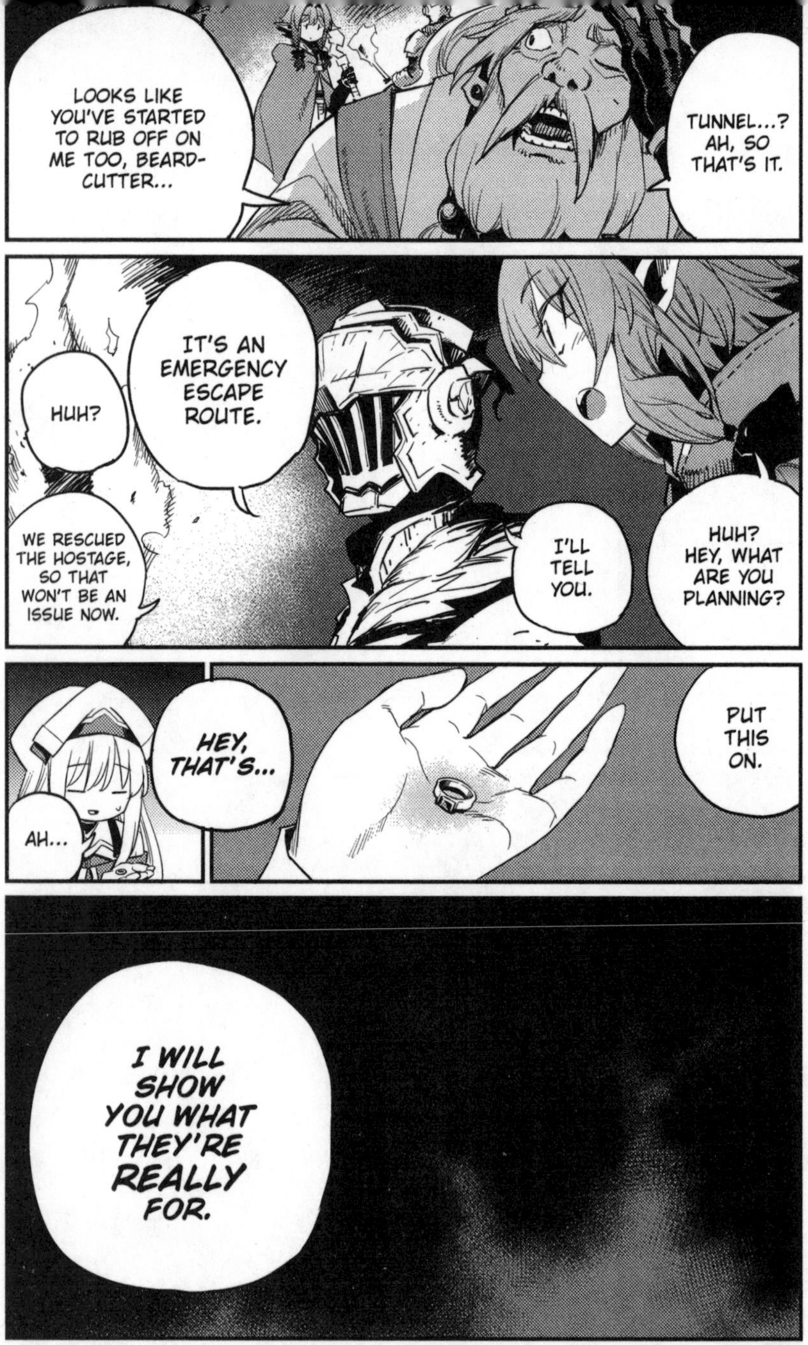
TUNNEL...? AH, SO THAT'S IT.
LOOKS LIKE YOU'VE STARTED TO RUB OFF ON ME TOO, BEARD-CUTTER...
HUH? HEY, WHAT ARE YOU PLANNING?
I'LL TELL YOU.
IT'S AN EMERGENCY ESCAPE ROUTE.
HUH?
WE RESCUED THE HOSTAGE, SO THAT WON'T BE AN ISSUE NOW.
PUT THIS ON.
HEY, THAT'S...
AH...
I WILL SHOW YOU WHAT THEY'RE REALLY FOR.

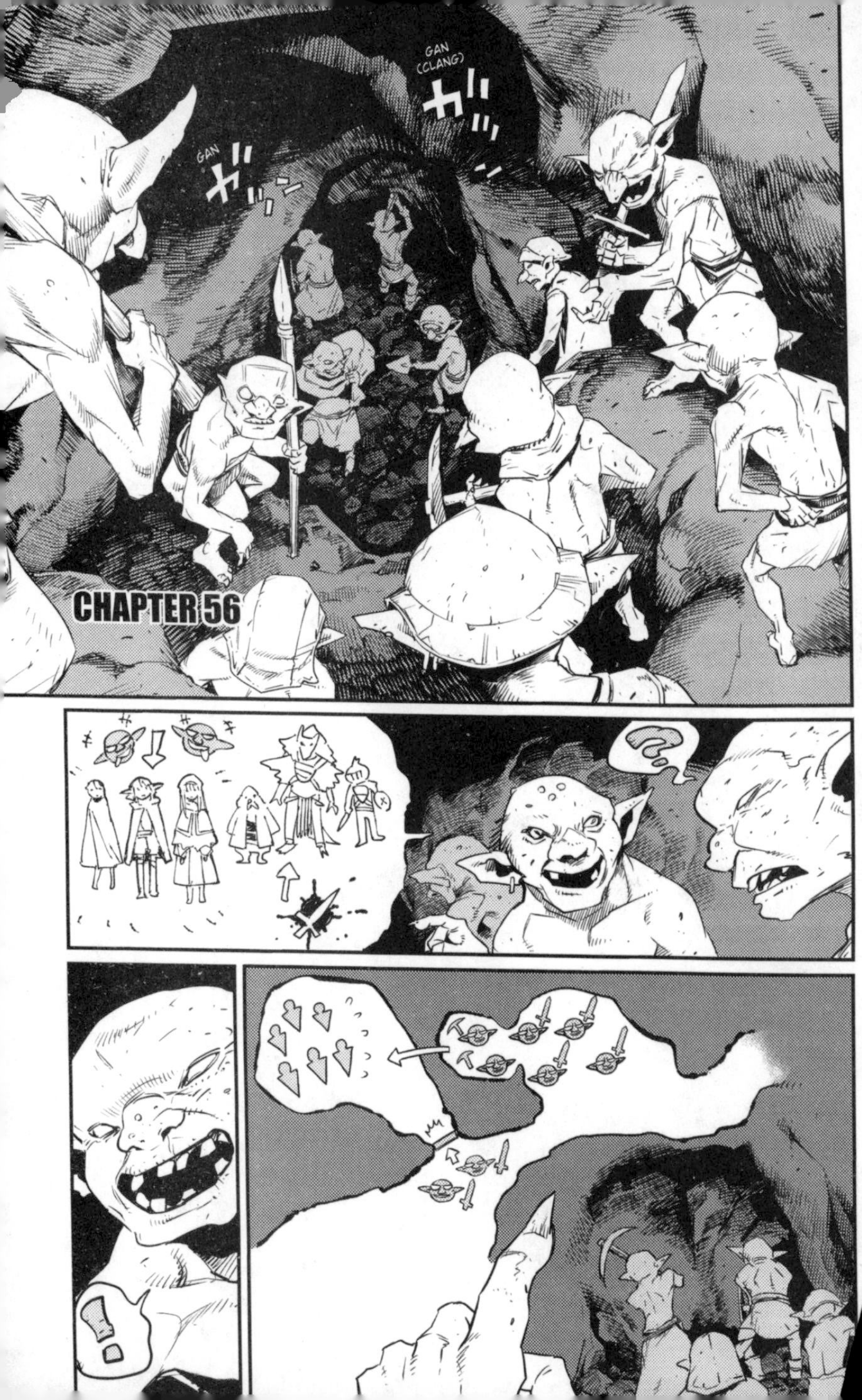
GAN
(CLANG)
GAN
CHAPTER 56

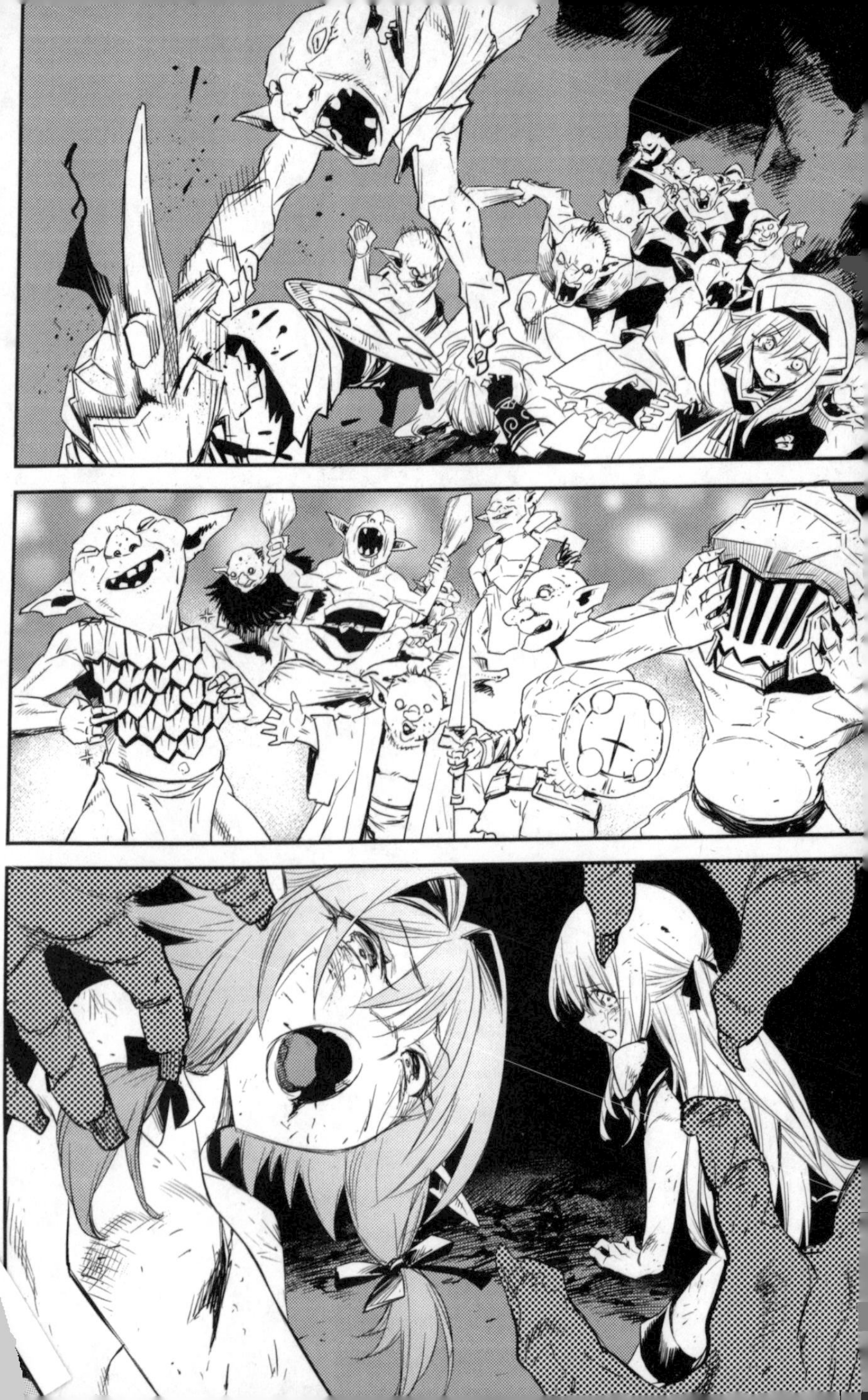

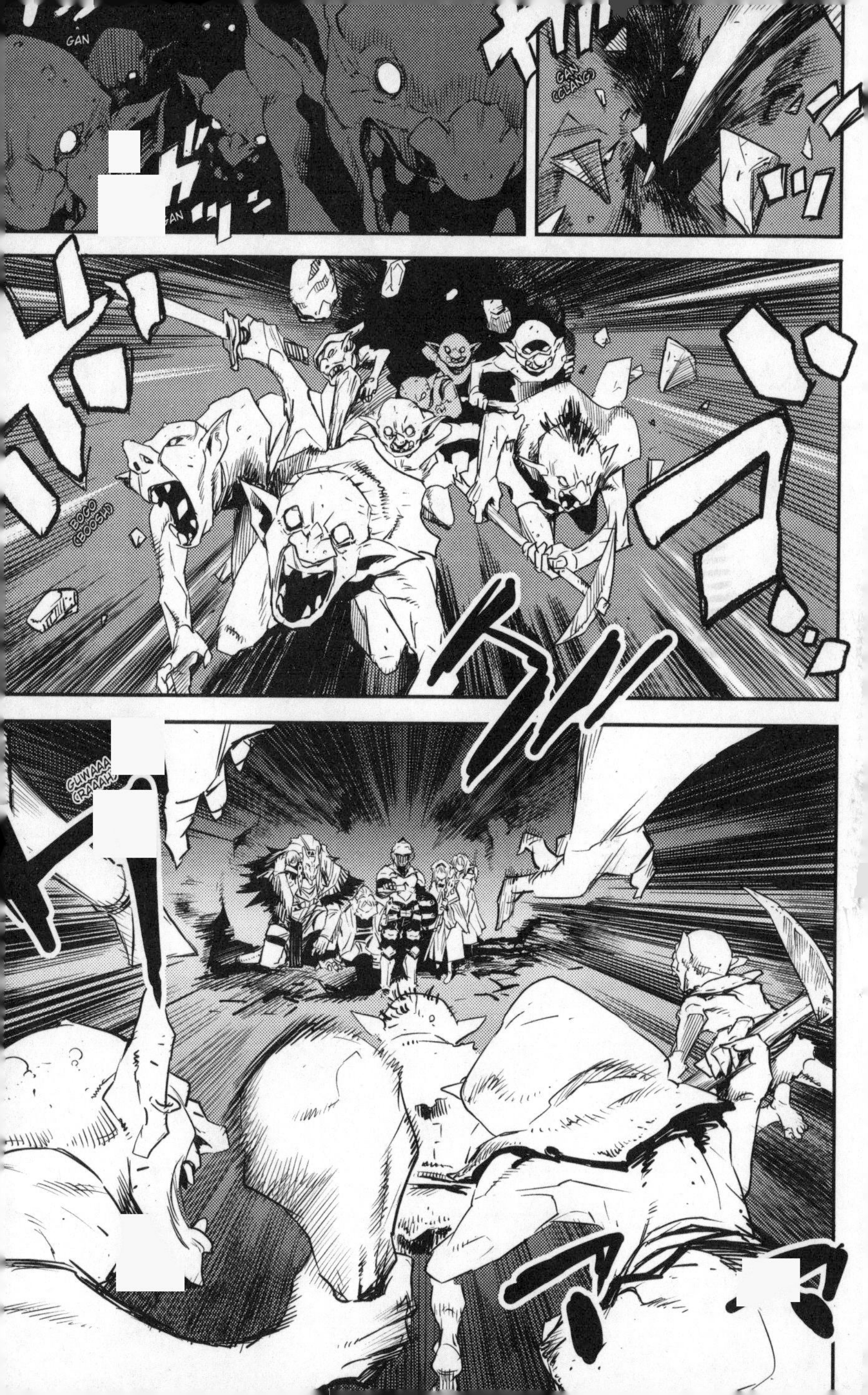
GAN
(CLANG)
GAN
BOGO
(BOOSH)
GUWAAA
(RAAAH)

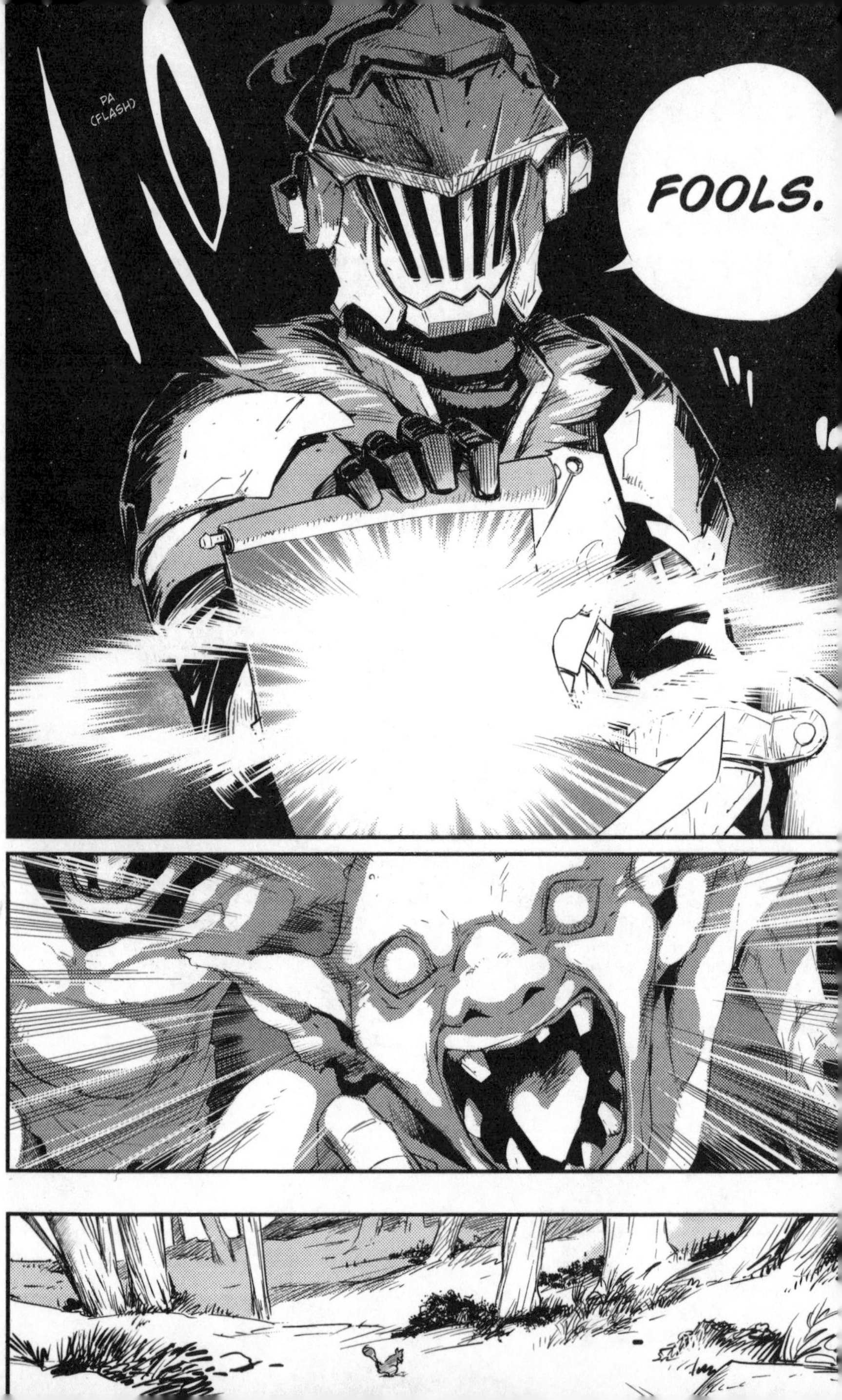
FOOLS.
PA (FLASH)

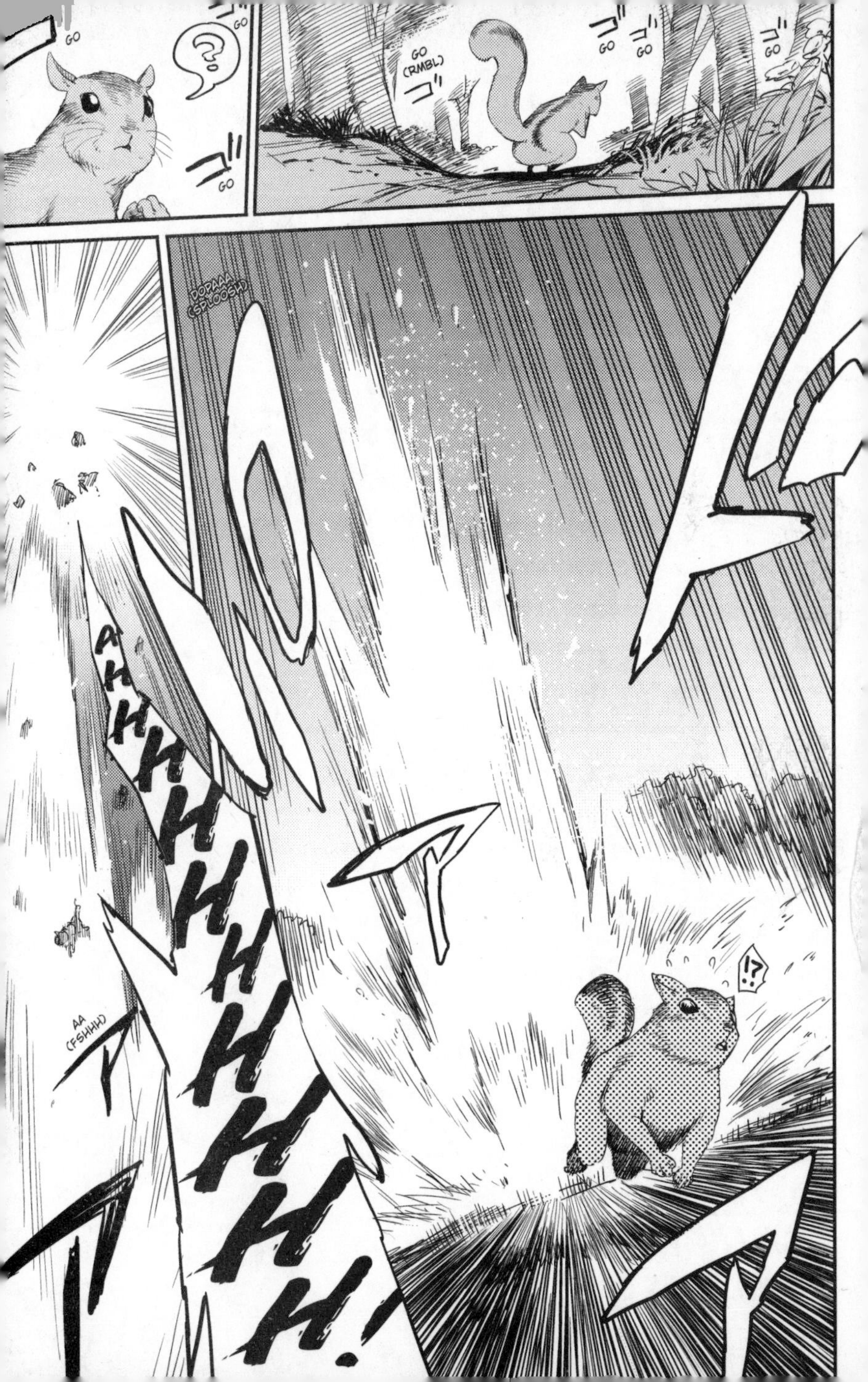
GO (RMBL)
GO
GO
GO
GO
?
GO
GO
DOPAAA (SPLOOSH)
!?
AA (FSHHH)
AHHHHHHHHHHHH!

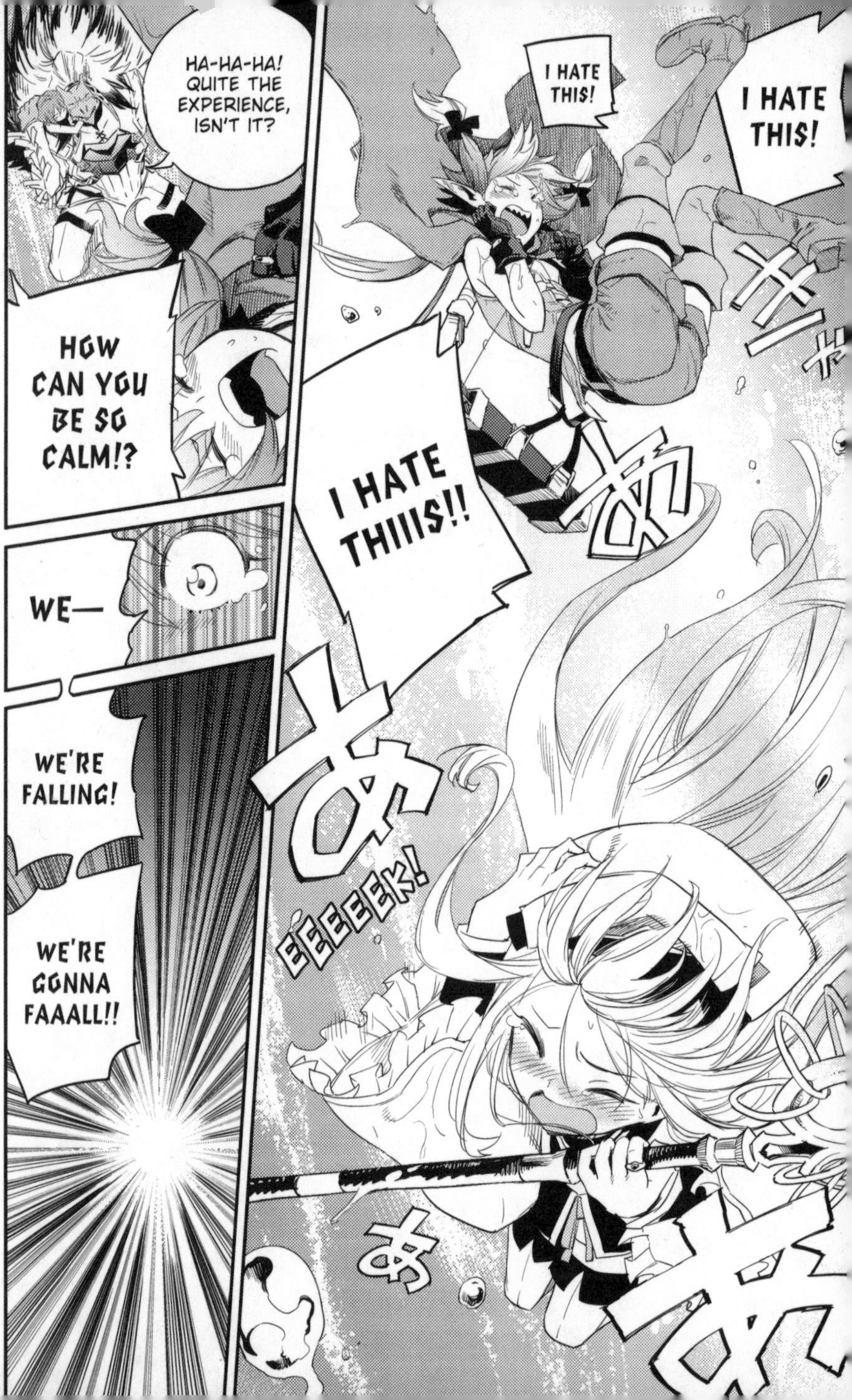
I HATE THIS!
I HATE THIS!
I HATE THIIIS!!
EEEEEK!
HA-HA-HA! QUITE THE EXPERIENCE, ISN'T IT?
HOW CAN YOU BE SO CALM!?
WE—
WE'RE FALLING!
WE'RE GONNA FAAALL!!

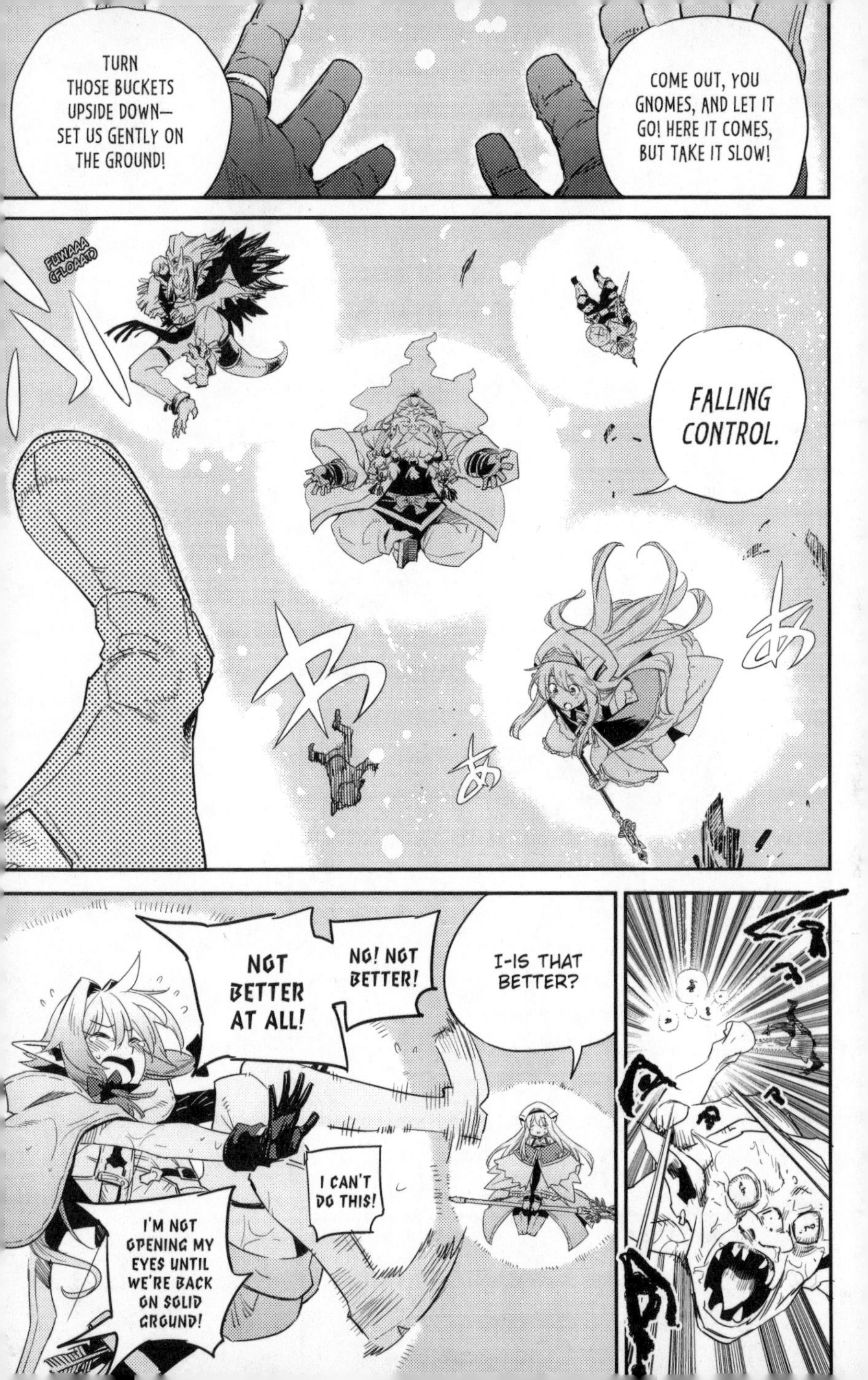
COME OUT, YOU GNOMES, AND LET IT GO! HERE IT COMES, BUT TAKE IT SLOW!
TURN THOSE BUCKETS UPSIDE DOWN—SET US GENTLY ON THE GROUND!
FALLING CONTROL.
FUWAAA (FLOAAT)
I-IS THAT BETTER?
NO! NOT BETTER!
NOT BETTER AT ALL!
I CAN'T DO THIS!
I'M NOT OPENING MY EYES UNTIL WE'RE BACK ON SOLID GROUND!

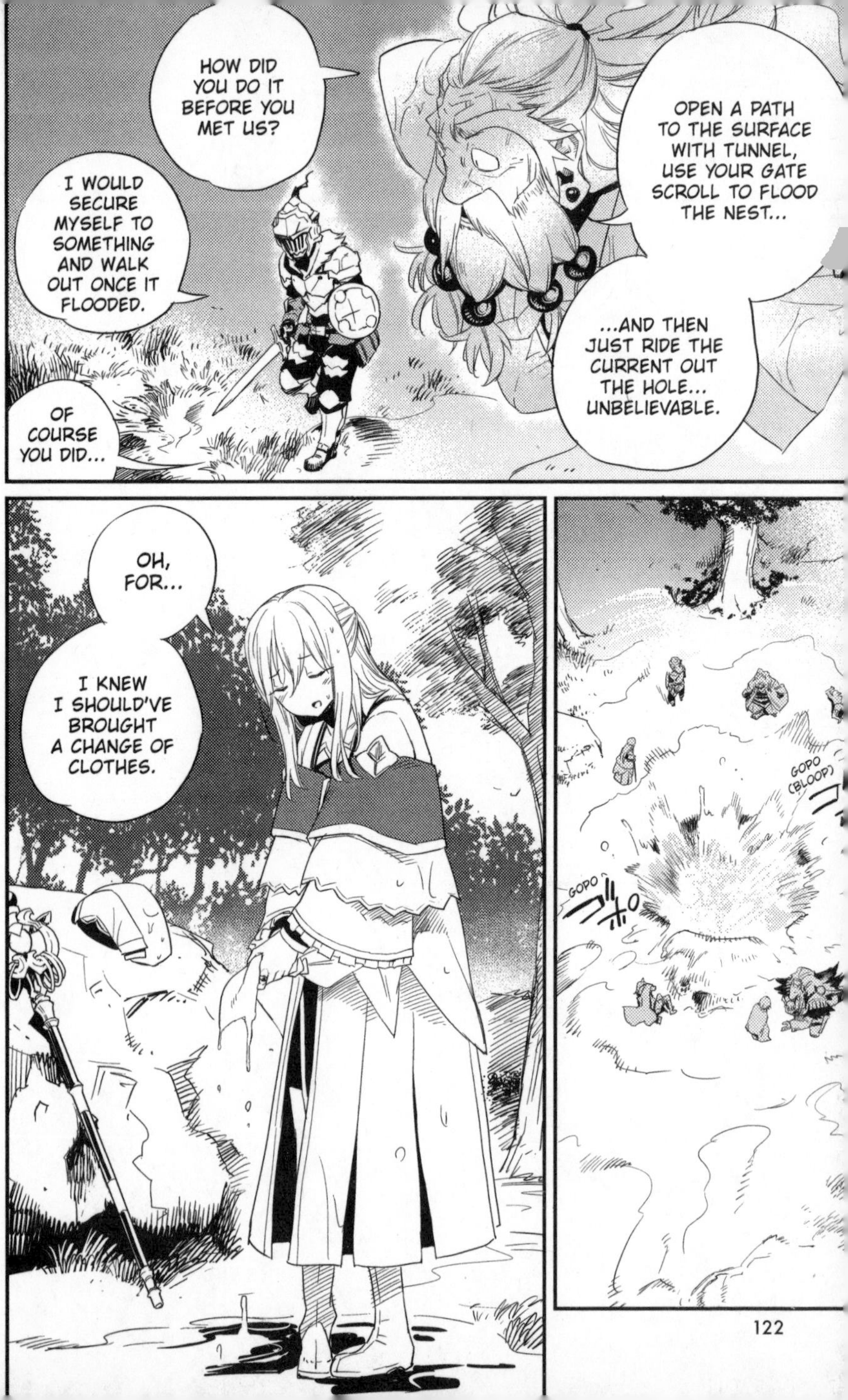
OPEN A PATH TO THE SURFACE WITH TUNNEL, USE YOUR GATE SCROLL TO FLOOD THE NEST...
...AND THEN JUST RIDE THE CURRENT OUT THE HOLE... UNBELIEVABLE.
HOW DID YOU DO IT BEFORE YOU MET US?
I WOULD SECURE MYSELF TO SOMETHING AND WALK OUT ONCE IT FLOODED.
OF COURSE YOU DID...
GOPO (BLOOP)
GOPO
OH, FOR...
I KNEW I SHOULD'VE BROUGHT A CHANGE OF CLOTHES.

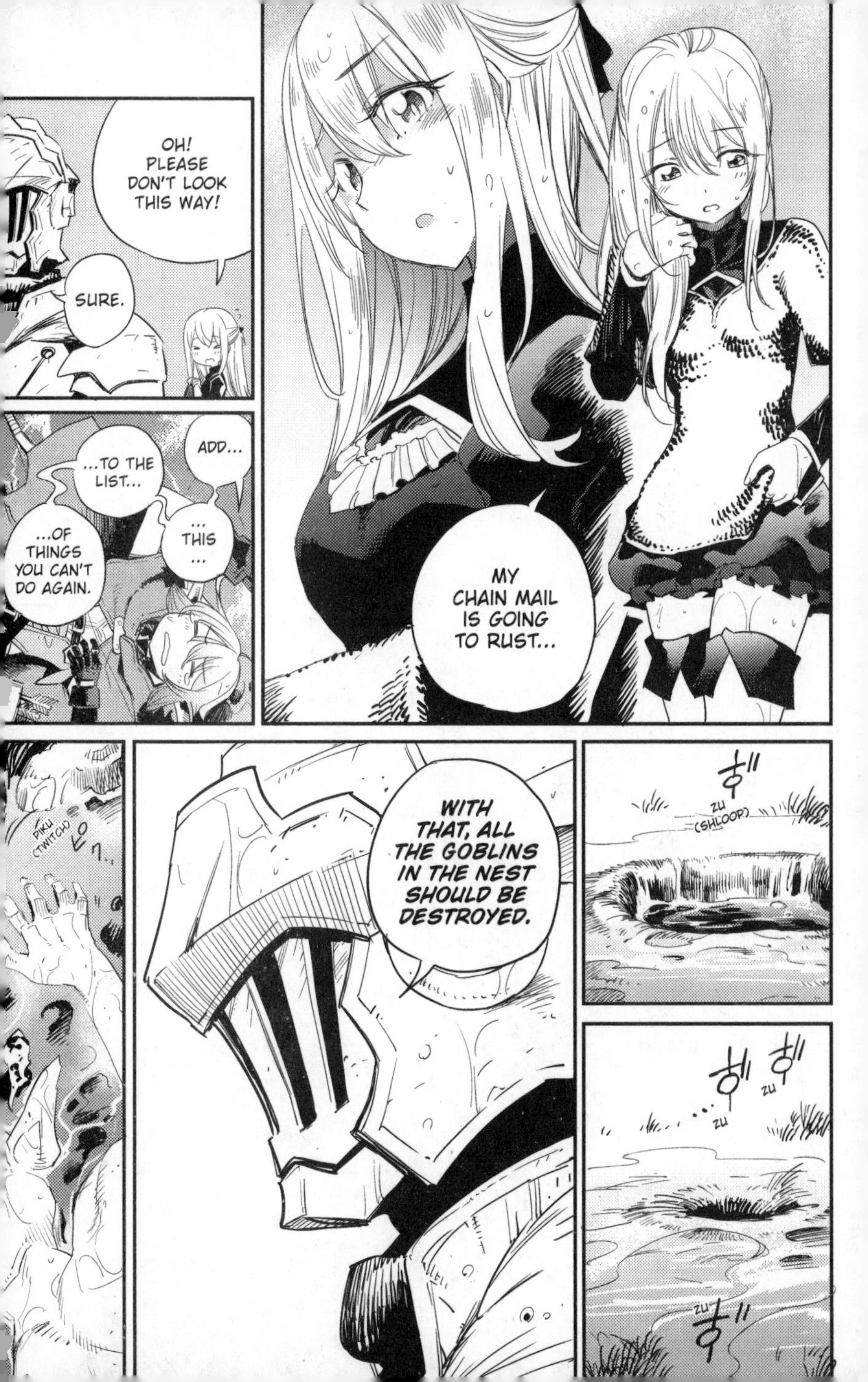
MY CHAIN MAIL IS GOING TO RUST...
OH! PLEASE DON'T LOOK THIS WAY!
SURE.
ADD...
...THIS...
...TO THE LIST...
...OF THINGS YOU CAN'T DO AGAIN.
ず
ZU (SHLOOP)
ず ず
ZU ZU
...
ZU ず
WITH THAT, ALL THE GOBLINS IN THE NEST SHOULD BE DESTROYED.
ピク
PIKU (TWITCH)

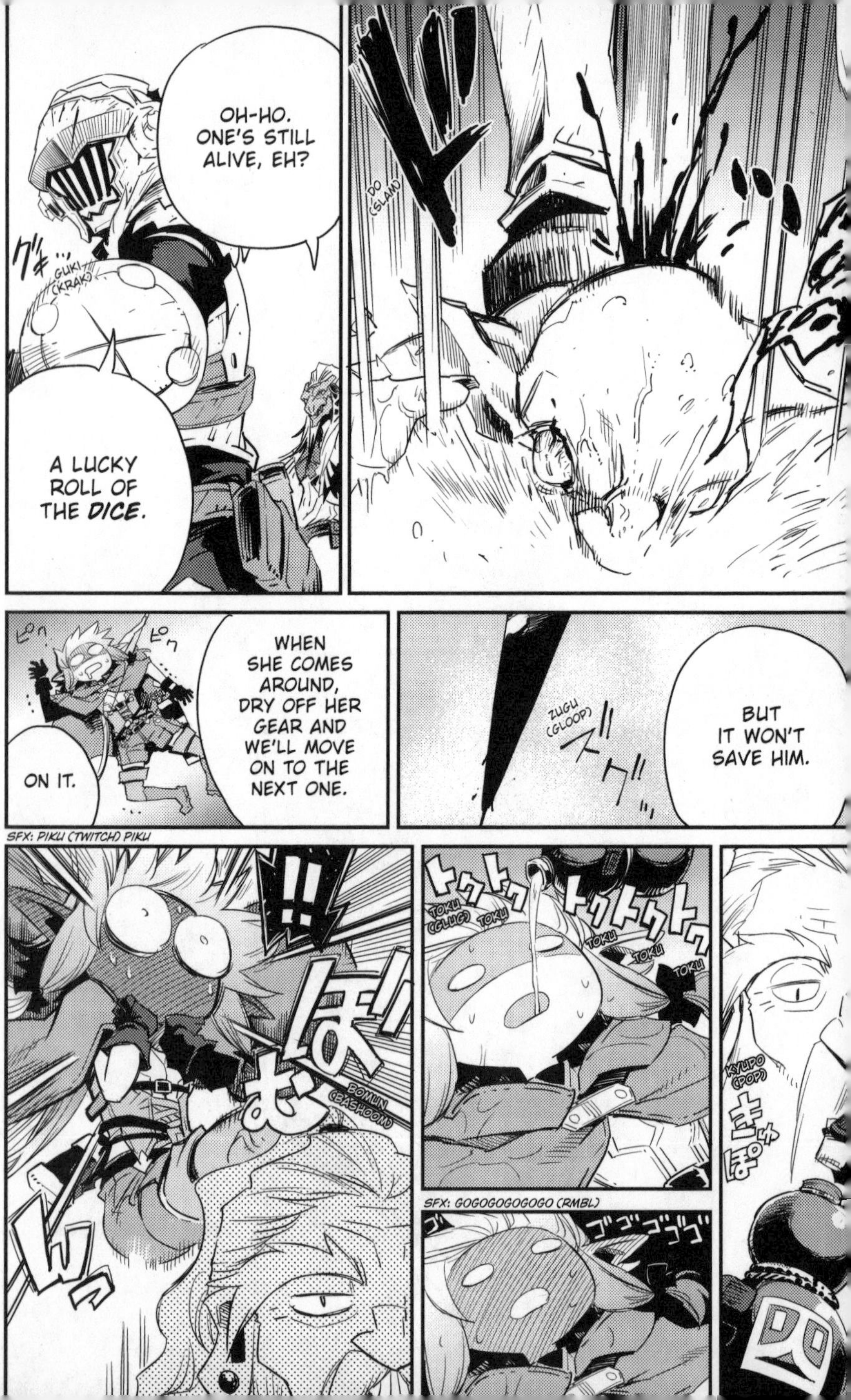
DO (SLAM)
OH-HO. ONE'S STILL ALIVE, EH?
GUKI (KRAK)
A LUCKY ROLL OF THE *DICE*.
ZUGU (GLOOP)
BUT IT WON'T SAVE HIM.
WHEN SHE COMES AROUND, DRY OFF HER GEAR AND WE'LL MOVE ON TO THE NEXT ONE.
ON IT.
SFX: PIKU (TWITCH) PIKU
KYUPO (POP)
TOKU (GLUG) TOKU
TOKU
TOKU
TOKU
SFX: GOGOGOGOGOGO (RMBL)
BOMUN (BASHOOM)

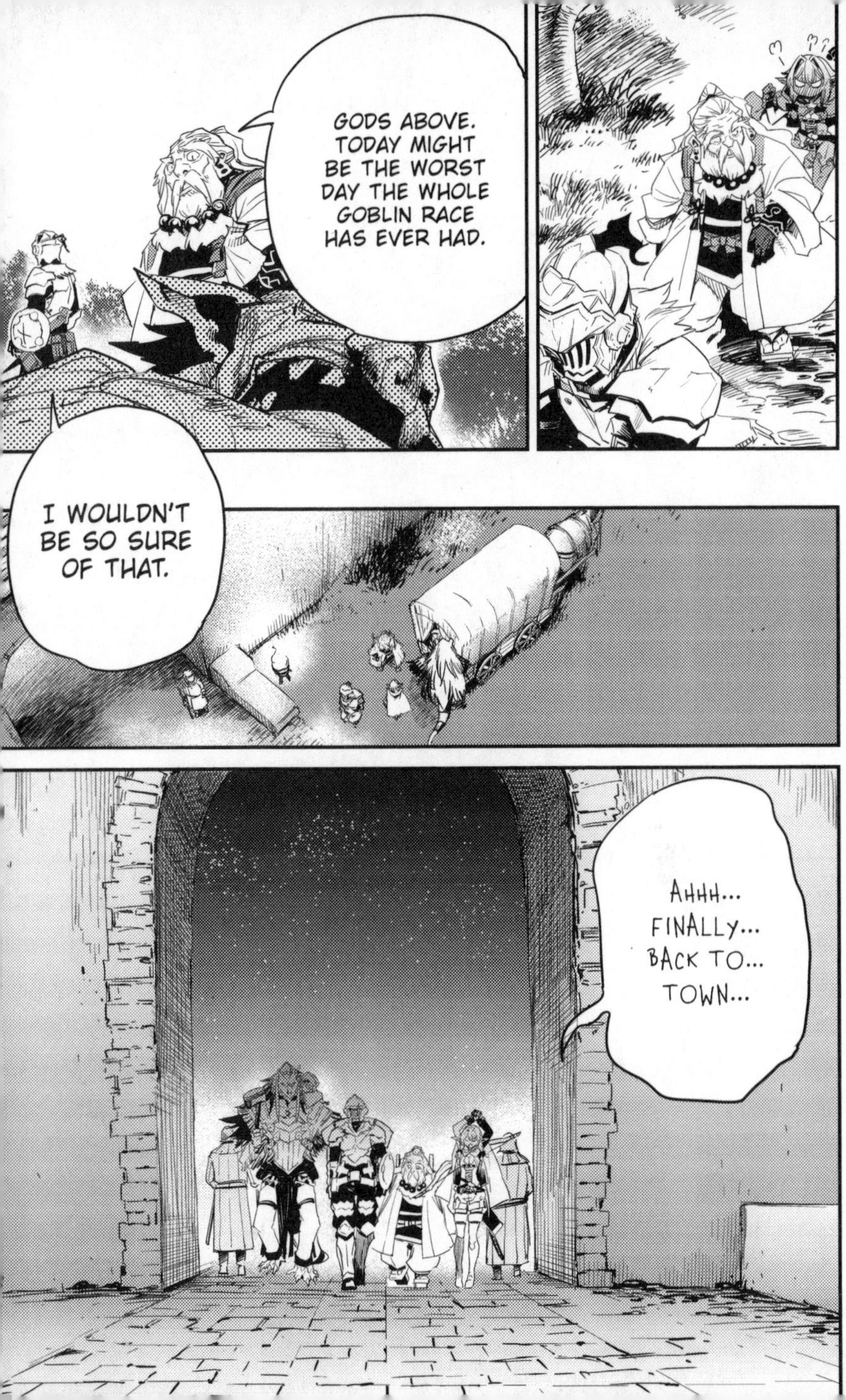
GODS ABOVE. TODAY MIGHT BE THE WORST DAY THE WHOLE GOBLIN RACE HAS EVER HAD.
I WOULDN'T BE SO SURE OF THAT.
AHHH... FINALLY... BACK TO... TOWN...

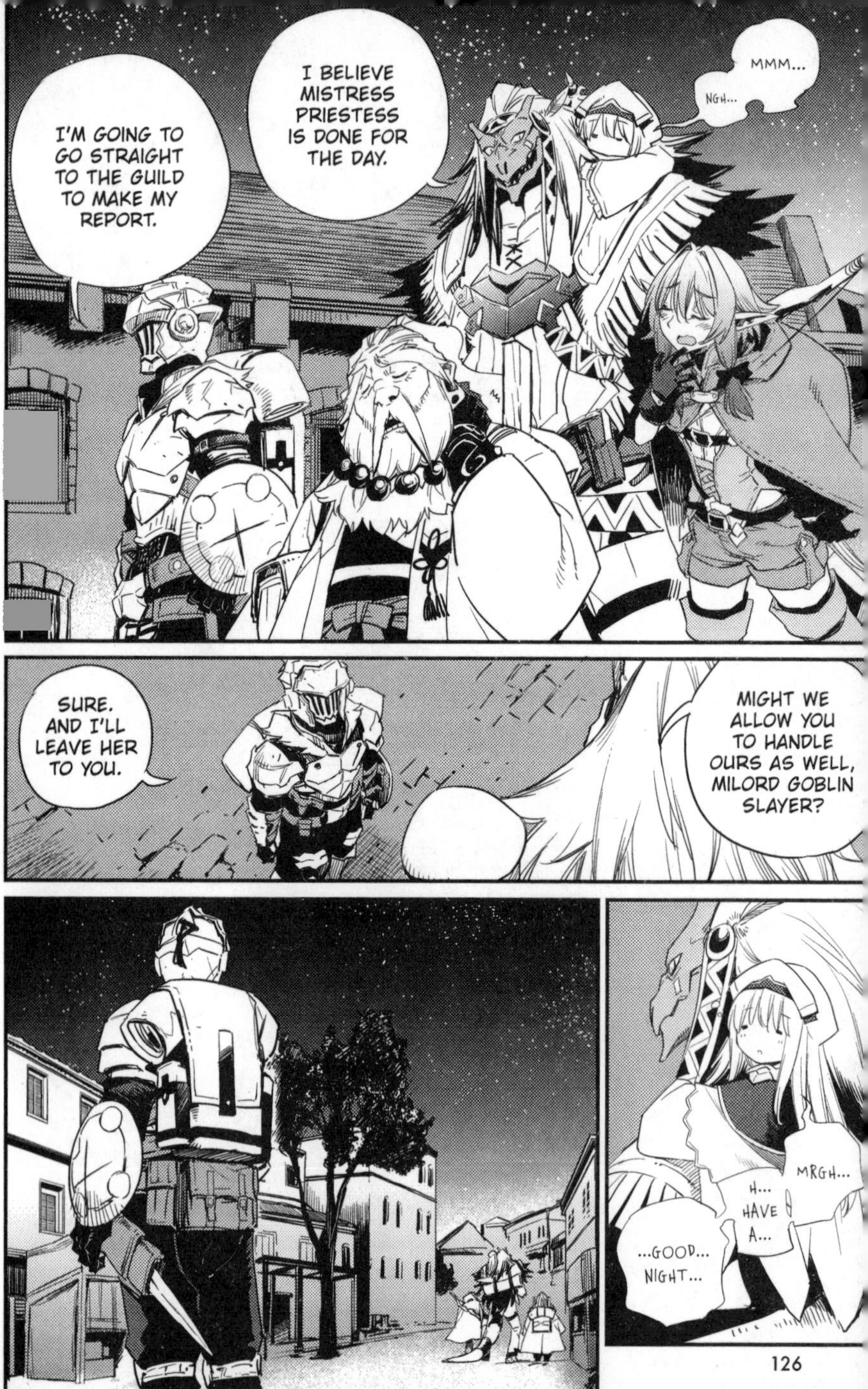
MMM...
NGH...
I BELIEVE MISTRESS PRIESTESS IS DONE FOR THE DAY.
I'M GOING TO GO STRAIGHT TO THE GUILD TO MAKE MY REPORT.
MIGHT WE ALLOW YOU TO HANDLE OURS AS WELL, MILORD GOBLIN SLAYER?
SURE. AND I'LL LEAVE HER TO YOU.
MRGH...
H... HAVE A...
...GOOD... NIGHT...

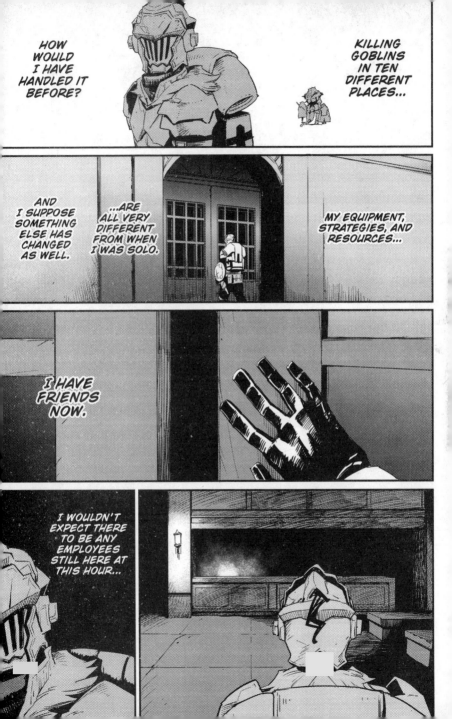

KILLING GOBLINS IN TEN DIFFERENT PLACES...

HOW WOULD I HAVE HANDLED IT BEFORE?

MY EQUIPMENT, STRATEGIES, AND RESOURCES...

...ARE ALL VERY DIFFERENT FROM WHEN I WAS SOLO.

AND I SUPPOSE SOMETHING ELSE HAS CHANGED AS WELL.

I HAVE FRIENDS NOW.

I WOULDN'T EXPECT THERE TO BE ANY EMPLOYEES STILL HERE AT THIS HOUR...

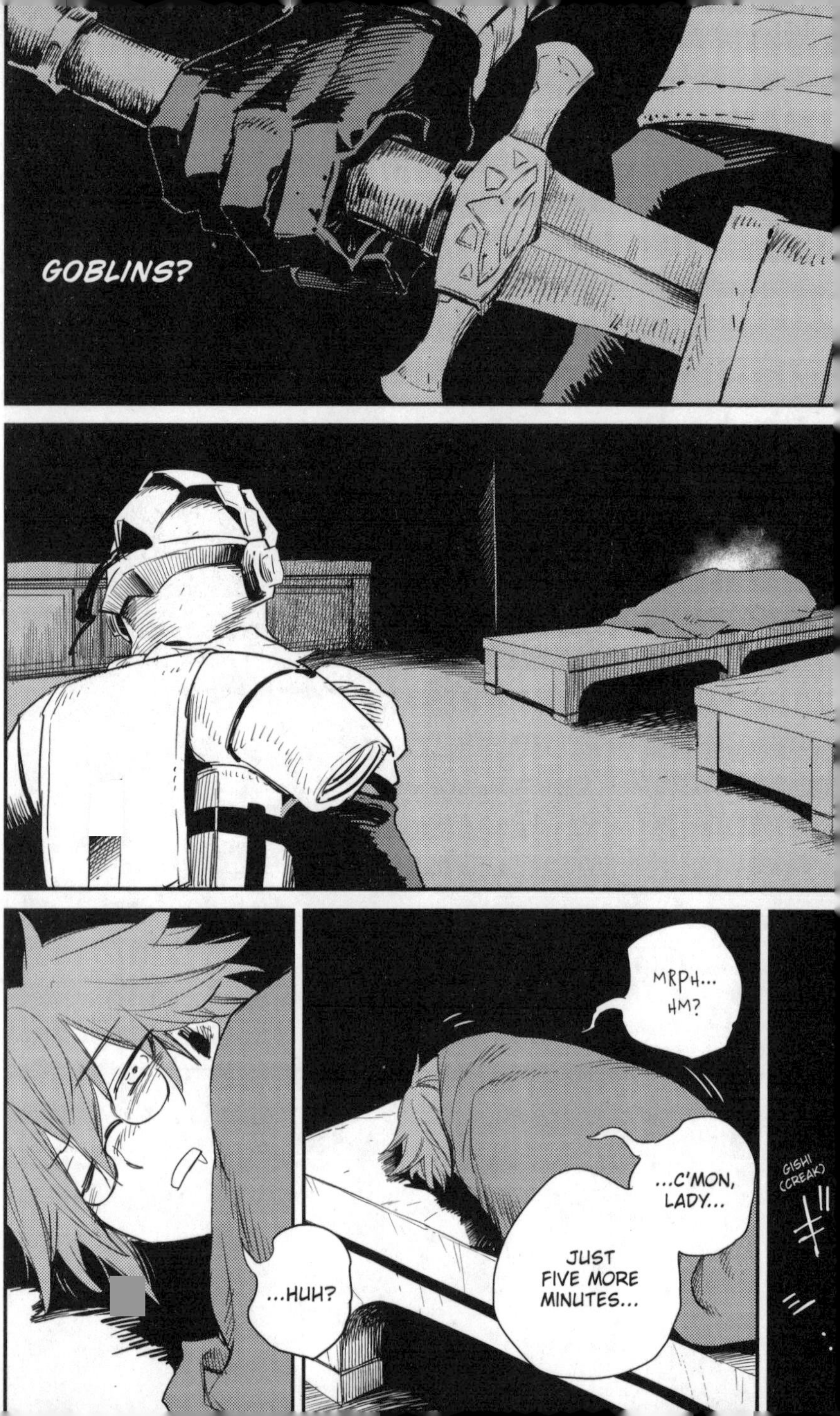
GOBLINS?
GISHI (CREAK)
MRPH... HM?
...C'MON, LADY...
JUST FIVE MORE MINUTES...
...HUH?

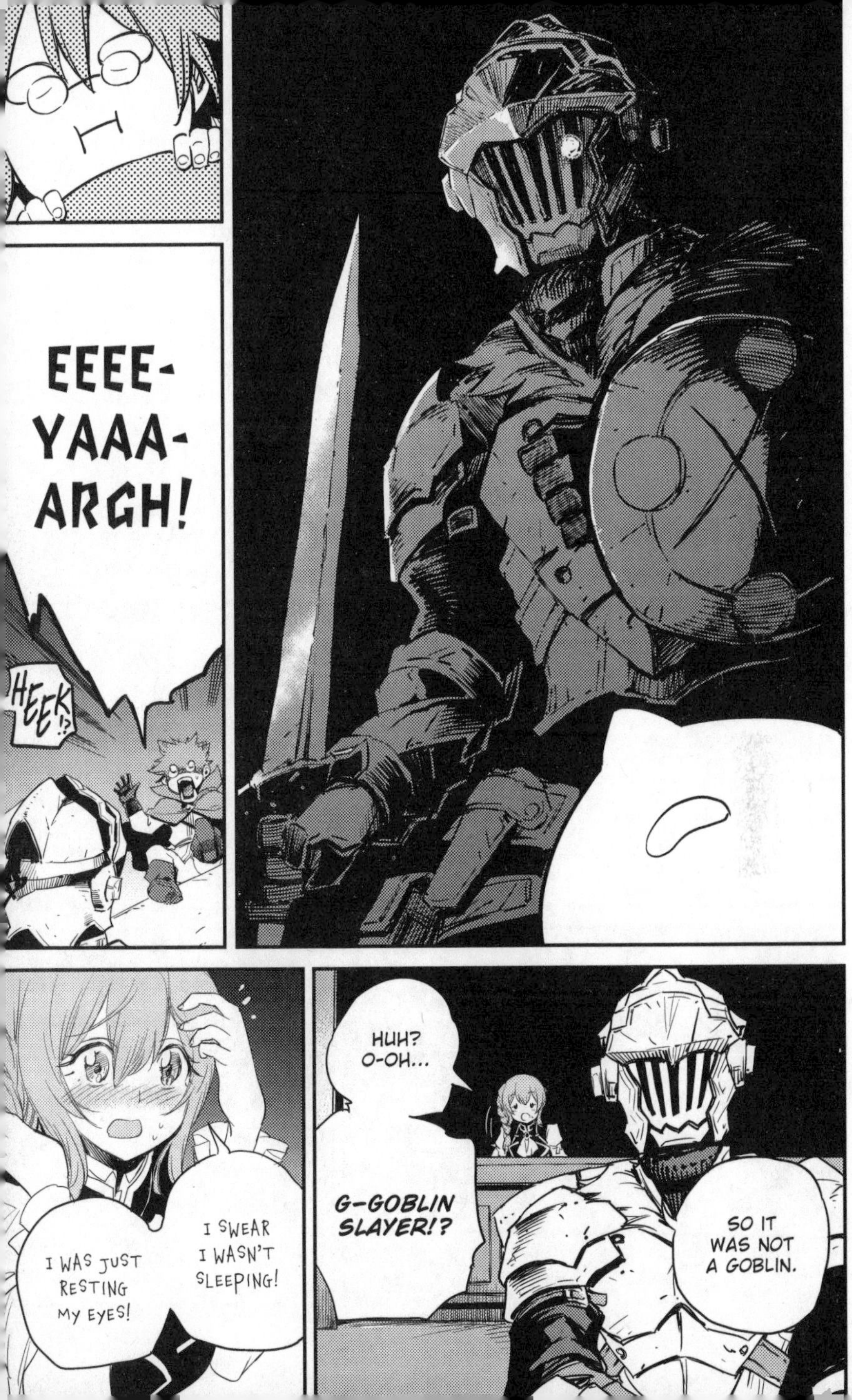
EEEE-YAAA-ARGH!
HEEK!?
HUH? O-OH...
G-GOBLIN SLAYER!?
SO IT WAS NOT A GOBLIN.
I SWEAR I WASN'T SLEEPING!
I WAS JUST RESTING MY EYES!

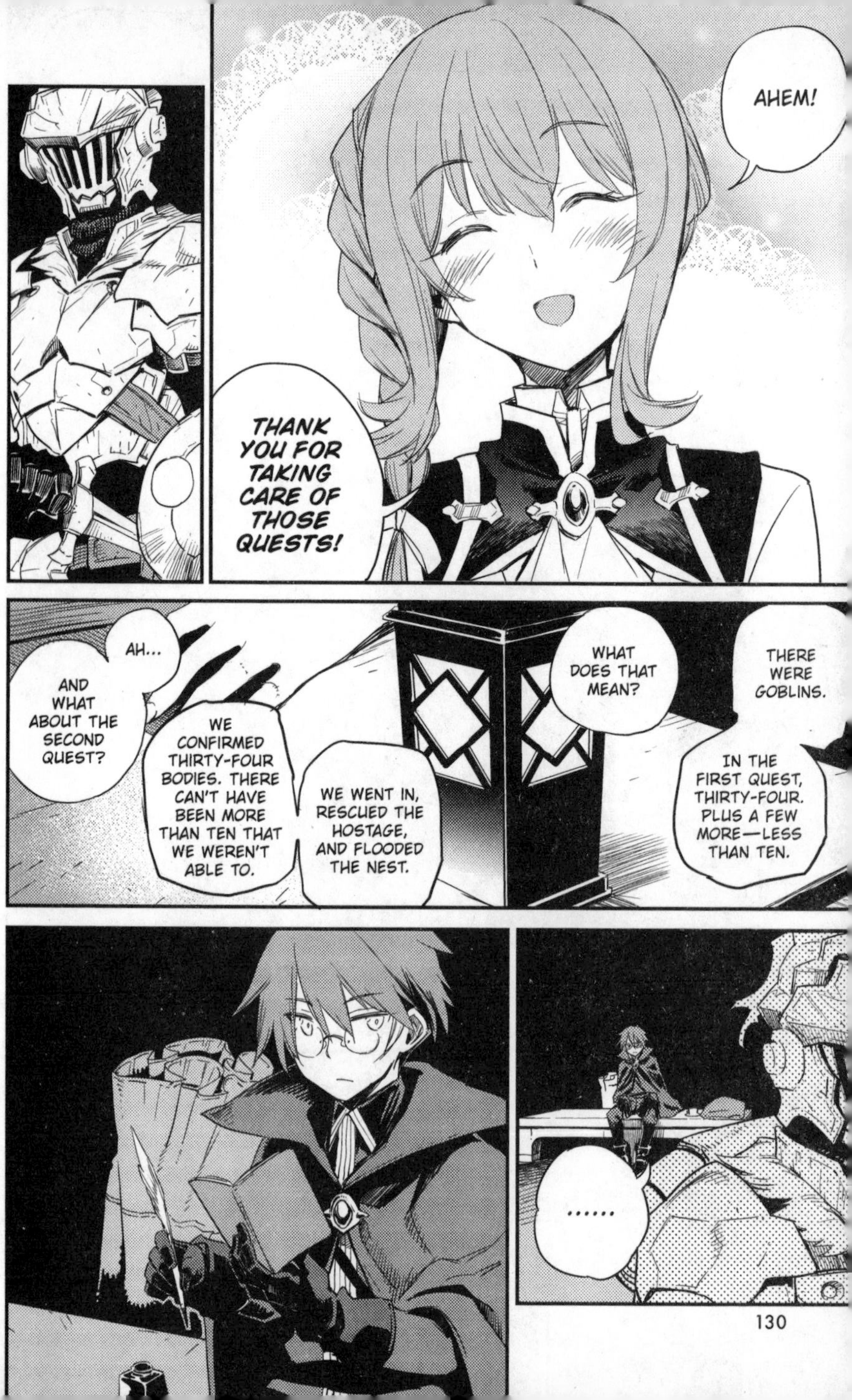
AHEM!
THANK YOU FOR TAKING CARE OF THOSE QUESTS!
THERE WERE GOBLINS.
IN THE FIRST QUEST, THIRTY-FOUR. PLUS A FEW MORE—LESS THAN TEN.
WHAT DOES THAT MEAN?
WE WENT IN, RESCUED THE HOSTAGE, AND FLOODED THE NEST.
WE CONFIRMED THIRTY-FOUR BODIES. THERE CAN'T HAVE BEEN MORE THAN TEN THAT WE WEREN'T ABLE TO.
AH...
AND WHAT ABOUT THE SECOND QUEST?
......

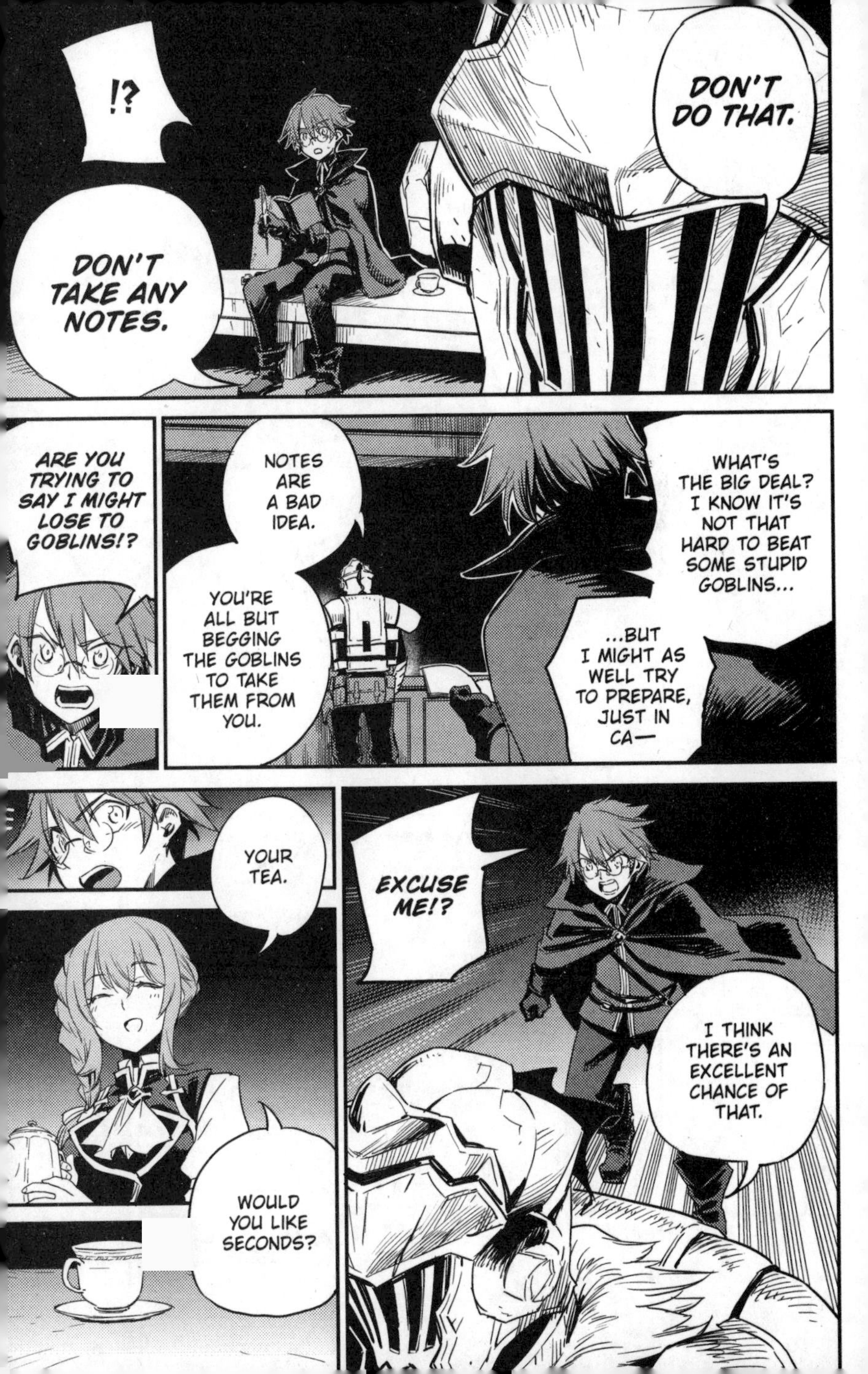
DON'T DO THAT.
!?
DON'T TAKE ANY NOTES.
WHAT'S THE BIG DEAL? I KNOW IT'S NOT THAT HARD TO BEAT SOME STUPID GOBLINS...
...BUT I MIGHT AS WELL TRY TO PREPARE, JUST IN CA—
NOTES ARE A BAD IDEA.
YOU'RE ALL BUT BEGGING THE GOBLINS TO TAKE THEM FROM YOU.
ARE YOU TRYING TO SAY I MIGHT LOSE TO GOBLINS!?
I THINK THERE'S AN EXCELLENT CHANCE OF THAT.
EXCUSE ME!?
YOUR TEA.
WOULD YOU LIKE SECONDS?

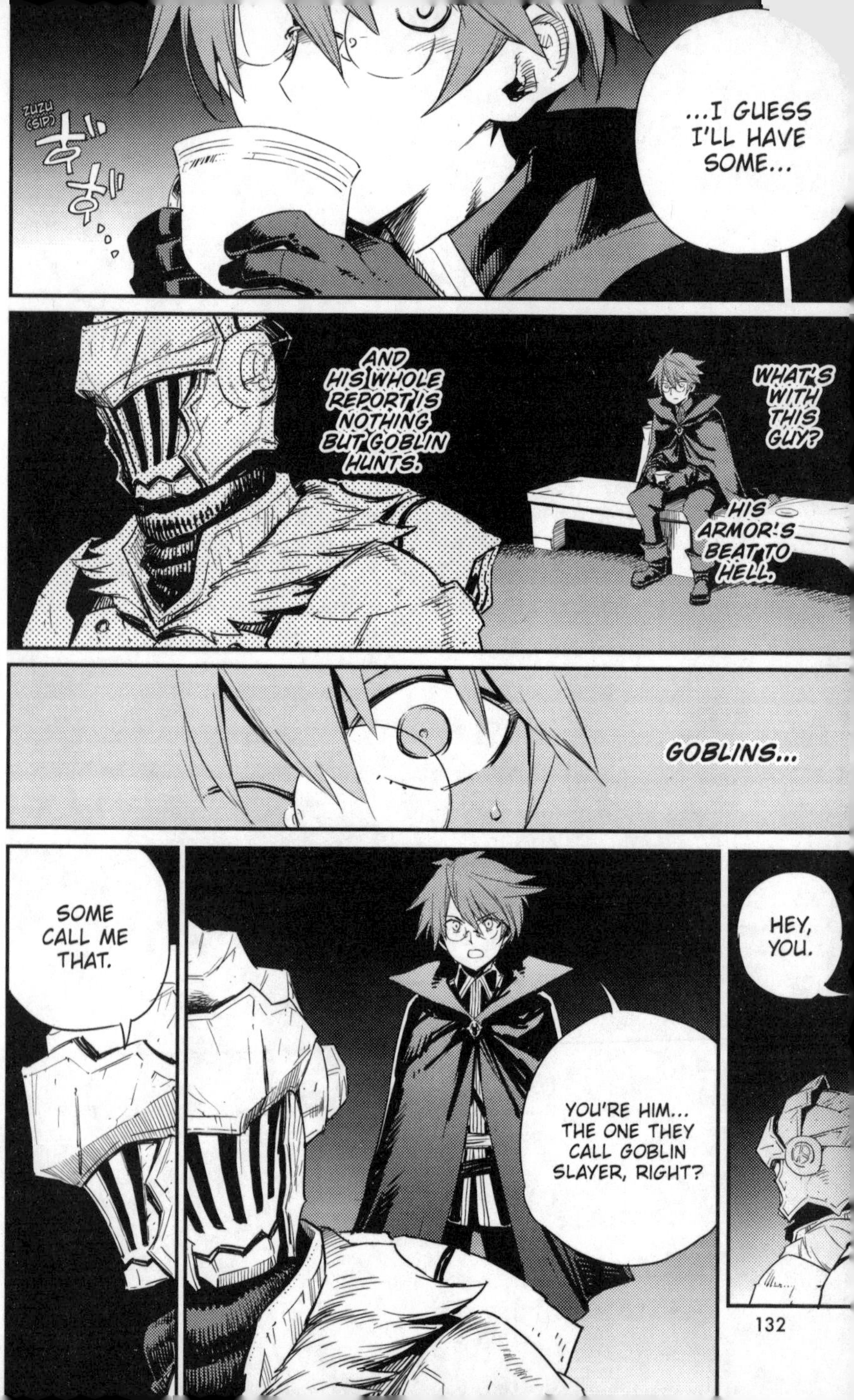
...I GUESS I'LL HAVE SOME...
ZUZU (SIP)
WHAT'S WITH THIS GUY?
HIS ARMOR'S BEAT TO HELL.
AND HIS WHOLE REPORT IS NOTHING BUT GOBLIN HUNTS.
GOBLINS...
HEY, YOU.
YOU'RE HIM... THE ONE THEY CALL GOBLIN SLAYER, RIGHT?
SOME CALL ME THAT.

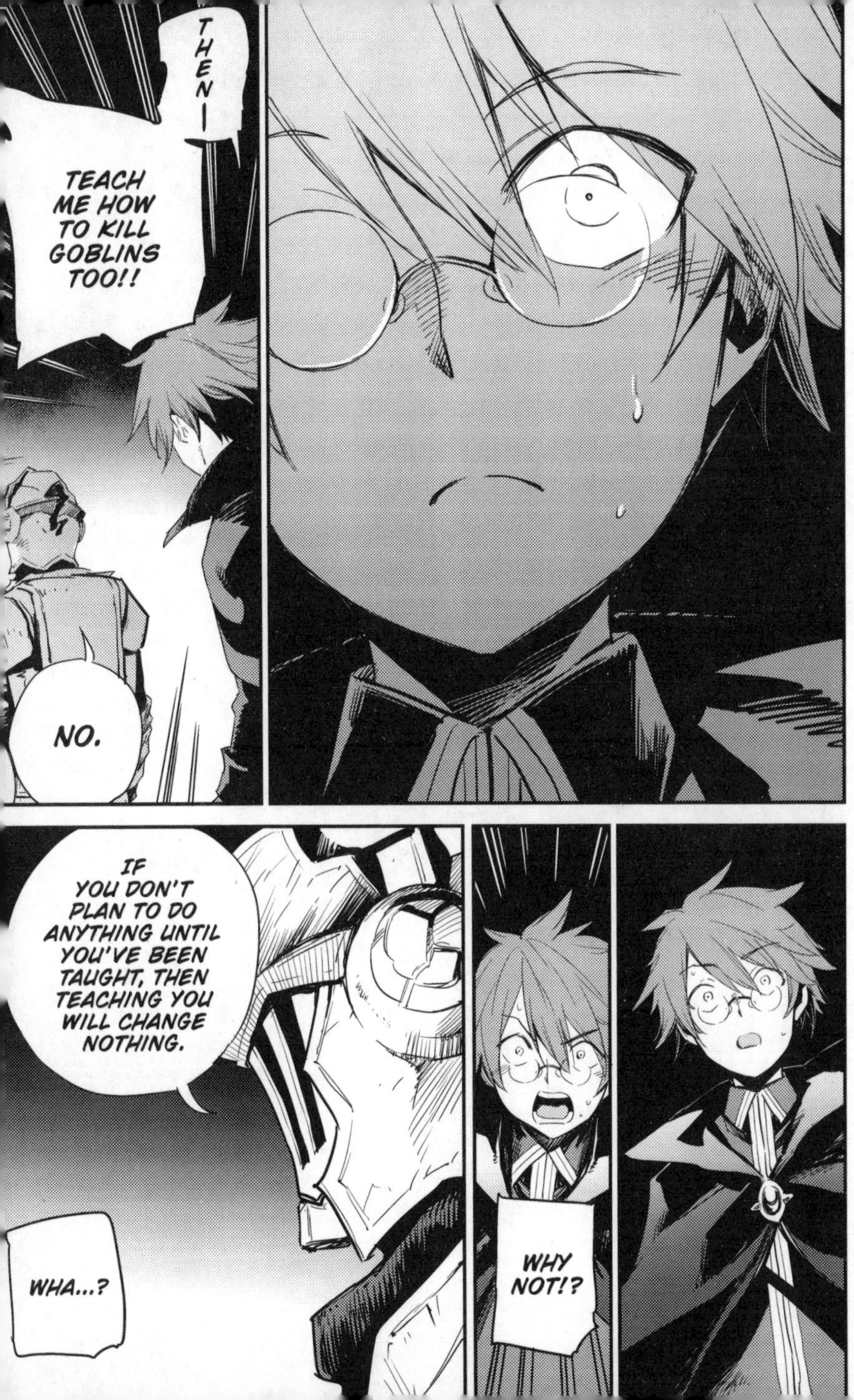
THEN I—
TEACH ME HOW TO KILL GOBLINS TOO!!
NO.
WHY NOT!?
IF YOU DON'T PLAN TO DO ANYTHING UNTIL YOU'VE BEEN TAUGHT, THEN TEACHING YOU WILL CHANGE NOTHING.
WHA...?

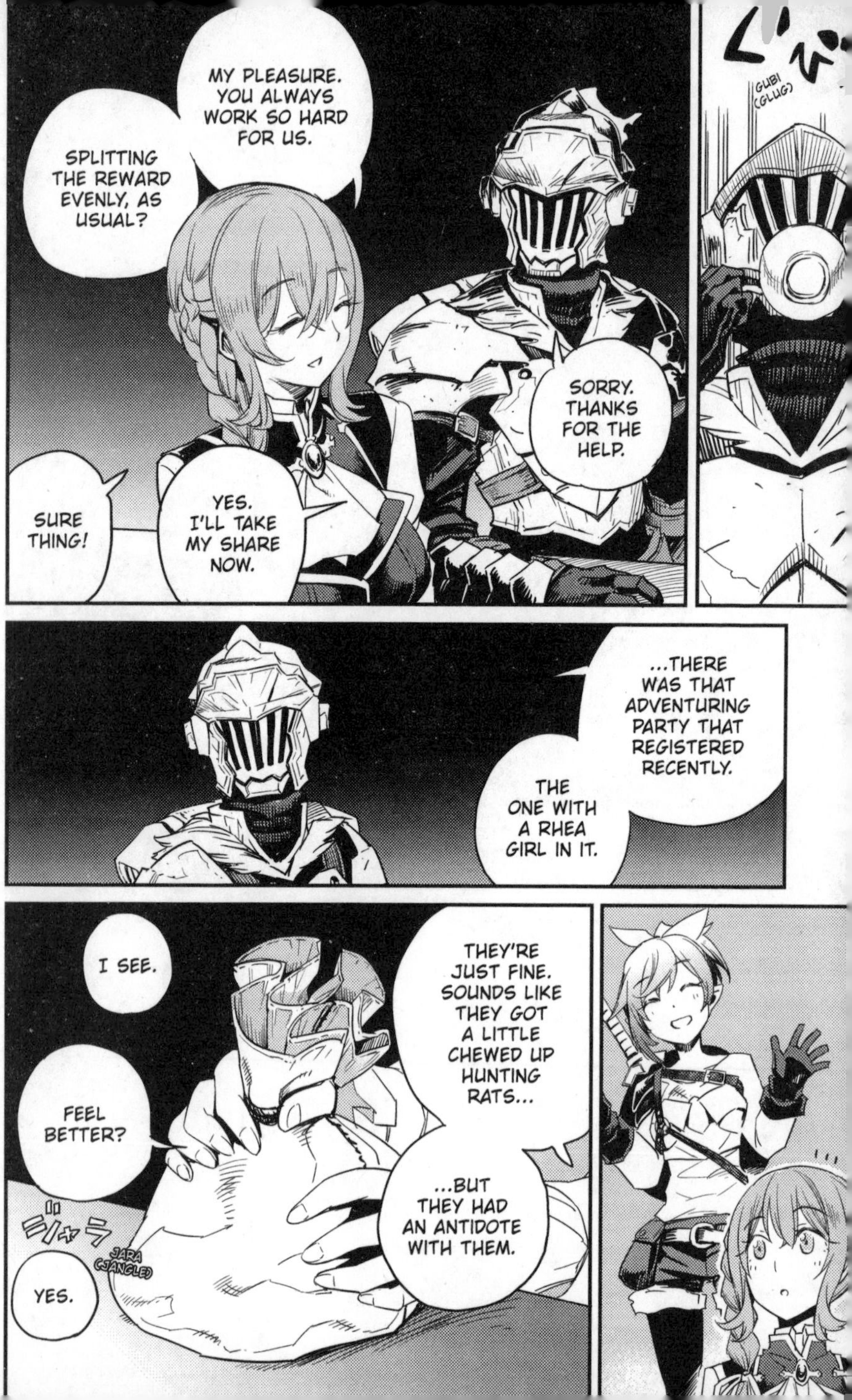
GUBI (GLUG)
MY PLEASURE. YOU ALWAYS WORK SO HARD FOR US.
SPLITTING THE REWARD EVENLY, AS USUAL?
SORRY. THANKS FOR THE HELP.
YES. I'LL TAKE MY SHARE NOW.
SURE THING!
...THERE WAS THAT ADVENTURING PARTY THAT REGISTERED RECENTLY.
THE ONE WITH A RHEA GIRL IN IT.
THEY'RE JUST FINE. SOUNDS LIKE THEY GOT A LITTLE CHEWED UP HUNTING RATS...
...BUT THEY HAD AN ANTIDOTE WITH THEM.
I SEE.
FEEL BETTER?
JARA (JANGLE)
YES.

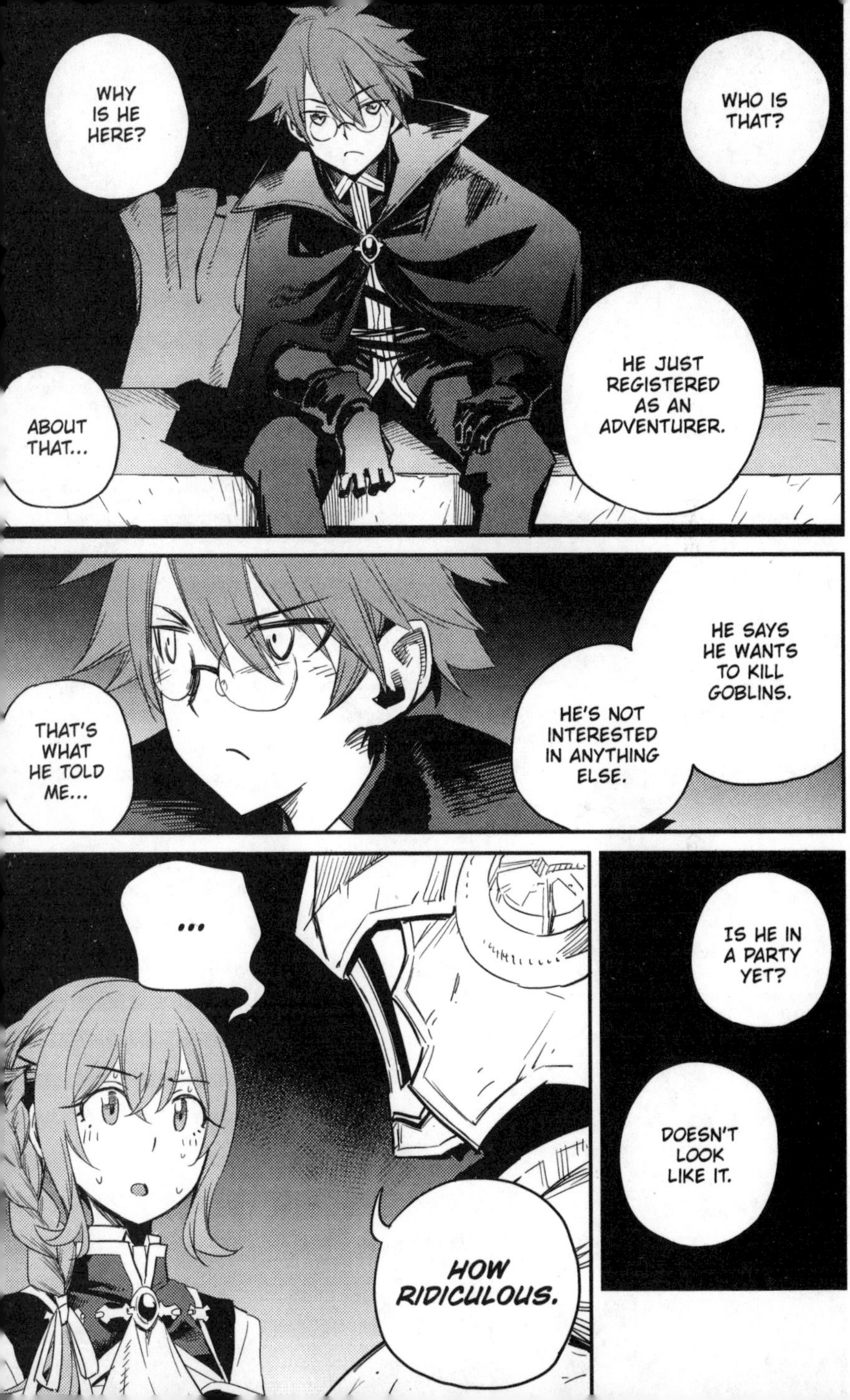
WHO IS THAT?
WHY IS HE HERE?
HE JUST REGISTERED AS AN ADVENTURER.
ABOUT THAT...
HE SAYS HE WANTS TO KILL GOBLINS.
HE'S NOT INTERESTED IN ANYTHING ELSE.
THAT'S WHAT HE TOLD ME...
IS HE IN A PARTY YET?
DOESN'T LOOK LIKE IT.
...
HOW RIDICULOUS.

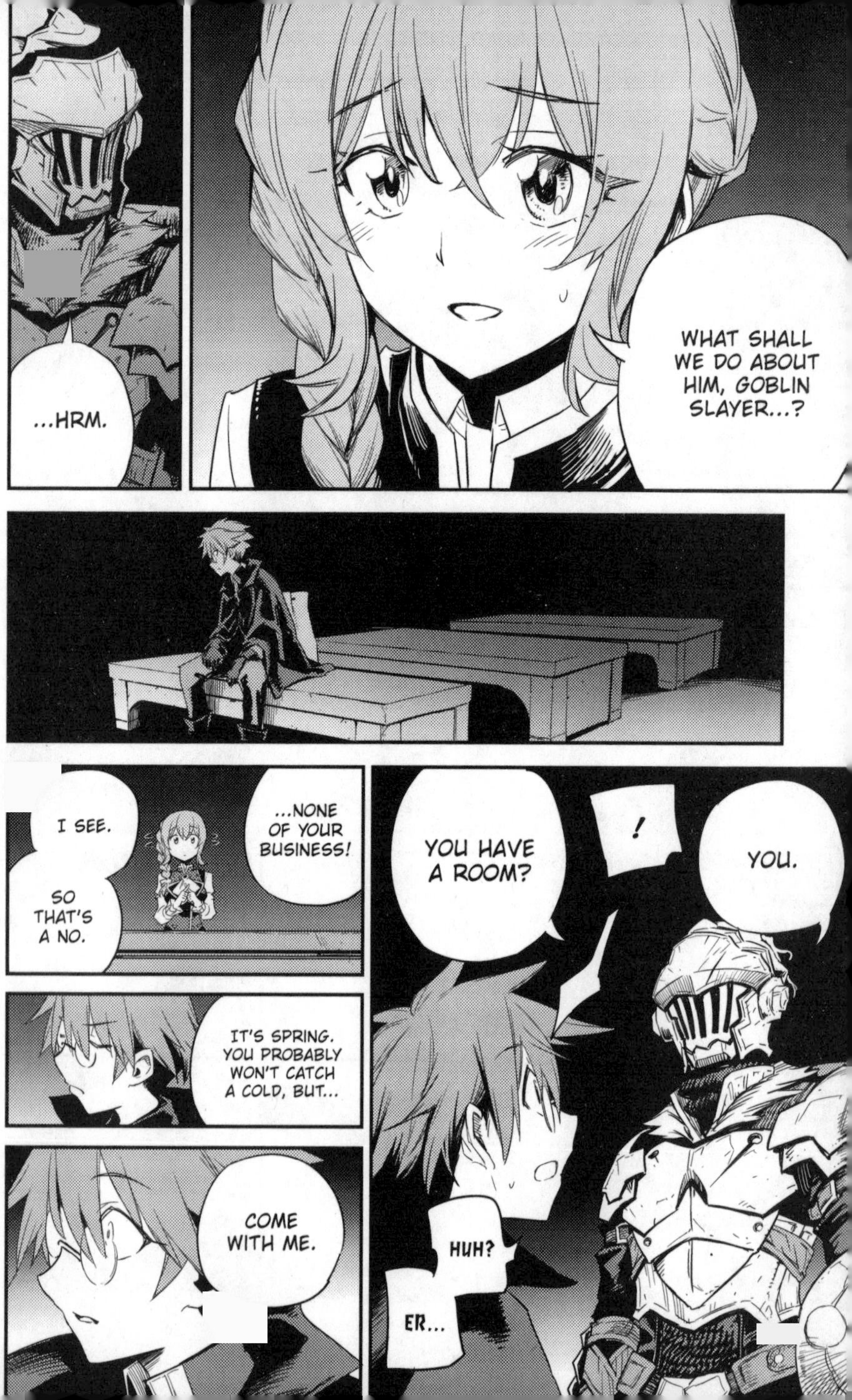
WHAT SHALL WE DO ABOUT HIM, GOBLIN SLAYER...?
...HRM.
YOU.
!
YOU HAVE A ROOM?
HUH?
ER...
...NONE OF YOUR BUSINESS!
I SEE.
SO THAT'S A NO.
IT'S SPRING. YOU PROBABLY WON'T CATCH A COLD, BUT...
COME WITH ME.

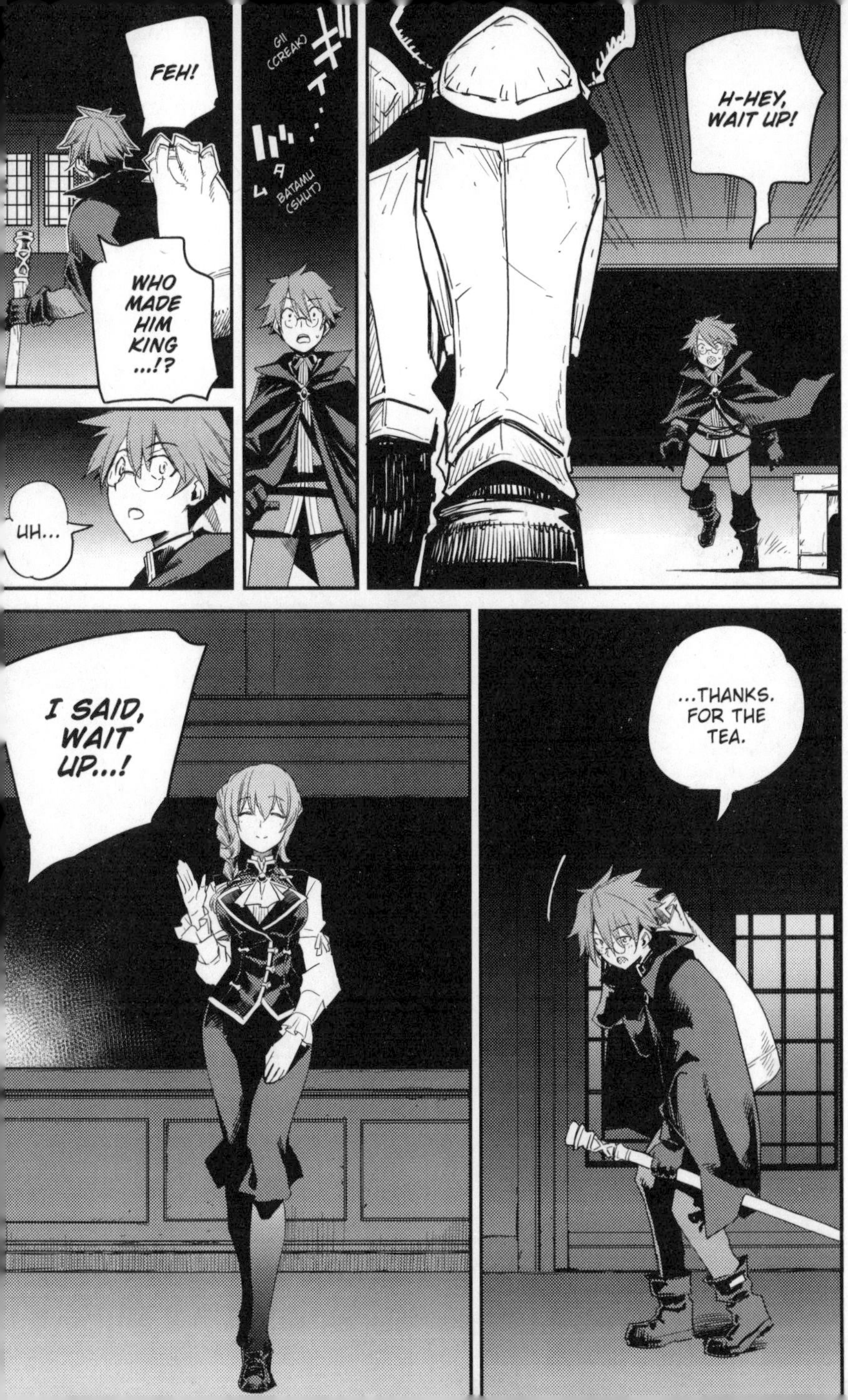
H-HEY, WAIT UP!
GII (CREAK)
BATAMU (SHUT)
FEH!
WHO MADE HIM KING ...!?
UH...
...THANKS. FOR THE TEA.
I SAID, WAIT UP...!

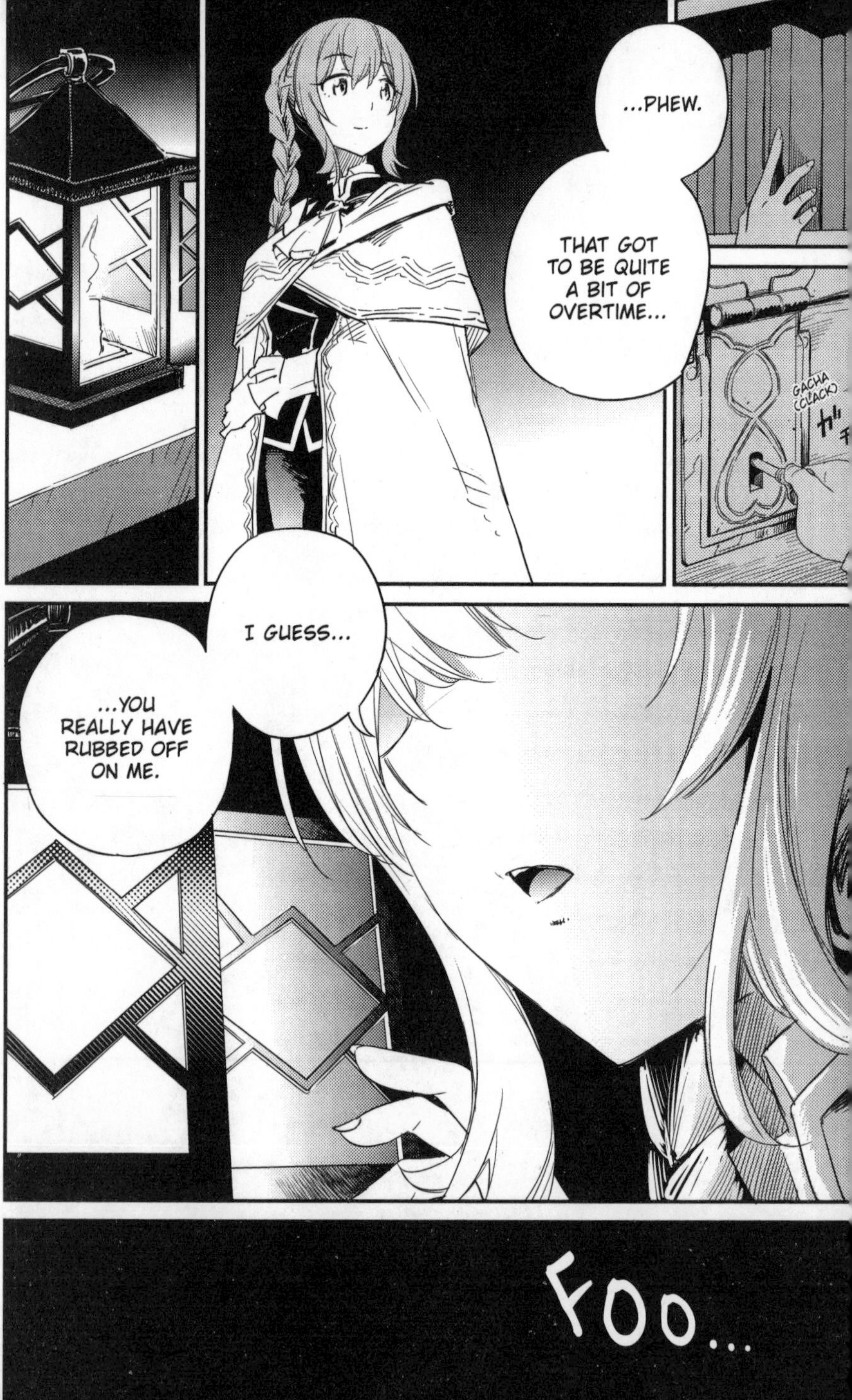
...PHEW.
THAT GOT TO BE QUITE A BIT OF OVERTIME...
GACHA (CLACK)
I GUESS...
...YOU REALLY HAVE RUBBED OFF ON ME.
FOO...

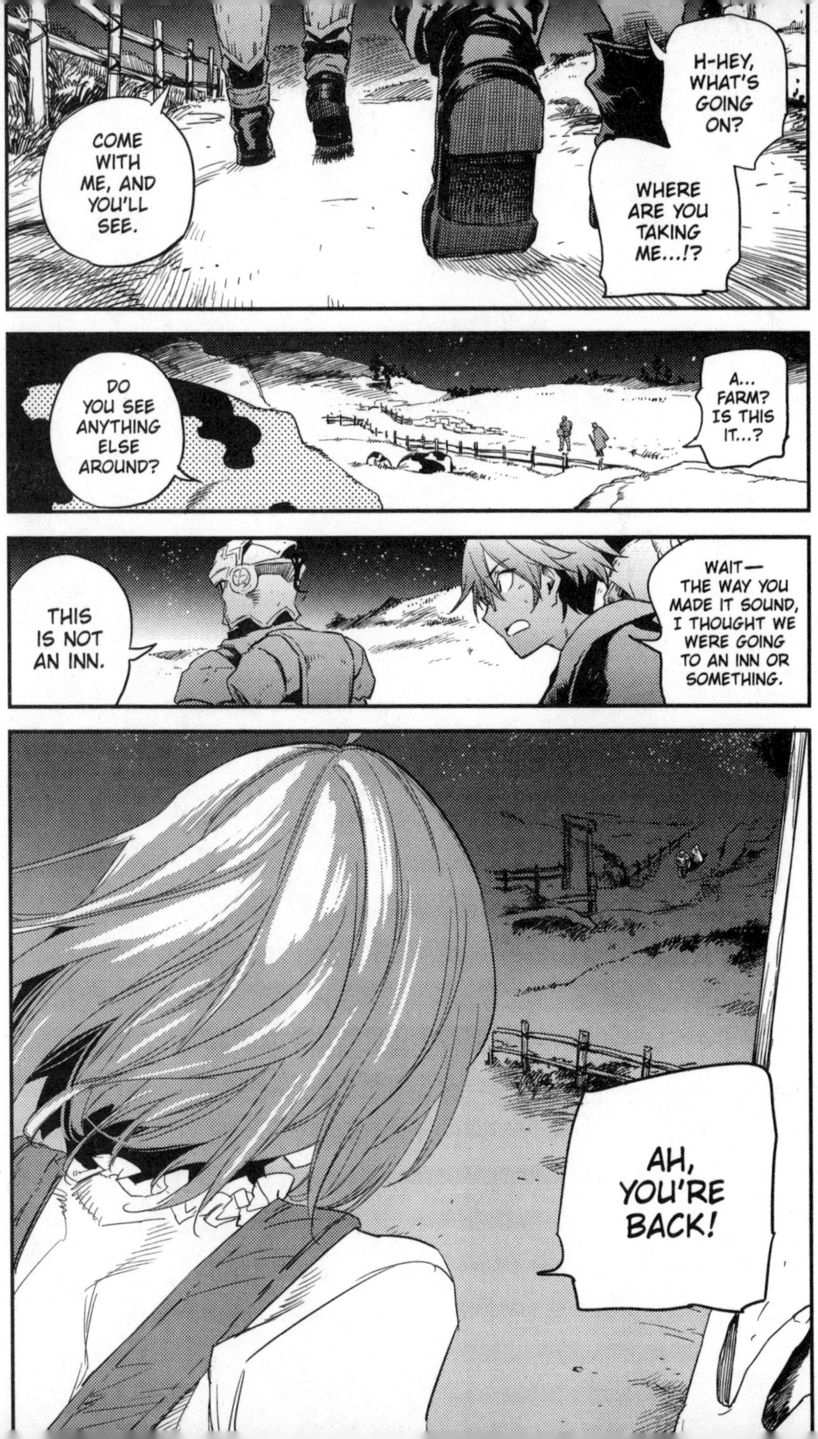
H-HEY, WHAT'S GOING ON?
WHERE ARE YOU TAKING ME...!?
COME WITH ME, AND YOU'LL SEE.
A... FARM? IS THIS IT...?
DO YOU SEE ANYTHING ELSE AROUND?
WAIT— THE WAY YOU MADE IT SOUND, I THOUGHT WE WERE GOING TO AN INN OR SOMETHING.
THIS IS NOT AN INN.
AH, YOU'RE BACK!

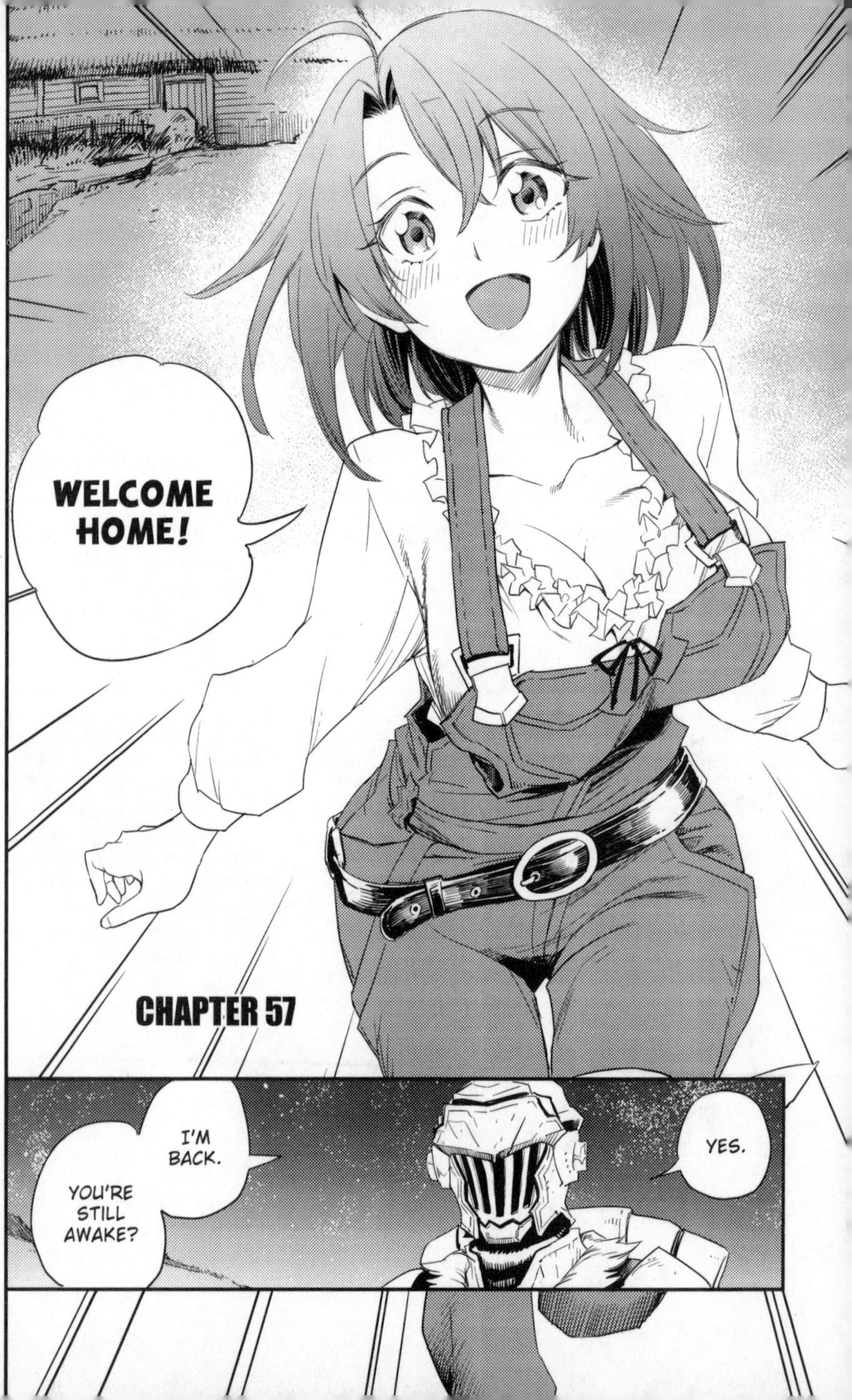
WELCOME HOME!
CHAPTER 57
YES.
I'M BACK.
YOU'RE STILL AWAKE?

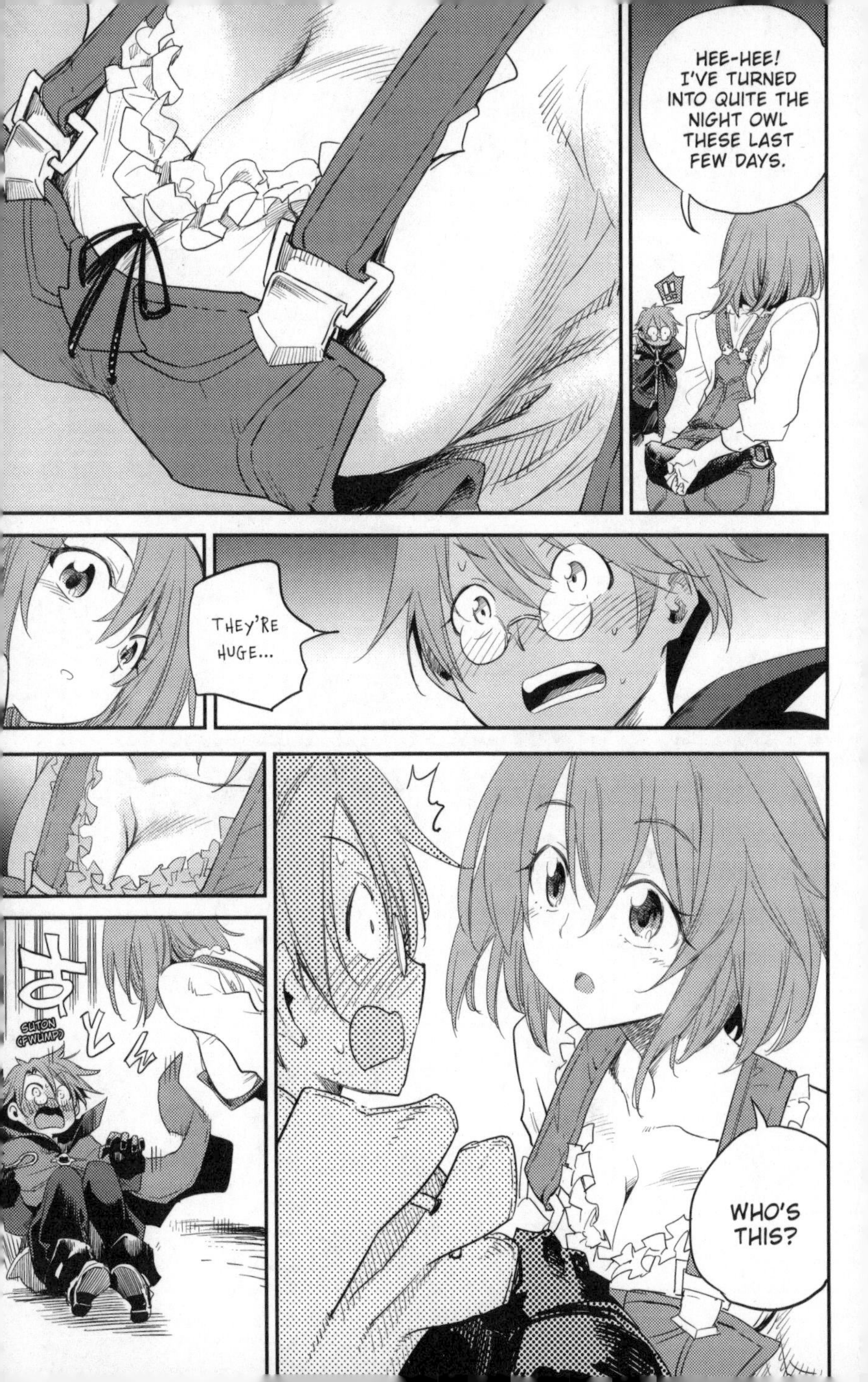
HEE-HEE! I'VE TURNED INTO QUITE THE NIGHT OWL THESE LAST FEW DAYS.
THEY'RE HUGE...
WHO'S THIS?
すとん
SUTON (FWUMP)

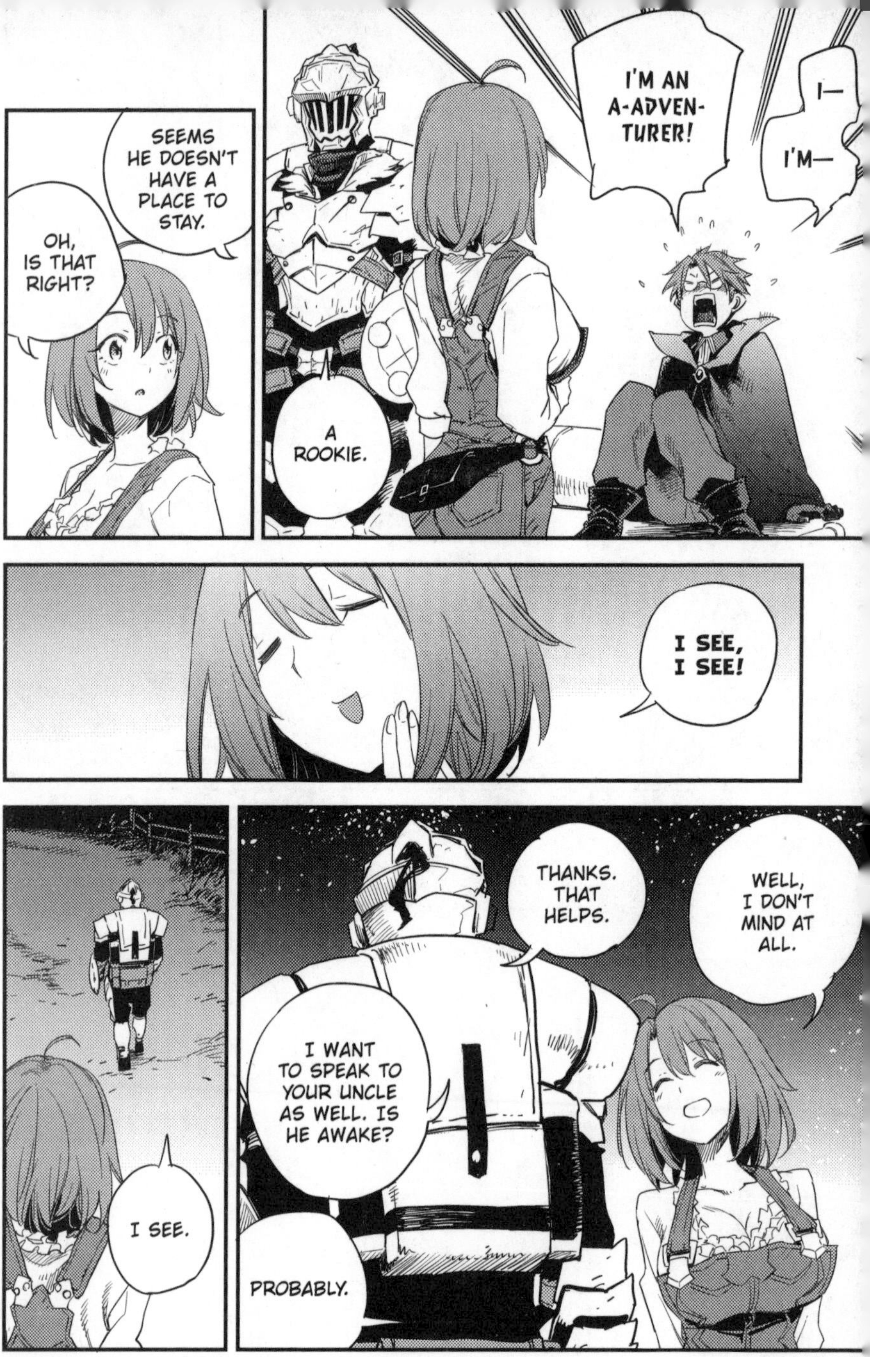
I— I'M—
I'M AN A-ADVENTURER!
A ROOKIE.
SEEMS HE DOESN'T HAVE A PLACE TO STAY.
OH, IS THAT RIGHT?
I SEE, I SEE!
WELL, I DON'T MIND AT ALL.
THANKS. THAT HELPS.
I WANT TO SPEAK TO YOUR UNCLE AS WELL. IS HE AWAKE?
PROBABLY.
I SEE.

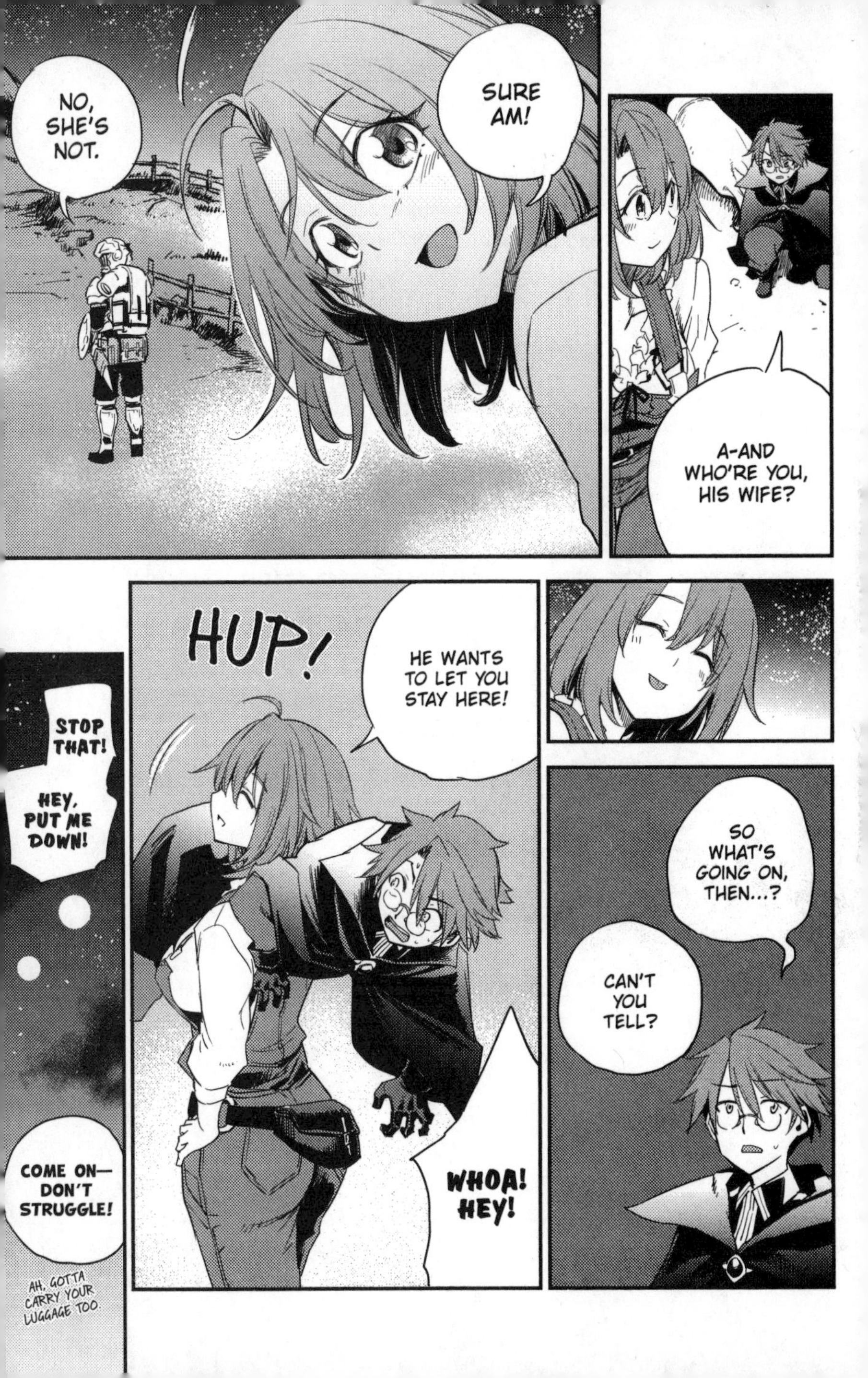
A-AND WHO'RE YOU, HIS WIFE?
SURE AM!
NO, SHE'S NOT.
SO WHAT'S GOING ON, THEN...?
CAN'T YOU TELL?
HE WANTS TO LET YOU STAY HERE!
HUP!
WHOA! HEY!
STOP THAT!
HEY, PUT ME DOWN!
COME ON— DON'T STRUGGLE!
AH, GOTTA CARRY YOUR LUGGAGE TOO.

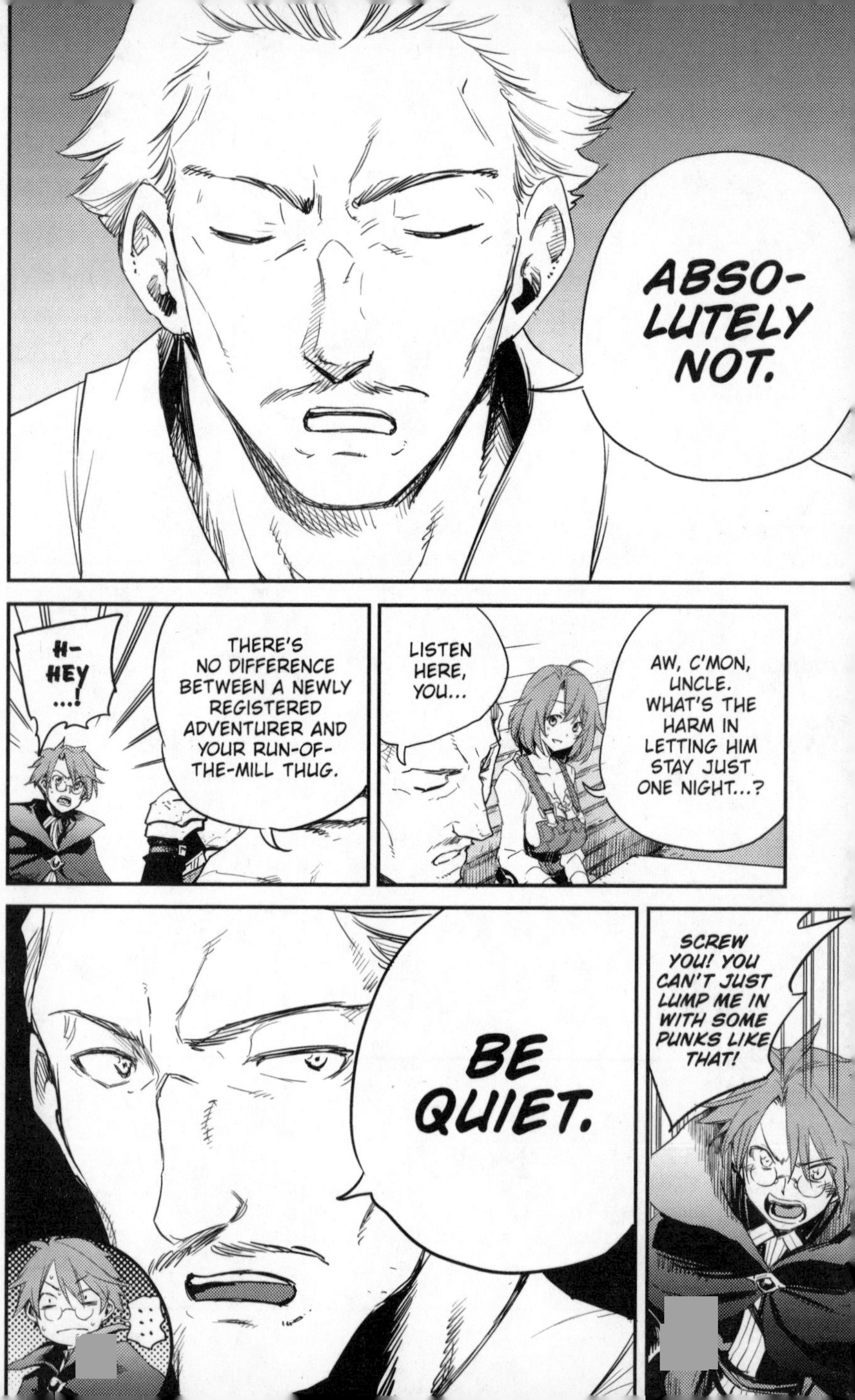
ABSO-LUTELY NOT.
AW, C'MON, UNCLE. WHAT'S THE HARM IN LETTING HIM STAY JUST ONE NIGHT...?
LISTEN HERE, YOU...
THERE'S NO DIFFERENCE BETWEEN A NEWLY REGISTERED ADVENTURER AND YOUR RUN-OF-THE-MILL THUG.
H-HEY...!
SCREW YOU! YOU CAN'T JUST LUMP ME IN WITH SOME PUNKS LIKE THAT!
BE QUIET.

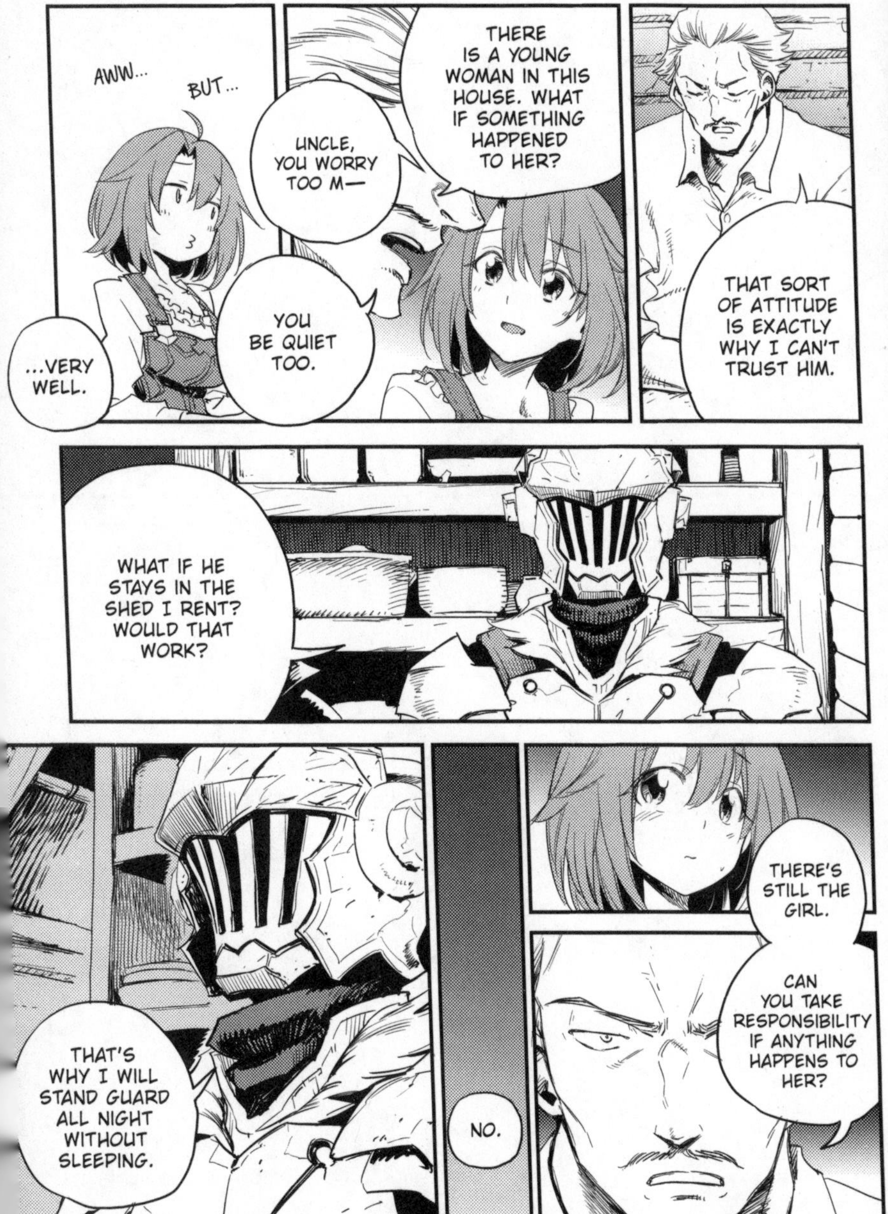
THAT SORT OF ATTITUDE IS EXACTLY WHY I CAN'T TRUST HIM.
THERE IS A YOUNG WOMAN IN THIS HOUSE. WHAT IF SOMETHING HAPPENED TO HER?
UNCLE, YOU WORRY TOO M—
YOU BE QUIET TOO.
AWW...
BUT...
...VERY WELL.
WHAT IF HE STAYS IN THE SHED I RENT? WOULD THAT WORK?
THERE'S STILL THE GIRL.
CAN YOU TAKE RESPONSIBILITY IF ANYTHING HAPPENS TO HER?
NO.
THAT'S WHY I WILL STAND GUARD ALL NIGHT WITHOUT SLEEPING.

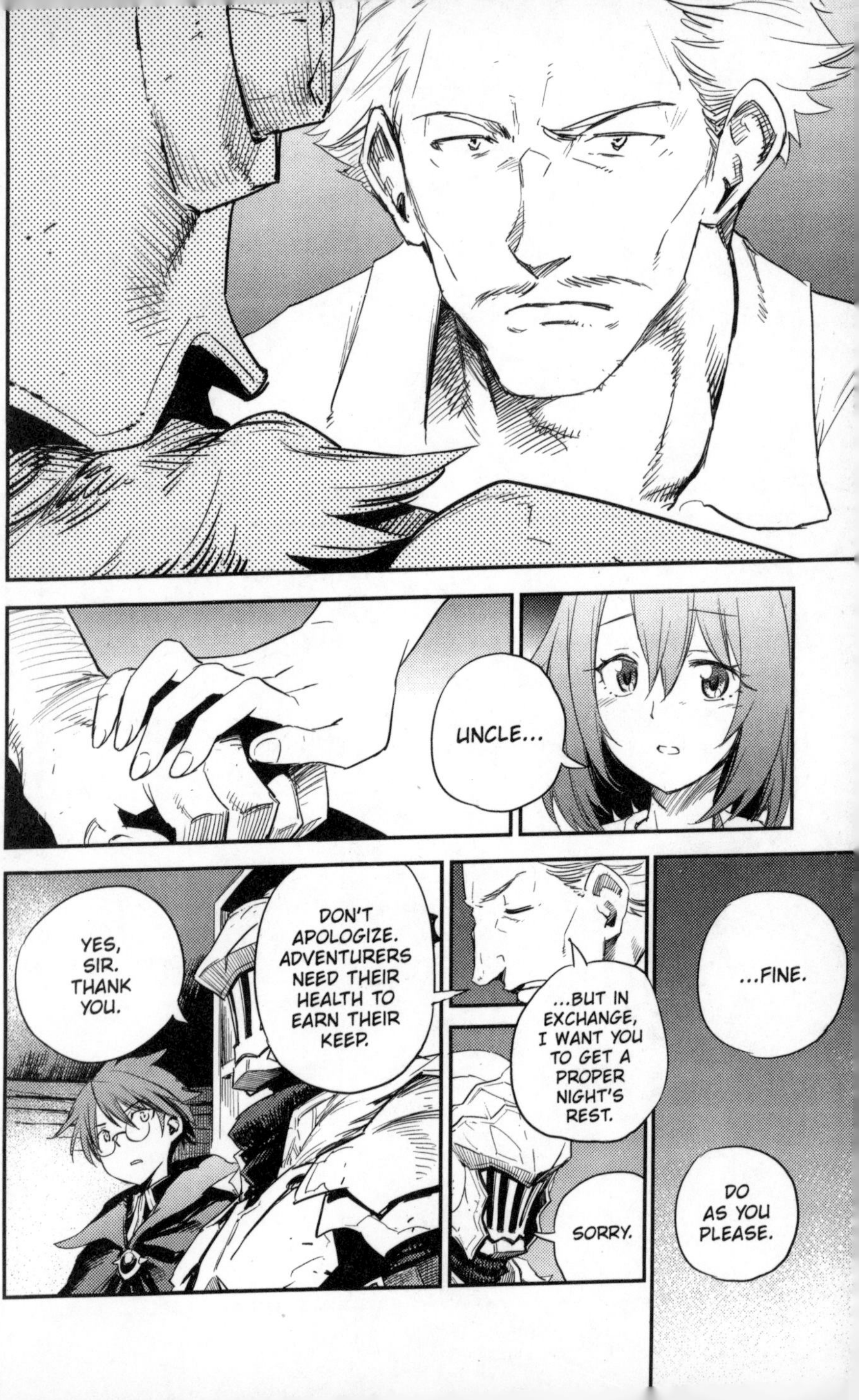
UNCLE...
...FINE.
DO AS YOU PLEASE.
...BUT IN EXCHANGE, I WANT YOU TO GET A PROPER NIGHT'S REST.
SORRY.
DON'T APOLOGIZE. ADVENTURERS NEED THEIR HEALTH TO EARN THEIR KEEP.
YES, SIR. THANK YOU.

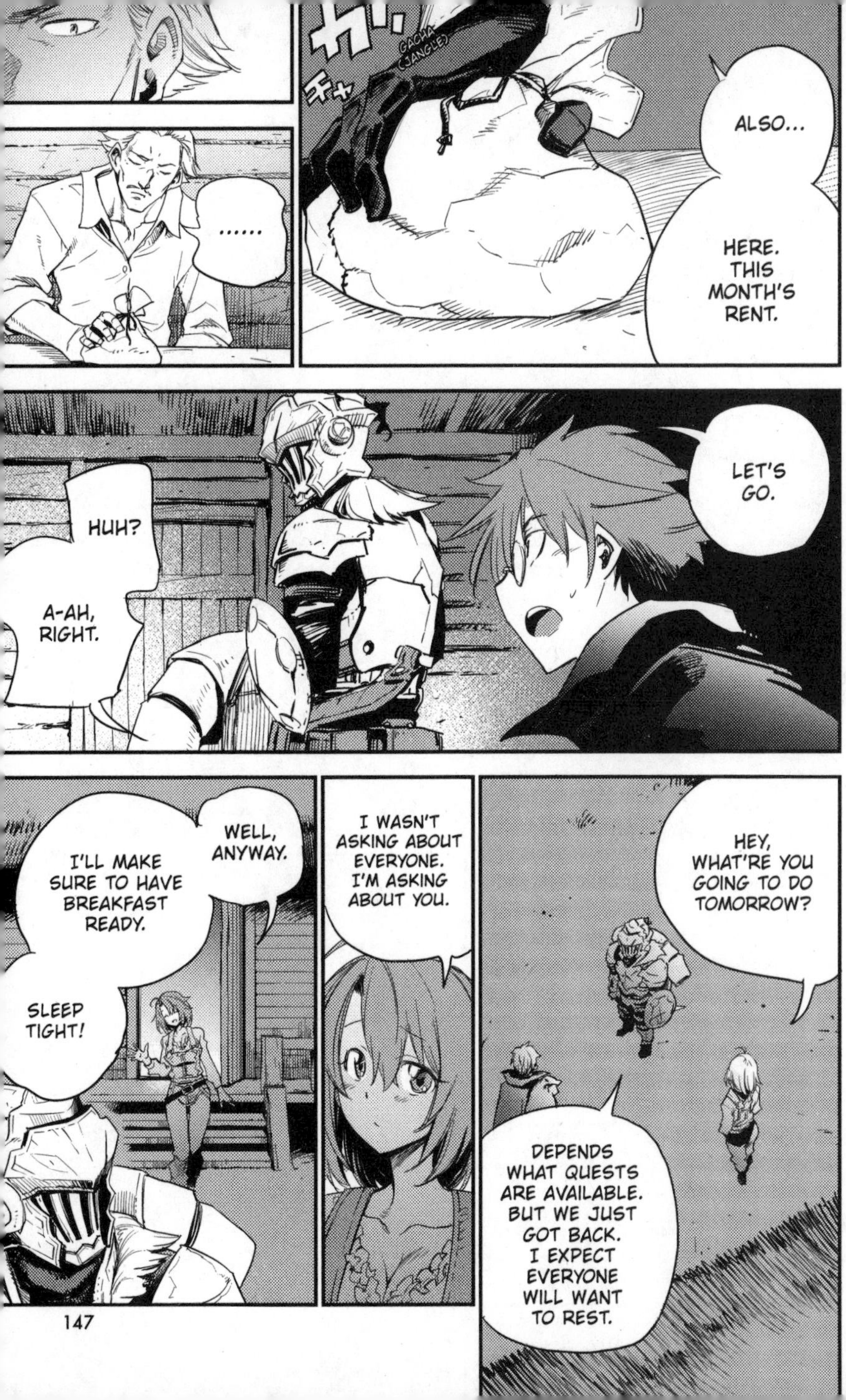
GACHA (JANGLE)
ALSO...
HERE. THIS MONTH'S RENT.
......
LET'S GO.
HUH?
A-AH, RIGHT.
HEY, WHAT'RE YOU GOING TO DO TOMORROW?
DEPENDS WHAT QUESTS ARE AVAILABLE. BUT WE JUST GOT BACK. I EXPECT EVERYONE WILL WANT TO REST.
I WASN'T ASKING ABOUT EVERYONE. I'M ASKING ABOUT YOU.
WELL, ANYWAY.
I'LL MAKE SURE TO HAVE BREAKFAST READY.
SLEEP TIGHT!

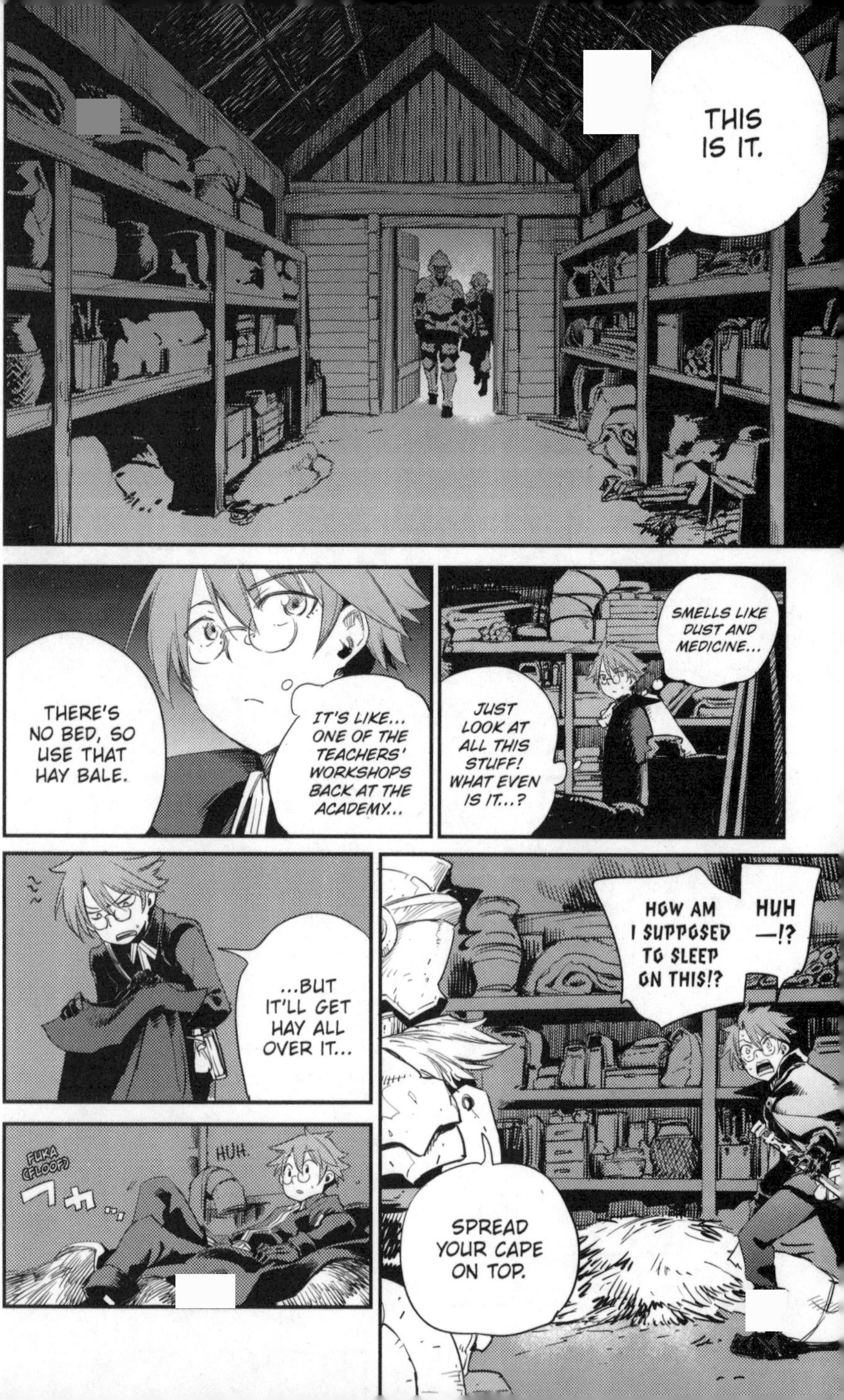
THIS IS IT.
SMELLS LIKE DUST AND MEDICINE...
JUST LOOK AT ALL THIS STUFF! WHAT EVEN IS IT...?
IT'S LIKE... ONE OF THE TEACHERS' WORKSHOPS BACK AT THE ACADEMY...
THERE'S NO BED, SO USE THAT HAY BALE.
HUH—!?
HOW AM I SUPPOSED TO SLEEP ON THIS!?
SPREAD YOUR CAPE ON TOP.
...BUT IT'LL GET HAY ALL OVER IT...
HUH.
FUKA (FLOOF)

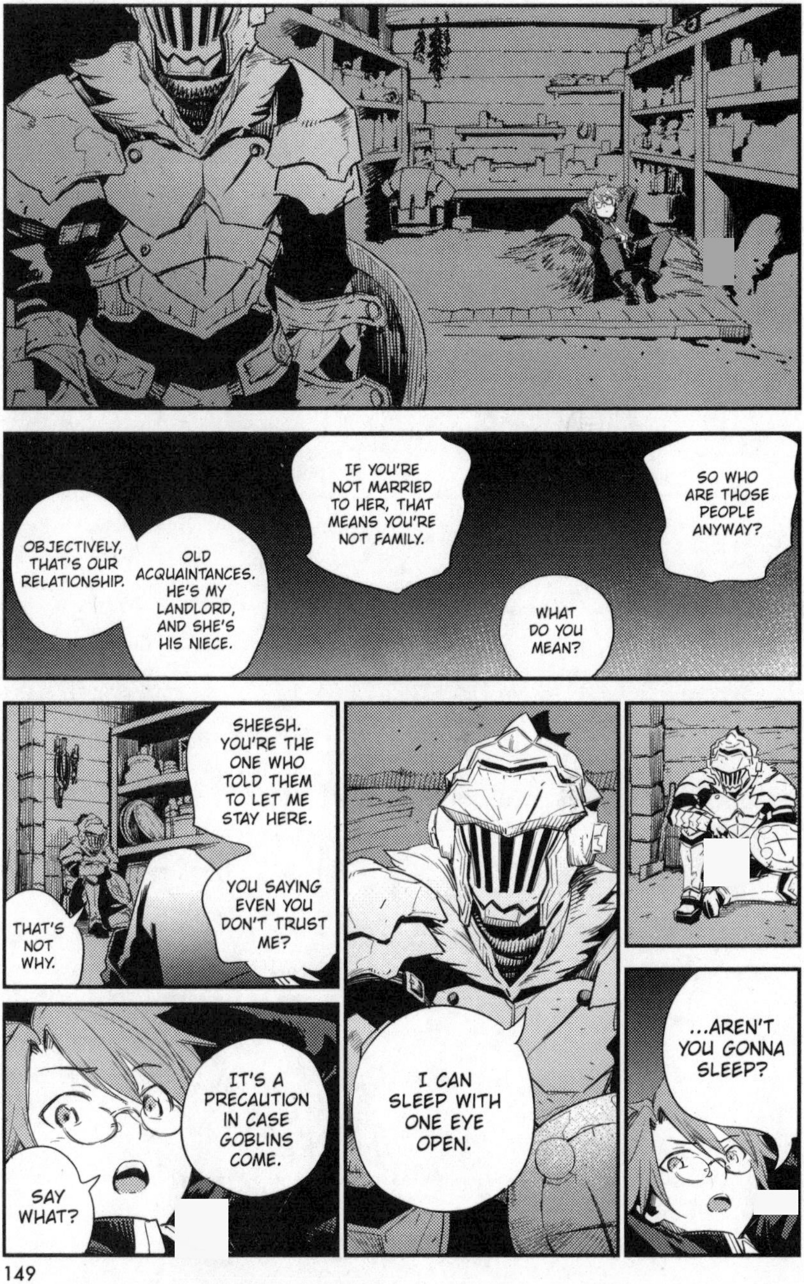
SO WHO ARE THOSE PEOPLE ANYWAY?
IF YOU'RE NOT MARRIED TO HER, THAT MEANS YOU'RE NOT FAMILY.
WHAT DO YOU MEAN?
OLD ACQUAINTANCES. HE'S MY LANDLORD, AND SHE'S HIS NIECE.
OBJECTIVELY, THAT'S OUR RELATIONSHIP.
...AREN'T YOU GONNA SLEEP?
I CAN SLEEP WITH ONE EYE OPEN.
SHEESH. YOU'RE THE ONE WHO TOLD THEM TO LET ME STAY HERE.
YOU SAYING EVEN YOU DON'T TRUST ME?
THAT'S NOT WHY.
IT'S A PRECAUTION IN CASE GOBLINS COME.
SAY WHAT?

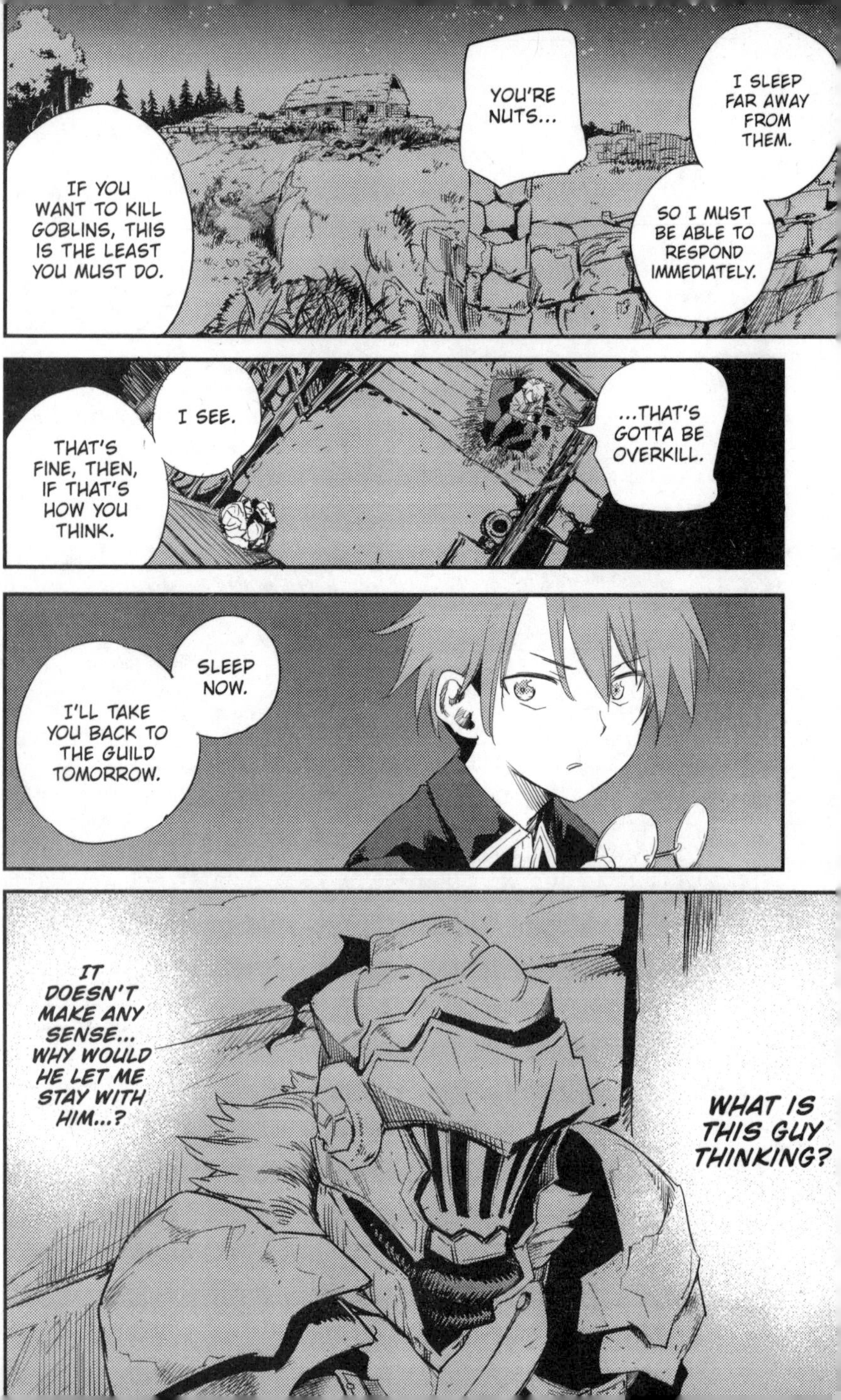
I SLEEP FAR AWAY FROM THEM.
SO I MUST BE ABLE TO RESPOND IMMEDIATELY.
YOU'RE NUTS...
IF YOU WANT TO KILL GOBLINS, THIS IS THE LEAST YOU MUST DO.
...THAT'S GOTTA BE OVERKILL.
I SEE.
THAT'S FINE, THEN, IF THAT'S HOW YOU THINK.
SLEEP NOW.
I'LL TAKE YOU BACK TO THE GUILD TOMORROW.
IT DOESN'T MAKE ANY SENSE... WHY WOULD HE LET ME STAY WITH HIM...?
WHAT IS THIS GUY THINKING?

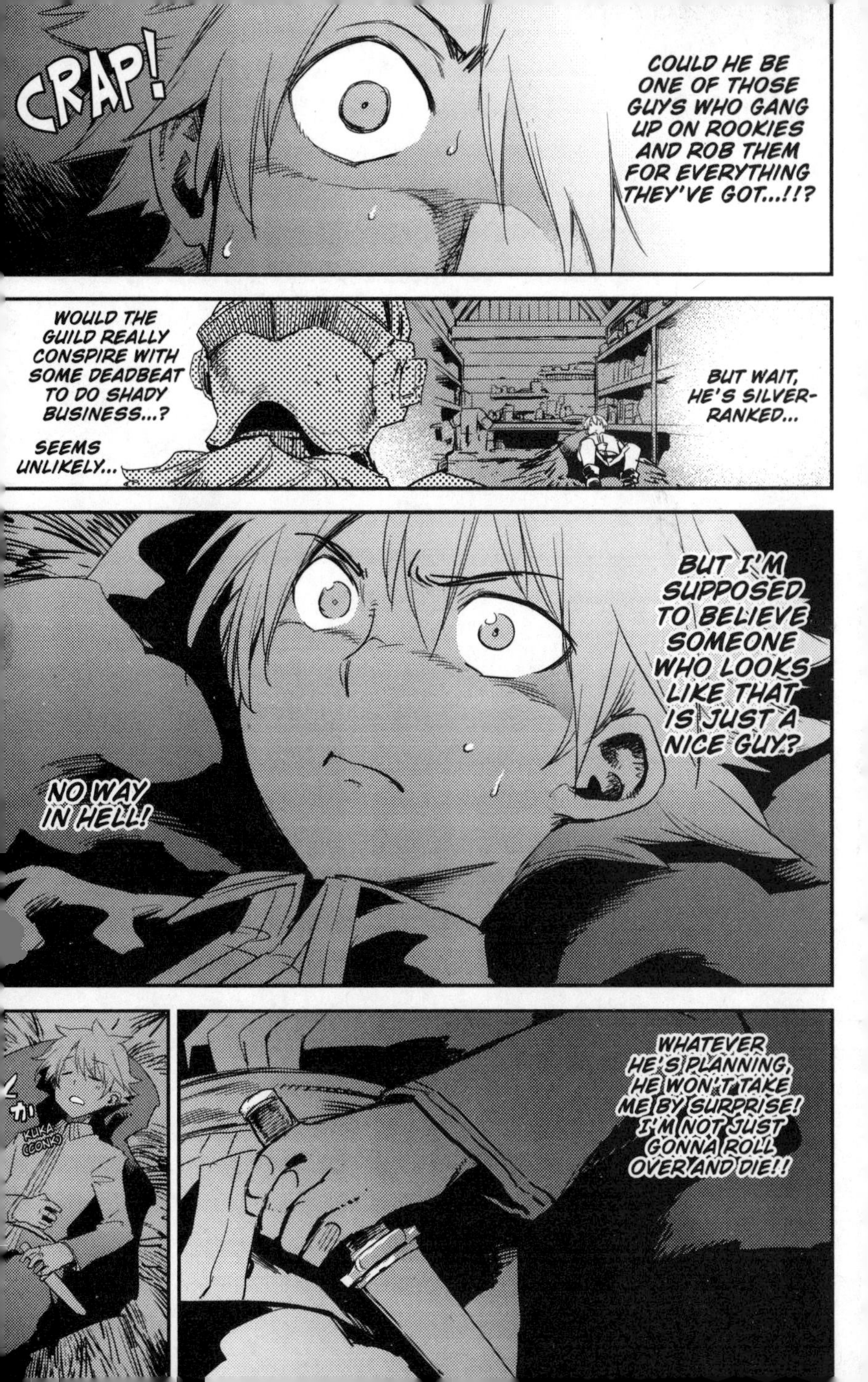
COULD HE BE ONE OF THOSE GUYS WHO GANG UP ON ROOKIES AND ROB THEM FOR EVERYTHING THEY'VE GOT...!!?
CRAP!
BUT WAIT, HE'S SILVER-RANKED...
WOULD THE GUILD REALLY CONSPIRE WITH SOME DEADBEAT TO DO SHADY BUSINESS...?
SEEMS UNLIKELY...
BUT I'M SUPPOSED TO BELIEVE SOMEONE WHO LOOKS LIKE THAT IS JUST A NICE GUY?
NO WAY IN HELL!
WHATEVER HE'S PLANNING, HE WON'T TAKE ME BY SURPRISE! I'M NOT JUST GONNA ROLL OVER AND DIE!!
KUKA (CONK)

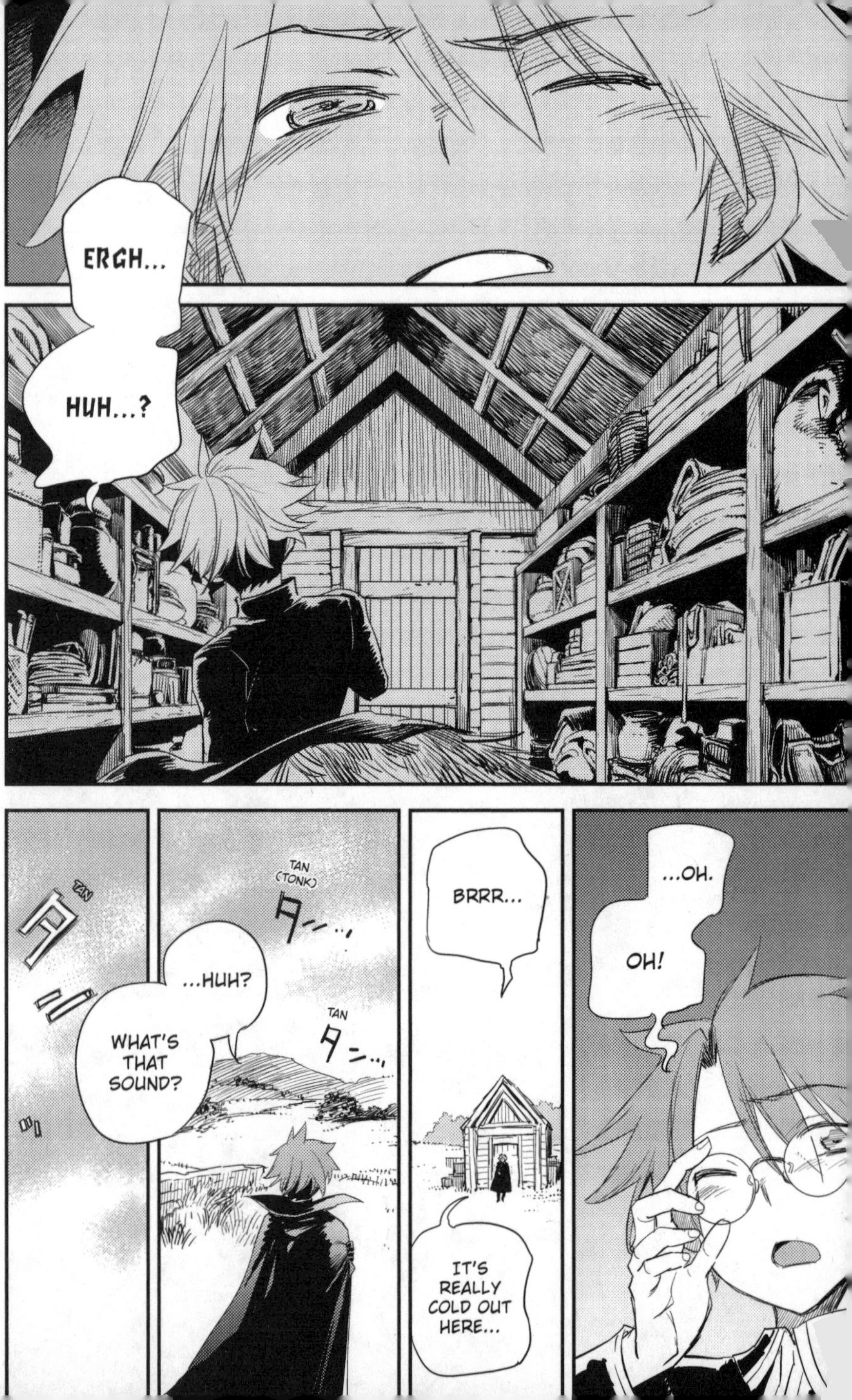
ERGH...
HUH...?
...OH.
OH!
BRRR...
IT'S REALLY COLD OUT HERE...
TAN (TONK)
...HUH?
WHAT'S THAT SOUND?
TAN
TAN

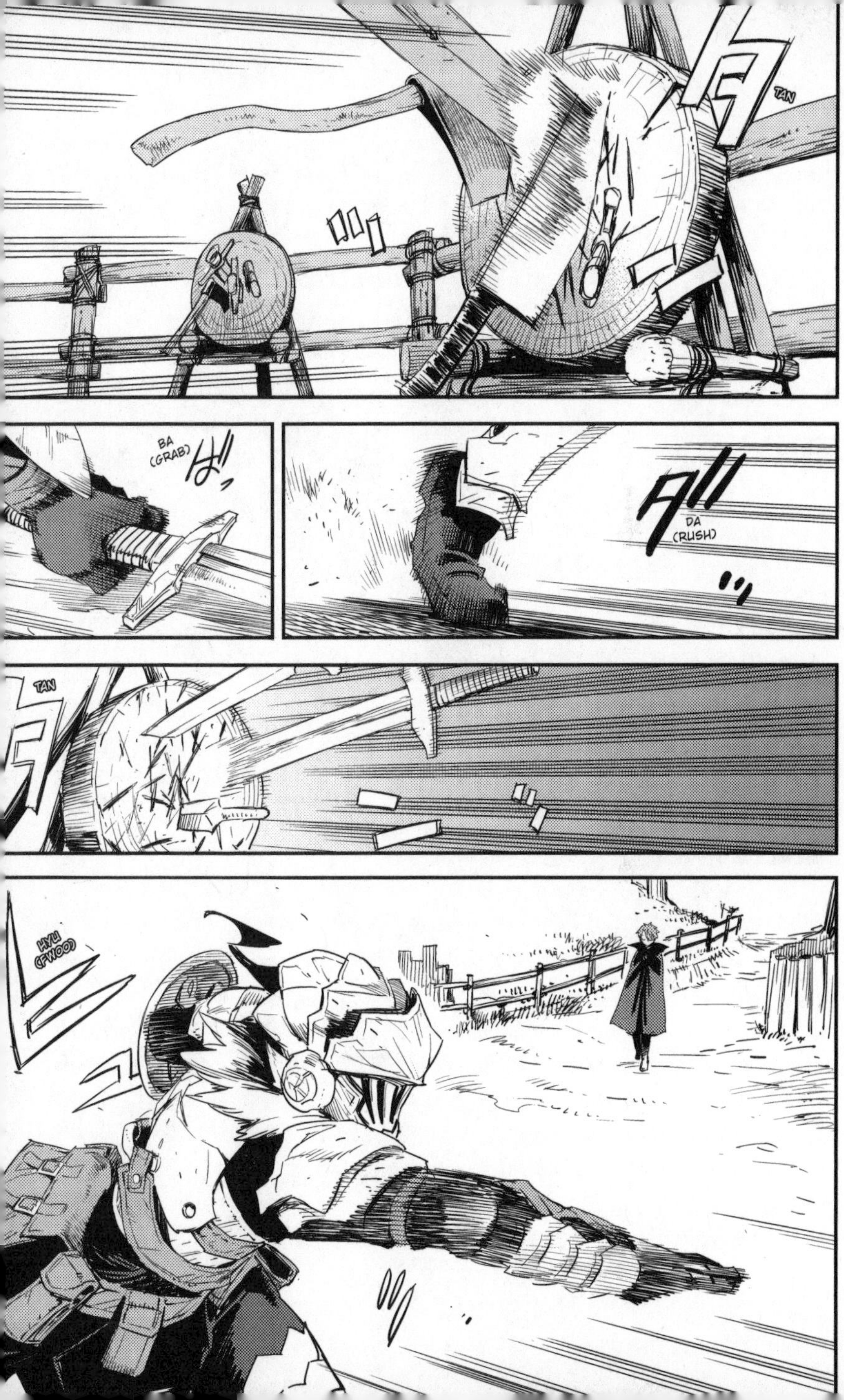
TAN
DA (RUSH)
BA (GRAB)
TAN
HYU (FWOO)

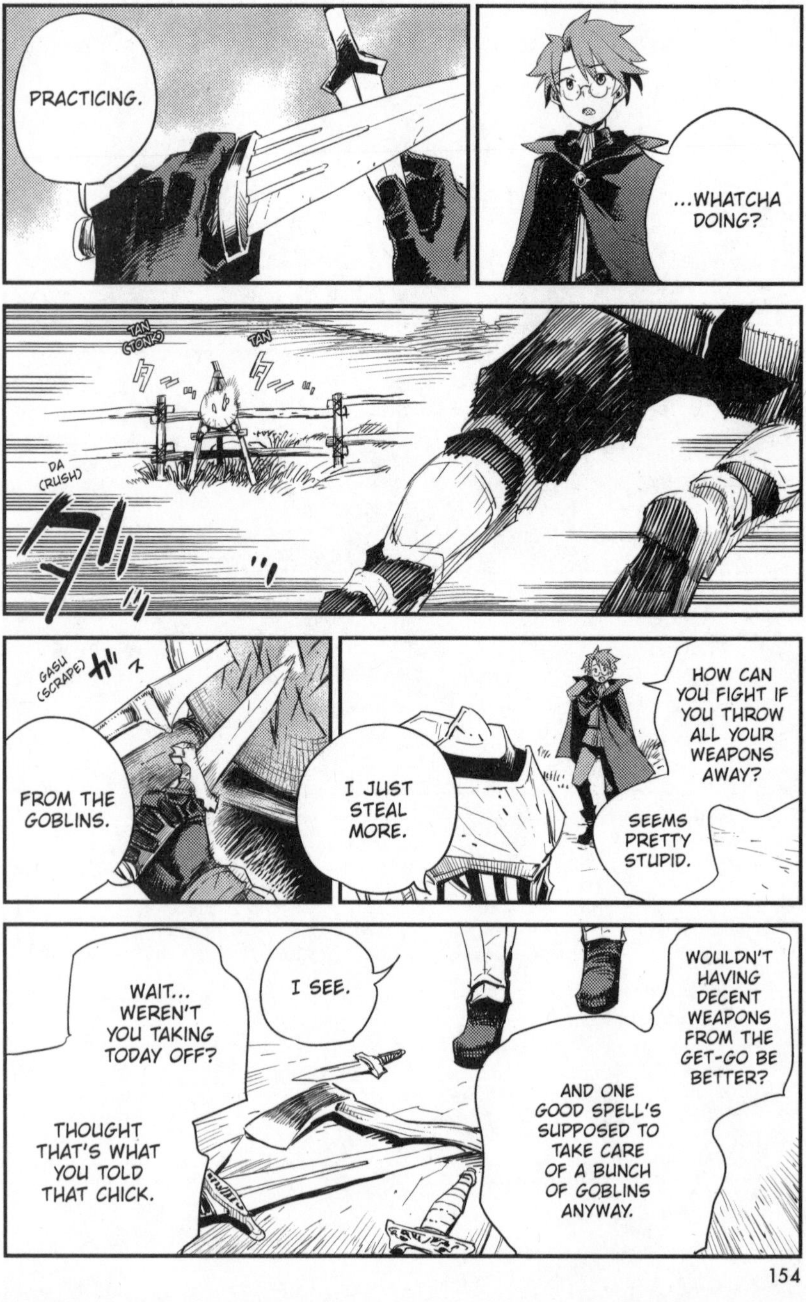
...WHATCHA DOING?
PRACTICING.
TAN
TAN (TONK)
DA (RUSH)
HOW CAN YOU FIGHT IF YOU THROW ALL YOUR WEAPONS AWAY?
SEEMS PRETTY STUPID.
I JUST STEAL MORE.
GASU (SCRAPE)
FROM THE GOBLINS.
WOULDN'T HAVING DECENT WEAPONS FROM THE GET-GO BE BETTER?
AND ONE GOOD SPELL'S SUPPOSED TO TAKE CARE OF A BUNCH OF GOBLINS ANYWAY.
I SEE.
WAIT... WEREN'T YOU TAKING TODAY OFF?
THOUGHT THAT'S WHAT YOU TOLD THAT CHICK.

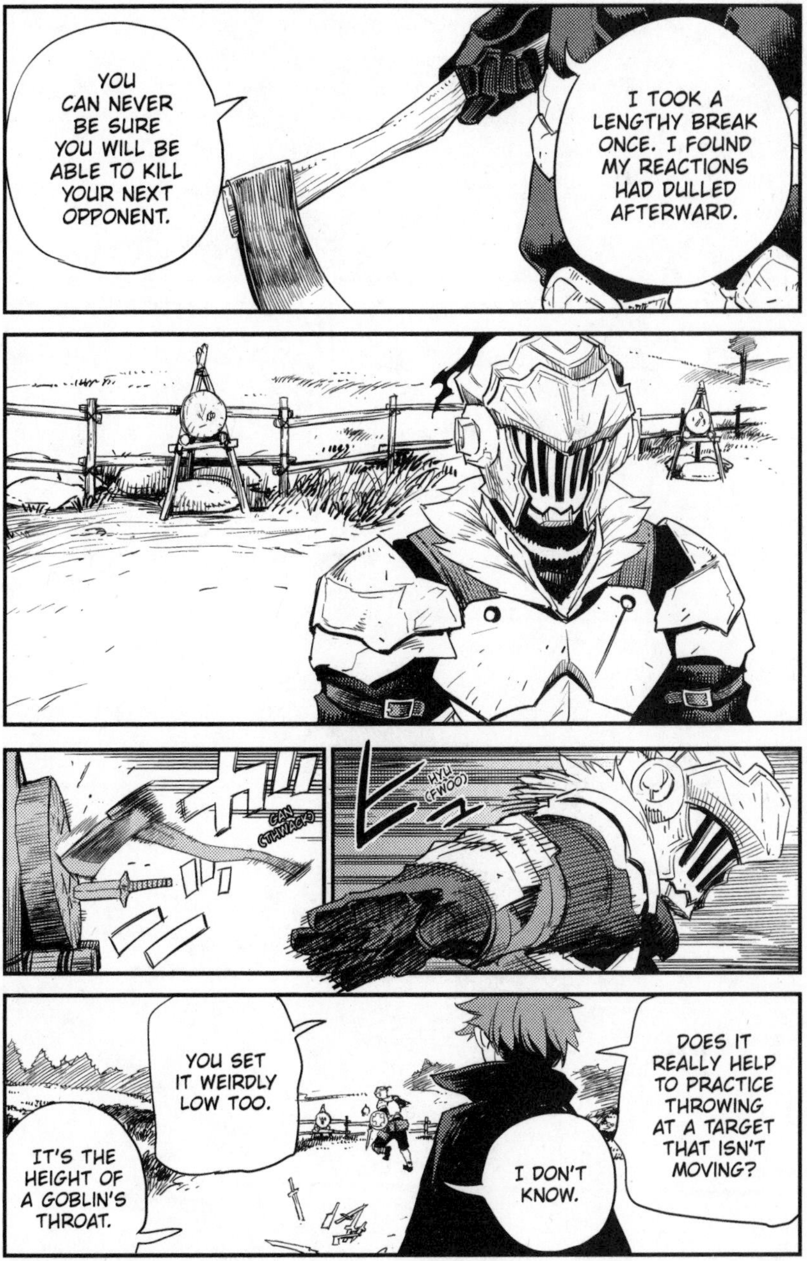
I TOOK A LENGTHY BREAK ONCE. I FOUND MY REACTIONS HAD DULLED AFTERWARD.
YOU CAN NEVER BE SURE YOU WILL BE ABLE TO KILL YOUR NEXT OPPONENT.
HYU (FWOO)
GAN (THWACK)
DOES IT REALLY HELP TO PRACTICE THROWING AT A TARGET THAT ISN'T MOVING?
I DON'T KNOW.
YOU SET IT WEIRDLY LOW TOO.
IT'S THE HEIGHT OF A GOBLIN'S THROAT.

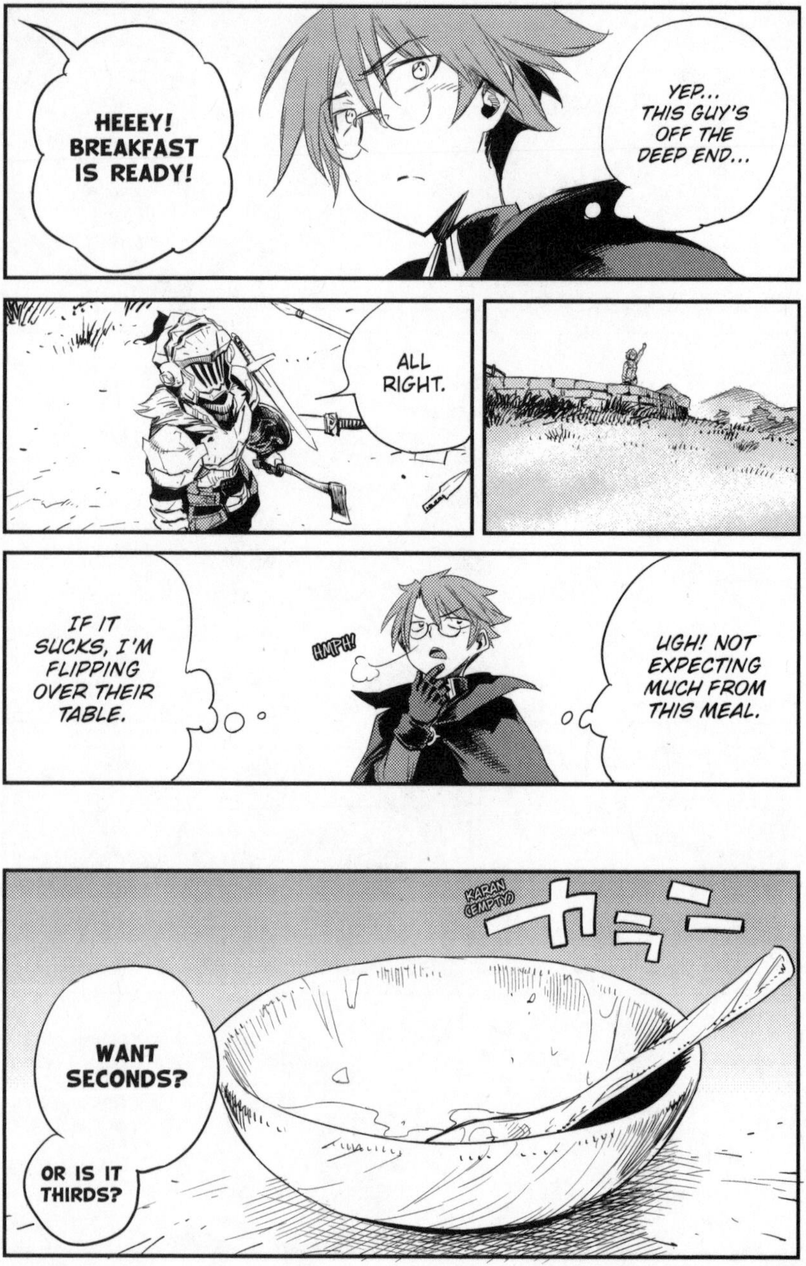
YEP... THIS GUY'S OFF THE DEEP END...
HEEEY! BREAKFAST IS READY!
ALL RIGHT.
UGH! NOT EXPECTING MUCH FROM THIS MEAL.
HMPH!
IF IT SUCKS, I'M FLIPPING OVER THEIR TABLE.
KARAN (EMPTY)
WANT SECONDS?
OR IS IT THIRDS?

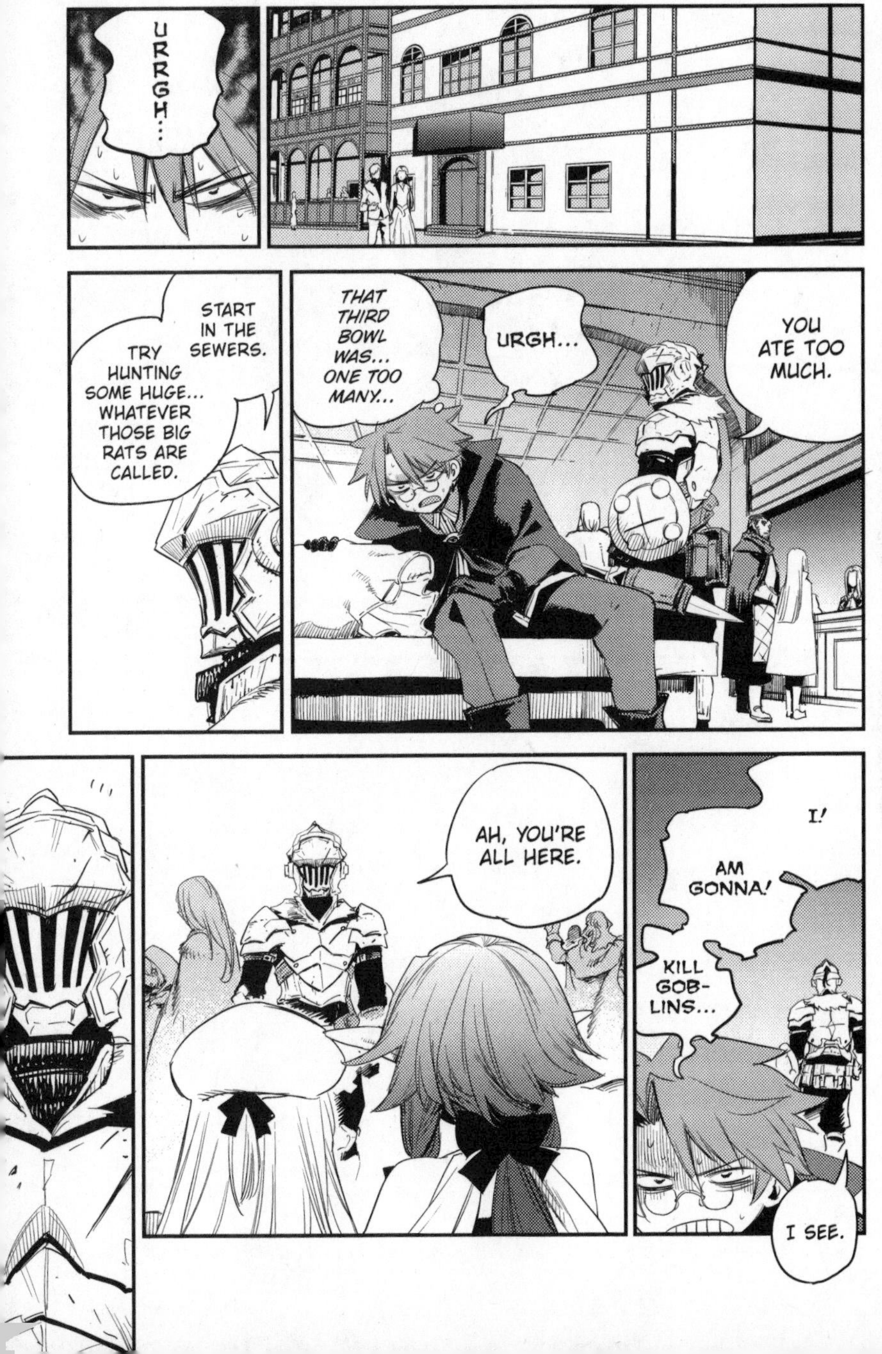
URRGH...
YOU ATE TOO MUCH.
URGH...
THAT THIRD BOWL WAS... ONE TOO MANY...
START IN THE SEWERS.
TRY HUNTING SOME HUGE... WHATEVER THOSE BIG RATS ARE CALLED.
I!
AM GONNA!
KILL GOB-LINS...
I SEE.
AH, YOU'RE ALL HERE.

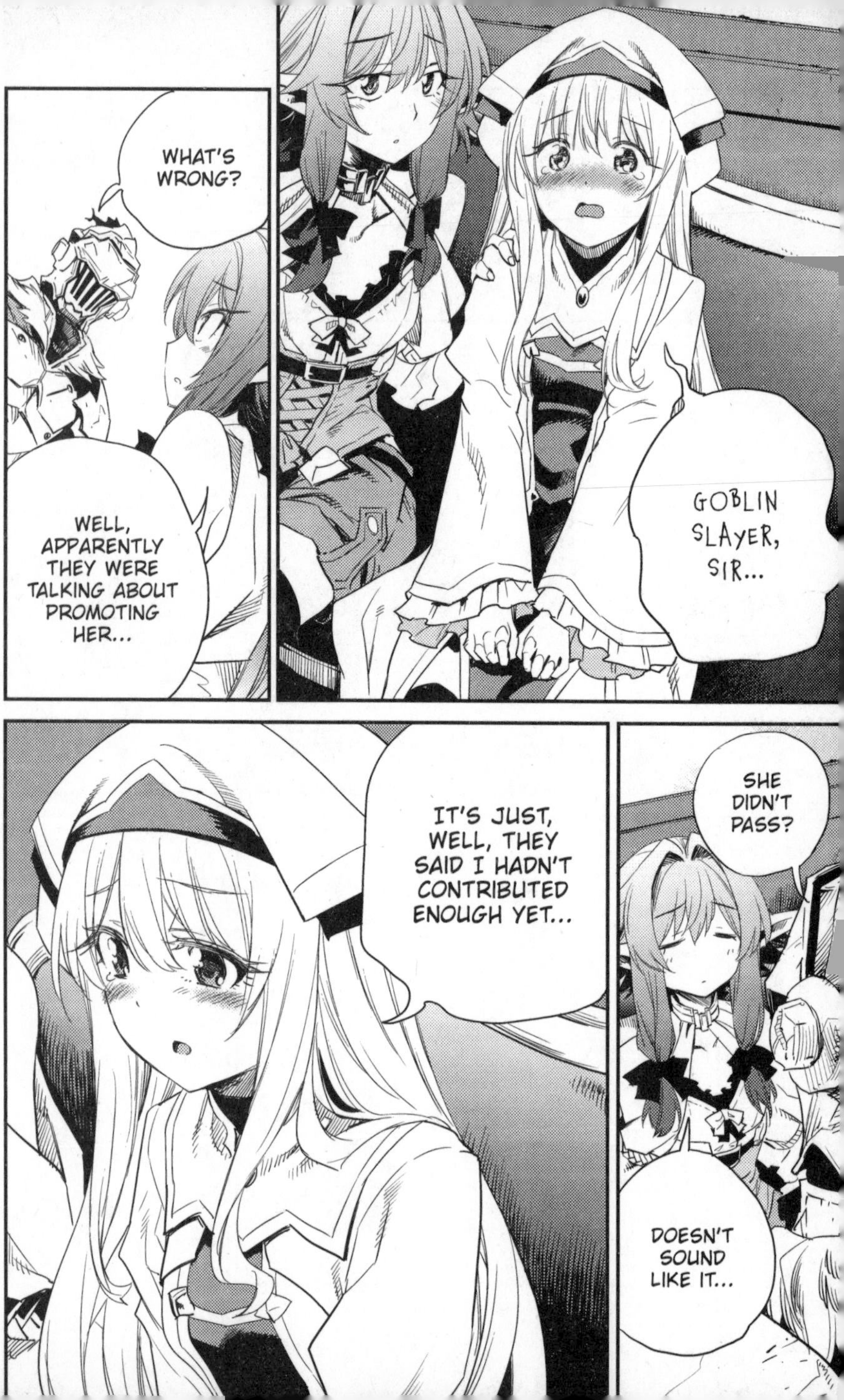
GOBLIN SLAYER, SIR...
WHAT'S WRONG?
WELL, APPARENTLY THEY WERE TALKING ABOUT PROMOTING HER...
SHE DIDN'T PASS?
DOESN'T SOUND LIKE IT...
IT'S JUST, WELL, THEY SAID I HADN'T CONTRIBUTED ENOUGH YET...

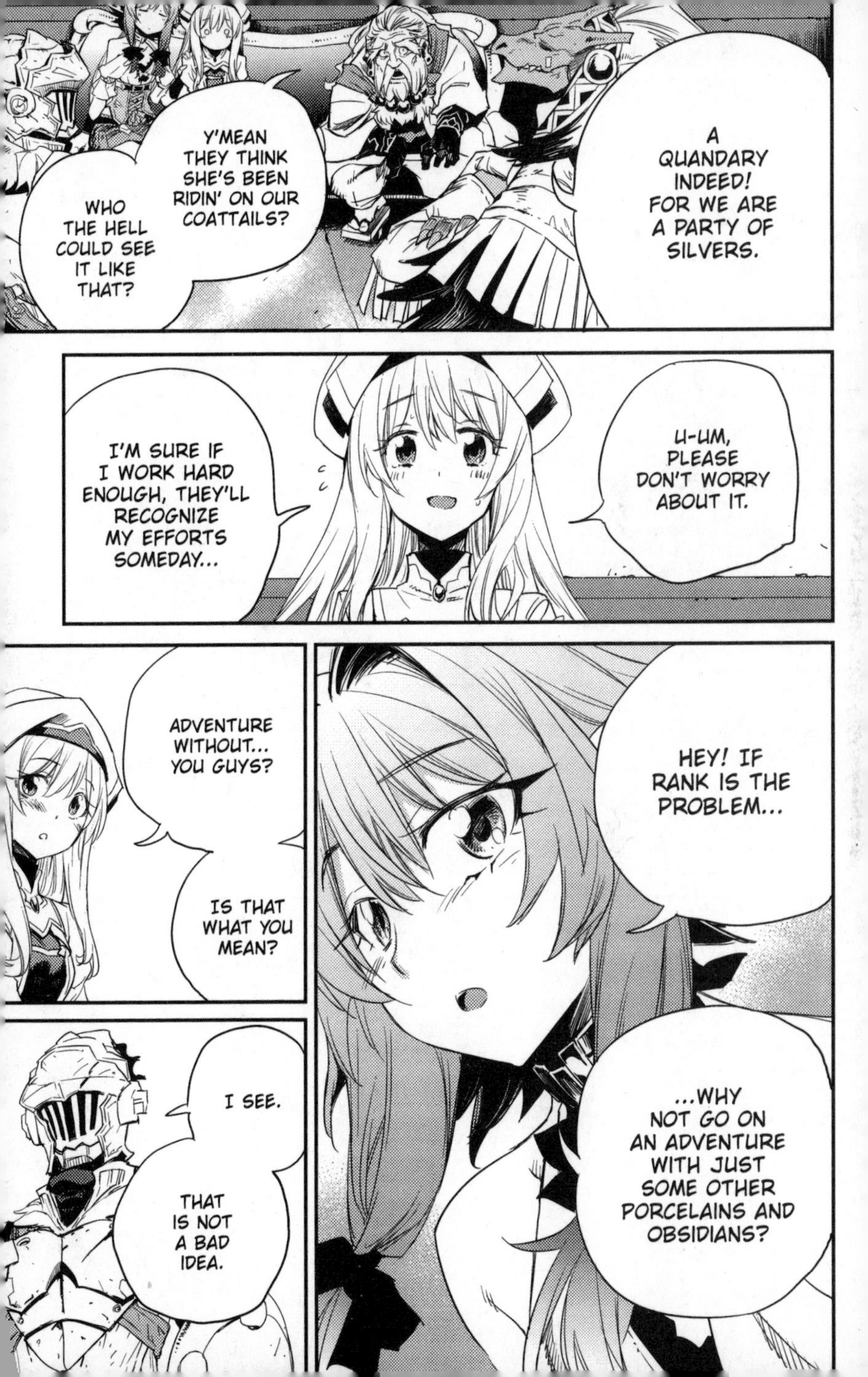
A QUANDARY INDEED! FOR WE ARE A PARTY OF SILVERS.
Y'MEAN THEY THINK SHE'S BEEN RIDIN' ON OUR COATTAILS?
WHO THE HELL COULD SEE IT LIKE THAT?
U-UM, PLEASE DON'T WORRY ABOUT IT.
I'M SURE IF I WORK HARD ENOUGH, THEY'LL RECOGNIZE MY EFFORTS SOMEDAY...
HEY! IF RANK IS THE PROBLEM...
...WHY NOT GO ON AN ADVENTURE WITH JUST SOME OTHER PORCELAINS AND OBSIDIANS?
ADVENTURE WITHOUT... YOU GUYS?
IS THAT WHAT YOU MEAN?
I SEE.
THAT IS NOT A BAD IDEA.

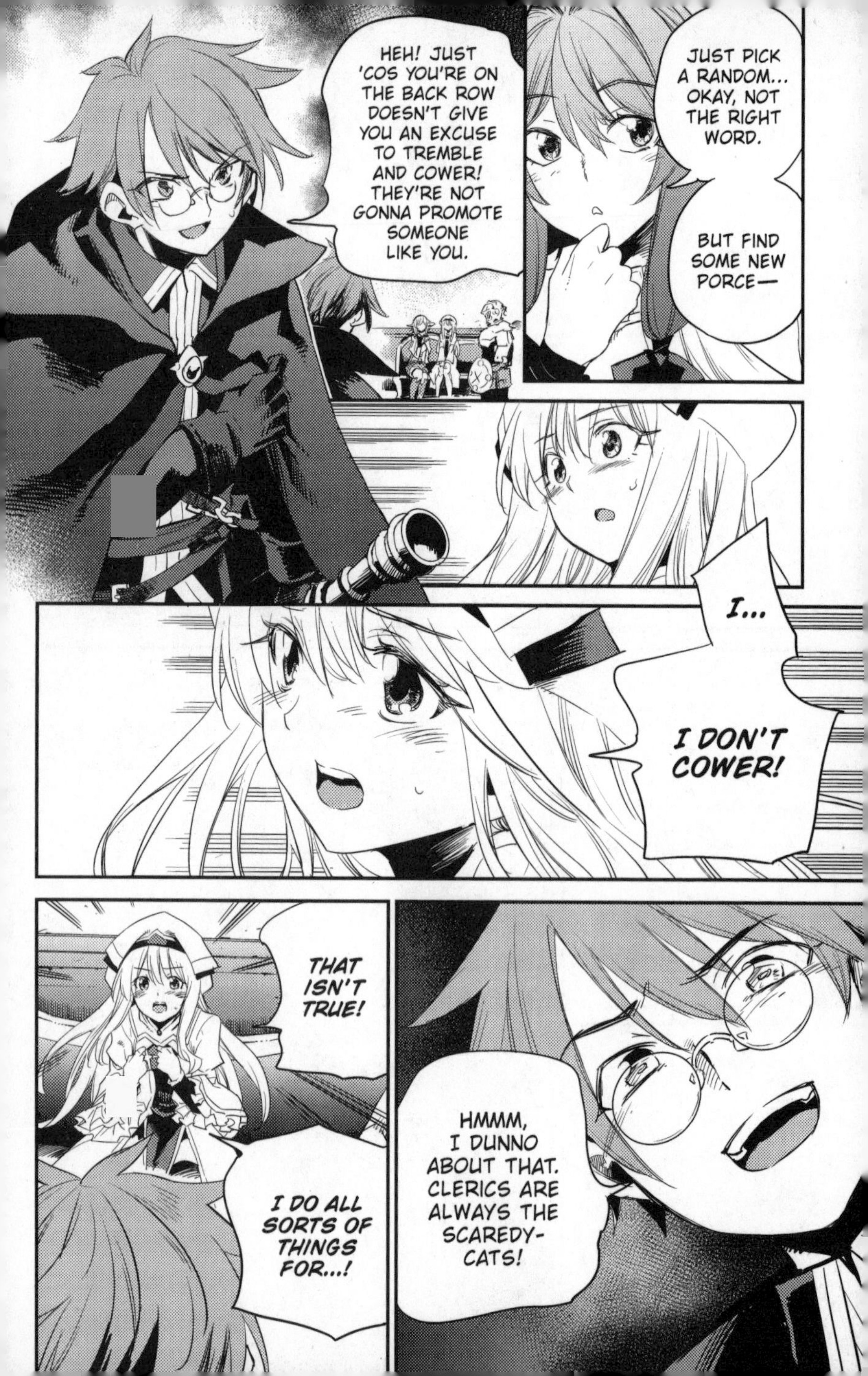
JUST PICK A RANDOM... OKAY, NOT THE RIGHT WORD.
BUT FIND SOME NEW PORCE—
HEH! JUST 'COS YOU'RE ON THE BACK ROW DOESN'T GIVE YOU AN EXCUSE TO TREMBLE AND COWER! THEY'RE NOT GONNA PROMOTE SOMEONE LIKE YOU.
I...
I DON'T COWER!
HMMM, I DUNNO ABOUT THAT. CLERICS ARE ALWAYS THE SCAREDY-CATS!
THAT ISN'T TRUE!
I DO ALL SORTS OF THINGS FOR...!

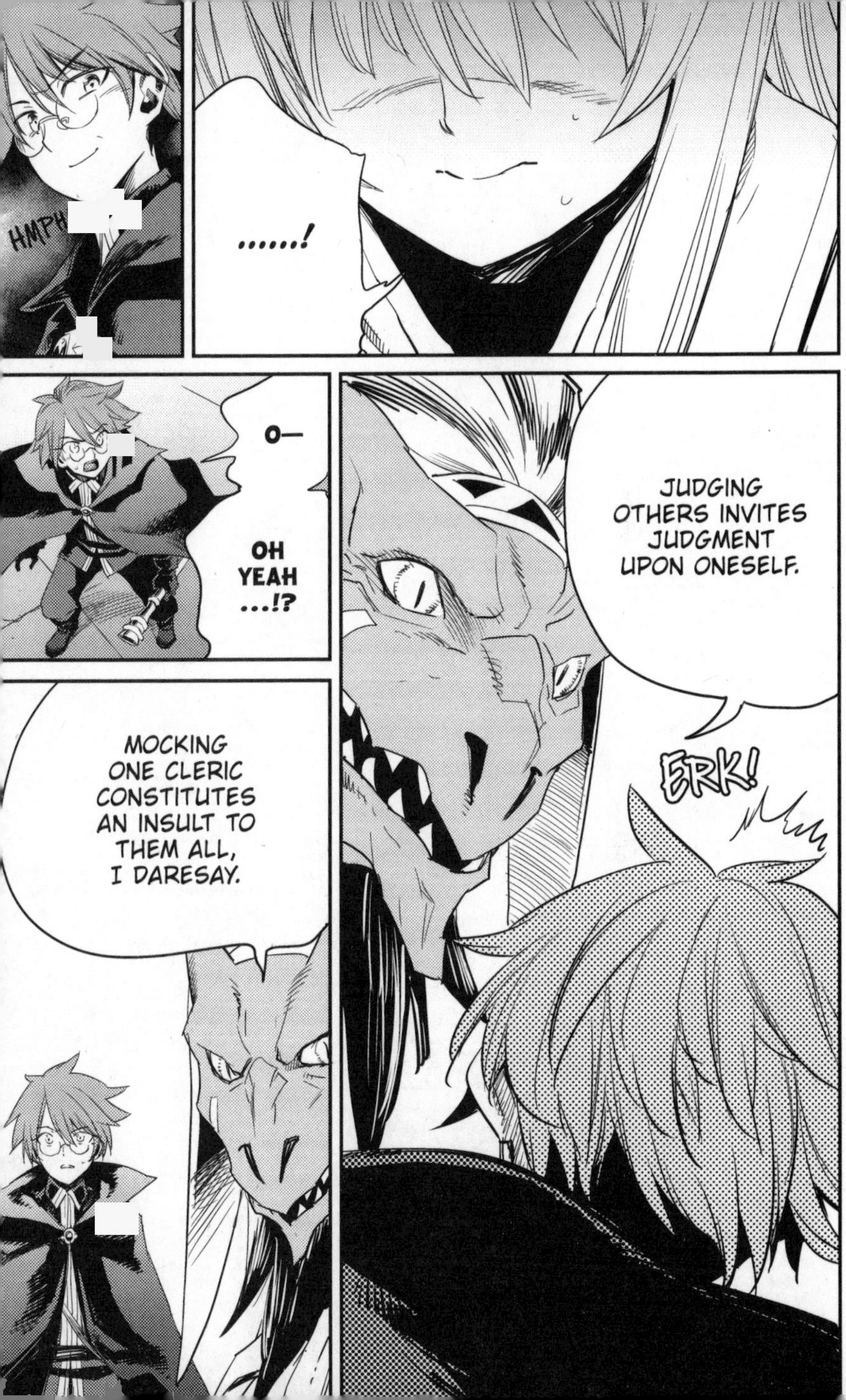
......!
HMPH
JUDGING OTHERS INVITES JUDGMENT UPON ONESELF.
ERK!
O—
OH YEAH ...!?
MOCKING ONE CLERIC CONSTITUTES AN INSULT TO THEM ALL, I DARESAY.

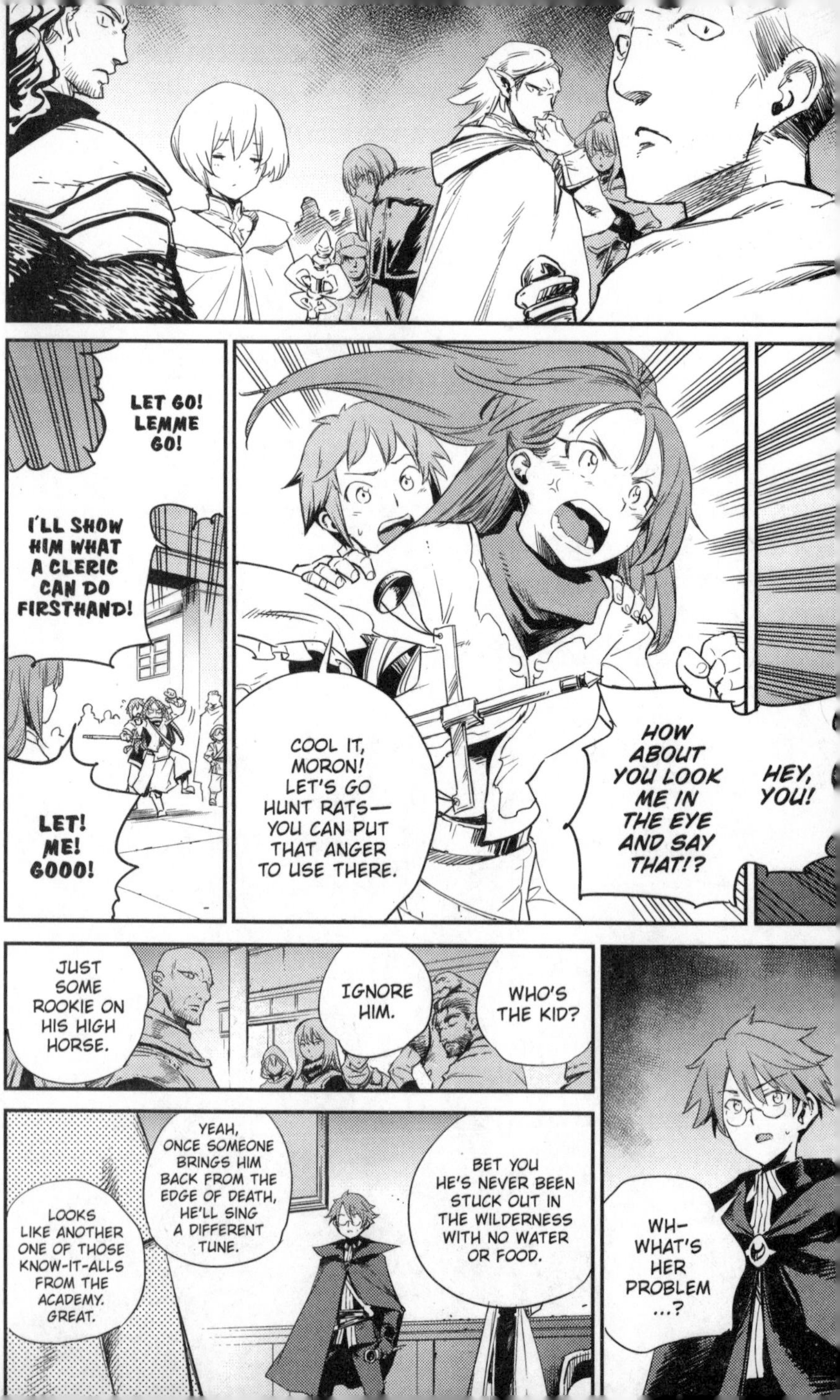

HEY, YOU!
HOW ABOUT YOU LOOK ME IN THE EYE AND SAY THAT!?
COOL IT, MORON! LET'S GO HUNT RATS—YOU CAN PUT THAT ANGER TO USE THERE.
LET GO! LEMME GO!
I'LL SHOW HIM WHAT A CLERIC CAN DO FIRSTHAND!
LET! ME! GOOO!
WH— WHAT'S HER PROBLEM …?
WHO'S THE KID?
IGNORE HIM.
JUST SOME ROOKIE ON HIS HIGH HORSE.
BET YOU HE'S NEVER BEEN STUCK OUT IN THE WILDERNESS WITH NO WATER OR FOOD.
YEAH, ONCE SOMEONE BRINGS HIM BACK FROM THE EDGE OF DEATH, HE'LL SING A DIFFERENT TUNE.
LOOKS LIKE ANOTHER ONE OF THOSE KNOW-IT-ALLS FROM THE ACADEMY. GREAT.

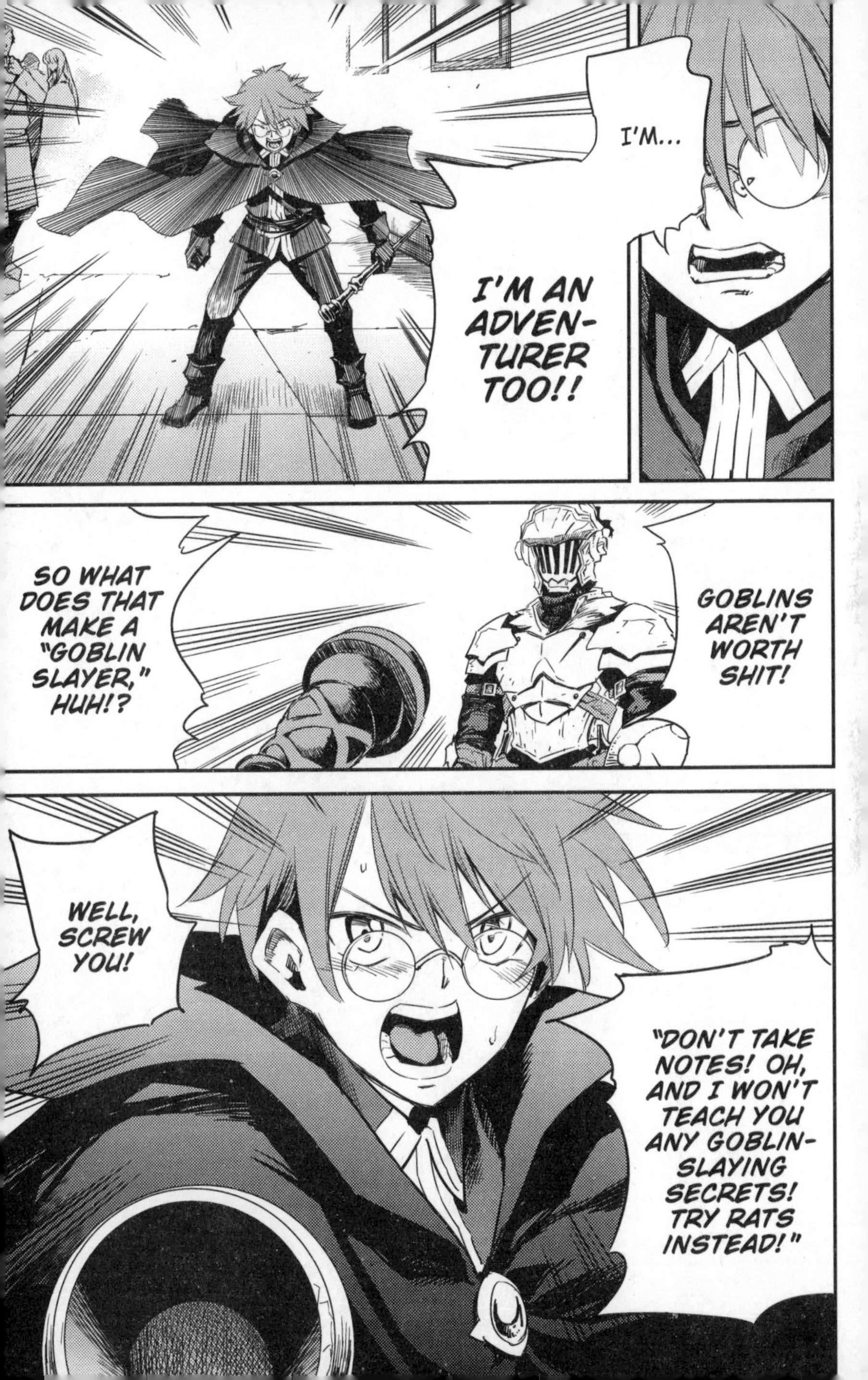
I'M...
I'M AN ADVENTURER TOO!!
GOBLINS AREN'T WORTH SHIT!
SO WHAT DOES THAT MAKE A "GOBLIN SLAYER," HUH!?
"DON'T TAKE NOTES! OH, AND I WON'T TEACH YOU ANY GOBLIN-SLAYING SECRETS! TRY RATS INSTEAD!"
WELL, SCREW YOU!

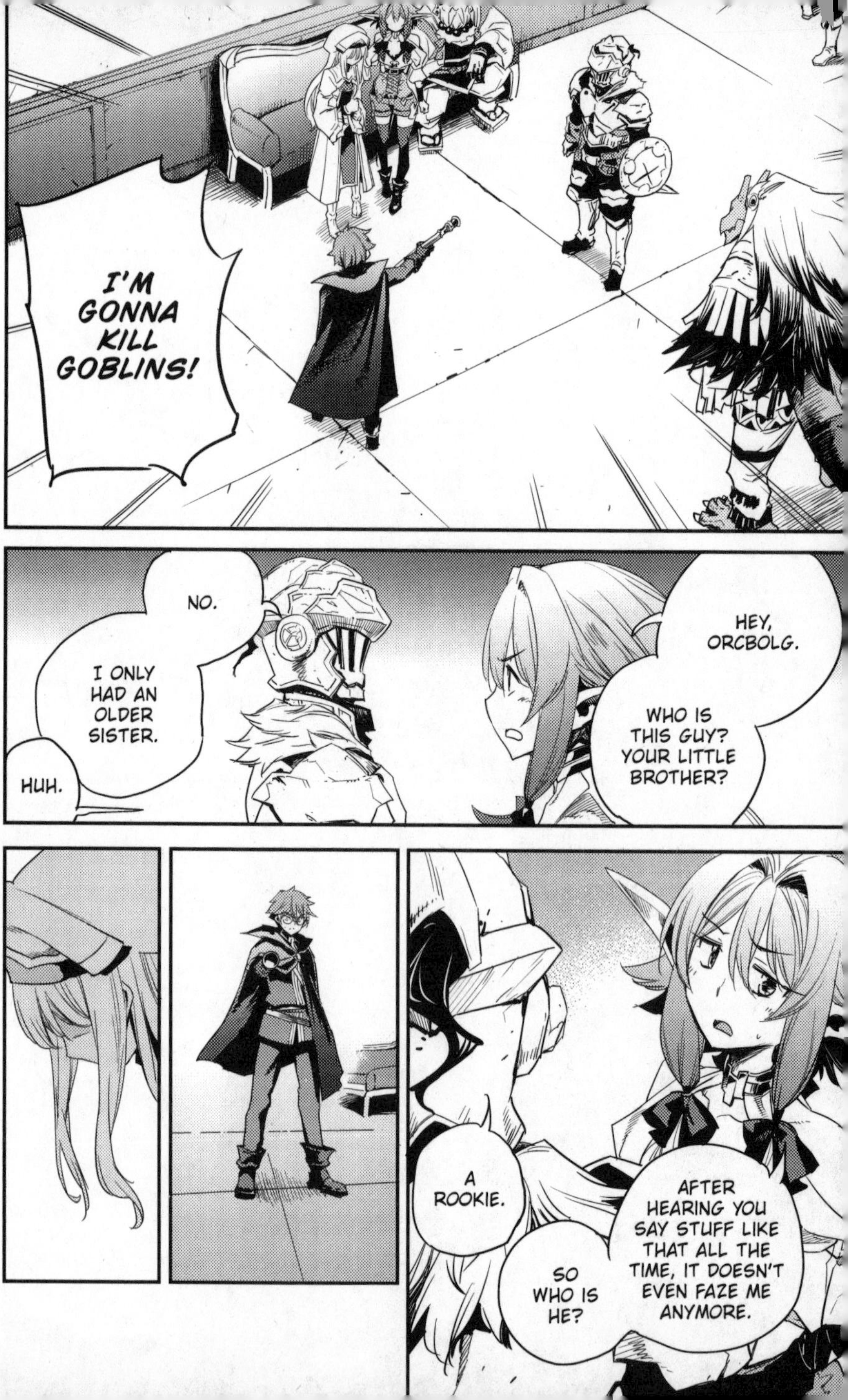
I'M GONNA KILL GOBLINS!
HEY, ORCBOLG.
WHO IS THIS GUY? YOUR LITTLE BROTHER?
NO.
I ONLY HAD AN OLDER SISTER.
HUH.
AFTER HEARING YOU SAY STUFF LIKE THAT ALL THE TIME, IT DOESN'T EVEN FAZE ME ANYMORE.
SO WHO IS HE?
A ROOKIE.

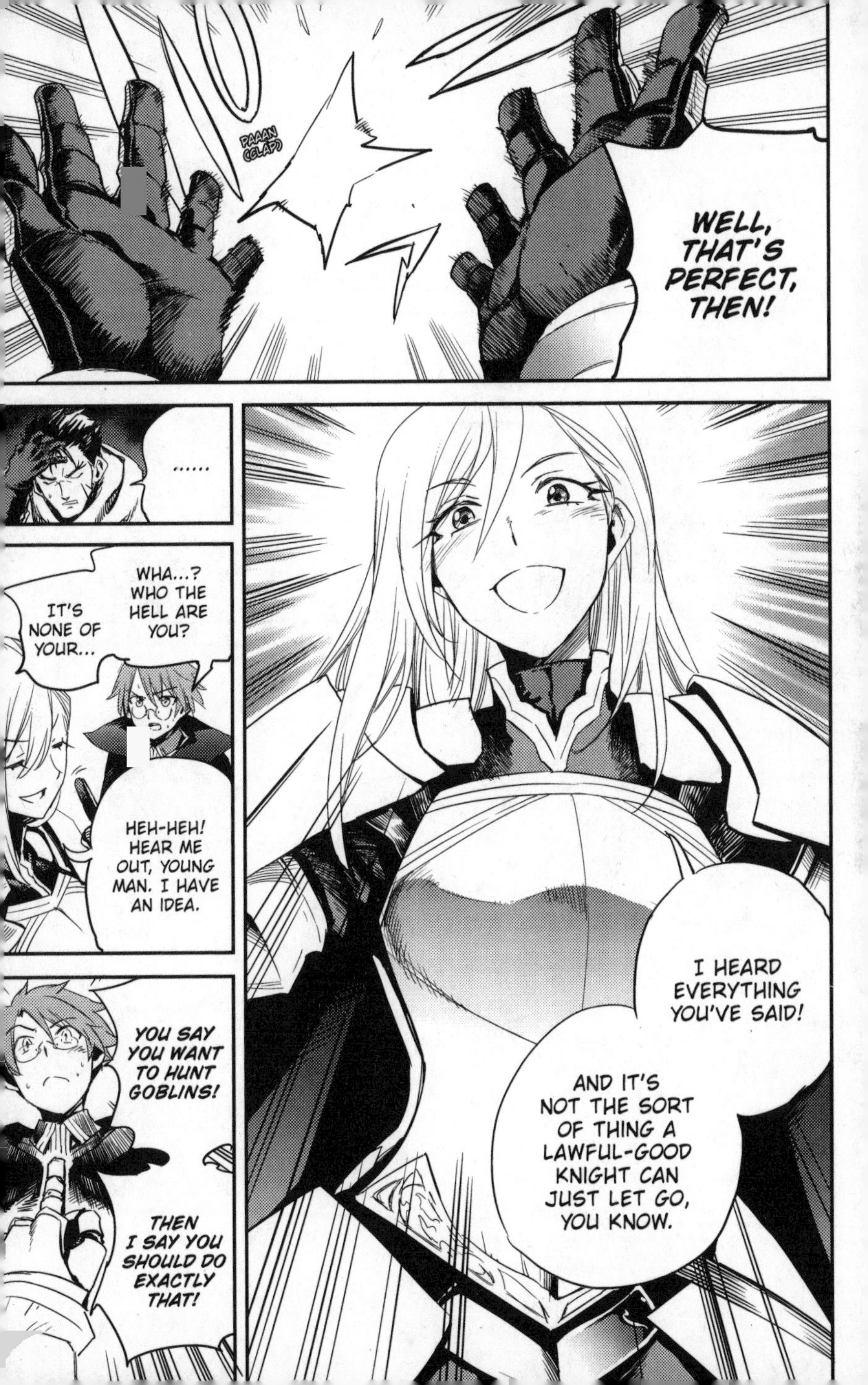
PAAAN (CLAP)
WELL, THAT'S PERFECT, THEN!
I HEARD EVERYTHING YOU'VE SAID!
AND IT'S NOT THE SORT OF THING A LAWFUL-GOOD KNIGHT CAN JUST LET GO, YOU KNOW.
......
WHA...? WHO THE HELL ARE YOU?
IT'S NONE OF YOUR...
HEH-HEH! HEAR ME OUT, YOUNG MAN. I HAVE AN IDEA.
YOU SAY YOU WANT TO HUNT GOBLINS!
THEN I SAY YOU SHOULD DO EXACTLY THAT!

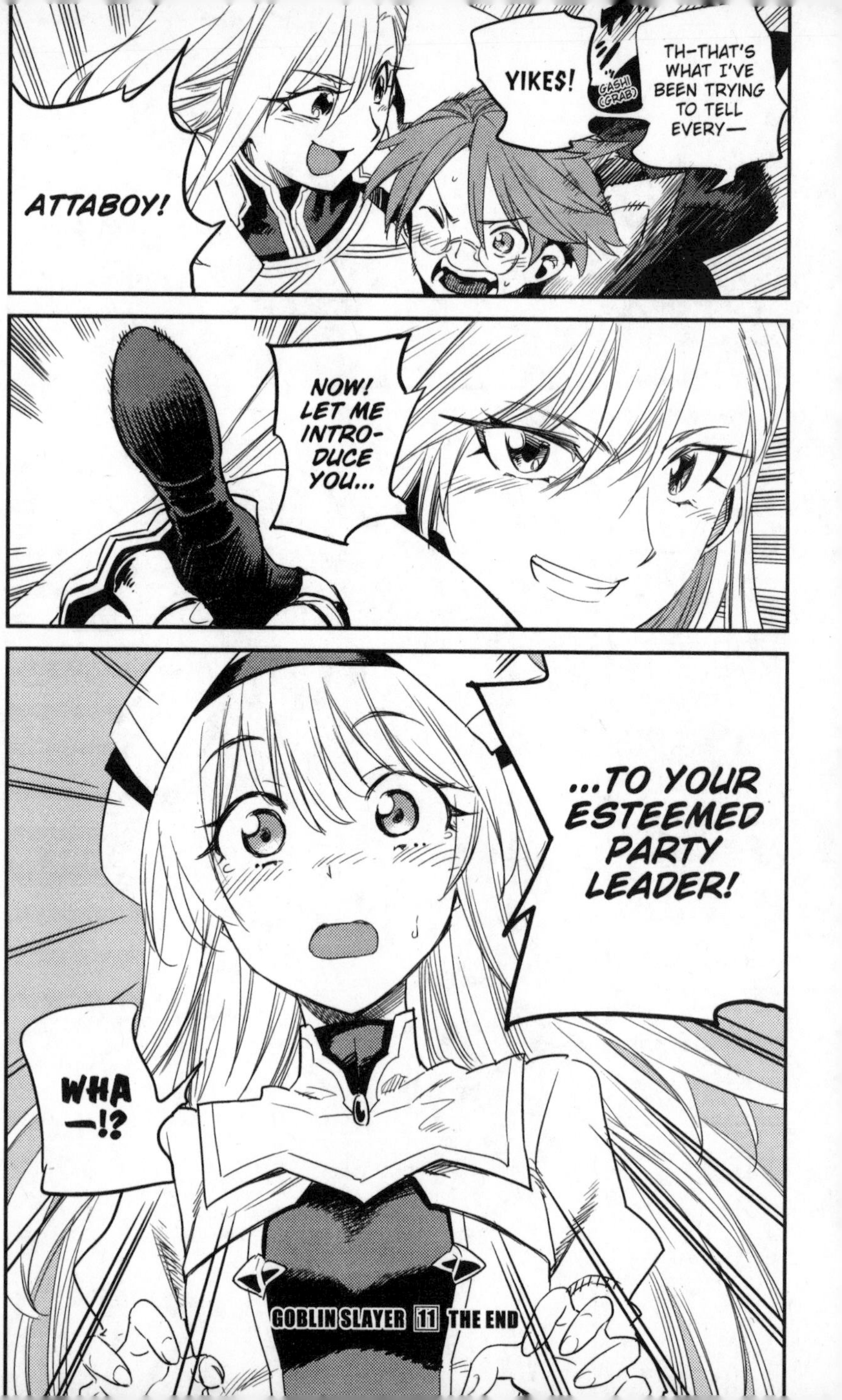
TH—THAT'S WHAT I'VE BEEN TRYING TO TELL EVERY—
GASHI (GRAB)
YIKES!
ATTABOY!
NOW! LET ME INTRO-DUCE YOU...
...TO YOUR ESTEEMED PARTY LEADER!
WHA —!?
GOBLIN SLAYER 11 THE END

Turn to the back of the
book for a short story by
Kumo Kagyu!

GOBLIN
SLAYER

GOBSLAY-SAN

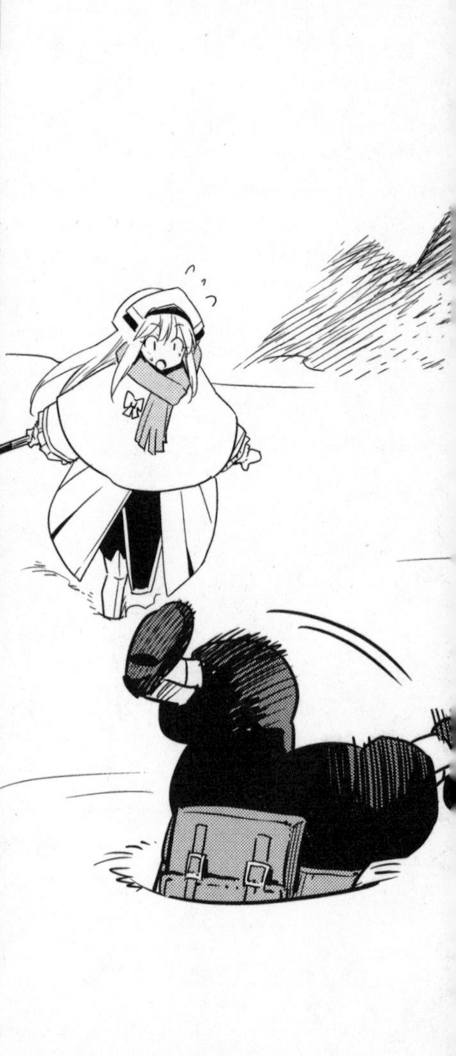

PLAYING ALONG

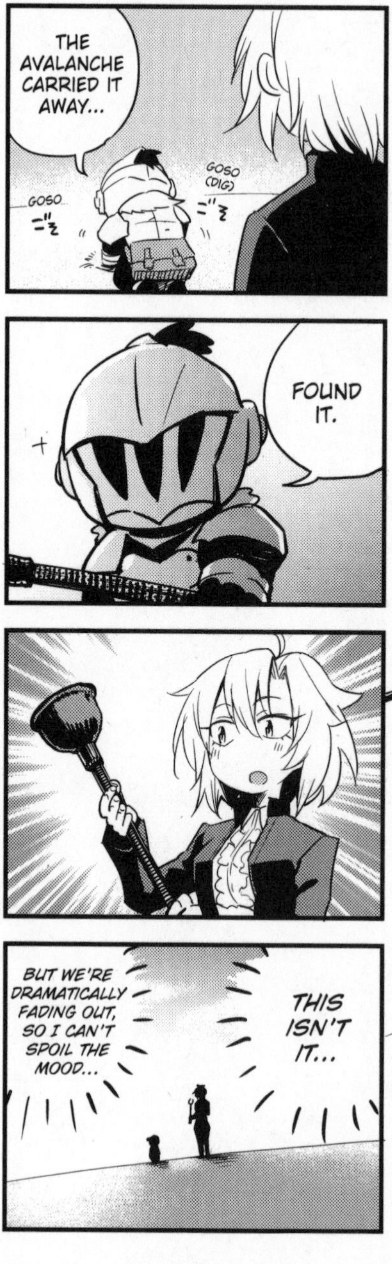
THE AVALANCHE CARRIED IT AWAY...
GOSO (DIG)
GOSO
FOUND IT.
THIS ISN'T IT...
BUT WE'RE DRAMATICALLY FADING OUT, SO I CAN'T SPOIL THE MOOD...

GROWING BOYS NEED SLEEP

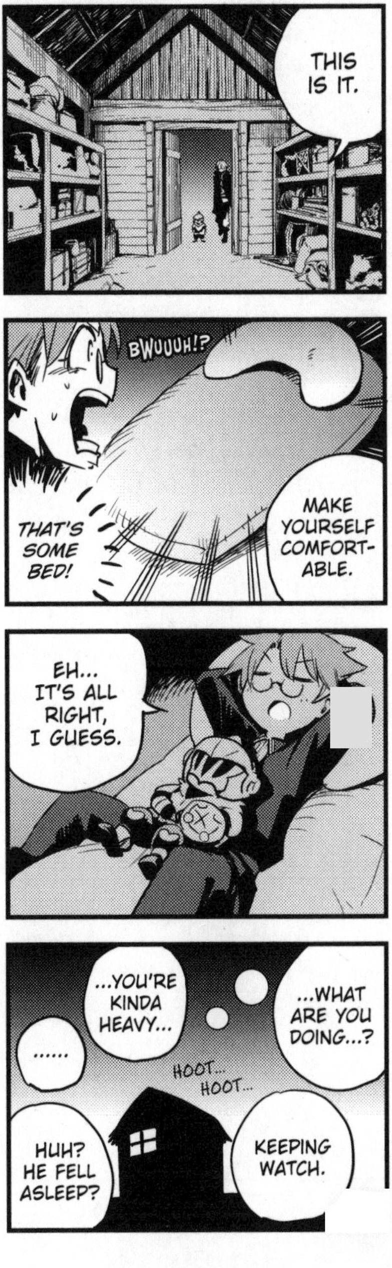
THIS IS IT.
BWUUUH!?
MAKE YOURSELF COMFORTABLE.
THAT'S SOME BED!
EH... IT'S ALL RIGHT, I GUESS.
...WHAT ARE YOU DOING...?
...YOU'RE KINDA HEAVY...
......
HOOT... HOOT...
KEEPING WATCH.
HUH? HE FELL ASLEEP?

BUMP IN THE NIGHT

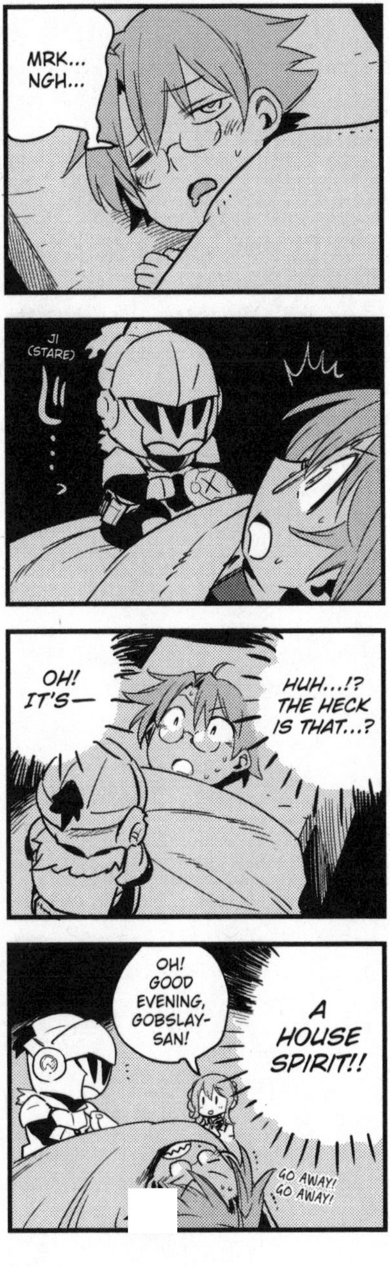
MRK... NGH...
JI (STARE)
HUH...!? THE HECK IS THAT...?
OH! IT'S—
A HOUSE SPIRIT!!
OH! GOOD EVENING, GOBSLAY-SAN!
GO AWAY! GO AWAY!

she said. The sword, once she had belted it to her waist, was so heavy that it made her lean to one side, but that didn't matter.

She steeled herself, put on a rucksack she'd packed full of whatever she thought she might need, and set out barefoot. She'd spent all day, every day, running around the rheas' shire, swinging her stick. Escaping it at night was no challenge. She even put the fence she had been sternly and repeatedly warned never to go beyond behind her with little more than a hop. It was almost too easy.

The girl could faintly hear shouting far in the distance behind her, so she turned around. She filled her ample chest full of air, and her shout echoed through the night: "I'm going to be the strongest in the world—you'll see!!!!!"

There was no one to laugh at her. She heard no ridicule, just the wind rushing past.

With a feeling of utter satisfaction, the girl set off running again and disappeared into the darkness.

"Where, then?"

"Undermountain," he said, a name the rhea girl didn't recognize, and then laughed, showing his teeth, for the first time she could remember.

§

In the end, it was just like her grandfather had said. People don't have to get hit with a stick to die. A nasty cold made the rounds that winter and claimed her grandfather's life just like that.

As part of the many details surrounding his funeral, people had started discussing what to do with his chest of belongings.

"Well, maybe now you'll finally get all these strange ideas out of your head and settle down with a man," her parents said—sounding downright grateful that the old man was dead—but that only strengthened the girl's resolve.

On the night of the funeral, she snuck into the old man's hole and pulled out the chest. It wasn't locked. Inside, there was no trace of the treasure everyone had speculated about—just a single pouch full of silver coins and an old, battered sword. The girl found herself smiling in spite of herself; it was almost as if he'd known who would open the chest and left exactly what she would need.

"I'll be borrowing these, if you don't mind, Gramps!"

children's game. Everyone had their own explanation.

The girl, huffing and puffing, stuck out her tongue at anyone who mocked her, but she also, nearly in tears, asked her grandfather, "Is there really a point to this?"

"None at all," he replied with his usual air of annoyance. "People die through sheer chance all the time. You still might be able to kill someone without doing any of this. And the only people liable to care how you kill someone are any rubberneckers who see you do it."

The girl screwed up her face and threw back her head, looking upside down at her grandfather. His face, floating in the air, wore its characteristic scowl. The girl pursed her lips.

"But it does have value," he said.

"...How so?"

"Because you found value in it. That's why you're doing it."

This time it was the girl who fell into a sullen silence. She slowly staggered to her feet and, with trembling hands she could barely make move, grasped her stick once more. She didn't like the way he said that—it was as though she would be an idiot if she decided to quit.

"...Gramps, did you really used to be an adventurer?"

"Mm."

"Did you go to the Dungeon of the Dead?"

"Never."

"Well...how about Firetop Mountain?"

"Nope."

GOBLIN
SLAYER

toward him without expecting much—and then gasped. He was showing her the underside of his left foot, the one he limped with. An ugly scar had been viciously gouged into it. She couldn't imagine what could have caused such an injury.

"...Does it hurt?"

"It doesn't hurt," her grandfather bluntly replied to her timid question. "Not anymore." He looked up at the sky as if he could see all the way to whatever lay beyond the horizon.

The girl followed his gaze, but all she saw was the familiar scenery of the shire—the fields, the comfortable little rhea holes, the sky and the hills. She had no idea what the old man was looking at.

"There wasn't a chance," he said, almost as if talking to himself—but then his piercing gaze turned to the girl. "But that's no reason not to try."

"......"

"Do you want to give it a shot?"

Without a moment's hesitation, she replied, "I do."

§

After that, her grandfather began to train her. That didn't keep people from laughing at her, though.

Specifically, the training consisted of shouting really loud and swinging a stick at a tree. Some people said she'd gone crazy; others, that it was some newfangled one thing or another—partly out of the goodness of their hearts, of course, but also with an eye on the old man's estate—were chased off with a stern glare.

Eventually, and perhaps inevitably, the people of the shire began to avoid and shun him. But for some reason, for all his quirks, the old man had taken a liking to his granddaughter. Or at least, he didn't laugh at the things she said. He would still firmly shake his head in the end, but he would hear her out first. That was more than her friends and the other adults did. More than anyone else did for her.

That was why, of all the times she had heard "Not a chance" that day, she felt she could demand to know why just this once. She knew she could trust her grandfather to explain himself—and lo and behold, he did.

"......"

But first, it was time for the umpteenth meal that day. Her grandfather sighed deeply, then slowly sat down on the edge of the footpath. He didn't seem to have brought any food with him.

The girl plopped herself down beside him and took out a pastry she'd swiped from the kitchen. "Want some?" she asked, holding out half to him, but when he replied with a curt "No," she stuffed both halves into her mouth, kicking her legs happily.

"...Look here."

Perhaps the low voice her grandfather muttered this in should have tipped her off, but she casually looked

"Yeah, but," the girl said, circling around him, "someone has to be the strongest in the world!"

"S'pose so."

"But they weren't the strongest when they were born, right?"

"Doubt it."

"So there!"

Her grandfather spoke oh so softly, but his words were no less piercing for it. "Not a chance."

Her grandfather was a strange, eccentric, and very un-rhea-ish man. In general, he seemed to have more in common with dwarves, though no one would truly mistake him for anything other than a rhea thanks to his bare feet.

He could always be found wandering the paths of the shire, one leg dragging slightly, with a pipe filled to the brim with tobacco clenched between his teeth. He couldn't have been more than ten years past his hundredth birthday, so the girl doubted he had gone senile quite yet. He had apparently been quite the rabble-rouser when he was young, even leaving the shire and only blowing back in on the wind one day decades later. Whenever anyone asked where he had been and what he'd been doing, he would simply shake his head and reply, "I was off somewhere, doing something."

He never seemed to have any trouble supporting himself, so there must have been a fair profit in whatever it was he had done. People who offered to help him with dejected as the day went on. And who could blame her? She'd finally worked up the nerve to tell people her dream, and they all laughed at her for it.

There was only one person who hadn't laughed: her grandfather. There wasn't even a hint of a smile on his wrinkled face as he listened to her carefully, nor when, once she had finished speaking, he told her, "Not a chance."

§

"Why not?!"

"Because the Four-Cornered World is far bigger than you even think it is."

Puff, puff. Smoke rings drifted from her grandfather's mouth and floated off toward the sky. The girl usually liked to watch them drift through the air until they lost shape and finally disappeared, but not today. Her grandfather only appeared to be leisurely strolling along a path between the fields, but she had to run after him as fast as she could to keep up.

"What do you mean, big...?"

"When I say big, I mean big," he grumbled, but at least his tone—like everything she said to him was an annoyance and he had expected nothing less—was nothing out of the usual for him. "Anyone who claims to know everything about the world turns out to only be familiar with a laughably small part of it."

Interlude:

Of Wanting to Be the Strongest in the World

– by Kumo Kagyu

"But there's no chance in hell that's gonna happen!"

When she boldly made her pronouncement, that's more or less what everyone said in response while looking at her like they thought she was an absolute fool. She got the same reaction from her parents, her brothers and sisters, her relatives, her neighbors—everyone who lived in the shire.

"Stop talking nonsense and try to be serious for once!" many of them then said with smug, self-satisfied looks plastered on their faces, claiming their advice was for her own good.

What part of what she said was nonsense? And she was being serious—but when she tried to tell them that, she only got scolded even more harshly for some reason. It was almost as if they seemed to think she was doing something wrong, which must have been why they were so stern with her.

Some replied, "Oh, really? That's nice, dear" instead. But the way they all said it with a smirk made it clear that what they really meant was "Not a chance."

The girl found herself becoming more and more

GOBLIN SLAYER 11

Original Story: Kumo Kagyu
Art: Kousuke Kurose
Character Design: Noboru Kannatuki

Translation: Kevin Steinbach ✤ Lettering: Bianca Pistillo

GOBLIN SLAYER Volume 11
©Kumo Kagyu/SB Creative Corp.
Original Character Designs:©Noboru Kannatuki/SB Creative Corp.
©2021 Kousuke Kurose/SQUARE ENIX CO., LTD. First published in Japan in 2021 by
SQUARE ENIX CO., LTD. English translation rights arranged with SQUARE ENIX CO.,
LTD. and YEN PRESS, LLC through Tuttle-Mori Agency, Inc., Tokyo.

English translation ©2022 by SQUARE ENIX CO., LTD.

Yen Press
150 West 30th Street, 19th Floor
New York, NY 10001

Visit us at yenpress.com
facebook.com/yenpress
twitter.com/yenpress
yenpress.tumblr.com
instagram.com/yenpress

First Yen Press Edition: April 2022
The chapters in this volume were originally published as ebooks by Yen Press.

Yen Press is an imprint of Yen Press, LLC.
The Yen Press name and logo are trademarks of Yen Press, LLC.

Library of Congress Control Number: 2017954163

ISBNs: 978-1-9753-3996-8 (paperback)
       978-1-9753-3997-5 (ebook)

10 9 8 7 6 5 4 3 2 1

WOR

Printed in the United States of America